Finally Retire from the Stage,

On which occasion the celebrated Artists announced, have in the kindest manner given their valuable services?

The Performances will commence with SHERIDAN's Comedy of The

RIVALS.

Sir Anthony Absolute,   Mr W. FARREN

Sir Lucius O'Trigger,   Mr HOWE

Captain Absolute,   -   Mr HENRY FARREN

Acres, -   Mr BEN' WEBSTER

Faulkland,   -   Mr LEIGH MURRAY

David,   -   -   Mr KEELEY

Fag,   -   -   Mr A. WIGAN

Coachman,   -   (on this occasion)   -   Mr GRANBY

Mr Acres' Servant, Mr ABBOTT   Mrs Malaprop's Servant, Mr GEOFFREY

Boy,   Master ABSALOM

Mrs. Malaprop,   -   Mrs. GLOVER

Julia, -   (on this occasion)   -   Miss HELEN FAUCIT

Lydia Languish,   Mrs NISBETT

Lucy,   -   (on this occasion)   -   Mrs KEELEY

Maid, Miss ISABEL ADAMS.

THEATRE ROYAL, DRURY LANE

To Laura Miller,

who understands,

approves & has a love

for Theatre Royal, Drury

Lane & who is consequently

a person of esteem & a

friend of mine.

With Every Good Wish

for always.

W. Maugham

1912.

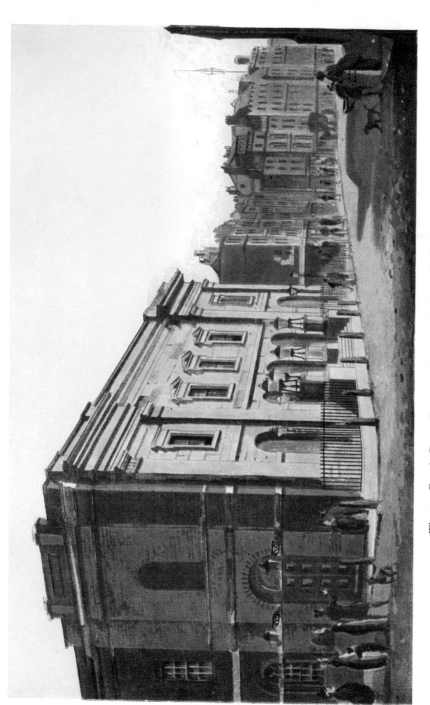

Theatre Royal, Drury Lane, as it appeared when rebuilt in 1812.
This is the present Theatre, the portico and the pillars in Gt. Russell Street being added later.

W. J. MACQUEEN POPE

THEATRE ROYAL DRURY LANE

W. H. ALLEN
LONDON

PUBLISHED BY W. H. ALLEN & CO. LTD.,
43 Essex Street, London, W.C.2.

Printed by CHARLES & READ LTD., LONDON.

To

MY WIFE

to place on record my
gratitude for a lifetime
of happiness.

CONTENTS

ILLUSTRATIONS

FOREWORD

:: By Ivor Novello .:

My Dear Popie,

    I am indeed most happy and flattered that you should ask me to write a foreword to your book on Drury Lane — happy because I now know that at last there is to be a book about Drury Lane — a long felt want ! I cannot in fact believe that there has never been a book devoted to this thrilling theatrical monument, identified as it has always been with the great names in the English Theatre.

    Drury Lane is not just a theatre — it is a tradition, a national treasure and should be included in the " musts " for every visitor to London. There will be millions who will come across the seas to see, not only the glorious scars on London's brave chest, but also those jewels that have so miraculously escaped, and one of the brightest jewels is the Theatre Royal, Drury Lane. Royal because Charles II. willed it so; while still the distant laugh of Mistress Nelly Gwynne rings down its corridors.

    If I were to visit the Temple of Karnak at Thebes I should very much like to be conducted round by one of the original High Priests, because I feel he'd know, and I feel much the same about being conducted round Drury Lane by you. In fact the first time I stepped upon that stage which was to be my most loved home for five years — you did conduct me round, and in about ten minutes told me more about Drury Lane than I had ever known, so you can imagine with what pleasure I am looking forward to your book.

You tell me, by reason of the paper shortage, that you can only give us an outline of the History. I can only say that Wells didn't do so badly on the same lines !

Good luck to you —

Yours affectionately,

FANFARE

THEATRE ROYAL, Drury Lane. A household word throughout this and other lands: the most famous theatre in the world. A place of memories, of dreams, of triumph and disaster; which has lived down through the years, and lives to-day, as strong as ever.

Theatres have come and gone, actors and actresses have played their parts; but the great playhouse stands, an enduring stronghold of the Drama.

Fire has consumed it, housebreakers have hewn it down; but part of it has always survived, and it has always risen again, stronger and more noble, to provide the greatest city in the world with the world's greatest theatre, and to furnish many generations with the first glimpse of that other world, the realm of make-believe, where men are governed by imagination, and where they remould life nearer to the heart's desire.

Drury Lane is a page of England's history, a gem-studded chapter in our life as a nation; where the famous and the infamous have foregathered, where Kings and Princes have sat enthralled, where memorable love stories have been unfolded, and monarchs have played their parts equally with the mummers. Orange girls, tragedians, comedians, buffoons, clowns, swindlers and men of high repute; immortal wits and dull fellows, achievement and failure, success and bankruptcy; riot, murder and suicide—all are interwoven in the fabric of Drury Lane.

The faithfulness of the Public, and its fickleness as well: these have their place. How actors who held London in the palm of their hand were yet howled down; how actresses came from the provinces to fail at Old Drury, to retire—yet to come back again and triumph. How actors with ragged clothes and soleless shoes drew all London to the theatre; how blood was shed, and the military called out. How a pastry cook became famous and made his name immortal; how an orange girl became mistress of a King; how a barmaid became the town's toast, and how a wine merchant wrote an immortal chapter of theatrical history—these are part of the record of Drury Lane.

11

The theatre cannot claim to have had Shakespeare himself under its roof, but there is a direct link with him, for his great-nephew Hart was its first star. Indeed, Hart trained Nell Gwynne for the stage. From the Restoration onwards, every great name in literature and acting came under the roof of Old Drury. Here is the place where it all happened, as things happen today; not a museum where memories live in glass cases, but a theatre going on with its work just as it did in the days of the Merry Monarch. It brings history to life; bare bones are covered with flesh and blood, and, at Drury Lane, those old times seem very near.

Here Charles II wooed and won Nell Gwynne, one of the world's supreme romances: from its stage other Royal Princes took lovers, some for happiness, some for sorrow. Here reigned David Garrick, one of the few great actors of all time. Here Richard Brinsley Sheridan wrote and produced a world-masterpiece; from here old Doggett instituted his Coat and Badge for Thames Watermen.

Its famous names are like a fanfare of trumpets—Dryden, Davenant, Killigrew, Sir Christopher Wren, Congreve, Betterton, Mrs. Bracegirdle, Mrs. Barry, Cibber, Wilks, Barton Booth, Nance Oldfield, Macklin, Garrick, Quin, Spranger Barry, Kitty Clive, Nell Gywnne, Susannah Maria Cibber, John Henderson, John Philip Kemble, Dora Jordan, Sarah Siddons, Perdita Robinson, Edmund Kean, Lord Byron, Doctor Johnson, Sir Walter Scott, Jane Pope, Grimaldi, Macready, Sir Augustus Harris, Dan Leno, Herbert Campbell, Henry Irving, Ellen Terry, Arthur Collins, Alfred Butt, Tom Arnold, Ivor Novello,—these are but a handful of the starry names met with in the saga of Drury Lane.

Drury Lane has often had managers as colourful and exciting as its actors. Some of them have bilked their artists. The brokers have been in times without number. Other managers have gone down in ruin, bankrupt and broken, to exist on charity. One, at least, committed suicide; others died penniless and friendless. Yet some made vast fortunes, were courted by Society, counted Crowned heads amongst their friends, and left records of upright dealing and honesty of purpose which shine like beacons in the darkness of a precarious profession

Drury Lane has known them all. Actors, wine merchants, bankers, money-lenders, newspaper proprietors, innkeepers, authors, musicians, poets,—all have taken a turn.

Drury Lane is Theatre Royal. Its Charter is the oldest of all, and still exists. Every Crowned head since Charles II has sat in the Royal Box. Many have had adventurous times there.

A King was there when the last invader of this country met his final defeat and Drury Lane announced the news. A King boxed the ears of his son and heir in the vestibule. A King narrowly escaped assassination there. Yet another King went there with his Queen and his family, to show by his personal example that at a time when national credit reeled and governments crashed, the Throne and Kingdom were secure.

Drury Lane has been everything which a theatre can be; a temple of Shakespeare, a circus, an opera house, a home of drama and comedy. It has known promenade concerts, wild beast shows, equestrian displays, nigger minstrel entertainments and oratorios. It has seen ballets, acrobatic displays, films and revue. Last but not least, it is the original home of pantomime in this country, if not in the world.

Structurally there have been four Drury Lane Theatres, but the same spirit permeated them all; the building has changed, but its soul has not altered. Its periods fall roughly into four parts: the Drury Lane of Killigrew and the Restoration down to the Triumvirate; the Drury Lane of Garrick, of Sheridan and Siddons, of Edmund Kean; and of Augustus Harris and Arthur Collins, and to-day.

To those of us who work there, who have the theatre in our blood, it is Drury Lane itself that matters. No other theatre makes such a claim upon its devotees, for one is conscious of being connected with something truly enduring.

It has stood there watching the ebb and flow of London, watching the patches and the powder pass, the sedan chairs being replaced by hackney coaches, by carriages, by hansoms, by four-wheelers and by cars and taxis; seeing the end of the gallants with swords and the ladies with hoops and crinolines, down to the heterogeneous fashions of to-day. It has watched the rise of England's greatness. It heard the crowds cheer and the bells ring for the victories of Marlborough, of Clive, of Wolfe, of Wellington, of Nelson. It saw us lose half America and gain one fifth of the entire world. The thunder of the guns and the bursting of bombs in the First World War—and some burst very near —left it quite unmoved.

13

When the Second World War came, Old Drury was still there and in the forefront, for it became the headquarters of the Entertainment National Service Association, and did national service itself. It stood up to the blitz of 1940-41, and later to the flying bombs, and to the rockets. It was struck by bombs, high explosive, and incendiary; but it withstood all shocks sturdily and never stopped work for a single day.

An attempt is made here to weave into a tapestry the tale of Drury Lane so that it may be preserved in permanent form for those who love to learn about the vast fabric, the threads of which make the story of London, of England and of the Drama—one of the most fascinating things in the world.

The Past will speak, so will the Present. The future no one knows. But may Theatre Royal, Drury Lane, continue to keep the past and the present always secure in its own future, right down the ages to come.

CHAPTER 1

FATHER OF OLD DRURY

IN the spacious vestibule of Drury Lane Theatre there is fastened on the wall a great tablet of mahogany, bearing in letters of gold the names of the men who have controlled its destinies. It begins with the statement " First Charter, 1639." That is not quite correct, the old building is not so ancient as that. The gap of 24 years between 1639 and its actual opening in 1663 is a small thing when reckoned in terms of centuries and of fame. For Drury Lane has them both.

To appreciate the greatness of Drury Lane Theatre, one must grasp the fact that it was the very first Theatre Royal; the very first theatre to have legal status conferred upon it. It was the real beginning of a regularised world of the theatre. It arose like a beacon from the twilight of the Drama, out of a period when all playhouses had been closed by Cromwell and Parliament, when actors had been oppressed and imprisoned and when the most determined attempt had been made to exterminate the Theatre altogether. It marked the emergence of Drama from the barn, the inn-yard, the wooden unroofed open-air structures, and the small, ill-equipped playhouses, into the dignity of proper equipment and public resort, and most important of all, into the realm of security of tenure. With Drury Lane, the theatre left behind its somewhat precarious and hole-and-corner existence and took its place in the life of the people, in the centre of town.

Up to the time of the Merry Monarch, the theatre had been an object of constant oppression. Actors were practically outcasts, rogues and vagabonds, and unless they were part of the retinue of some great noble (as was so often the case) they were treated like vermin. Established authority did its best to kill the theatre and drama as soon as it showed itself. The usual excuse was that by drawing crowds of undesirables together it caused riots and breaches of the peace, but more potent was the claim that owing to the concourse of playgoers, it spread the risk of infection of the Plague.

The first London theatre was erected in Shoreditch; built and opened in 1576, it was called The Theatre; the second, close by, opened in 1577, was called The Curtain. This had nothing to do with a drop-curtain, but was local nomenclature, for it stood where Curtain Road is to-day, and took its name from Curtain Yard. But even there, civic authority reached them and theatres and play-going were removed to Bankside, outside the city's jurisdiction. James I. allowed Burbage's company, which had been known as The Lord Chamberlain's, to call themselves The King's Servants, and they were enrolled in the Royal Household; each man (there were no women) being allowed as livery four yards of "bastard scarlet" and a quarter of a yard of velvet for a cape. The Royal favour does not appear to have done much for them, except perhaps to give them status in their profession, otherwise its effect seems to have been as skimpy as the allowance of velvet.

It is ironical that the first monarch to have his own company of players and to encourage the drama was Richard III, who himself was to become the drama's arch-villain.

Under Charles I theatres were again built across the river on the Middlesex side, and in the town proper. The Red Bull was there in Clerkenwell, probably converted from an inn yard, a place much derided by its contemporaries, and which seems to have been a species of "blood tub."

15

There is some suggestion of a theatre at White Friars, but the evidence is slight and it seems more probable that the great hall or refectory of the Carmelite Monastery was the site in which plays were given. The theatre at Black Friars was a very different concern. It was a fashionable house, but constantly in trouble. It stood where now stand the offices of "The Times," and Playhouse Yard commemorates it. It was a " private theatre," which meant that it had a roof and that the pit was reserved for wealthy people, mostly of the peerage, who also had the privilege of sitting on the stage. So high did its prestige stand that musicians would play there for nothing in the hope of attracting the attention of the noble patrons.

Then there was The Cockpit (afterwards The Phoenix) in Drury Lane, a small roofed theatre which saw many vicissitudes and made much history. It closed finally before the might of Drury Lane Theatre.

Another theatre, built in 1629, was in Salisbury Court; this was the last playhouse constructed prior to the Restoration. It stood on a portion of the site of Dorset House, where is now Salisbury Square, Fleet Street. It had many famous actors and tenants. Suppressed in 1644, it got into bad repair, was rebuilt in 1660, and burnt down in the Great Fire of 1666.

When Drury Lane was opened, London had only these three theatres—The Cockpit (or The Phoenix), The Red Bull, and Salisbury Court.

That Drury Lane ever got its Charter, was ever built, or indeed that the theatre ever succeeded in overcoming its attempted extermination by the Puritans, is largely due to one man, Sir William Davenant. His father, John Davenant, was a vintner of Oxford and master of the Crown Inn; his mother was a beautiful and witty woman. A very frequent visitor to their house was William Shakespeare. There is a legend that William Davenant was indeed the son of Shakespeare. It was said that when the great William visited, young William Davenant would rush home from school to be with him, and that he referred to him as his godfather, though some told him jokingly not to take the name of God in vain. No less an authority than Montague Summers, doyen of historical and Restoration research, says he sees no reason why the story should not be accepted.

On leaving Lincoln College, Oxford, Davenant became page to Frances, first Duchess of Richmond. But—and

16

again it seems to bear out the Shakespeare legend—Davenant had the theatre in his blood. He went to Court, wrote plays, and so high did he stand in the King's favour that on the death of Ben Jonson he was appointed Poet Laureate by Charles I—or perhaps Court Poet is the better term—at a yearly salary of £100. That was in 1637.

In 1639 he took an important step. He obtained from Charles I, on the 26th March of that year, a Royal Patent under the Great Seal of England, to erect a theatre. It was to stand "upon a parcel of ground lying near unto or behind The Three Kings Ordinary in Fleet Street, in the Parish of St. Dunstans in the West, London, or in St. Bride's, London, or in either of them; or in any other ground in or about that place, or in the whole street afore-said, already allotted to him for that use, or in any other place that is or hereafter shall be assigned or allotted out to the said William Davenant by our right trusty and right well beloved cousin and counsellor, Thomas, Earl of Arundel and Surrey, Earl Marshal of England, or any other of our commissioners for building for that time being in our behalf."

This was something new, nobody else had ever received such a wide charter. There was a stipulation that the theatre was to have the necessary tiring and retiring rooms, and other places convenient "containing in the whole forty yards square at the most, wherein plays, musical entertain-ments, scenes and other like presentments may be presented. Note that word "presented." After a gap of three hundred years Charles Frohman, the great American impresario, "presented" plays, and the phrase was thought to be new. Had Mr. Frohman been delving into old documents?

But Sir William Davenant never built his theatre. It would appear that, owing to the uncertainty of the times, his "backers" backed out, a thing which theatrical backers have been doing ever since! So Fleet Street never got its theatre. If it had, the mighty presses may well have roared elsewhere, for theatres are gregarious, and the Street of Ink might have become the Street of Greasepaint. So, too, the history of the Strand and Shaftesbury Avenue might have been altered.

Already Davenant had reforms for the theatre in mind, he had visualised what he eventually introduced, painted pictorial scenery and a proscenium.

He did not surrender his patent rights. With that document in his pocket he entered into management, taking over the Cockpit Theatre, becoming the Governor of it when William Beeston lost the job. He ran the little theatre—it was only forty-six feet broad and about one hundred and forty feet long—very well indeed. The prospects of Davenant, Court Poet, accepted wit and playwright, Governor of the Cockpit, now looked rosy, but the Civil War broke out and spoiled Davenant's plans.

Although the playhouses had been closed, the appetite of the public for plays still remained, and surreptitious and private performances were being given. The condition of actors at this time was terrible. They lived as best they could, by odd jobs; they hung around the bookshop of old Rhodes, who had been at the Blackfriars Theatre; they gave furtive performances at private residences, like Holland House, where collections were made for them, and managed by these means to scrape together a few odd shillings. Yet the urge to act never left them, so consuming is the calling of the Drama.

Davenant got into touch with numerous sympathisers who wanted the theatre back, and in his own home, Rutland House, Charterhouse Yard, he started to present plays. He had a scheme to build a theatre, but this had to be dropped. So long as he gave his performances privately, nothing much was said. He knew the difficulties. His old theatre, the Cockpit, had tried to open. In 1649 they had given a show but the soldiers raided the theatre and dismantled it.

In 1658, however, the public were getting tired of " controls " and restrictions. The time was about ripe for Davenant, and he worked quickly. He found a weak spot in the Puritan armour of Cromwell, and that blind spot was hatred of the Spaniards. In spite of all opposition he gave a show at the Cockpit, " The Cruelty of the Spaniards in Peru. Represented at the Cockpit in Drury Lane at three after noon punctually."

It was a success, this curious entertainment. It was not a play—oh, no, Sir William Davenant would not break the law. It was entertainment, a mixture of songs, music and declamation and some dancing, although he had to be careful about that. It might be opera, but definitely it was not a play. It drew the town, and was a bigger step forward in dramatic representation than had been his " Siege of Rhodes " privately produced at Rutland House,

18

in which Mrs. Coleman had played or sung "Ianthe" and very nearly won for herself the crown of being the first English actress. Like "The Siege," "The Cruelty" had painted backcloths, another advance in technique. Davenant had been clever. He threw dirt at the Spaniards, whom the Lord Protector loathed, and thereby got his favour, for Cromwell smiled upon such propaganda.

Davenant now saw his way clearly. He presented another show of his own devising, "The History of Sir Francis Drake," again anti-Spanish in character. Whereas "The Cruelty" had been a mixture of scenes, songs and horrors, "Drake" was much closer knit and was almost a musical melodrama, with continuity of action and theme. London liked it, and its scenery, for flats were used as well as backcloths, and, much emboldened, he showed the public his "Siege of Rhodes." But this time he overdid it. The Puritans were on the watch, and at last succeeded in closing down the theatre for some weeks. But it soon reopened, for John Evelyn saw "The Siege of Rhodes" in May of the same year.

Shortly afterwards, owing to the disturbed state of the country, the authorities acted, and Davenant and many other Royalists were put in prison. But even whilst in prison, shows were still given at his theatre, and there is on record an instance of troopers raiding the Phoenix whilst a performance was taking place and fining the audience on the spot. The playgoers "were mulcted there and then of three pounds, eight shillings and sixpence."

Davenant soon got out of prison, and the return of the King became imminent. Sir William knew this would mean the theatres reopening. He treated with Thomas Lisle for the use of his Tennis Court in Portugal Street, Lincoln's Inn Fields, with the idea of turning it into a theatre. Later it became one and made history. But Davenant did not pursue the matter then. He decided to go abroad and join the King and re-establish himself in Royal favour. And this he did, returning with Charles II as a person of considerable influence and prestige. He still had that Patent which Charles I had bestowed upon him. Here was a precedent, a thing beloved of the Law all the world over. And from that seed sprang Theatre Royal, Drury Lane. Had the patent not been granted, the idea of the Royal Charter might never have been thought of.

On arrival at the Court in exile of Charles II, Davenant

19

found another man of the theatre there already. This was Thomas Killigrew, the Father of Drury Lane—the man who made and built it.

Thomas Killigrew, born in 1612, came of a distinguished Cornish family of courtiers renowned for their loyalty to the Crown. His father was Sir Robert Killigrew, and Thomas was the fourth son. The theatre must have been in the Killigrew blood, for two of Thomas's brothers wrote plays, and in his early days Thomas showed his love of all things theatrical.

Killigrew never went to a university, but straight to Court as a Page of Honour to Charles I. Therefore he never had the cultural polish considered so necessary in those days. Indeed, he often referred to himself as "the illiterate courtier." But his natural talent and wit, added to his considerable reading, more than made good the deficiencies in his scholastic education, and in the outcome he succeeded in becoming a firm favourite of the King.

A friendly partnership sprang up between Davenant and Killigrew. And soon they began, no doubt, to plan ahead those future happenings which meant so much to theatrical history. Killigrew—and probably Davenant too—was on the " Royal Charles " when it bore its Royal namesake back to his throne on 23rd May, 1660; for Pepys — always on the lookout — chronicles that amongst the notabilities he saw "Thomas Killigrew, a merry droll but a gentleman of great esteem with the King."

Back in England, the two great men of the theatre found three companies acting, in spite of the persecutions. There was Rhodes with his players at the Cockpit, there was the persistent Red Bull, and Beeston at Salisbury Court. All had been fined and harried but were carrying on. With the return of the King, persecution ceased; but Sir Henry Herbert, a gentleman who was to make a lot of trouble, came into the limelight. Whilst the King had been away, he had laid low, but he now resumed his title and powers as Master of the King's Revels. He would only issue a licence to allow actors to perform in return for payment. He made the three playhouses pay him £4 per week each if they wished to keep open. He made many other vexatious charges in addition.

The King had told Killigrew he was his Master of the Revels, and here was Sir Henry Herbert doubling the part. Killigrew lost no time in grappling with an impossible situation. As early as 9th July, 1660, he obtained a warrant from the King "to erect one company of players, which shall be our own company." He and Davenant together could do more: they went to work and decided to get the King to grant them a monopoly of London theatres, to get a company each, to build a theatre each and squash all opposition. Davenant then played as his card the Patent of 1639, and Killigrew backed him up by agreeing that Sir William should have a company as well as the one granted to him (Killigrew) by the King. So great was their influence and so well did they go about it that on 21st August, 1660, the King passed through the Privy Signet an order which gave these two managers a complete monopoly over the London theatre. Not only could they have companies but they could build theatres, have complete jurisdiction over them, and also act as censors on all plays.

Now one of the two theatres built under that agreement was Old Drury, and the charter of 1639 played a big part in the negotiations.

Sir Henry Herbert did not sit down under this state of affairs. Killigrew and Davenant acted swiftly, and advised all the players that they were now the masters. Sir Henry fought back, making a great outcry. He represented to the King that Killigrew and Davenant had misled His Majesty by saying that he had agreed to their having power. He had done no such thing. Nor would he, with all respect! He drew the King's attention to the fact that he held the appointment of Master of the Revels, which was one of great antiquity (actually it dated from Henry VIII). Nobody had dismissed him, and he was entitled to his rights. The King took the easy way. He handed the matter over to the Attorney-General, hoping no doubt that it would solve itself. Much argument followed.

Small wonder that the bewildered actors themselves petitioned the Throne. They presented "The Humble Petition of Michael Mohun, Robert Shatterell, Charles Hart, Nicholas Burt, Wm. Cartwright, Walter Clun, and William Wintersel," who complained that Herbert persecuted them until it "ended in soe much per weeke to him" and then his promised protection was of no use, for here were Killigrew and Davenant, under a Royal Warrant, saying they would close the actors down unless they bound themselves to the new patentees, "to act in a new theatre, with

21

women" (which was obviously a bitter pill) "and habits according to our sceanes."

The King sided with Killigrew and Davenant. Those two worthies, to force the issue, went into joint management at the Cockpit. They opened on 8th October, 1660, with the pick of all the companies, including all the actors mentioned in the petition, and Baxter, Loveday, Betterton and Kynaston as well. Having thus established themselves, they played until the end of the month, and then split into two companies, one under Killigrew and one under Davenant. They were the dictators of Theatreland. Killigrew moved into a tennis court fitted up as a theatre in Vere Street, Clare Market, and on 8th November, 1660, they played Henry IV, Part 1. Now, Killigrew's company, it should be remembered, was "The King's Company of Players," so that theatre, long since forgotten and swept away, might claim to be the first Theatre Royal. But the patent given to Killigrew and Davenant applied to new theatres to be built by them, so Vere Street must forego its claim.

Yet it did make history, for the first actress to tread the boards of the English stage did so there, on 8th December, 1660. She played Desdemona. Unfortunately we are not sure of her name. There are various claimants and on the available evidence the most likely of these seems to have been Mrs. Hughes. Jordan wrote a prologue mentioning this historic occasion, but he does not mention the lady by name. There have been many suggestions, such as claims for Anne Marshall and for Mrs. Corey, but Margaret Hughes, afterwards to be courted by the famous and gallant Prince Rupert, was in all probability our first professional actress.

It was expressly provided in Killigrew's and Davenant's charter that they could employ actresses, which was a revolutionary move, but since women had never appeared on the stage before, one might ask where did those enrolled by Killigrew and Davenant get their training? We know they were good actresses. It may be that they had played without being announced, and the public had taken them for boys. It may be that they were wives or connections of the company and received no payment. It may be—and this is probable—that they played with the strolling players and normally dressed as men to escape observation in private life. When Killigrew started employing actresses

22

he had plenty to choose from, and indeed in 1664, at Drury Lane, he presented " Parson's Plague " with an all-woman cast.

Killigrew was going ahead but he was not yet clear of his enemy, Sir Henry Herbert. Now that Killigrew and Davenant had parted company, Herbert saw his chance. He attacked the weaker man, the easy-going, jolly Killigrew. The shrewder and harder-headed opponent he left alone.

Herbert had, in 1661, filed a suit against Davenant and Killigrew for infringement of his rights. He lost it and the defendants got £25 damages and costs. Now the division had taken place, Herbert went after Killigrew with vigour. In 1662, Killigrew, weary of the continuous battle, made terms with him. Killigrew was well beaten, but he should not have been. He agreed to pay Herbert all licensing fees for plays dated back from 1660, at the rate of £2 for new plays and £1 for revivals. He paid all his legal expenses, and gave him £50 for himself. In return Herbert promised not to molest him any more and gave him his patronage. Killigrew promised to stand by Herbert and aid him against Sir William Davenant. This he never did, and he must have had his tongue in his cheek, for he had a gentleman's agreement with his old friend, which he respected. It was tantamount to blackmail on the part of Herbert, but Killigrew's surrender was probably due to the fact that he was actually busy on preparations for his new theatre, which was to be Drury Lane. He wanted an undivided mind and the ground clear. He had got his site, and the playhouse which was to make so much history, and which still exists to-day, was on the verge of being built.

CHAPTER 2

THE THEATRE IS BORN

KILLIGREW leased from the Earl of Bedford the site which was to become so important, so permanent, as the home of Theatre Royal. Joined with Killigrew in the lease were Sir Robert Howard, and eight actors, Hart, Mohun, Burt, Lacy, Robert Shatterell, Clun, Cartwright, and Wintershall. Joined also in the lease were William Hewett and Robert Clayton. The site was "a piece or parcell of ground scituate in Pach, Sct Martin's-in-the-Ffields and St. Paule, Covent Garden, known by the name of the Rideing Yard." From east to west it measured 112 feet; it was 59 feet wide at its eastern end, and 58 feet wide at its western end. The lease was dated 20th December, 1661, and the condition was that by Christmas 1662 £1,500 should be spent on building a theatre on the site. The ground rent was £50.

On 28th January, 1662, Hewett and Clayton sold out: it is not known why. The property was then divided into 36 parts, nine to Killigrew, nine to Sir Robert Howard, four to Lacy, and two each to Mohun, Hart, Burt, Shatterell, Clun, Cartwright and Wintershall: at the same time the company was extended to include Theophilus Bird, Richard Baxter, Edward Kynaston, Nicholas Blagden, and Thomas Loveday. These, with the before-mentioned actor-participants, bound themselves to play at this theatre exclusively. They further agreed that the original partners in the building scheme should receive £3 10 0, for "every day the theatre was open for the presentation of plays, or every acting day" as they called it.

The building of this theatre must have caused quite a stir. London was still a comparatively small city. Its playgoing public was still smaller. But, in their newly-found freedom from the amusement-suppressing Puritans, the erection of a Theatre Royal was an event.

The playhouse became known as Theatre Royal, Bridges Street. It stood actually in a field approached by a pathway from Drury Lane to Bridges Street, which is now Catherine Street. It faced Bridges Street and was therefore so called. But it was Drury Lane. It was Theatre Royal. The charter which made it so important is still in existence. It must be held by whoever holds Drury Lane. The present company possesses it, and it is kept at the bank, and inspected annually by the auditors. It is in a state of perfect preservation. But it has had some ups and downs and changes in value. Sheridan charged his shareholders £30,000 for it, and once it changed hands for the sum of 10s., so low had the drama fallen. It stands in the balance sheet of the present company at £7,520 10s 7d. It has been lost and found again; it has been in jeopardy of cancellation and has been renewed by successive sovereigns. Its true power was taken from it in the 19th century, but still it plays its part at Theatre Royal. We shall meet it often.

Even before his theatre opened, Killigrew seems to have deputed the actual management to the chief actors, Mohun, Hart and Lacy. This was to lead to much trouble. Killigrew probably did not want to be bothered by detail, but the true duty of a manager is to preserve discipline, hold a balance and have the last word. This the gay Tom never did.

Drury Lane was then an aristocratic part, of the town: it was surrounded by the houses of noblemen. Its name came from the Drury family who lived there; and in and around it dwelt the Earl of Craven and Clare, the Marquis of Argyll, the Earl of Anglesey and many others. It had even boasted a Queen—the Queen of Bohemia, mother of Prince Rupert, before she moved to Leicester Fields. Thus, in Killigrew's day, it was what we now call a West End theatre, as against the old theatres on Bankside and in the City. True, it was not too safe at nights around there, but playgoing was early. By the reign of Queen Anne, the neighbourhood had deteriorated and become disgraceful and unsafe. Playgoers of the higher ranks came attended by their running footmen, part of whose duties was to be able to fight. For quite a while these servants were admitted to the gallery free, to await their employers, and they caused frequent riots in return for this concession.

Before the first night there was much for Killigrew to do. He had to get certain of the company " sworn in " as members of the King's Household. They were entitled " Gentlemen of the Great Chamber," and each had ten yards of scarlet cloth and a proper quantity of lace allowed them for their liveries. Ten of them were given warrants for this honourable appointment from the Lord Chamberlain, though which ten we are not quite sure. They wore their Royal livery with an air, and regarded it as a privilege. The last actor to wear it was Robert Baddeley.

All the men and women who constituted His Majesty's Company of Comedians in Drury Lane, as they styled themselves, had to take the oath of allegiance to the Sovereign. This gave them a new standing. Elizabeth had a company, but they played anywhere, not in a Theatre Royal. James I and his " Servants " have been mentioned, and Beeston's players as well, but here was a company who were the King's own players housed in a Theatre Royal.

The first company of players at Drury Lane consisted of:

MEN

Theophilus Bird
Charles Hart
Michael Mohun
John Lacy
Nicholas Burt
William Cartwright
Walter Clun
Richard Baxter

Robert Shatterel
William Shatterel
Mr. Duke (Marmaduke Watson)
Thomas Hancock
Edward Kynaston
William Wintersel (spelt several
Thomas Bateman   ways)
Nicholas Blagden

WOMEN

Mrs. Corey
Mrs. Anne Marshall
Mrs. Eastland
Mrs. Weaver

Mrs. Uphill
Mrs. Knep or Knip
Mrs. Hughes

What manner of men and women were these original Drury Lane players? A great deal about their qualifications, strengths and weaknesses is known. The two great stars were Charles Hart and Michael Mohun. They shone with equal brilliance, and when they played together, even when age and infirmity were beating them, they never failed to fill the house. Charles Hart should come first, for to him Killigrew deputed the duty of "Keeper of the House," its General Manager, in other words, and he probably lived on the premises, as did Betterton at the Duke's, Drury Lane's rival to come.

Hart was a grand-nephew of Shakespeare, so that there is a direct link between the world's greatest playwright and the world's greatest theatre. He was a very fine actor. He created the part of "Alexander the Great" in Nathaniel Lee's play of that name, and it was said of him in it that no Prince in Europe might have been ashamed to copy him. The observant and witty Rochester called him the Roscius and Mohun the Aesopius of the stage of that time. Another writer goes even further and puts this on record: "Were I a poet—nay, a Fletcher, a Shakespeare— I would quit my own title to immortality so that one actor (Hart) might never die. This I may modestly say of him, nor is it my own particular opinion, but the sense of all mankind, that the best tragedies on the English stage have received their lustre from Mr. Hart's performance." What would not a star actor to-day give for such a "notice." In Hart's day tragedians ruled the stage, but he could be as good a comedian as he was a tragedian. Steele wrote in "The Tatler" about the joint stars: "My old friends, Hart and Mohun, the one by his natural and proper force, the

26

other by his great skill and acts, never failed to send me home full of such ideas as affected my behaviour, and made me insensibly more courteous and humane to my friends and acquaintances."

Hart was a very early lover of Mistress Nell Gwynne. It was he who trained her for the stage, so he seems to have been a sharer in Royal favours as well as chief of His Majesty's Company of Comedians.

Hart was a very handsome man, and had a fine voice. When playing he became quite unconscious of his audience, so absorbed was he in the part he portrayed. No matter how great the applause, he never stepped out of character. He gave every part the most careful and meticulous study. His earnings were probably about £1,000 a year. He retired in 1682, and was the recipient of a half-salary pension (about 30/-).

Michael Mohun, his co-star, was a man of small stature but great art and power. He had fought for his King in the Civil War and become a major, a title he always used and treasured. He had a pleasant manner, and was always the peacemaker when disptes and strife rose—which, as Drury Lane was a theatre, was very often. He was modest, too, for once when Lee, a well-known playwright of the period, was reading a play to him, Mohun put the script gently aside and said: "Unless I could play the part as beautifully as you read it, it were vain to try it at all." The playwright returned the compliment for he wrote parts in every play for Mohun. Lee paid him a handsome tribute, too, after seeing him in "Mithridates": "Thou little man of mettle," exclaimed the dramatist, "if I should write a hundred plays I would write a part for thy mouth in every one."

Theophilus Bird was related by marriage to Beeston, who had been so prominent in theatrical affairs and had very nearly had a Theatre Royal himself. He stood well in stage circles and had influence. He had one share in the undertaking at Drury Lane, but not in the original building scheme. Little is known of him as an actor, except that he played Prospero at Drury Lane in 1663.

John Lacy was a very good actor indeed. He was a famous "Falstaff," and his "Bayes" in "The Rehearsal" was one of his greatest successes. Charles II also held him in high regard, and had a picture painted of Lacy in three of his famous parts ("Teague" in "The Committee," "Mr. Scruple" in "The Cheats," and "M. Gaillard" in "The Variety.") It was originally in Windsor Castle and is now at Hampton Court.

Nicholas Burt came from the Red Bull Theatre, and had a whole share in Drury Lane. He was a man of means, for he lent £160 to the theatre company, as represented by Killigrew, Dryden, Hart and Mohun. Subsequently he sued Killigrew for detaining his share of the wardrobe, scenes and books in the theatre. He had probably left the theatre by 1680, for his name does not occur after that. He was excellent as "Cicero" in "Cataline." The production of this play throws a sidelight on theatrical business of that time, for Charles II gave £500 towards the clothing needed for the play. Burt was a great "Iago," rivalling Mohun in the part. He was also a celebrated "Subtle" in "The Alchemist."

William Cartwright, who had formerly played at Salisbury Court Theatre, was a man of substance as well as being a good actor. Besides playing principal parts Cartwright was a man of high influence, for when trouble arose between Killigrew and his son, the Lord Chamberlain appointed Cartwright together with Hart, Mohun and Kynaston, to see that the theatre was properly run.

Walter Clun met with a tragic end. He was a first-rate actor, who had, like Kynaston, graduated from women's parts. He was murdered on 3rd August, 1664, on his way home to his country lodgings in Kentish Town. Clun had dined well, and it is rumoured that he had a lady with him. Pepys heard the news at the theatre the following day, and he writes: "Clun, one of their best actors, was, the last night, going out of town after he had acted 'The Alchemist,' wherein was one of the best parts that he acts, to his country house, set upon and murdered; one of the rogues taken, an Irish fellow. It seems most cruelly butchered and bound. The house will have a great miss of him."

Other less prominent members of the original company were Richard Baxter, who was sworn a gentleman of the Great Chamber, and had a new livery in 1665; Robert Shatterell, a soldier like Mohun and Burt; William Wintersell, who had belonged to Queen Henrietta Maria's company at Salisbury Court—he was a famous "Slender"—Nicholas Blagden, Thomas Hancock, Marmaduke Watson (who adopted the stage name of Duke, surely one of the first actors to do so). Thomas Bateman, who played small parts, joined in the first year.

There remains one of the most famous of them all, Edward Kynaston. He is one of the few "boys" who played women's parts, before the arrival of actresses on the stage, whose name has lived. He was originally with Rhodes, at the Cockpit, where his success as a girl was phenomenal. Pepys was in ecstasies about him, in "The Loyal Subject" in 1660—"where one Kinaston, a boy, acted the Duke's sister, but made the loveliest lady that ever I saw in my life." And Pepys was no bad judge of feminine charms. Later on, he saw Kynaston in Ben Jonson's "Epicene" and reports: "Among other things here, Kynaston, the boy, had the good turn to appear in three shapes; first as a poor woman in ordinary clothes, to please Morose; then in fine clothes, as a gallant, and in them was clearly the prettiest woman in the whole house; and lastly as a man; and then likewise did appear the handsomest man in the house." Downes tells us that the critics debated as to whether any of the actresses of the day touched the heart so deeply by their acting as Kynaston had done when he was a girl.

As "Henry IV," one of Kynaston's finest parts, Cibber's comment is : " Every sentiment came from him as if it had been his own, as if he had himself that instant conceived it, as if he had lost the player, and were the real king he impersonated." High praise indeed, from an authority on acting.

These then were the Gentlemen of the King's Company of Comedians whom Tom Killigrew picked for Theatre Royal. A fine team, too. He had taken the more mature. Davenant relied on youth.

And what about the ladies?

CHAPTER 3

LADIES OF OLD DRURY

IN Restoration times, the name of every actress was prefixed by the word "Mrs." or "Mistress"—never "Miss." For the latter word in that period had another disreputable meaning, which the former word has now displaced. In the time of Charles II, when people wanted to say that a lady was living under a gentleman's "protection" they would remark, "Oh, she is Lord Soandso's Miss." Thus the actresses, wishing to keep up a show of respectability, were always announced as "Mistress".

Mistress Catherine Corey, one of the first to tread the boards at Old Drury, was a good character actress, whose biggest success was probably in "The Alchemist". She played many parts and excelled in those in which she had to represent age. She caused a real uproar at Drury Lane once. Egged on by Lady Castlemaine, who mixed much with the Drury Lane company, she made up like a certain Lady Harvey, against whom the Castlemaine had a grudge. Not only did she make up like her, but she gave an imitation of her, which must have been good, for the lady herself recognized it, although Mrs. Corey was purporting to play "Sempronia" in "Cataline." The outraged victim got the actress arrested, but Lady Castlemaine obtained her release and told her to do it all over again, apparently before the King, whilst hirelings of Lady Harvey pelted her with oranges and hisses as hard as they could. The stage was an exciting career in those days; players were always in trouble for giving imitations of important people, and yet continued to do so for years. Mrs. Corey is heard of no more after 1692. In 1689 she had been in some sort of trouble and had then sworn that she was the first, and was now the last survivor, of the actresses who took the Royal Oath at Drury Lane's beginning, and that she had been on the stage for 27 years.

Ann Marshall was, with her sister Rebecca, one of the Drury Lane company's first leading ladies. As their names were never printed separately on the playbills, but both were announced as "Mrs. Marshall" it is impossible to say with any certainty which parts they played. Pepys supplies us with some gossip about them, when Rebecca had words with Nell Gwynne. He was then told that they were the daughters of Stephen Marshall, a great Presbyterian.

Mrs. Eastland was a player of small parts. Mrs. Weaver had her name on the list of liveries in 1666, but was not on the list the following year. She seems to have been frequently in trouble over money matters. She sued Drury Lane for wrongful dismissal on one occasion, and it was pleaded against her that she had handed in all her scripts, and refused to act with the company again, although she was asked to do so. An early example of temperament, it would seem. Pepys hints that she had an affaire with the King, another very likely event, and that this had spoiled her. When amenable she was a good actress.

Mrs. Uphill was of no great talent, and is generally supposed to have been the mistress of Sir Robert Howard, whom she eventually married.

Mrs. Knip, or Knep, is more familiar to the public through the pages of Pepys, who had a great admiration for her; he writes—" Pretty enough, but the most excellent mad humoured thing and sings the noblest that ever I heard in my life." He described her husband as a "kind of jockey. An ill, melancholy, jealous looking fellow." She was a mistress of Sir Charles Sedley, and played parts in his comedies. Killigrew thought highly of her talent and told Pepys "Knip is likely to be the best actor that ever came upon the stage, she understanding so well." She got a rise of £30 per annum, considerable money then.

The final name in that first company is that of Mrs. Hughes. She has the most right to be called the "first actress," for it is probable that she was the anonymous Desdemona at Vere Street. Margaret Hughes created many important roles, and finally went over to the rival theatre, the Duke's house. Pepys has said of her "a mighty pretty woman and seems, but is not, modest." But he was glad to give her a kiss! From which it may be gathered that she was a bit of a minx. She was mistress of Sedley, who had a roving fancy, but it was left to her to captivate and subdue that stern soldier Prince Rupert from his scientific research, to which he had turned when there was no more need to lead cavalry charges, and who wooed her with great determination. The Court rejoiced over his back-sliding. She bore him a daughter, but she ruined him, and at the end her extravagance ruined her. She had to sell off her jewels which the Prince had given her, some of which Nell Gwynne bought.

That was the female team, but the men were the strongest side.

Let us now observe the playhouse. By the early spring of 1663, Killigrew was ready to open the great new playhouse which was destined to become historic. It had, as yet, no definite name. It was referred to as "The new theatre now building," "The new theatre in Covent Garden,"

31

and even when it was finally opened one finds it referred to as either The King's House, or Theatre Royal, Bridges Street (now Catherine Street). The name Drury Lane crept in later and still remains.

In May, Killigrew was ready. He had engaged his players and arranged terms with them. He had got his staff together, with Charles Hart as his "Keeper of the House" or General Manager, and also leading man, and Charles Booth as his prompter and stage director. The theatre was commercial, then as now, and Killigrew wanted to make as much money as possible. Nowadays, the bars, cloak-rooms and programme concessions of most theatres are let to contractors. Killigrew had no programmes as we know them now, only bills of the play, and he had no cloak-rooms, and no bars. But he had a chance of making money by selling or letting the concession for the sale of fruit and refreshments in the theatre, and over this he did a deal. So he and his partners entered into an agreement with Mrs. Mary Meggs (known generally as "Orange Moll"), who lived in the parish of St. Paul, Covent Garden. For her concession she paid £100 down and received "full, free and sole liberty, licence, power and authority to vend, utter and sell oranges, lemons, fruit, sweetmeats and all manner of fruiterers and confectioners wares and commodities." She could exercise her right all over the house except in the upper gallery. She paid 6/8 per day as rent, and had a lease for 39 years. The restriction placed on the upper gallery was probably on account of the tendency of the patrons of that part of the house to use fruit as a missile rather than an eatable, and so, by not being able to buy it on the spot, and having to bring it with them, the supply of ammunition would be limited. Orange Moll supplied the orange girls who were such a feature of the time. It must have been she who engaged Nell Gwynne, if indeed this delightful person did sell oranges in Theatre Royal, which is doubtful. Moll was the centre of all gossip and news; she seems to have been a kind of private broadcasting station for scandal. She was a woman of resource, as will appear, and she spent a good deal of her time, very likely extremely profitably, in arranging liaisons and carrying messages relating to these, as did her girls. The current price of an orange was 6d. and the girl expected a tip as well. They bandied jokes with the gallants, they "palmed" notes and the accompanying "pecuniary compli-

32

THOMAS KILLIGREW, the Father of Drury Lane, the man who conceived, built and first managed the world-famous Theatre. He opened it in 1663.

(Reproduced by kind permission of Messrs. Arthur Tooth and Sons, Ltd., 31 Bruton St., W.1.)

Above.
CHARLES MACKLIN, a great Drury Lane
figure who startled all London with
his Shylock there in 1741. He also
killed a brother actor in the Green
Room.

Below.
SARAH SIDDONS, the greatest Drury
Lane actress, as *Queen Catherine*

Top right.
COLLEY CIBBER, actor-dramatis
manager-poet-laureate, one
the famous Triumvirate whic
won Drury Lane such glory.

In oval.
ALEXANDER POPE, famous act
at Drury Lane, who so ofte
played leading parts wi
EDMUND KEAN.

ments ", to be passed diplomatically to this lady or that gentleman. They were quick-witted, ready-tongued women of that world.

Orange Moll was well known to Pepys, as to everyone else, who often refers to her. When the union of the Theatre Royal and the Duke's house took place, the new management put in a nominee of their own, to the exclusion of Orange Moll, which led to a suit in 1684 and more trouble in 1690. Before the litigation was over Orange Moll died. Her quickness of thought and action saved at least one life in the great theatre, and Pepys duly reports it. He was watching " Henry IV ", and relates that " a gentleman of good habit, sitting just before us, eating some fruit in the midst of the play, did drop down as dead, being choked, but with much ado Orange Moll did thrust her finger down his throat and brought him to life again ". An early example of rough but effective first aid in the theatre.

The entire size of the first Theatre Royal, Drury Lane, was almost exactly the same area as the stage of the present one. In the basement to-day is a tiny room, the walls of which are believed to be part of the original fabric, and which goes by the name of Nell Gwynne's dressing room, though it never was; it is possible that the " tiring room " as the common dressing room for the actresses was called, may have been on this spot.

The building which cost £2,400, was a three-tier house, divided into boxes, which were on the first tier, middle gallery, also made into boxes, and upper gallery, which was just a plain gallery. The entire floor of the theatre was taken up by the pit; such things as stalls were still in the dust sheets of the future! The floor of the pit was steeply raked, and at the back it reached so near to the boxes that their occupants could chat, on level terms as it were, with people standing on the floor. The pit benches were covered with green cloth. There are no details of the scheme of decoration, but a French gentleman visiting the theatre on 22nd May, 1663, a fortnight after its opening, said it was the best playhouse he had ever seen.

Pepys, alas, was not present at the first performance ever given in Drury Lane; but he was there the following day and he wrote this: " The house is made with extraordinary good contrivance, and yet hath some faults, as the narrowness of the passages in and out of the pit, and

c

the distance from the stage to the boxes, which I am confident cannot hear; but for all other things it is well, only above all, the musique being below, and most of it sounding under the very stage, there is no hearing of it the bases at all nor very well the trebles, which sure must be mended."

What Pepys meant was that the orchestra pit was where we have it now, only not extending right across the proscenium, but occupying only the centre; also of course, the stage was an apron stage, and protruded into the auditorium as did the old Tudor stages. Later the position of the orchestra was altered and it went aloft, its position being on a platform in what are now called the "flies". For years it only descended to floor level when opera was being performed, otherwise it remained above the stage.

In Colley Cibber's time, however, it was back on the floor again, for the actors, when not appearing, would slip into the orchestra pit and watch the show, and a few privileged people were allowed in as well.

The lighting was supplied by pendant chandeliers, which hung from the proscenium arch. It seems difficult to assess their exact position; Pepys, who had trouble with his eyes (eventually they failed the poor man) complains that the light from the chandeliers hurt them. There were no footlights when the Lane first opened. They appeared nearly forty years later as little oil lamps. Then they were transformed into "floats" (a word the conservative theatre still uses for them), which were wicks run through circular pieces of cork, which floated in a shallow trough of iron or tin, let into the stage and filled with oil. It has been stated that Garrick was the inventor of footlights. He was not, but he improved them.

In the days of the first Drury Lane, the plays were given in the afternoon, and that affected the lighting. For the theatre had a glazed cupola over the pit which let in the light—and the rain too—and gave Pepys a cold in the June of 1663 by reason of drips and draught. There were windows as well. Magolotti, describing the theatre, says "Plenty of light on the stage and on the walls to enable the spectators to see the scenes and the performances." The light on the stage would be from candles and that on the wall from the windows. There was music before the show started, just as we have it now. As an overture they played three pieces, of varying nature, which were called "First

34

Music ", " Second Music " and " Third Music ". These were used as cues for calling the players, and during the Third Music the prompter, who was also stage manager, would give the call "Third Music ", the equivalent of " Overture and Beginners " to-day. You can see these cues marked on old scripts, and these music terms lasted for over 100 years. It was customary for " First Music " to be a Rustic Air, " Second Music " to be a Minuet, and "Third Music " to be a Coranto. Third Music was also called, back stage, "The Curtain Tune ". There were signs also that music was played in the intervals. At the end of the show, they played the audience out with a lively march. Things are much the same to-day.

The Third Music being finished, the Prologue was spoken and then the curtain went up. At the first Old Drury and for a long time after, having once gone up, its curtain did not descend until the end of the show. Intervals were marked by the stage being left empty. There were doors in front of the curtain line, through which actors made their entrance on to the apron stage, and through which they took their calls at the end. In the first Drury Lane Theatre, there were six of them, three on each side. In the second they were reduced to four, two aside. These proscenium doors lasted for many years and were very useful.

Back stage, the visitors would find scenery at which to gape, for it was still a great novelty. And there would be the " tiring rooms " to visit. It is doubtful how many there were of these, probably one for the men and one for the women, although some lines in a play of the period, in which the character had an adventure with a pretty girl during the course of the show, seems to indicate that there were some other and more private rooms as well. Audiences wandered all over the stage and behind the scenes The privacy of a dressing room in those days was not the valued thing it is now, for the theatre was a good deal more intimate. The Green Room was the centre of theatrical life, where the players waited for their cues and chatted with their friends and members of the public. Why Green Room? That also is in some doubt. Some authorities say it had a green baize carpet and green hangings. Others claim the name to be a derivation of "Scene Room," as indeed it was sometimes called in the early days, meaning the place in which the actors waited for their "scenes." It was much easier to "call" them from there than from their private dressing room of to-day

The word "green" is used in rhyming slang to indicate the stage, which is referred to by those who speak it (largely music-hall performers) as the "greengage," shortened by experts into "green." "To be on the green" is to be acting. Yet green is in theatrical superstition an unlucky colour in spite of the fact that there was "The Green Room," that act-drops were made of green baize, that the same material was spread on the stage, and unrolled for tragic heroes and heroines to die on, (so as to save their costumes from getting dirty,) and that uniformed stage attendants wore green livery coats and are still referred to as "green coats."

That Green Room is most likely a corruption of "Scene Room," is attested by Pepys who tells us that Knip took him to "the scene room" and that they sat there whilst he heard her go through her part. In the epilogue to Nat Lee's "Mithridates" produced at Drury Lane in 1678, these lines occur:—

"Faith, I'll go scour the scene room and engage
Some Toy within to save the falling stage"

The toy was probably a pretty actress whose glamour might appeal more than the tragedy. Yet in 1697, the year before, in the Drury Lane production of "The Female Wits" it is spoken of as The Green Room. In the same play the call boy is referred to, the first mention of this functionary in theatrical history. In 1700, Green Room was the accepted term. In Cibber's success, "Love Makes a Man", at Drury Lane, "Clodio" says "I know London pretty well, sir, and the side box, sir, and behind the scenes; aye, and the Green Room, and all the girls and women actresses there!"

A murder in the Green Room of Drury Lane, comes into our story, and in the court evidence this place is referred to as "The Scene Room." That was in 1735. In 1775, William Cooke in "Elements of Dramatic Criticism" maintained that men of rank and fashion should be encouraged to visit the Green Room, so that the players might learn deportment and gentlemanly behaviour from them." There was a special etiquette about the Green Room, too. Players of low rank and small salary could not use it. So, often, there were two Green Rooms, one for the principals and one for the smaller part people.

36

It was not only the players who were bound by Green
Room etiquette: it applied to visitors too. Speaking of 1818,
Joe Cowell, the comedian says " During this season the
principal Green Room was conducted with all the etiquette
in an apartment designed for the same purpose in private
life, and very properly too. There was an obsolete forfeit
of one guinea for anyone entering it in undress, unless of
course, in character. This being understood perfectly was
never likely to be incurred, but Alderman Cox, one of the
committee (of Drury Lane), in defiance of this well-known
rule, dropped in one evening in a riding dress with very
muddy boots and spurs, Julia's train getting entangled in
one of them, Oxberry good-naturedly reminded the alderman of the forfeit, which he appeared to take (and I think
he did) in high dudgeon; but the next day a note was
addressed to the gentlemen of the Green Room, begging
them to accept a dozen of very fine madeira in lieu of the
guinea forfeit, pleasantly stating that as he was a bad actor,
he must be a member of the second Green Room, if of
any, and therefore did not consider himself amenable to
the laws of the first."

That novelty, the scenery, was fairly simple, consisting
merely of flats and shutters at the back which drew across
the stage. Flats would be pushed across and joined up,
and drawn away again to show another scene behind them.
There were some " relieves," that is, scenes with moulding
on them, and some " cuts " which showed perspective behind
them. The scenes were all stock ones doing duty over and
over again. Much of the important action took place on
the apron, to bring the actors as near the public as possible.
How the changes of lighting were effected is not so easy
to understand. Moonlight was often achieved by " trans-
parencies ", and dark scenes by putting out certain of the
candles. These candles were a constant source of worry.
They were attended to by " snuffers " whose job it was
to watch them, and snuff them as soon as they smoked
or guttered, and to replace and relight if need arose. The
audience enjoyed this, and gave them all possible, if un-
desired, assistance. Let a candle start to smoke, and from
the auditorium arose the yell of " Snuffer, snuffer!" and
that functionary thereupon shuffled on the stage and did
his work, without any regard to the action of the play,
even though it might be in the middle of a tense scene
or death agony.

The Royal Box at Drury Lane was the very first there had ever been. It is not perhaps generally recognised that Charles II, the patron of Drury Lane, was the very first monarch ever to attend a theatre. His predecessors had the theatre brought to them.

The first Royal visit to a theatre was not, alas, to Drury Lane but to Davenant's theatre in Lincoln's Inn before the Lane was opened. But at Old Drury the King had his box, from which to observe his own company of comedians, who wore his own livery, who were officials of his own Court, and whose chief, Tom Killigrew was Groom of His Majesty's Bedchamber. Every crowned Monarch of this realm has occupied that box since. Whatever Charles's shortcomings as a King may have been, and they were many, the Theatre owes much to him.

All these theatre details are mentioned here because, although in many cases they had come into being before Theatre Royal opened, yet it was there that they first had "a local habitation and a name". It was at Drury Lane that they, and the Theatre as a whole, first had real permanence.

CHAPTER 4

THE CURTAIN GOES UP

THE great day dawned. Outside the theatre on May 7, 1663 there was a considerable crowd, jostling and pushing at the gallery door, for queueing was unknown and it was each man for himself.

There was another crowd for the pit, even larger, and a third for the middle gallery, but a more orderly one. The patrons of first-tier boxes came later, as befitted their importance. There was also a mob of spectators, such as one always finds in London, who had no idea of going inside, but wanted the free show made by watching those who were —the ancestors of those extraordinary people who to-day stand outside theatres on a " first night" to gape, and jostle the celebrities. There were some, too, who hung round the stage door to see the actors, although most of these lived in the neighbourhood (nobody lived far from their work in those days of sparse transport).

38

To-day those actors were going to play for the first time at Drury Lane, and they had taken on the stature of heroes. Very likely the least disturbed people were the players themselves. First-night nerves were not affecting them, they knew all about their play. But doubtless there was some additional pressure on their arteries, for this was a great venture, which meant much to them.

Killigrew, for all his easy-going ways, was on his mettle. Well to the fore, he was fussing about, consulting with Hart, and with Booth, the prompter-librarian-treasurer, stage director and everything else. The "machines" were given a last look over, the staff of scene-shifters, carpenter, candle-snuffers all inspected and sent to their posts. The orchestra were in their pit; Orange Moll in her room below stage, giving out the oranges and confectionery to her orange girls, who were preening themselves. The money-takers were sent to their positions. For some days past, bills of the play had been stuck on all the available posts in the town (hence the word "posters") and delivered to all the nobility and gentry living in the vicinity. In the coffee-houses in Covent Garden the fops were sharpening their wits and showing off their clothes, looking forward to the opportunity of airing both in the new playhouse. The playbill, beyond giving the name of the play to be presented, offered little information. The cast was not given. However, word of mouth supplied this item. There was the date but not the year. Some years ago a spurious bill, purporting to be that of the first performance at Drury Lane, got into circulation, but to the expert eye it was full of mistakes and was soon discredited.

What those playgoers were to see, as the first play performed at Drury Lane (or Theatre Royal, Brydges Street, or The King's House—either of which they might have called it), was Beaumont and Fletcher's " The Humourous Lieutenant," and the cast was as follows:

King	...	...	...	...	Mr. Wintersal
Demetrius	...	...	...	...	Mr. Hart
Seleucus	...	...	...	...	Mr. Burt
Leontius	...	...	...	...	Mr. Mohun
Lieutenant	...	...	...	...	Mr. Clun
Celia	...	...	...	...	Mrs. Marshall

Ann Marshall was thus the first leading lady of that famous and glittering procession which has crossed the stage at Drury Lane all down the years.

All being ready inside, Killigrew gave the word to open. That would be shortly after noon—say twelve-thirty. The rush commenced. There would certainly be trouble at the doors, for the money-takers were notoriously dishonest and would cheat the playgoers over change if they had the chance. Even careful Sam Pepys was " done " by a money-taker, who before his very eyes made away with one shilling out of the six tendered for three admissions, and made the irate Pepys pay up again. Pepys says he was overborne by the cool grave way the man did the trick.

Killigrew and Davenant tried to put a stop to this by using metal checks issued to the public on payment (much the same as the Accurate Checktaker business of to-day) stamped with the name of the theatre and the part to which it admitted. This might have worked well as a check on the amount taken, but there was a monstrous system in vogue which defeated it. This was the privilege granted to playgoers of "sampling." They could see an act, and if they did not like the play when the first act was over, they could have their money back and go away. Even that might have worked but for the gallants and fops who considered it too much trouble to pay at the doors and then have the fatigue of getting it back again if they did not fancy the show. They made such a fuss about this, that rather than offend them, the management decreed that the boxkeeper should collect from them in the interval. Later Garrick was to attempt reforms by instituting a "numberer' who counted the house. No doubt, complications like these added to the confusion of the opening day.

When the audience got inside, there was a great noise. Nor did attempts to gate-crash help to make things any smoother. The gallery audience rushed to their places and began to shout and whistle. The pittites, the backbone of the theatre, scrambled to their seats, climbing over the backs of the benches, jumping over obstacles in their hurry. Then the fops came strolling in. Everyone was examining the house and exclaiming about it. The smart young men called out to each other and hailed their friends in the boxes.

The orange girls cried their wares, which the men would buy and in turn present to the nearest " Vizard " to take their fancy. "Vizards" were the ladies of the town, who wore black masks from which they took their name—they had other names, too, such as Cyprians, Bona-Robas and Fireships, and a still shorter one of Biblical origin.

They had stolen this mask idea from the fashionable ladies who wore a vizard, they said, to hide their blushes caused by the general lewdness of the plays presented. Pepys saw Lady Mary Cromwell put on a vizard, and was so charmed that he bought one for his wife. It was a point of honour for a man about town never to haggle about the price of an orange but to give a tip as well. The ordinary people in the house had many disputes with the orange wenches, and Pepys once got landed with six oranges he did not want, and paid up rather than risk a row. Much of this would be happening whilst that first afternoon audience waited for the curtain to rise at Drury Lane for the first time.

Then the celebrities began to enter the boxes, to the accompaniment of more chatter. The fops were picking out their special coign of vantage, to become known as Fops' Alley, where they could best see and be seen. The First Music was played, followed by the Second Music, barely heard above the din except by those in the very front row. The Third Music began and Booth called his company.

Now there is tension backstage as well, and Killigrew takes an anxious survey of the whole house, hoping and wondering, but fairly well pleased with everything. The Company stands ready, the last strains die away—and " The Humourous Lieutenant " begins . . . Drury Lane is open.

As the play progresses, it pleases. It is familiar, but the acting is as good as the play. There is applause for the favourites, and the public have the pleasure of seeing Hart and Mohun play together. The audience, in the fashion of the period, is as colourful as the stage scene. The fops are on the stage, swelling the crowd of people already there who consider it their privilege, and one which, incidentally, they were not to lose until Garrick drove them away. Suits are shown off, new clothes flash before the public eye; silks, laces, fine ribbons and lovelocks these men display. But the play goes on, for the company are used to all this. And then, at last, it is over, to great applause—and the public stream out, to spread the fame of the new theatre by word of mouth—the only real form of publicity in those days. The new theatre, the play, and the company, are a definite success. The same play and the same players continued for twelve successive days. Then came new recruits to the King's Company of Comedians. They included Mr. Hains, Mr. Griffin, Mr. Goodman, Mr. Lyddoll, Mr. Charleton, Mr. Sherly, Mr. Beeston, and, according to Downes, four were

41

bred up from boys under the Master Actors—Bell, Reeves, Hughs and Harris. Of the new actresses there were six—Mrs. Boutel, Mrs. James, Mrs. Rebecca Marshall (already mentioned), Mrs. Rutter, Mrs. Verjuice and Mrs. Reeves.

Joe Hains was a fine low comedian, singer and dancer, an excellent speaker of Prologues and Epilogues, and above all an inveterate joker. Pepys saw him first in " The Spanish Gypsy " at Drury Lane on March 7th, 1667-8. He did not like the play but he liked Hains. " A very silly play," says the forthright critic, " only great variety of dances, and those most excellently done, especially one part by Hains (which he spells Hanes) only lately come hither from the Nursery, an understanding fellow but yet they say hath spent £1,000 a year before he came hither."

Hains once engaged an unsuspecting and simple clergyman as " Chaplain to the Theatre Royal " and sent him to the theatre ringing a bell to call the players to prayers. To pull the leg of Sunderland, during the reign of James II, when Roman Catholicism was very much in the air, he pretended that the Virgin Mary had appeared to him saying " Joe, arise." But Sunderland was not to be caught. " She would have said Joseph," he replied, " if only out of respect to her husband." He then pretended to recant, which he did on the stage of Drury Lane, wearing a white sheet, holding a candle and repeating some nonsense rhymes as only he could. The audience pardoned him, for they loved his " Roger " in " Aesop " and his " Tom Errand " in Farquhar's " Constant Couple."

Hart, his manager and leading man, once cast him for a small part in " Cataline " which was Hart's " chef d'oeuvre." Annoyed at this, Hains sat on the stage with a comic dress on, holding a pipe and pot in his hands, and made faces at Hart behind his back. This caused roars of laughter. It did not disturb Hart, who sustained his performance until the end, without turning a hair, but when he came off he promptly sacked the over-funny comedian Hains. He remained on the stage until 1701, when he died of a fever and was buried in the churchyard of St. Paul's, Covent Garden, where the remains of so many actors lie.

Hains was irrepressible. He visited Paris with a Peer of the Realm, assumed there the character of an English lord, got into debt and into prison. On his release he came home and claimed that he had received the title of Count. This did not impress people much, least of all a couple of bailiffs who wanted him for a trifling matter of £20 and caught him on Holborn Hill. Still Hains was undefeated; he saw a carriage coming along and knew to whom it belonged. Said he to the bailiffs: " Here comes the carriage of my cousin, the Bishop of Ely—let me speak to him; I am sure he will satisfy you on this matter." More impressed by the Bishop than the so-called Count, the bailiffs consented. Hains poked his head through the window and told the Bishop, whom he did not know from Adam, that with him were two Roman Catholics who had leanings towards Protestancy but still retained scruples. The Bishop was vastly intrigued. " My friends," he called out to the men, who had not heard what Hains had said, " if you will presently come to my house, I will satisfy you in this matter." He drove on. Hains was released. The bailiffs went to the Bishop's house and the truth came out. And for very shame, the Bishop paid the comedian's debt.

Philip Griffin was another actor of considerable merit. Old Downes thought a lot of him. He had a long career at the Lane. He would appear to have been the lover of Orange Moll inasmuch as he was her executor and there was a picture of him in her lodgings. Although he lodged with Scum Goodman, the bad man of the theatre, he appears himself to have been a man of good character, who was well received in Society. Later in the Lane's career he was manager for Christopher Rich, and Cibber puts his name alongside such people as Betterton, Smith, Mountford, Mrs. Bracegirdle and Mrs. Oldfield for social position and decency. Among new men, sworn in after the opening, Cardonnel Goodman is worthy of a great deal of attention. His nickname was Scum, and he deserved it. Scum was a bad man through and through. He will be referred to later.

Meanwhile, things at the Lane went very well. It was easily the first theatre in town, as it should be, with the best actors and actresses. Its great rival, The Duke's Theatre, had not yet arisen, and things looked very prosperous for Killigrew and his company. Notable plays presented by Killigrew were " Rule a Wife and Have a Wife"; Jonson's " Volpone," with Mohun as " Volpone " and Hart as " Mosca "; " The Silent Woman," " The Alchemist," " The Maid's Tragedy," " King or No King," and many more. Business was good, the house popular, and the audiences as unruly and vociferous as usual. Hart had a bad experience one night in a play which demanded the use of a baby in the action. The title is believed to have been " All Mistaken " (and if so, the title was right). There was no baby in the theatre outfit, but Hart, who liked to do things as well as possible, went to the length of borrowing one from a woman in the audience. He made his entrance with the child in his arms, but the infant, missing its mother and not knowing Hart's face, began to wail and cry most pitifully. The actor, usually oblivious of his surroundings when playing, could not disregard this hullabaloo right under his nose, and tried to quieten the baby, who now, thoroughly upset, redoubled its yells and made the theatre resound, much to the joy of the audience but to the horror of the mother, who could stand it no longer. She rushed up on to the stage, seized her precious brat, dragged it from the arms of Hart, and ran off the stage with it.

It was one occasion on which the imperturbable Hart was put out of countenance.

CHAPTER 5

NELL GWYNNE

TWO names of great account now enter our saga, the one a dramatist, Dryden, and the other an actress who has become one of the most romantic figures in the land, Mistress Eleanor, Ellin, or as is mostly preferred, Nell Gwynne.

Her story is romance itself. Where did she come from, this girl who captured all hearts, ruled a King and kept his love, swore like a trooper, lived an unmoral life yet delighted to do good. Who proved herself one of the most delightful comediennes the stage has ever seen, who left a line of Dukes to succeed her, and may have been instrumental in founding Chelsea Hospital; and who, more than anyone else in its long story, is bound up in the popular imagination with Old Drury, though her career there was so short?

Who was her father? He may have been a tradesman in Hereford, an Army Captain in Oxford or a fruiterer in Covent Garden. Who knows? Probably not even her mother, Madame Gwynne herself knew, for she was a lady of the easiest virtue, with a taste for the bottle right up to her last day on earth. Nor can anyone be sure that the name was really Gwynne or Gwyn, or Gwin, as variously spelt.

Nell was illiterate, and would hardly know herself. There is more than a suggestion that her name was really Symcott, for in a list of Charitable Bequests to the Prisoners on the Common Side of King's Bench Prison, there is an entry:

> " Mrs. Margaret Symcott (i.e Eleanor Gwyn) sixty-five penny loaves every eight weeks.
> " Charitable Donation to the Prisoners in the Marshalsea; Mrs. Margaret Symcott (i.e. King Charles' Eleanor Gwinn) 65 penny loaves every eight weeks, paid to the Chamberlain £2. 0. 0."

Now these are just the sort of bequests that Nelly would have made. But why Symcott? Did she wish to do good anonymously? That was unlike her, she was never ashamed of what she did. It is probable that the gifts were paid for out of public funds—she spent quite a deal this way—and that the officials did not want this known or were unwilling to show too heavy expenditure by the King's Mistress. Not that £2 was much; she had far heavier items against her from public funds for luxuries and the like. In 1752 there was a book published anonymously under the title of " Memoirs of the Life of Eleanor Gwinn, a Celebrated Courtesan of the Reign of Charles II and Mistress of that Monarch," and in it there is the following paragraph:

> " and who, for the comfort of old soldiers, was the cause of erecting Chelsea Hospital, with an account of many charities she left and good deeds she performed in her retirement from public life and the stage (as Lady Simcott)."

The Simcott idea, in its various spellings like Gwynne, seems to have been prevalent, but no proof of any kind can be found; nor does the name occur in her Will. But what does it matter? Nell Gwynne she was, and Nell Gwynne she will remain forever. This girl of doubtful parentage, whose father is unknown and whose mother was a loose liver, a procuress and a drunkard, had a great heart and she has left a glowing memory.

Nell is first met with in a common brothel run by Mother Ross in Lewknor Lane (now Macklin Street) off Drury Lane, which was a famous street for such establishments. Here she fetched strong drink for the customers, ran errands, sold herrings to eke things out and sang bawdy songs at tavern doors. She had a lover, a link-boy named Richard, when she was an ill-clad and ill-fed child, and he gave her stockings to cover her chilblain-stricken feet. At the age of thirteen she had a windfall. She became possessed by some means or other of the enormous sum of Two Guineas.

Longing to act and feeling independent Nell went to Orange Moll, to get as near to the theatre as possible. She suited Moll and so sold oranges before she became an actress and won a King. Very likely she was on duty at the opening. She soon attracted the attention of Hart, who became her lover. He and Lacy trained her as an actress and found her an apt pupil. If it is correct that she was born in 1650, then she was fifteen when she made her début.

She first appeared on the stage in Drury Lane Theatre in April 1665, playing " Cydaria " in Dryden's tragedy " The Indian Emperor " with Montezuma as its hero. It was the fourth play of his to be produced at Drury Lane, although it is somewhat doubtful if one of them, " The Mistaken Husband " was really his when first produced. No reports exist to show how Nell was received. She must have been woefully mis-cast, for she was never a tragedienne and at that time she was quite inexperienced. We have some knowledge of a later performance of hers in this play, for Pepys, who saw her in it on August 22nd, 1667, says " where I found Nell come again, which I was glad of; but was most infinitely displeased with her being put to act the Emperor's daughter, which is a great and serious part, which she does most basely." That is straight talking. Nor did she improve, for on a further visit, the diarist reports " To the King's Playhouse and there saw 'The Indian Emperor,' a good play, but not so good as people cry it up. I think though above all things, Nell's ill-speaking of a great part made me mad ".

Two fallacies about her must be cleared up at once. One is that when Charles II first met her she was selling oranges at the Lane. Actually she had been on the stage for some time and had another noble lover before she took the King's eye. The other, far more important to the theatre, is the legend that she it was who persuaded Charles to grant Drury Lane its Charter. It had been given to Killigrew three years before she ever appeared on its stage.

46

Nell's stage career was a short one, and it had two considerable interruptions. But it must be always linked with another of the gods of Drury Lane's Valhalla, the great John Dryden, poet, dramatist and Poet Laureate. John Dryden was unquestionably the greatest of the early dramatists of Drury Lane and one whose name will always be associated with it, although he seceded later to the Duke's House. His early fame as a dramatist was made at Old Drury, and Nell Gwynn was leading lady in his first success, "The Indian Emperor".

Other early dramatists at Drury Lane were Thomas Porter, Richard Rhodes, John Wilson (The Cheats), Edward Howard, and Robert Howard.

With its fine company, its dramatists, its Royal standing, the noble playhouse was sailing with a fair wind, when suddenly the Great Plague smote the City and the playhouses closed down. This was indeed a desperate blow. The Plague had always been the actors' enemy, indirectly if not directly. For many generations it had been the plea of the authorities that the crowds going to the play spread infection, but now it fell on all alike, and on Drury Lane in the flood tide of its initial success.

The King's House closed, and His Majesty's Comedians and servants were all out of work.

CHAPTER 6
PLAGUE AND FIRE

BECAUSE of the Plague, the playhouses remained closed from 5th June, 1665, when the Special Order was issued, until 29th November, 1666. On the latter date Drury Lane reopened and so did Lincoln's Inn Theatre, Davenant's House and Old Drury's only rival. They were opened on condition that a large percentage of the takings were given to charity. They had tried to open on the Day of National Thanksgiving, 20th November, 1666, but this was stopped by the Archbishop of Canterbury. Apparently the public, who had been thoroughly frightened, were on his side, for they murmured that Thanksgiving was being hurried forward "to get grounds for plays to be publicly acted, which the Bishops would not suffer until the Plague was over." The public knew the hold the theatre had upon the King.

47

That Closing Order was unique. Save for set periods of mourning for Royal Demise, it was the only general closing order in respect of places of amusement until 3rd September, 1939, nearly three hundred years later, when the Second World War broke out.

Both actors and actresses suffered in 1666. The actors probably came off worse; for the women of that period almost certainly found kind gentlemen to see that they lacked little. Killigrew, however, did not waste his time in vain regrets. He used the period to make alterations in his theatre and to widen the stage. For Davenant was going in more and more for spectacles, and Killigrew wanted to keep even.

Pepys visited the empty theatre on 19th March, 1666. His curiosity urged him on; he tells us what he saw.

> "After dinner we walked to the King's Playhouse, all in dirt, they being altering the stage to make it wider. But God knows when they will begin to act again; but my business here was to see the inside of the stage and all the tiring rooms and machines; and indeed it was a sight worth seeing. But to see their clothes, and the various sorts, and what a mixture of things there was; here a wooden leg, there a ruff, here a hobby horse, there a crown, would make a man split himself with laughing; and particularly Lacy's wardrobe and Shatterell's. But then again, to think how fine they show upon the stage by candle light, and how poor things they are to look at too near at hand, is not pleasant at all. The machines are fine, and the paintings very pretty."

Poor Pepys was having his illusions shattered by going back stage at the wrong time. He was not the first and by no means the last.

The plague and the closing must have hit Tom Killigrew, never a rich man, pretty hard. He complained that since the Plague and the Great Fire which followed, business had never been so good as before. Yet the Lane was still pre-eminent. It had the stars, it had the glamour of being the King's House; (the other theatre was now spoken of as The Duke's, being under the patronage of the Duke of York), it had Dryden, and, of course, it had Nell Gwynne. Its rival had Betterton and the younger actors and actresses, and it was soon to challenge the supremacy of Drury Lane in reality.

In the December of 1666 they were open again and Nell Gwynne appeared in James Howard's " The English Monsieur ". This time it was a comedy and she made a real success. We have Pepys' report on it: " To the King's House, and there did see a good part of 'The English

Top.

Mrs. PATRICK CAMPBELL, who played at Drury Lane in 1906 in *The Bondman.*

Centre.

JOHN PHILIP KEMBLE, brother of Mrs. SIDDONS, who did wonderful work at Drury Lane as actor and as manager.

Below.

MICHAEL MOHUN, who had been a Major in the Cavalier Army. One of the first stars at Drury Lane when it opened in 1663.

At left.

JANE POPE, famous Drury Lane actress who played there for fifty years. Leading lady with GARRICK and afterwards under SHERIDAN. Amongst other things she created " Mrs. Candour " in *The School for Scandal.*

Below.

DAVID GARRICK, Drury Lane's greatest man, who did so much for the stage in general and who wrote such a wonderful page of Drury Lane's history.

Monsieur,' which is a mighty pretty play, very witty and pleasant. And the women do very well, but above all little Nelly; that I am mightily pleased with the play and much with the House, the women doing better than I expected; and very fair women."

When the same authority saw her in Beaumont and Fletcher's "The Humourous Lieutenant" with which the Lane had reopened and in which she played "Celia" (played at the opening by Ann Marshall), he had a big thrill. It was not the play which gave it to him, for: "Thence to the King's House (the date is 23 January, 1667) and there saw 'the Humourous Lieutenant'; a silly play, I think; only the spirit in it that grows very tall, and then sinks again to nothing, having two heads breeding upon one, and then Knipp's singing did please me. Here in a box above, we spied Mrs. Pierce; and going out, they called us all in and brought us to Nelly, a most pretty woman, who acted the great part of Celia to-day very fine, and did it pretty well; I kissed her, and so did my wife, a mighty pretty soul she is."

In the same year Dryden provided Drury Lane with a play called "Secret Love, or The Maiden Queen." This time no mistake was made about Mistress Gwynne's capabilities, she was cast for a comic part, that of "Florimel" playing opposite her tutor-lover Hart, who played "Celadon." It was a triumph for the two of them and for the dramatist as well. The King was in his box at the first performance, and the gossips whispered that he himself had suggested the plot to the poet-dramatist, so it was really a Royal play in Theatre Royal. The Duke of York, the Royal brother and future James II came as well, sitting with the King. We have again the benefit of Pepys, who was present on that important occasion, 2nd March 1667. "After dinner, with my wife to the King's House to see 'The Maiden Queen,' a new play of Dryden's, mightily commended for the regularity of it, and the strain and wit; the truth is, there is a comical part done by Nell, which is Florimel, that I never can hope ever to see the like done by man or woman. The King and Duke of York were at the play. But so great a performance of a comical part was never, I believe, in the world before as Nell does this both as a mad girl, then most and best of all when she came in like a young gallant, and hath the motions and carriage of a spark the most that ever I saw any man have. It makes me, I confess, admire her." That was a pretty good notice from a " choosy " experienced man.

Although it is said that the King suggested the plot to Dryden, it is on record that Charles objected to the sentiments about their marriage made by " Celadon " and " Florimel " and uttered before the Queen. This comes well from that faithful husband! The lines had extra point because the audience knew that the two performers who uttered them were living together. Nell had a jig in this play which she danced divinely in boy's clothes, and also spoke the Epilogue which Dryden wrote specially for her. She excelled in Epilogues and would send the audience away happily. Dawns said of her " she acted the most spirited and fantastic parts, and she spoke a prologue or an epilogue with admirable address. Indeed it was sometimes carried to extravagance, but even her highest flights were so natural that they rather provoked laughter than excited disgust." She was the darling of her audiences. She made a delightful boy and looked so attractive in male attire that she started a fashion, for the fine ladies of Whitehall took to wearing it. Probably Nell was the first actress to influence female fashion.

Having attained so quickly an assured stage position, she was already preparing to leave it. She was beginning a liaison with Charles Sackville, Lord Buckhurst, afterwards 6th Earl of Dorset and first Earl of Middlesex. She was at the time lodging at the " Cock and Pie," in Drury Lane, which as No. 88 in that famous street, existed until 1880. Pepys had a glimpse of her there on May Day in 1667, which he enshrines for us in a vignette of Restoration Spring " Thence to Westminster; in the way meeting many milkmaids with the garlands upon their pails, dancing with a fiddler before them; and saw pretty Nelly, standing at her lodgings door in Drury Lane in her smock sleeves and bodice, looking upon one; she seemed a mighty pretty creature."

Buckhurst carried her away from Drury Lane in the July, and took her off to Epsom: he was very much in love with her. A talented man, he has left a lovely song by which to remember him called " To All You Ladies Now on Land," composed when he was at sea with the Fleet fighting the Dutch.

The love affair did not last long. Either Nell wearied of Epsom where Buckhurst installed her and where they kept " a merry house," or else the two did not hit it off. Anyway she was back at Drury Lane in the August, for she played in " The Indian Emperor " there in that month, on the 22nd and four days later Pepys saw her again, this time in " The Surprisal" which he did not like, and as to which he reports an empty house. Orange Moll supplied him with the latest scandal, especially about Mistress Nell. Moll told him " that Nell is already left by My Lord Buckhurst and that he makes sport of her, and swears she hath all she could get of him; and Hart, her great admirer, now hates her and that she is very poor and hath lost My Lady Castlemaine, who was her great friend also, but she is come to the House but is neglected by them all."

Business was evidently still bad, for Pepys mentions it when he went to Drury Lane on 5th October—" And so to the King's House, and there going in, met with Knipp and she took me up to the tiring rooms; and to the women's shift, where Nell was dressing herself and was all unready, and is very pretty, prettier than I thought. And so walked all up and down the house above and then below into the scene room and there sat down and she gave us fruit; and here read the questions to Knipp, while she answered me, through all her part of Flora's Vagaries, which was acted to-day. But Lord, to see how they were both painted would have make a man mad and did make me loathe them; and what base company of men comes along them and how lewdly they talk—and how poor the men are in clothes and yet what a show they make on the stage by candlelight, is very observable . . . . But to see how Nelly cursed for having so few people in the pit, was very pretty; the other house carrying away all the people at the new play, and is said nowadays to have generally the most company as being better players. By and by into the pit, and there saw the play, which is pretty good, but my belly was full of what I had seen in the house, and so, the play being done, away home and there to writing my letters and so home to supper and bed."

Nelly was now coming into Royal favour. She had attracted the King, who was also casting a very friendly—a too friendly—eye on Moll Davies at the Duke's or Lincoln's Inn Theatre. Mistress Davies was also a dancer, and according to some a better dancer than Nelly. She also appeared as a boy and looked charming. The King had given her a ring worth £700, and a house in Suffolk Street.

51

But at the same time he " sent several times for Nelly." Nell was " on to " Moll Davies. Hearing that she had been told to visit the King late at night, she sent for Moll in a friendly fashion and gave her some sweets which were filled with jalap. Very like Nelly.

In 1669 she played in Dryden's "Tyrannic Love, or The Royal Martyr." This was a tragedy, so she was given a very humorous epilogue to speak, as a comic climax. Nell lay dead on the ground as "Valeria" and bearers entered to carry her away. They placed her on the bier when she revived and cried

> " Hold, are you mad, you damn'd confounded dog
> I am to rise, and speak the Epilogue.":

In the following year, 1770, she put this final blow right home to the heart of the King. The play was Dryden's "Almanzor and Almahide, or The Conquest of Granada by the Spaniards." This enabled Nell to bring off a double event. At the Duke's House, Nokes, a great comedian, had appeared in a very large hat which was received with much laughter and created a great deal of talk. Dryden and Killigrew went one better. They put Nell into boys' clothes and they gave her a hat larger than the largest cartwheel ever seen, and on she danced to speak the Prologue. The effect was electrical. Nell's tiny figure and piquant face in her gay gallant's clothes beneath this enormous hat sent the audience into convulsions and made even the actors roar with laughter. She rattled off the Prologue, a brilliant one, as only she could, and the King was vastly delighted. He was, it is stated, almost suffocated with laughter. That night he carried her home in his coach and from then on she ruled him as his mistress. But his gain was Drury's loss. Nell never returned to the stage. She had her hands full with her Royal lover.

What did this captivating woman look like? There are scores of her portraits in existence, for artists loved to paint her. But how could they catch that rich personality, that mobile mind which made her face change every second as thoughts and feelings crossed it? Could they convey the spirit of the true actress and born charmer? She was very pretty; not beautiful in the accepted sense, but she possessed charm; something far better. She was short but she had an exquisite figure, rather full, as the saying—and the taste—was in those days. She was no scraggy hop

52

pole of a girl, but extremely feminine. She had reddish brown hair, and her eyes twinkled like stars. When she smiled, and she smiled nearly always, her eyes nearly closed, to open again suddenly and with vivid effect. This was no trick, but a natural grace. She had the smallest hands and feet, tremendous vitality and personality, and a sense of humour which never deserted her. When she died, having lived every minute of her thirty-six years, she was buried in St. Martin's-in-the-Fields, and Dr. Thomas Tennison—afterwards Archbishop of Canterbury—preached the funeral oration.

The romance which surrounds her memory hides much that is sordid and squalid, but let that go. What remains is affection and even respect. For she never pretended to be other than she was. She possessed a loyalty and truthfulness which would have graced her so-called betters; she loved her country; and in her own way, and by her own means, she worked for it. She loved her sister Rose, although she was a convicted felon; she loved her mother, to whom she owed nothing save birth, and she loved her King. She held him longer and more closely than any of the women he dallied with, and his last thoughts were of her to the exclusion of all else. "Don't let poor Nelly starve" he breathed to James, when that worthy was waiting to become King—and to James's credit, he did not. Nell only outlived her King Charles by two years.

*　　*　　*　　*

Killigrew was not finding things easy. The players at the Duke's and the growing power of Betterton were luring the public away from the Lane, in spite of a startling new attraction. For in 1668 something which was to become the policy of the great theatre, a forerunner of those realistic dramas which were to add to its fame, and create the phrase "Drury Lane Drama," had made its appearance. It was in a play called "Hide Park" and in it real horses appeared, to the astonishment, joy and delight of all beholders. Give an audience something on the stage they can see for nothing outside and the result in success. Killigrew knew it, and all Drury Lane managers since have known it also. Killigrew was going in for Spectacle when "Cataline" was staged on 18th December 1688, with Hart in his most famous part, and Mohun and the entire strength of the company to support him. There was much ado. The

53

King had promised them £500 to be spent on costumes, and the thing was done in slap-up style. There were no fewer than sixteen scarlet robes in the Senate scene, and the battle was done with the greatest care. It made a sensation. Indeed, it appears to have been a production such as Tree might have handled with pride.

Another most important theatrical event followed. For years the brilliant George Villers, Duke of Buckingham, had been preparing a play which should be a satire on the cult of the heroic drama and the stage in general, to say nothing of the public taste. He gave it to Killigrew and it was produced at Drury Lane on 7th December 1671. This was "The Rehearsal." The chief character is one "Bayes," and the play was almost a play within a play, for it showed the last rehearsal of an alleged play just to be produced, by no means a new device. It was the progenitor of Sheridan's "The Critic."

This part of Bayes was almost certainly a composite portrait, but it was generally considered that Dryden was the man aimed at, for he was the arch-exponent of the heroic school. At the first performance it is said that Dryden was induced to sit in a box between Buckingham and the Earl of Dorset (presumably Nell Gwynne's old lover), and watch and listen to the burlesque of himself. Lacy, that fine comedian, played Bayes, specially rehearsed by the author, and the cast included Cartwright, Kynaston and Mrs. Reeves, who is supposed to have been Dryden's mistress. "The Rehearsal" is theatrical history, and it belongs to Drury Lane. It was a success and has held the stage for centuries. The role of Bayes was a famous part of Garrick's and Samuel Foote made his first big success in it. Old Farren played it in 1819.

In spite of the success of "The Rehearsal," matters were far from good at Drury Lane with a strong rival in the great playhouse which Davenant had dreamed but had not lived to see built. The Duke's House, or Dorset Gardens Theatre, had opened on 9th November 1671 (old calendar). It stood on the river side just by what is now Salisbury Square. Designed by Wren, it was ornate and modern. It had better lighting, better machinery (or so they said) and a fine company headed by the great Betterton himself, who was "Keeper" as well. It was a sensation. Betterton did things well,

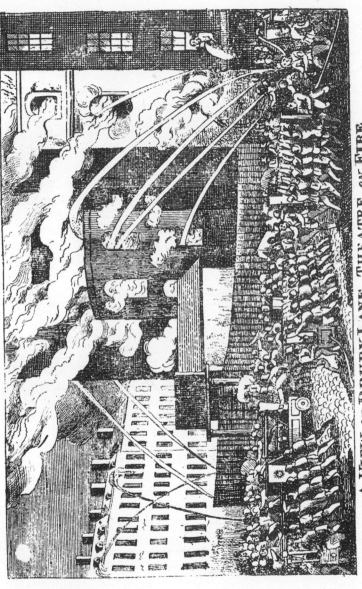

A VIEW OF DRURY LANE THEATRE ON FIRE

This superb Edifice with its scenery and dresses &c was totally destroyed by Fire on the night of Feb 24 1809 & cost 200,000 Pounds building

Published March 3 1809 by J. Pitts 14 Great St andrew Street Seven Dials

The fire of 1809, which nearly ended the career of Theatre Royal.

A contemporary print gives a lively representation of the scene.

55

and drew the public which then as now—perhaps more than then—always flocked to any novelty. It made history, it gained fame, but in the end, for all its glory, it had to amalgamate with the King's Theatre,—our Drury Lane. All that remains of it now is a plaque on a wall in John Carpenter Street, to mark the site.

Then out of a clear sky came destruction. It was on the evening of 25th January 1672. The play was over, the audience and players had gone home. Suddenly the cry of "Fire, fire" thrilled through the neighbourhood: it brought a head out of every window, and thronged the streets as if by magic. For fire was a deadly catastrophe then, and the memory of the Great Conflagration in 1666 was fresh in every mind.

Drury Lane Theatre was afire and burning briskly. The fire had started below stage, beneath the stairs in the room where Orange Moll kept her stores. Here was highly inflammable material, and as nothing was fireproofed in those days, the place was like a tinder box. The outbreak was discovered between six and seven p.m. on that Thursday evening, and it spread rapidly. Fire-fighting was rudimentary and the flames obtained a sure hold. All the scenery and the wardrobes and half the theatre was destroyed. The fire spread with terrific rapidity, wiping out all the houses from the Rose Tavern in Russell Street, on the corner of Drury Lane and Vinegar Yard, and many of the houses in Vinegar Yard itself.

So dangerous did the spread of the flames prove that the old method of checking them was resorted to, and gunpowder was used to blow up houses standing in the direct course of the fire. As usual this did more harm than the fire. In this case it did worse, for in an explosion died the young Drury Lane actor, Richard Bell, come doubtless to try and render aid and to save what he could from the wreck.

One can imagine the company, Hart, Mohun, and the rest, and Killigrew with his sons, gazing with grief and dismay at the blackened ruins of their playhouse,—of their very livelihood, for all they knew. For when morning dawned, there was just a heap of smoking ruins where once had stood the Theatre Royal. The first chapter of the great playhouse was over.

56

CHAPTER 7

WREN REBUILDS THE THEATRE

WITH their theatre burned down, all their properties and wardrobe destroyed, and damage done to the extent of £20,000—a crippling sum then—Killigrew and his company still had to act, in order to live.

They had the agony of mind of seeing their rivals installed in the handsome new theatre in Dorset Gardens, with a clear field before them. All they could do was to go up to Lincoln's Inn Fields, the old Duke's Theatre, Davenant's house, which had been abandoned by their competitors for their new playhouse. The position of the two companies was now reversed, the Duke's Players had the big theatre, the King's men had to go to the old, inconvenient, smaller place which had been Lisle's Tennis Court.

But Killigrew was not beaten. He at once set about raising money to rebuild Drury Lane. He was not in too good shape in that direction. In spite of the previous playhouse's initial success, he was heavily involved. It seems as if he had no head for figures or grasp of business matters.

Indeed, early in 1663, before his first playhouse opened, he had already assigned his shares elsewhere. He borrowed £950 on them in 1673, and negotiated another loan in the same year for £1,600. This did not make for financial stability when the new house was finally opened.

Meanwhile the whole company had to work. They opened at Lincoln's Inn on 26th February, 1672. They announced themselves as " The Shipwrecked Mariners " to gain public sympathy for their plight and the play was "Wit Without Money," a very apt title in the circumstances. They had to rely on old stock plays for some time, to suit the small amount of costumes they had been able to buy, beg or borrow, and their Royal Master does not seem to have helped them at all.

Their lot was made doubly hard by the arrival in London and the success of a company of French players, who took much custom from them, and who made them very angry by exhibiting bills printed in red and black on white, which outshone the ordinary plain black on white bills of the conservative English players. The King's Company either could not or would not alter their bills to compete. But they resented the foreign invasion when they were fighting almost for their very lives, and their spokesman, Dryden, inveighed against the Frenchmen in a prologue which he wrote for a revival of " Arviragus and Philicia " :

> " A brisk French troop is grown your dear delight
> Who with broad bloody bills call you each day
> To laugh and break your buttons at their play."

That French company played at the old Cockpit, and very successful they were. The King supported them by many favours, which added to the discomfiture and anger of his own Comedians.

They do not seem to have tried a new play at all until they produced Dryden's " Marriage à La Mode." That was an immense success and brought them back some prosperity and favour. It is difficult to trace all their doings at Lincoln's Inn. But meanwhile the new theatre was building, and there is no reason to suppose that during the period which elapsed between the summer of 1673 and the spring of 1674, when the new Drury Lane opened, the Royal Company were unemployed.

Killigrew was not above learning from the new Dorset Gardens Theatre. The architect of that playhouse, now enjoying great prosperity, was Christopher Wren, the rebuilder of London. So Killigrew had Wren build his new theatre too. It was very much larger than the old one. It was indeed practically the Drury Lane we know to-day. It stood upon the same site, occupied the same amount of ground, and some of it, at any rate, stands there now, for the great arches under the theatre upon which the structure now rests are those which Wren erected to support the second Drury Lane Theatre, or Theatre Royal, Brydges Street, in 1674; and they carry the theatre to-day, as sound and as steady as when Sir Christopher first built them. "The Crypt," as it is called, was used as an air raid shelter and Home Guard sleeping quarters during the Second World War, until another and more commodious shelter was built adjoining it; and not one flake or particle of mortar of Wren's work was stirred by the bombs which hit the building.

In addition to the theatre, Killigrew built a " scene house " in Vinegar Yard, behind the theatre, where he could make and paint scenery. The cost of this, together with that of the scenery, costumes, machines and the like, was found by the actor-sharers in the concern. Drury Lane still has its scene room and paint frame. But the new building was really owned by the outside people who had invested their money in it.

Killigrew, of course, held the all-powerful Charter or Patent, but he had mortgaged it for the building fund. The cost of the building was about £4,000, which sum probably included the scene room.

All was ready on 26th March, 1674, and Theatre Royal, Drury Lane, reopened its doors for the second time.

Architecturally it could not compete with the magnificence of the Dorset Gardens house — there had not been enough money for that. But it was a fine workable theatre, and it was Theatre Royal. The opening night, March 26th, 1674, was duly celebrated by the attendance of the King and Queen. The play was "The Beggar's Bush," an old favourite and a sure card. It was by Beaumont and Fletcher, one of whose plays had opened the First Theatre. There was, of course, a Prologue written by Dryden, as was right and proper, in which he cleverly contrasted the plainness of the new theatre with the grandeur of its competitor, at which he jeered because it had forsaken, to a large extent, the drama proper and gone in for opera.

This, then, was the theatre which was to stand for 117 years, through six reigns, to become the home of Betterton, Booth, Wilks, Cibber, Dogget, Mrs. Barry, Mrs. Bracegirdle, Nance Oldfield, Garrick, Peg Woffington, Kitty Clive, Mrs. Abington and many others.

We have a vivid picture of the interior from Colley Cibber. The stage at the new Old Drury projected right forward in a semi-oval to the front benches of the pit, with side wings instead of stage boxes, so that, if need be, the whole action could be carried out on the apron, in front of the proscenium. This enabled the players to get over their subtle effects of expression and whispers, which otherwise would not have been seen or heard.

Despite its brilliant opening, all was not well at Drury Lane. Hart and Mohun were ageing, the younger people getting restive, salaries were small, and becoming smaller. Later they were to become irregular too. The old men still had all the good parts. Good as they were, their continued appearances were palling on the public. Some of the company deserted to Dorset Gardens. It was now Killigrew's turn to appeal to the Lord Chamberlain to intervene.

But Mohun and Hart had entire control; Killigrew doing little, although he was still Patentee (and so all-powerful if it came to any vital decision) and also Master of the King's Revels, having wrested that title from his old enemy, the crooked, grasping Sir Henry Herbert. In 1676, the troubles in the theatre had grown so acute that the company shut themselves down, so bad was the disagreement. A Royal Mandate immediately bade them reopen, and they did so. Trouble between Killigrew and his son Charles caused much confusion. Charles wanted his father to retire, in order to succeed him. The Lord Chamberlain, who must have been heartily sick of them all, cut the Gordian knot and made Hart and Mohun, Kynaston and Cartwright managers, and responsible to him. This, however, does not appear to have worked very well, and finally, Hart became sole and responsible manager, though he was getting old and suffering from the stone. Mohun was ageing, too, and a victim to gout. Still, when the two appeared together they exercised their old magic, and the house was good.

Real desertions began in 1676. The two leading ladies, Mrs. Marshall (Ann) and Mrs. Hughes, skipped off to Dorset Gardens, which already had Mrs. Sanderson and Mrs. Barry. Then on 22nd February, 1677, Killigrew, who felt the burden had become too great for him—he was becoming an old man—resigned his Patent and power to his son Charles, and gave up to the King his title of Master of the Revels. He had proved himself a man of brains and wit, of initiative and ideas. He had done much for the theatre. But he was not strong-willed enough to rule with power nor could he cope with trouble and disagreement. Thomas Killigrew, gentleman, wit, playwright, courtier, actor, Gentleman of the Bedchamber, ambassador, Master of the Revels, died on 19th March, 1683, and was buried in Westminster Abbey. His memory lives for ever as the Man Who Gave Us Drury Lane.

The Lane did not flourish under Charles Killigrew in spite of some new blood amongst the players—especially Mrs. Boutel and above all Cardonnel Goodman.

Mrs. Boutel is described in Betterton's History of the Stage, as follows: " Mrs. Boutel was likewise a very considerable actress; she was low of stature, had very agreeable features, a good complexion but a childish look. Her voice was weak but very mellow; she generally acted the young, innocent lady whom all the heroes are mad in love with; she was a favourite of the town." Add to this that she had very blue eyes and chestnut hair, and you have a pretty complete picture of her.

And now for the "bad-man" of the theatre, Scum Goodman. He took to the stage because no other calling was left to him, as so many of his sort have done since, and because no references were asked or given. That he was a good actor was lucky for him and for Drury Lane, and had he wished, he could have earned an honest living in the theatre. On and off the stage he fulfilled the Shakespearean dictum of playing many parts in his time, and it was no fault of his that he escaped his just due—the gallows.

He had been an undergraduate at Cambridge. He made no mark there as a scholar, but a considerable one by his devotion to and extravagance in fashionable dress. He was a handsome, dashing fellow His career at the university was brought to a close when he chose, for no discernible reason, to slash to pieces the portrait of the Duke of Monmouth, who was the Chancellor. Sent down from Cambridge, with no calling or influence of any kind, he enrolled at Drury Lane.

Early in his career (in 1678) we find him joined with Charles Killigrew, Hart, Burt and Mohun, petitioning the Lord Chamberlain that Lee and Dryden should not be allowed to take their new play, "Oedipus," to Dorset Gardens. They besought his Lordship to protect them, for these two men, they said, were their last poets.

A quarrel between the Killigrew brothers, Charles and Henry, brought things to such a pass that Drury Lane closed down in 1678. This was the cue for Scum and his youngsters, and they took it. Goodman, Clarke, Hains, and Gray, the theatre's treasurer, seceded in a body and took with them Mrs. Corey. They could not open in opposition in London, for the Patent prevented them. Nor did they want to. They went off to Edinburgh, and played in a house in the Canongate which was used as a theatre. Soon after their arrival the High Commissioner for Scotland, His Royal Highness the Duke of York, heir to the Throne (afterwards James II) reached the Scottish capital. Like his brother Charles, the Duke loved the Theatre and was patron

61

of Drury Lane's successful rival in Dorset Gardens. He and his Court made much of the rebels from the Lane, who called themselves, without the slightest right to the title, "His Majesty's Comedians."

Killigrew still wanted those young men, and he wanted his good actress. He made them all sorts of promises, even offering to pay their expenses for the long journey home. The Duke of York returned to London in 1680, and the errant players came back with him, no doubt travelling in his entourage. It is pretty certain they never got those expenses from Killigrew, although peace was made between them, but on their return to Old Drury they found things worse than before they left.

Goodman and his fellows were in a bad plight. Scum had never had more than £2 per week, and he was a leading actor. Now he could not get even that. He, who loved finery and soft living, found himself reduced to sharing an attic with Griffin, who was faring no better. The two men had only one decent shirt between them, and had to wear it turn and turn about, as occasion demanded. But the day, or the night, arrived when both wanted it at the same time. Both had an appointment with a lady. Friendly arguments failed. There was a quarrel which developed into a fight. Swords flashed out in that attic and in the duel which resulted, both contestants were hurt, and worst of all, the shirt itself was destroyed.

Scum needed money desperately : there was none to be had at the theatre, but there was one means of getting some ready cash if you were courageous, reckless and dare-devil, and that was by becoming a highwayman. To this adventurous, if dangerous, course, Scum turned without hesitation. He got hold of a horse and some pistols, and at nightfall "took to the road." But although he was successful as an actor, he was a failure as a highwayman. He was captured and accommodated with free board and lodging in Newgate, with the gallows being set for the last act. He was about to quit the boards of the stage for the boards of the scaffold when help came from high quarters. James II was King. The Duke of Monmouth had been in rebellion and before being defeated and captured had given the King some very anxious moments. Scum was the man who had put a great and public affront upon the defeated Pretender. Somehow Scum must have got word through to the King, who remembered the story and their meeting in Scotland. He was pardoned.

There seems to have been no question about his returning to Drury Lane. Doubtless the management thought it no bad thing from a publicity point of view. He now succeeded to many of the parts which had been Hart's. He was a big success as " Alexander the Great " and as " Julius Caesar," and he played the name-part in Rochester's " Valentinian." Success smiled on him in other directions, and financial gain, of a kind not at all distasteful to him, was soon to follow. For a Duchess, a faded and middle-aged Duchess maybe, but still a Duchess, fell in love with this reckless young actor. The Duchess of Cleveland had plenty of money. That was what appealed to Scum. He grew more impudent and overbearing than ever. He " played " to the Duchess at Drury Lane as if she were the only person in the house. He ignored the rest of the audience.

Now Queen Mary was a Stuart, and so loved the theatre, which she attended frequently. Once, when Queen Mary was coming to occupy the Royal Box, Scum refused to go on or have the play start until his Duchess was seated. " Has my Duchess arrived? " he demanded, and when an anxious management told him " No " he flatly refused to allow the play to proceed. The Queen was already in the box and to keep her waiting was to risk scandal and trouble. But Scum was adamant; the management terrified. Fortunately the Duchess turned up in the nick of time and a crisis was averted.

His life having fallen on easy lines, he ought to have been reasonably content. But no; the scum rose to the surface again. Two of his Duchess's children annoyed him. In his easy, high-handed way, he arranged to have them poisoned. A hireling was procured to do this deed, but the plot was discovered. Scum was arrested and stood his trial. Even then his luck held. He was not tried for attempted murder but only for a misdemeanour. He managed to escape even imprisonment, but he was fined so heavily that it crippled him for the rest of his life in England. Another source of income was at hand, however. He was hired by Jacobites to assassinate King William. Probably he was paid in advance. But the secret leaked out; he was arrested and to save his life he turned King's evidence. He was then in danger from the plotters, who feared that he might make further dangerous revelations. They offered him a pension of £500 a year to leave the country. He went to France, and there were rumours that he ended up in the Bastille. He was a thorough scoundrel but he loved Drury Lane: and one good action to his credit will be told a little further on in the story.

CHAPTER 8

SCANDALOUS TIMES

THINGS were going from bad to worse at Old Drury. At the beginning of the year 1681, the brothers Killigrew could not meet their debts and for a time the theatre closed down. That fine old theatrical custom of a " cut " came into operation. A " cut " means that everyone connected with the theatre agrees to take a reduction in salary, to help over bad times.

Everyone took a cut, even the shareholders in the theatre, who expected their share weekly, and not in the form of dividends half-yearly, or yearly, as to-day. They reopened, but business did not improve. During the months of May and June they were glad to play to £4 per performance. Sometimes the audiences were so small that the money was refunded and no show was given. In the autumn they did have success with John Bank's "The Unhappy Favourite, or The Earl of Essex" but it was a drop in the ocean. A new dramatist, Thomas Southerne, was then tried, and his play, "The Loyal Brother, or The Persian Prince," was acclaimed. It had a fine cast, Scum Goodman, Clarke—a splendid actor when sober—Mrs. Corey, Sarah Cook, Ann Quinn (often confounded with Nell Gwynne) and Mohun himself. All were well suited and at the top of their form. In those days, it was an all star cast. But, alas, it was only a flash in the pan, and the temporary end was near.

Theatre Royal could not compete with the times. The steps downwards are easy to mark! The disgraceful management of the unruly, unreliable Charles and Henry Killigrew, libertines both! the constant war and intrigues of Goodman and Clarke against Hart and Mohun, and the gradual falling out by death and retirement of the best of the older men. Wintershal died and Burt retired in 1679; Lacy, a tower of strength as actor and as dramatist, died in 1681. Cartwright was an invalid and out of action.

64

Internal strife, and political plots and sensations brought down the curtain at Drury Lane in 1682. They had blamed the Duke's House in Dorset Gardens for their downfall. But despite fine acting and good plays and first class dramatists, things were very little better even there. The times were bad and affected everyone. Davenant's widow and son, and Betterton, as Keeper of the House and general art director and producer, had run it to the best of their great ability. Their company was a brilliant one; their dramatists superb, for they included at this time Dryden and Lee, renegades from the King's House, Thomas Otway, Aphra Behn and many others. But, whilst generally they were in a better position than the King's House, their position was not strong and they were worried. It was not surprising, therefore, to find that those two "old timers" Hart and Kynaston, seeing their parlous state, had put out feelers about a union as early as 1681.

The result was satisfactory. The Duke's House had long been attempting to undermine Drury Lane, and had already seduced away Dryden and Lee, two of its chief pillars. They found that Hart and Kynaston were also considering the possibility of a merger. At first sight this might sound somewhat traitorous, but most certainly it was not. Hart was concerned with the continued existence of the theatre he loved, and Kynaston had feelings of the same kind, with the added inducement to safeguard himself. So these two men came to an agreement with the Duke's Theatre whereby they undertook to use their best endeavours to bring about a union. The document, which is an important one in Drury Lane history, is here given in full.

" MEMORANDUM. It was then agreed upon between Dr. Charles Davenant, Thomas Betterton, gent., and Willie Smith, gent., of the one part, and Charles Hart, gent., and Edward Kynaston, gent., of the other part, that the said Charles Davenant, Thomas Betterton, and Willie Smith, do pay or cause to be paid, out of the profits of acting, unto Charles Hart and Edward Kynaston, five shillings apiece for every day there shall be any tragedies or comedies, or other representations, acted at the Duke's Theatre in Salisbury Court, wherever the company shall act during the respective lives of the said Charles Hart or Edward Kynaston, excepting on the days the young men or young women play for their own profit only; but this agreement to cease if Charles Hart or Edward Kynaston shall at any time play among or effectually assist the King's company or actors; and for as long as this is paid they both covenant and promise not to play at the King's Theatre.

"If Mr. Kynaston shall hereafter be free to act at the Duke's Theatre, this agreement with him, as to his pension, shall also cease.

"Mr. Hart and Mr. Kynaston do promise to make over within a month after sealing of this, unto Charles Davenant, Thomas Betterton, and Willie Smith, all the right, title, and claim which they or either of them may have to any plays, books, clothes and scenes in the King's Playhouse. Mr. Hart and Mr. Kynaston do also promise, within a month after the sealing hereof, to make over to the said Charles Davenant, Thomas Betterton and Willie Smith, all the title which they each of them have to six and three-pence apiece for every day there shall be any playing at the King's Theatre.

"Mr. Hart and Mr. Kynaston do both also promise to promote with all their power and interest an agreement between both playhouses; and Mr. Kynaston, for himself, promises to endeavour as much as he can to get free that he may act at the Duke's playhouse, but he is not obliged to play unless he have ten shillings a day for his acting, and his pension then to cease.

"Mr. Hart and Mr. Kynaston promise to go to law with Mr. Killigrew to have these articles performed, and are to be at the expense of the suit.

"In witness of this agreement all the parties have hereunto set their hands this 14th day of October, 1681."

That was the agreement which has been commented on as being treachery to the King's House (Drury Lane). But was it? Both men knew that their theatre was doomed unless something was done, and this was the only possible course. Hart made the sacrifice—he accepted 5/- a day and forfeited six and threepence. This 5/- pension he would have had from King's House anyway, plus his shares and could have got a salary as well. It is certain that his motive was the saving of Drury Lane. Kynaston fared better. If he played at the Duke's he got 10/-, but he never did so. But he did continue to play at the Lane after the Union.

The triumph of the old Theatre was complete, for the Duke's House lingered on only for a few years, going down and down in the scale, becoming merely a house for light opera, a home of tumblers, acrobats and wire walkers. Eventually, it shut down for ever some time in 1706.

When Drury Lane reopened on 16th November 1682, under the new regime, most of the old actors who had formed the first company of The King's Comedians had vanished from the stage. Hart retired: he could not compete with Betterton. Although his nominal salary had been £3 or £3 10 0 per week—never more than £4,—his profits in the good times as shareholder had brought him in £1,000

66

a year, a fortune then. Now full of years and honours, he bade farewell to the public and to the theatre he had served so well.

The case of poor, gentle, talented Mohun was different. He still tried to carry on, gout stricken and old as he was. He was poor and needy, and had a family of five. But the "young men" now in charge of the Lane brushed him aside. In desperation he appealed to his King-Master. He reminded Charles that he was an old Cavalier, and that he had fought for his father. For once, Charles remembered. More, one feels sure, because of Mohun the actor, than of Mohun the old Cavalier. He sent peremptory orders that Mohun should enjoy the same privileges as those accorded to Hart and Kynaston. Mohun did not live long after leaving Drury Lane. He died in a house in Brownlow Street, near the theatre, in 1684. By a strange trick of fate, that street is now called Betterton Street, and so perpetuates the memory of the actor who eclipsed Major Mohun, soldier, actor and gentleman.

Betterton stepped into the shoes of Hart, and though some of the old company lingered, most of the actors and actresses were from the Duke's Theatre. The opening was an occasion of some importance. The King and Queen attended in state.

There was now only one theatre in London in possession of a patent, so new terms were imposed on the actors. The profits were divided up into twenty shares, ten of which went to the company, in proportions according to their standing, and there was probably much haggling before agreement amongst the participants was reached. The other half went to the shareholders in the concern, who appear to have disposed of them to speculators wanting a flutter in the theatre business.

With Betterton at its head, the King's House received an infusion of new blood, which so far as acting was concerned, was the best in the kingdom. It included Montford, Sandford, Noakes (Robert), Underhill and Anthony Leigh, and Mrs. Betterton, Mrs. Barry, Mrs. Leigh, Mrs. Butler, Mrs. Montford and Mrs. Bracegirdle. With Kynaston and the rest of the King's Company who remained on it was the finest team Old Drury had ever had.

After Betterton, the brightest and most popular stars were the two women Mrs. Bracegirdle and Mrs. Barry, whose stories are to a large extent interwoven with those

67

of the great actor. During the period now under review, it is the history of Betterton that is the history of Drury Lane. He shines like a star of honesty, and clean living, in a brutal, licentious age. His fellow actors and actresses, whether of Drury Lane, Lincoln's Inn or the Duke's Theatre, were of their age, and that age was a loose one. Nor did the poets and dramatists endeavour to improve it. The mere title "Restoration Comedy" tells us what to expect. Dryden had a play "Mr. Limberham, or The Kind Keeper," withdrawn because of its lewdness. Sedley, Etheredge, Wycherley, Congreve (who comes into the saga very soon now) all salted their wit with salacity. Amongst it all, four-square to the dirt and scandal, stands the immortal figure of Thomas Betterton. He proved that it is possible to touch dirt and not be defiled, that it is possible to preserve honour and gain self-respect even when all things noble are held up to ridicule. Throughout his long life, there was no breath of scandal against Betterton.

He was the son of Matthew Betterton, generally supposed to have been an under-cook to Charles I and he was born in Tothill Street, Westminster in 1635, being christened at St. Margarets on 11th August of that year. He was apprenticed to a bookseller, and later stepped straight into leading parts. Old Downes, who worshipped Betterton, says of him that "Mr. Betterton, being then but 22 years old, was highly applauded for his acting in all these plays, but especially for 'The Loyal Subject,' 'The Mad Lover,' 'Pericles,' 'The Bondman,' 'Deflores in The Changeling'; his voice being then so audibly strong, full and articulate, as in the prime of his acting."

Davenant took over this company intact from Rhodes and made them the Duke's Servants at the old Lincoln's Inn playhouse, and it was here that Betterton rose to real fame. In 1660 (5th November) he and other actors were bound to Davenant by contract, under his patent. It was there Betterton was to play "Hamlet" and to give such a performance as the English stage had never before seen. Downes, who should know, says: "Hamlet being performed by Mr. Betterton. Sir William (Davenant), having seen Mr. Taylor of the Blackfriars Company act it, who being instructed by the author, Mr. Shakespeare, taught Mr. Betterton in every Particle of it, gained him esteem and reputation, Superlative to all other plays."

Pepys, who saw him play it several times says, "Above

all, Betterton did the Prince's part beyond imagination "—
he follows with several other instances of the actor's greatness in this test part for actors; his praise rose to a
crescendo when he saw Betterton play it again some years
later. "The Duke of York's Playhouse and saw 'Hamlet,'
which we have not seen this year before or more, and
mightily pleased with it, but above all, with Betterton, the
best part, I believe, that ever man acted."

His "Ophelia" was Mrs. Sanderson, which gave added
zest to the early performances of "Hamlet" at Lincoln's
Inn, for all the town knew that these two performers were
in love; very shortly after they married.

Other Betterton triumphs were his Henry VIII and
"Bosola" in Webster's tragedy "The Duchess of Malfi."
He showed his versatility, for this greatest of Hamlets was a
particularly successful Sir Toby Belch: he scored also as
Captain Jolly in a comedy "The Cutter of Coleman Street."
He also played Macbeth, which nobody seemed like, not even
King Charles, who fell foul of the fact that the Two
Murderers were made up as very dark men. He himself
was extremely swarthy and he made the classic criticism
about this: "Pray, what is the meaning that we never see
a rogue in a play but odsfish they always clap on him a
black periwig when it is well known one of the greatest
rogues in England wears a fair one?" This was a cut at
the Earl of Shaftesbury, but also a defence of the monarch's
own black periwig.

Pepys considered Betterton the finest actor in the world.
Those who desire to hear the greatest eulogy one actor
ever wrote about another should turn up Colley Cibber's
Apology, and there read in full what he says of this man.
It is an amazing tribute, too long to quote, for he dissects
the performance of Hamlet. But his summing up is "I
never heard a line of tragedy come from Betterton wherein
my judgment, my ear and my imagination were not fully
satisfied." Of how many could that be said? And how
many actors would say it? Even though they were not
contemporaries and rivals.

When Dorset Gardens was opened, Betterton shone in
full glory. He was now the chief, his old master Davenant
being dead, and Betterton's honesty, wisdom and judgment,
guided Davenant's widow and orphans along the perilous
path of theatre management. He opened the theatre with
a play which had gained immense success at the old play-

house lately vacated, "Sir Martin Mar-all," in which he himself had no part. This may have been intended as an act of modest abstention on the part of the greatest actor of the day, but it turned out to be a very wise one, for it left him free to concentrate all his great skill on the multifarious duties which, as Keeper of the House, must have been particularly onerous at the opening of a new venture.

All his life he worked hard and took little rest. He was a just man in all his dealings, he was an ideal husband, he returned good for evil. When a friend of his persuaded him to invest his savings, which he had worked so hard to gain, in a disastrous venture, Betterton adopted the daughter of the man who had almost ruined him and brought her up as his own. He never showed jealousy yet often he would stand down and play inferior parts to give rising actors a chance. Four Royal Personages honoured him, Charles II, James II, William's Queen Mary, and Anne. His highest salary was £5 per week, and even that included £1 per week for his wife when she retired in 1694. He stood up for his profession, he fought injustice and oppression, and won. He had the greatest Benefit in his old age that any actor had ever had; a solemn and touching occasion. He died in 1710 and his body was buried in the eastern cloister of Westminster Abbey. Mrs. Betterton survived him but lost her reason. The story of the Bettertons is the story of the stage and its players in its happiest, most attractive light.

Like all or most of the great actors, Betterton had to contend with physical disabilities. His face, as painted by Kneller, shows dignity combined with sweetness of expression and extreme intelligence. Yet it seems that in real life he was pock-marked, had a large head, and a short thick neck. He was barely above middle height, but he had a fine strong athletic figure and his voice was full and manly, though at times rumbling and low; he could so manage it that he could command the attention of the most unruly house, and houses in his time were unruly.

Cibber's farewell to him is taken from that play in which perhaps he most excelled,—Hamlet, for he says " He was a man, take him for all in all, I cannot look upon his like again."

In Mrs. Barry and Mrs. Bracegirdle, to say nothing of his wife, Mrs. Saunderson, he had three of the best actresses of the English stage, of then or any other time. Mrs.

Bracegirdle owed much to the Bettertons, and to one who should have been her rival, Mrs. Barry. But this great actress early saw the promise of the other, and gave her every encouragement.

Mrs. Bracegirdle seems to have been a most respectable woman, although she had plenty of mud thrown at her. She was as good as she was beautiful. Cibber says her virtues made her the delight of the town. Audiences loved her youth, her cheerful gaiety, her delightful voice and her grace of manner and movement. Her figure was perfect, she had dark brown hair and eyebrows and eyes of the same colour. It was said that she never left the stage without the audience feeling that they had all moulded their faces into an imitation of hers. She was very charitable, and the poor of the neighbourhood adored her. She lived to be over 80.

Elizabeth Barry, born in 1658, was a girl who made a bad start in her profession. She was a failure at first and was dismissed from the company. She returned in triumph and gave some magnificent performances. Dryden said of her that when she played Cassandra in one of his plays: "Mrs. Barry, always excellent, has in this tragedy excelled herself, and gained a reputation beyond any woman whom I have ever seen in the theatre." She was the daughter of a man who had ruined himself for King Charles I. She had a wonderful list of parts to her credit, creating many great roles.

Such were the stars who were to rebuild the fortunes of Old Drury at the Union.

CHAPTER 9

FOPS, VIZARDS AND ROGUES

BY the union of the two theatres, Drury Lane became the only playhouse in the town possessing a Patent or Charter. Those holding a patent could, and did, prevent other playhouses from performing not only Shakespeare but the legitimate drama and any performances other than opera, plays with music, or in dumb show. It was a monopoly or part monopoly.

71

In the later half of the eighteenth century, Foote got a limited Patent for the Haymarket, but this only enabled him to open when the other two Patent Houses were closed in the summer, and was granted for his life only. The Lyceum was refused a dramatic licence for years owing to the opposition of Drury Lane. It was not until about 1846 that the exclusive right of the Patent in this respect was finally broken. The Patent put its holder above all authorities save that of the Crown, as represented by the Lord Chamberlain, and many were the injustices it wrought. Of the Patent Theatres of London, Lincoln's Inn-Theatre is no more, the Dorset Gardens Theatre is gone, Covent Garden is an opera house; Drury Lane still remains the only true Theatre Royal, given over to the drama entirely. The Haymarket, that delightful and beautiful playhouse, has no real claim to the title " Royal," for its patent died with Foote. Perhaps because Betterton wanted to test himself and show his mettle, Drury Lane opened with a round of old favourites, "Othello," Wycherley's " Plain Dealer," Dryden's "Evening Love," Ben Jonson's " Bartholomew Fair " (of which Pepys thought so highly), "Julius Caesar," in which Betterton was a magnificent Brutus, were among these revivals. The King and Queen were at the first night, and there was a topical prologue written specially for the occasion by Dryden.

The theatre had changed little from the days of the first opening. The time of performance was now a little later, at half-past three in the afternoon; soon it was as late as five, and in the early days of the fast approaching 18th century the performances were at six.

The pit benches were still backless, and people scrambled over them. In the second Drury Lane, by means of the apron, the actors were at least ten feet nearer the audience than they had been before. The nobility and gentry sent their footmen to keep their places. These men were allowed free in the upper gallery and abused their privilege, often creating uproars.

The middle gallery, admission 1s 6d, had an unenviable reputation, for it was the haunt of the women of the town —the Vizards. In an epilogue Dryden says:

" But stay, methinks some vizard mask I see
Cast out her lure from the mid-gallery;
About her all the fluttering sparks are ranged,
The noise continues though the scene is changed;
Now growling, sputtering, wauling, such a clutter
'Tis just like puss defendant in a gutter."

But apparently it went further than just fluttering around, for in the prologue to " The Island Princess " we have the following reference :

> " Ye gallery haunters, who love to lie snug
> And munch apples or cakes whilst some neighbour you hug."

The pit held the interested playgoers and those who came to the play for their own benefit. Those who really wanted to see and hear the performance—if they could—seem to have banded themselves together in the middle and to have held it against all comers, which would suit the fops and their lady friends quite well, for they liked the end seats because they were always on the move.

Special word-games were played by the idle people in theatres—too gross even for modern ears. All this went on whilst great plays were being greatly acted.

Fops' Corner, down the front of the pit near the stage, was the centre of criticism and disturbance. Often the criticism was so loudly uttered that not only the audience but the poor players heard it as well. The attitude of the foppish gentry to the play is well illustrated in the following dialogue :

> " Come, Dick," says I, " damme, let's to the play. " Rot me," says he, " 'tis a dull one." " Damme," says I, " I value not the play, my province lies in the boxes ogling my half-crown away, or running from side box to side box, to the inviting incognitas in black faces, or else wittily crying out loud in the pit ' Bough ' or ' Boyta ' and then to be prettily answered by the rest of the Wits in the same note, like musical instruments tuned to the same pitch."

At any rate, he was willing to pay his half-crown.

The stage itself had improved. The scenery was much better. There were many "traps." There were "traverses" too, curtains running on rods which when drawn aside showed another scene set.

The front of the orchestra pit and the stage boxes were spiked to prevent people from leaping on the stage. These spikes sometimes aroused a spirit of emulation in the fops, as the following extract from the *Tatler* shows :

> " There was a very lusty fellow but withal a sort of Beau, who getting into one of the side boxes on the stage before the curtain drew, was disposed to show the whole audience his activity by leaping over the spikes; he passed from thence to one of the entering doors, where he took snuff with a tolerable good grace, displayed his fine cloaths, made one or two feint passes at the curtain with his cane, then faced about and appeared at the other door. He here affected to survey the whole house, bowed and smiled at random, then showed his teeth, which were, some of them, very white; after this he retired behind the curtain and obliged us with several views of his person from every opening."

73

There were some actors new to Drury Lane when the companies united. William Montford, or Mountford (it was spelt both ways), is described by Cibber as being the most affecting stage lover he ever saw, the ideal " juvenile lead." " He had a particular talent for giving life to *bon mots* and repartees; the wit of the poet seemed always to come from him extempore, and sharpened into more wit from his brilliant manner of delivering it." In other words, he was an actor who thought as well as spoke. Poor Will Mountford, his tragic end cast a gloom over Drury Lane. For a certain Captain Hill, a very disreputable character, had fallen in love with the chaste Mrs. Bracegirdle and, like everyone else, failed to win her. He and a Lord Mohun, one of the worst characters in London and a confirmed duellist, tried to carry her off one night when she was walking home, but their attempt failed. Their resentment fell upon Mountford, who, they thought quite wrongly, was her lover. So they decided to " liquidate " him. On the night of the 9th November, 1692, they lay in wait for Mountford with their swords drawn. Towards midnight they met him in Norfolk Street, Strand, where he lived, and Mohun stopped him in a friendly manner and got into conversation. Mountford, enquiring what his lordship was doing there at that hour of the night, was asked if he had not heard "of the affair of the woman"? to which he replied " What woman? " and the answer was " Mrs. Bracegirdle." Mountford did not lack for courage and said : " I hope, my lord, that you do not encourage Captain Hill in his attempt on Mrs. Bracegirdle, which, however, is no affair of mine." As he said so, blows from a bludgeon rained on his head from the redoubtable Hill, who had crept up behind him whilst Mohun engaged his attention. Mountford staggered and made some attempt to draw his sword but Hill ran him through the body and killed him.

Mohun was tried by his peers and acquitted. Hill fled the country. Mountford was buried in St. Clement Danes.

Smith, the Willie Smith of the union agreement, was another fine actor. He was the original " Chamont " in Otway's " Orphan " and " Pierre " in the same dramatist's very famous " Venice Preserv'd."

Charles Sandford, short and hump-backed, was an ideal stage villain. He was a nice man but his physical deformities condemned him to villainy on the stage, and the audience revelled in his " crimes." Once he was cast for

74

the part of an honest man and the audience, thinking his apparent honesty was a cloak for desperate villainy to come, considered themselves hoaxed when they found he was honest all through. They damned the play with hoots and derision.

Robert Nokes was the crack low comedian. His manner and appearance were so amusing that he always got applause on entering, even before he opened his mouth. He was one of those grave, morose comedians, and the more laughs he got the more serious and puzzled he became. He was perhaps the Alfred Lester of his time. He had a long and brilliant career.

Leigh was also a comedian, but of the gay, bright order and was a particular favourite of Charles II.

Cave Underhill was another comedian, whose speciality was the simulation of stolid stupidity. On the stage he was the quintessence of wooden-headed simplicity, with a perfectly expressionless face and vacant eye — what the Americans to-day call a "dead-pan." He died a pensioner of the theatre.

Dick Estcourt, who joined a little later, was a better mimic than actor, and finally became the landlord of The Bumper Tavern in St. James's Street. He is buried in St. Paul's, Covent Garden.

Of the ladies, Betterton's wife, Mrs. Sanderson, was a very good actress and singer.

Mrs. Mountford, who afterwards married Verbruggen (a fine actor), was first class. She was versatile. She could play bouncing country wenches, or fine ladies full of whimsies and airs, with equal perfection. She was also popular in "breeches parts," for which her figure was well suited.

That was the team which Betterton now led at Drury Lane. It was one which should have ensured success for years. They had the best players, the best plays and a clear field.

Politics were rife; they were referred to in the theatre, the battles of the Whigs and Tories were made the point of references in prologues, epilogues and even obliquely in entire dramas. The popularity of Charles was contrasted with the unpopularity of the heir, his brother James. Shadwell, Dryden, D'Urfey and Otway lashed out in all directions. Crowne, the dramatist, had grown tired of the theatre and asked the King for a place at Court, which that Monarch (who seldom said "No") duly promised on condition that Crowne wrote one more play for Theatre Royal. Much as Charles liked the drama, he did not appreciate Shakespeare, and so for this period his works had disappeared almost entirely. But the Merry Monarch liked Crowne, and when they had this interview, he handed the dramatist a Spanish play, suggesting that it should be adapted. This was done and the play was put into rehearsal. The day before the first performance, Crowne met Underhill leaving the theatre and rebuked him for leaving so early. Underhill took no notice of the rebuke; he was too distressed. "We are all undone," he cried. "How?" asked the astonished playwright. "Is the playhouse on fire?" "The whole nation will quickly be so" retorted Underhill, "for the King is dead." Crowne saw the end of his hopes. That was in 1685, only three years after the Union.

The play was "Sir Courtley Nice, or It Cannot Be." Charles's death delayed its production, which did not take place until May 4th. It was fitting that Drury Lane, Charles's theatre, should give a representation of "Albion and Albanius," by Dryden, in which Charles's memory was lauded to the skies and his brother glorified. The play had no luck and lost a lot of money.

Meanwhile, Betterton was leading man, manager, and stage director, giving great performances and doing plays by Aphra Behn, Thomas D'Urfey, William Mountford, the actor who was murdered, Charles Sedley, Nahum Tate, Nathaniel Lee, Dryden, and Shadwell, names which live to-day. What a glorious chapter this should have been in the history of the Theatre.

But bad management, like Shakespeare's "worm in the bud," undid all that the players were doing. Davenant the younger had not inherited his Father's genius for the Theatre.

Plays were getting dirtier too, and a woman dramatist Aphra Behn, who was a remarkable personage with a strange story, was the worst offender, particularly in "The Lucky Chance," in which Betterton made a big success. Yet in another, "The Emperor of the Moon" she supplied what might be almost the first Drury Lane pantomine. Shadwell's "Squire of Alsatia" was one of the few successes of the time. Even bloodstained Judge Jeffreys came to

76

applaud, and on the third night, it turned away money from the house; Shadwell gives the figure of £130, a vast sum when the top price seats were 4/-.

Protests which came to a head before long, arose at the indecency of the plays. Politics were affecting the theatre, both outwardly and inwardly. Dramatists took sides, Dryden and Crowne were rank Tories and Elkanah Settle was a rank Whig.

These difficulties proved too much for Charles Davenant and his brother Alexander, so when Christopher Rich, a lawyer, offered to buy them out, they lent a ready ear to his proposals. Rich, who found affairs at Drury Lane in a muddle was to leave them long after, in a worse one. He was one of the greatest blackguards in the history of the theatre. He defrauded, lied, oppressed, and stole. He had no love for the theatre, as such; he regarded it and the actors solely as a means of enriching himself. He took everything out and put nothing back.

This wily gentleman got around the Davenants and secured their interest and the Patent for the sum of Eighty Pounds, thus becoming Patentee and Manager of the great Theatre Royal. He had many pretty little ideas to put into operation. One was to enlist volunteers, young stage-struck men whom he promised to teach and to pay them 10/- per week; which they never got! One of them left us an admirable picture of Christopher Rich:

> " He was as sly a tyrant as ever was set at the head of a theatre; for he gave the actors more liberty and fewer days' pay than any of his predecessors; he would laugh with them over a bottle, and bite them in their bargains. He kept them poor that they might not rebel, and sometimes merry that they might not think of it. All their articles of agreement had a clause in them that he could creep out at."

Rich was the progenitor of all crook managers. He diverted actors' wages into his own pocket. He always paid short, promising to pay right up to date "when the money came into the house." By way of establishing good will for himself he would, occasionally, overpay slight sums! But actors were then, and now, trusting folk. They had no organisation to fight their battles.

Yet, amongst the crowd of poor boys, whom he paid by promises and used for walk-ons, supers and small part people, was one who was to bring about Rich's downfall. That man of destiny was Colley Cibber, soon to become joint patentee of Drury Lane, its leading man, its chief dramatist and eventually Poet Laureate.

At this time the Theatre Royal had the best of everything in Europe, but *per contra* it had Christopher Rich The nation had recently been torn by rebellion. The National Theatre was to follow suit.

CHAPTER 10

CIVIL WAR IN THEATRELAND

ONE summer's day in the year 1692, a young man with a play in his pocket, presented himself at the stage door of Drury Lane. Such visitors were by no means uncommon but this call was destined to become historical.

The young man was conducted to Rich and Betterton and, impressed by the author's story—he had written a novel at the age of 17—the two men asked him to read his script aloud. It is to the credit of the astute, wily lawyer and the discerning actor-manager that they promptly accepted the work.

Rich evidently recognised that a genius had walked in on them, for he did something, which was most unusual for him—he became suddenly generous. To the overjoyed and slightly bewildered playwright he offered a free permit to the theatre. It was a privilege only bestowed on authors when their plays were actually produced.

The young man—he was William Congreve—had, within the space of a couple of hours, hitched his wagon to the star of Old Drury. At a time when it sorely needed help the theatre had received a gift from the gods of fortune. Without seeking it, Drury Lane had acquired one of the greatest jewels that ever glittered in its crown.

Congreve left his play—"The Old Bachelor"—with the two men who in turn showed it to other dramatists attached to the house. Southerne read it and passed it on to Dryden. They saw its worth and decided that "though the stuff was rich it still needed the fashionable cut." And to the delight of Congreve, three first-rank dramatists— Southerne, Maynard and Dryden — proceeded to give the work the lapidary attention it required to ensure

its success. It was a graceful act which only a deep love
for the theatre could have inspired.

"The Old Bachelor" was produced in January 1693. It
had been a bad winter. Internal strife was again tearing at
the vitals of Drury Lane, for Rich continued his oppressive
methods. Mountford had been murdered, Nokes, the great
low comedian, was dead, as was Leigh, his opposite number
in lighter comedy. His Majesty's Servants could ill afford
such losses. The lack of these departed actors made casting
difficult too.

The Patentee and Betterton allotted the part of
"Fondlewife" (to become one of the great stage characters
for centuries) to a young actor from Dublin, one Thomas
Doggett, who had been hanging about playing small parts
and hoping for just such a chance. Betterton played
"Heartwell," the Old Bachelor himself.

What an all-star cast this first play by a new
author was given: Betterton, Mrs. Bracegirdle, Mrs. Barry,
Mrs. Mountford, Mrs. Bowman and Thomas Doggett.

The production was a memorable event in theatrical
history. It introduced a new actor, destined for greatness, in
Doggett, it provided Betterton with a part worthy of him,
it fitted the fair and brilliant women better than their own
gloves, and it brought a gifted dramatist before the public.
It was one of the great days of Old Drury. Mrs. Bracegirdle spoke the prologue with consummate art. It was a
clever prologue, for she had to pretend to "dry up" and
finally run off the stage in confusion without ever breaking
the cadence of the verse. The first act was a test for the
endurance of the playgoers of that day. It was almost without action, just a conversation between four men in a London
street, no women in it. But the play held, and backstage
the women stars waited for their cues. And when they
came, triumph began. Mrs. Mountford was "Belinda," and
the one and only Bracegirdle was "Araminta" the innocent,
the fair, the pure. Powel, afterwards to be the star of the
Lane, played "Bellmour."

Young Doggett, as "Fondlewife" (the Puritan banker,
fair game then) took the house by storm and laid a sure
and firm foundation for his career. The final scene was
triumphant, the great Mrs. Barry spoke the epilogue to an
excited and enthusiastic audience.

"The Old Bachelor" ran for fourteen consecutive performances—an unprecedented run. Congreve was in the

front rank at the age of twenty-three. The Lane was itself again.

Waiting about the stage was a young man named Cibber, dreaming his dreams on an empty stomach, but inflexible in his aim and ambition. Up in his room Rich rubbed his hands, worked out schemes whereby actors and authors might get as little as possible, and set about tying Congreve to Drury Lane. Congreve, handsome, young and flushed with success, plunged into the gaieties of the town and began undermining that delicate constitution which led him to a premature grave. The fops were full of praise, the coffee houses were buzzing, and Congreve was being pressed by Rich and Betterton to " do it again."

Meanwhile the eager, hungry young Cibber was on the way up. An accident made him. He had been given a tiny part opposite the great Betterton himself. In his over-anxiety he made a mess of the scene and got off as best he could. When the great star had finished he bore down upon old Downes, the prompter, with thunder on his brow. "Who was the young fool who muffed that scene?" he demanded. "We call him Master Colley," replied Downes. "Then forfeit him five shillings" snapped the angry Betterton. "I am afraid that is impossible" answered Downes, "for he gets no salary." This gave Betterton pause; he knew all about Rich and his tricks. But Betterton had power in the house, and its direction. "Oh, does he not?" he said, with a twinkle in his eye, "then pay him ten shillings and forfeit him five of them."

Master Colley never forgot. He learned his lesson and his admiration for Betterton knew no bounds. The contretemps got Cibber into notice. He had another part allotted to him, the chaplain in Otway's "Orphan," despite his "insufficient voice and meagre person and dismal pale complexion (his own description). Next day at rehearsal he saw a handsome man, whom he knew by name and reputation for a fine actor who had now left the stage. The ex-actor had been " in front " the previous day and was discussing the play with Mountford. "Who was the new young fellow who played 'The Chaplain' yesterday?" he enquired. "That's he, behind you; Colley Cibber," replied Mountford. The ex-star turned—and, in Cibber's own words,—"looked earnestly at me, and after some pause, clapping me on the shoulder, rejoined—' If he does not make a good actor, I'll be damned.'"

THE OLD THEATRE, DRURY LANE.

This Front which stood in Bridges Street, was built by order of Mr. Garrick, previous to parting with his share of the Theatre.

See Pennants London.

Publish'd June 1. 1794, by N. Smith Mays Buildings St. Martins Lane.

BY COMMAND OF
Their MAJESTIES.

At the Theatre Royal in Drury-Lane,
This preſent WEDNESDAY, June 5, 1776,

KING RICHARD the THIRD.

King Richard by Mr. GARRICK,
Richmond by Mr. PALMER,
Buckingham by Mr. JEFFERSON,
Treſſel by Mr. DAVIES,
Lord Stanley by Mr. BRANSBY,
Norfolk by Mr. HURST,
Cateſby by Mr. PACKER,
Prince Edward by Miſs P. HOPKINS,
Duke of York Maſter PULLEY, Lord Mayor Mr GRIFFITHS,
Ratcliffe by Mr. WRIGHT, Lieutenant by Mr. FAWCETT,
King Henry by Mr. REDDISH,
Lady Anne by Mrs. SIDDONS,
Dutcheſs of York by Mrs. JOHNSTON,
Queen by Mrs. HOPKINS.

To which (by Comm n) will be added a Comedy of 2 Acts, call'd
BON TON, or HIGH LIFE ABOVE STAIRS.

The original Prologue to be ſpoken by Mr. KING.
The CHARACTERS by
Mr. KING,
Mr. DODD,
Mr. PARSONS, Mr DAVIES, Mr. LAMASH,
Mrs. KING,
And Mrs. ABINGTON.

Ladies are deſired to ſend their Servants a little after 5 to keep Places, to prevent Confuſion.
The Doors will be opened at HALF after FIVE o'Clock.
To begin at Half an Hour after Six. Vivant Rex & Regina.

The Bill of the Play when Mrs. SIDDONS made her second appearance
with DAVID GARRICK in 1776, during her ill-fated debut
at Drury Lane, when she failed completely.

The man who spoke those words of praise was Scum Goodman! It was the one good deed that we can put to his credit. And Scum's judgment was right. Cibber did become a good actor; but Scum, was damned, nevertheless. Meanwhile, Congreve had been working on a successor to "The Old Bachelor." It was now ready, and "The Double Dealer" was produced (as we say) or "brought upon the stage" (as was then the phrase) in the October of 1693.

Expectation ran high. It is not an easy matter to top a success. Perhaps it was bad policy to follow up the triumphs of "The Old Bachelor" too soon. But a magnificent cast was again assembled. Betterton brought all his art to bear on the scurrilous character of "Maskwell." Doggett was in his best form as "Sir Paul Plyant." Mrs. Bracegirdle, Mrs. Barry, Mrs. Mountford and Mrs. Leigh were all there, doing their excellent best. The actor Williams was perhaps not quite good enough for "Mellefont," but Kynaston showed them that he could still be handsome and still play with the same sureness of authority as "Lord Touchwood."

The audience did not react. Congreve's theme was too true, too near home; his dialogue was too pointed, the satire too direct. It annoyed the men, and it thoroughly upset the women, by its frankness. It had not the run of "The Old Bachelor" but the brilliance of Congreve and the excellence of the acting ensured its place on the stage and it was frequently revived.

On the afternoon before Queen Mary was due to see "The Double Dealer," the company was thrown into consternation. Kynaston was too ill to play "Lord Touchwood." It was a chance for the ambitious young Cibber. Congreve had spotted him, and suggested him to Betterton who, like a good judge, did not demur. Cibber rushed home to his room, steeped himself in the part and was ready to play it, word perfect, before he went to sleep. Cibber scored a success and he tells us: "Mr. Congreve made me the compliment of saying that I had not only answered but had exceeded his expectations, and that he would show me he was sincere by his saying more of me to my masters. He was as good as his word, and the next pay-day I found my salary of fifteen was then advanced to twenty shillings a week."

But he was to learn, as many have learnt since, that the understudy who steps into the breach and makes a success, gets nothing except a few more shillings. Hard as that may seem, it is just. Stars are not made by repetition of other people's performances, but by creations of their own. So Cibber found; for he bewails "not a step further could I get, till the company was again divided; when the desertion of the best actors left a clear stage for younger champions to mount, and show their best pretentions to favour." He had not long to wait.

Queen Mary, as ardent a playgoer as her gracious namesake of our day, was so pleased with "The Double Dealer" that she asked for "The Old Bachelor" to be staged specially for her. Congreve wrote a new prologue, risking much, for in it he hinted how advantageous it would be if Royalty patronised the drama more often. On the strength of his success, Congreve was appointed Licensor of Hackney Carriages, a sinecure carrying about £100 per annum as salary, and he celebrated his accession to the post by leaving town for a holiday.

Meanwhile at Drury Lane storms tore the skies. Betterton and his actor friends had been led into a commercial venture. The ship foundered, or rather was captured by a French privateer, and they were penniless. Rich was quick to take advantage of this situation. To save money, he gave star parts to the smaller fry. By so doing he hoped to achieve several things; to make the actors realise that he was their master; to share the prestige of Betterton, whom he feared; and to build up around him a set of younger men bound to him by gratitude if not by money. The public, however, showed what they thought about it by staying away from Drury Lane. Rich never learnt, till his dying day, that though he was Master of Drury Lane, the public, in its turn, was his master and had the last word.

He became more overbearing, more slippery in his dealings, and his treasurer, Zaccary Bagges, performed more sleight-of-hand with the salary lists and balance sheets.

Betterton called his followers together and they took up a firm stand against the Patentee. The Patentee rallied his party, the younger men and women. There was civil war.

Betterton's friends in high circles espoused his cause. They promised support; they even told the King about it, and he referred the matter to Lord Dorset, the Lord Chamberlain. His lordship reported that there was nothing to prevent William issuing another Patent, if he so desired, to a really responsible person. This was what Betterton wanted, for he and his party had determined on leaving Rich, and Drury Lane. They adored the playhouse but detested the manager.

There were two interested onlookers, Colley Cibber, the great opportunist, and William Congreve, the great dramatist. Cibber threw in his lot with Rich. Congreve, as a dramatist, wanted the best cast for his plays. Betterton had it. He therefore joined Betterton's camp.

Betterton besought an audience with King William. The monarch, anxious to be fair, and perhaps a little curious to see at close quarters the marvellous people of whom he had heard so much from his Queen, granted the request. The upshot was that he granted them a licence to perform elsewhere than at Theatre Royal, Drury Lane. It was issued to Thomas Betterton, Elizabeth Barry, Anne Bracegirdle, John Bowman, Joseph Williams, Cave Underhill, Thomas Doggett, William Bowen, Susan Verbruggen, Elizabeth (or Elinor) Leigh, and George Bright. By it, they could play any sort of play at any sort of place.

But Betterton had neither theatre, nor money. His friends the noblemen put this right, and sufficient was collected to put into use of the old Tennis Court in Lincoln's Inn Fields once again. The site was in Portugal Street, covered now by the Royal College of Surgeons.

Drury Lane had to accept the challenge. The team they had was weak, but Colley Cibber had got a further 10/- rise out of the trouble. His salary was now 30/- per week. They scoured the country for talent—cheap talent—amongst the strolling players. The biggest fish they netted this way were Benjamin Johnson, a good character actor, who was particularly good in the plays of his great namesake, and William Bullock, a large and boisterous low comedian, good but much addicted to " gagging." Neither was up to the Drury Lane standard. Then they received an unexpected windfall, for two of the rebels, Mrs. Vanbruggen and Joseph Williams, left Betterton and returned to the Lane.

But Lincoln's Inn gained a victory which more than offset the desertions. Congreve signed a contract by which he undertook to supply Betterton with a new play every year, if his health permitted. And in pledge of good faith, he gave him the one just fresh from his pen. Betterton, highly delighted, decided to open his theatre with it. That was a bad shaking up for Rich.

Drury Lane got in first. On Easter Monday, April 1695, they opened with Aphra Behn's " Adelazar " or "The Moor's Revenge " to a full house. Rich rubbed his hands, but his glee was premature. On the second night, the house was empty. And so it remained, open, it is true, but playing to sparce audiences.

On April 30th the rebels opened up with Congreve's "Love for Love," originally intended for Drury Lane, but lost through Rich's avarice. It played for thirteen consecutive performances, and no other new play was required that season. They alternated " Love for Love " with " The Old Bachelor " and their popular stock plays. Rich was up against it. He was doing no business and his rivals were playing to capacity. It was battle royal between Theatres Royal.

It came to Rich's knowledge that Betterton was to perform "Hamlet" (his greatest part) on a certain Tuesday night. Powel, who now ran the Lane for Rich (skulking with a pain in his pocket), decided to beat Lincoln's Inn Fields to it. He decreed that Drury Lane should perform "Hamlet" on the Monday night, thus getting in ahead.

News travels fast in theatreland. The Lincoln's Inn camp altered their plans, advanced their "Hamlet" for Monday also!

There was consternation at Drury Lane. What were they to do now? It was up to Powel, as chief, to save his company. He called a council of war. He was an artful man, if a drunkard, and he proposed a bold and daring counter stroke. They would put on " The Old Bachelor " instead of "Hamlet." He (Powel) would play Betterton's part and mimic the great actor all through it. This was received with cheers, and Cibber comments "as whatever can be supposed to ridicule merit generally gives joy to those who want it." They got out bills announcing " The Part of the Old Bachelor to be performed in Imitation of the Original." They felt triumphant, but an unforeseen snag arose. There was nobody who could play " Fondlewife," the role in which Doggett had made such an immense hit. Here was the opportunity for the opportunist. Cibber volunteered for the job. " If the fool has a mind to blow himself up at once, let us even give him a clear stage for it," sneered Powel.

The part was given to Cibber. He knew every line and move of it.

Curiosity drew a good house, and Powel got applause for his mimicry of Betterton, but Colley Cibber stole the show. He had made up so exactly like Doggett that the audience were in two minds as to whether this was not Doggett himself returned to the Lane. It was a night of triumph for Cibber, for Doggett himself was in the pit spying out the land for Betterton.

Cibber however, had "typed" himself. Whenever he asked for a good part in a forthcoming play, he was told curtly: "That is not in your way." His reply is one of the great utterances of the Theatre. Said Colley Cibber: "I thought anything, naturally written, ought to be in every one's way that pretended to be an actor."

These words ought to be emblazoned on every call board and in every dressing room, not only in Theatre Royal, Drury Lane, where they were most fittingly spoken, but in the office of every manager who produces plays. For they enshrine one of the great truths of the Theatre. Cibber was told that it was a vain impracticable conceit of his own. The same idea still obtains. Yet it was a very great truth, Cibber himself was to prove it, for unable to get the role he wanted the opportunist-optimist decided to become a playwright and write a part for himself.

CHAPTER 11

DRURY LANE'S GHOST

IN the battle between the two theatres, Drury Lane was doing a little better. Southerne, who remained faithful to it, had provided it with "Oroonoko," a play which was so successful that it held the stage, off and on, for years.

There was a little trouble over this, however, for Powel, as leading man, had taken it as his own. He was prevented, however, by Lord Halifax, then Lord Chamberlain, who insisted on Verbruggen playing it, and who said that "Jack was the unpolished hero and would do it best." It seems strange for the Lord Chamberlain to take a hand in casting plays, and one wonders what would happen if he did so to-day. But in this instance his lordship was right. Verbruggen was a rough but very strong and effective actor. He could roar like a lion, as Bully Bottom desired to do, and thrilled his audiences. Mrs. Rogers played the lead, and Mrs. Verbruggen played " Charlot Weldon." This she was at first loath to do, for it meant assuming male attire, which she had never done, but so well did she look, and act, that success was assured.

Meanwhile, Colley Cibber was playing his round of small parts, and getting on with his play. He says it was first performed in 1695 but his memory tricks him. It was first seen in January, 1696. It was called " Love's Last Shift," or "The Fool in Fashion," and with his authority as author, he cast himself for the leading part, "Sir Novelty Fashion." He tells us that Southerne, to whom he read his play in order to gain approval for its production, said: " Young man, I pronounce thy play a good one! I will answer for its success, if thou dost not soil it by thy own action."

Nobody but Colley Cibber believed in the acting of Colley Cibber. But his self reliance was such that he stuck to his guns. " Love's Last Shift " was a big success, and Master Cibber, as " Sir Novelty," was a success of equal dimensions.

This play may be said to be a milestone in Drury Lane's history, for it brought another great name into its story. This was Sir John Vanbrugh, who was so impressed by it, that he wrote a sequel, called " The Relapse; or Virtue in Danger," and promoted " Sir Novelty " to the peerage by making him " Lord Foppington." It is strange for one author to write a sequel to a play by another, but these were strange times. Cibber was much honoured by Vanbrugh's condescension, and made a tremendous success in the part.

The success of these two plays did much to improve the status of Drury Lane. Money began to come in again, to be swept into the pockets of the rapacious Rich, for the company saw little of it. " The Relapse " also precipitated another crisis, this time an artistic one. It was customary in those times for tragedians to take precedence of mere comedians particularly in the matter of expensive costumes. The tragic actor was the star, the comedian, a mere though necessary excrescence on the dramatic scene, whose main object was to create shade against which light of the tragedian might shine more strongly.

Now Cibber, the purveyor of laughter, had seen to it that, as "Sir Novelty Fashion" in his own play, and as "Lord Foppington" in "The Relapse," he wore clothes which were as gorgeous, good and fashionable as any of the leading fops of the day, whom he was satirising on the stage. Powel, the chief tragedian, could not stomach this.

This trouble was not confined to Drury Lane; the same thing was going on at Lincoln's Inn, only in the reverse direction. Up there, when Betterton was about to produce a tragedy, the comedians, led by Doggett, would grumble at the expense. In their view (and they were probably right) "they were the men who drew the money in; the audiences were sick of tragedy and wanted to laugh—all the old traditional theatrical grumbles on both sides—still in force to-day—would be trotted out. So, whenever the plumes and trappings of tragedy were brought out, they being no use to him, he would grouse and make trouble. A little later, he left Lincoln's Inn and returned to Drury Lane.

The possession of three good new plays, and the promise of more from the pen of Vanbrugh; the success of Cibber as actor-playwright; the popularity of Verbruggen as commenced in "Oroonoko," and the return of Doggett; has stabilised Drury Lane, which was now getting ahead of its young rival round the corner.

There had been another upheaval, too. A gentleman called Jeremy Collier wrote "A View of the Immorality and Profaneness of the English Stage," which caused a tremendous sensation. The actors of course considered themselves outraged, and the dramatists considered themselves libelled. Congreve wrote a scathing reply. Dryden kept silent at the moment, but Collier stuck to his guns. Battle was joined and the officials had to take some notice of it. A cleaning up was speedily ordered. The great Betterton and Mrs. Bracegirdle were fined.

The battle thus started by Collier raged furiously. Informers almost wore themselves out by going to the play, laughing uproariously at the dirty jokes, and then speeding to the Justices to lay information. So over anxious did the Censorship become that Cibber tells us that when he submitted his own version of Shakespeare's "Richard III" to the Censor, that worthy expunged the entire first act. He might have done worse than expunge the lot, for Cibber took great liberties with Shakespeare. It was he who inserted the famous "off with his head, so much for Buckingham" into the above-mentioned play. These informers worked for a so-called religious association which named itself "The Society for the Reformation of Manners."

Good Queen Anne, who had then ascended the throne, understood the situation, which was getting out of hand. She knew the informers were not actuated by high moral feelings, but from a desire to cause trouble and gain a fee. She put a stop to the whole thing.

Meanwhile, the only one who came through unscathed and indeed with credit, was Cibber. His play, "Love's Last Shift," though written two years before, had been a " clean " and moral play in which Virtue shone and Vice was defeated, where purity and chastity were lauded and were victorious over debauchery and lust. It was a wonderful instance of " flair." Much kudos accrued to him, and Drury Lane shone in reflected glory.

Vanbrugh, too, had given the Lane " Aesop," which was another success. The battle between the two theatres, fanned by Doggett's desertion, was conducted with bitterness and considerable venom. As actors sneered at each other, they also besmirched each other from the stage, with withering sarcasm in Prologues.

Apart from Cibber and Vanbrugh, nothing of dramatic importance had occurred for some time at Drury Lane. The other house still had Congreve, but his ill-health had prevented him writing anything since "The Mourning Bride," and "The Way of the World" had not yet appeared. So things were bad all round.

But in 1698, Drury Lane got another recruit who was to bring glory. This was George Farquhar, whose comedies " Love and a Bottle " and " The Constant Couple " or " A Trip to the Jubilee " (1699) were to bring great success. Although Gildon the critic said the latter was only fit for footmen, it ran for so long that the author got three benefits out of it.

One reason why Drury Lane was more than holding its own is a paradox. Its bad manager was in reality the means whereby it held together. Infamous, thieving, grasping, penny-snatching as he was, he still was master and maintained some sort of discipline, if only by fear. At Lincoln's Inn everyone was of equal rank and all gave contradictory orders.

Rich was still pursuing his cheeseparing methods. He was still mystifying and robbing the actors, and by now he had got complete control. His main backer, Sir Thomas Skipworth, who should have known better, had got tired of the whole thing and made a present of his share in the Patent to one Colonel Brett, who, to make it legal, paid Skipworth a consideration of 10/-.

Rich spent more of his time contriving how to alter the house so as to squeeze in a few more seats, tinkering with this part, then with that, taking away some of the entering doors on the stage to establish stage boxes, than he did in trying to get good plays and seeing that they were well acted. He had the whip hand of his wretched company financially. If he sacked them they had nowhere to go save Lincoln's Inn, where they would not be welcome.

They did try. Verbruggen deserted to Lincoln's Inn as Doggett had done to the Lane. Rich immediately screamed the place down, flew to the Lord Chamberlain, quoted his Patent and asked for his lordship's support. Strangely enough, he got it. Verbruggen was peremptorily ordered to return to Drury Lane, there to remain until 1697 —a year's sentence—after which he was told he could act where he liked. But no action was taken to make Doggett return to Lincoln's Inn. He would have been a rare handful of trouble, which perhaps the Chamberlain knew.

It is to this mania for structural alterations which obsessed Rich that Drury Lane, in all probability, owes its Ghost. For a phantom does indeed haunt the great old theatre,—a phantom of a most curious kind. It is a strange story, but one very appropriate to Drury Lane. It is natural that the grand theatre, so rich in history, so full of years, so colourful of story, should have its own supernatural inhabitant.

The story begins long ago, and generations of men and women have beheld the ghostly visitor. Nobody knows anything about him, but the one certainty—that he walks at Drury Lane. He is a daytime ghost, in itself a remarkable thing. He has never been seen at night, or later than six in the evening. All the recorded accounts of his appearance are between nine a.m and six p.m. Also he haunts only one part of the building. He is not an exclusive spectre, preferring his own company in the witching hours of night, nor does he take pleasure in scaring the wits out of unsuspecting people who see him. He keeps himself to himself; he neither approaches, nor allows you to approach too near; but so far from shunning company, he seems to prefer it. For he has been seen clearly during a matinee performance to a packed house, he has been seen when the stage has been full of people rehearsing, and he has been seen when the theatre has been full of people hurrying from department to department during the occupation of Drury Lane by ENSA.

And no matter who sees him, the description is always the same. He is a man of medium height, dressed in a long grey riding cloak of the early 18th century, wearing a powdered wig of the period and a three-cornered hat; the cloak covers most of him, but he has a sword which can be seen under it, as it swings at his side, and he has high riding boots. Sometimes he carries the hat in his hand. He has been approached near enough for his features to be visible, and they are those of a handsome man with a squarish chain, somewhat resembling the late Sir George Alexander (but it is not the spirit of that great actor). He is clearly visible, although slightly misty on occasions, as if he had a " gauze " between him and the beholder; yet in the strongest light he is the most clearly seen.

The present historian wishes to put it on record that he has seen this apparition on numerous occasions. He has excellent sight, is not troubled mentally, has not a fantastic mind, and is not a Spiritualistic medium.

On one occasion, which may be quoted out of the many, a cleaner entered the upper circle to begin her work shortly after ten o'clock a.m. A rehearsal was in progress on the stage. She saw, sitting in the end seat on the centre gangway of the fourth row, a figure of a man in grey, wearing a hat, gazing down at the stage. She thought it one of the actors, who had assumed his costume, but also thought she had better make sure. She therefore put down her pail and her broom and went to speak to the figure. As she neared it, it seemed to vanish, and then reappeared at the exit door on the right hand side of the circle, through which it passed. She imagined it was some trick of the eyes, this vanishing, so she did nothing about it, except to report it later. The authority on the ghost was sent for to cross-question the woman. She had never heard of the ghost before in her life, but gave a description of it which tallied accurately with all the others.

On another occasion, during the matinée performance

90

of a big musical play not many years before the recent war, a lady in the upper circle asked an attendant if this was the sort of play where the actors came out amongst the audience. The girl told her no, and asked the reason for her enquiry. The playgoer said she had seen a man in a long grey cloak, with a white wig and cocked hat, pass through the entrance door just ahead of her. The attendant assured her there was nothing like that in the play, and suggested that the figure in grey might have been a nurse in grey uniform, but the lady was sure of her story. Again the expert on the ghost scrutinised the whole house, division by division. No nurse of any kind was present. What that lady visitor had seen was the ghost.

One autumn evening in 1942, Mr. Stephen Williams, Broadcasting officer of Ensa at the time, saw the ghost clearly whilst he was on the grand staircase near the upper circle entrance. Another Ensa official said he saw it in the Green Room; but if so, this is its only recorded appearance back stage. There are scores of other examples, and always the description is the same.

Who is this uneasy spirit and why does he walk? That again, nobody knows. He is as unique as Drury Lane. But there is a clue. About a century ago, when some work was proceeding in the theatre, workmen employed on the Russell Street side of the upper circle of Drury Lane (left hand side facing stage) came upon a portion of what seemed to them the main wall, which rang hollow. They called the attention of the foreman in charge to this, and he decided to break through and see what was wrong. It was far more wrong than he had imagined. For when the workmen had hewed their way through the wall, they found themselves suddenly bursting into a small room, which had been bricked up. In that room was a skeleton, and in that skeleton's ribs was a dagger.

The dagger was of Cromwellian design, but that proved nothing. An inquest was held, an open verdict returned; and the skeleton, which was that of a male, was interred in the little graveyard on the corner of Russell Street and Drury Lane, believed to be the graveyard mentioned by Dickens in " Bleak House."

Again, who was he, this man who was done to death and buried in the walls of the great playhouse, which holds so many secrets? That he was not a member of the company or staff of the theatre is certain, for his disappearance would have caused talk or search, and there is no record of such a thing. The present writer has his own theory. It is that the victim of the murder was a young man from the country, possessed of some means, who came up to town to see the sights and cut a dash. Naturally he gravitated to the playhouse and probably, as was the manner of those days, was one of those who invaded the stage to show himself off, to see and be seen. Maybe he got too friendly with one of the girls, and her lover had him quietly put out of the way, and hid him in the little room which was, to his knowledge, to be bricked up. If this idea is right, he at least became a part of the romance of Old Drury.

Before proceeding to the part played by George Farquhar in the history of the playhouse, let us take note of another figure now entering the story who is, like that playwright, to bear a most important and an even more prominent part in its history. This is the figure of Robert Wilks, destined with our firm friends Colley Cibber and Thomas Doggett to write a page which is now one of the brightest in the tale, not only of Drury Lane, but of the whole history of the British Theatre.

Robert Wilks, like his future partners Cibber and Doggett, had been one of those young men whom Rich persuaded to hang about the theatre, walk on, play small parts and be generally useful in minor ways for a very minor salary. He however, was rather more impatient for fame and fortune than either of the other two. He was of good birth. Son of one of the Pursuivants to the Lord Lieutenant of Ireland, he had been trained for a career in the Civil Service, and been employed in the office of the Secretary of State for his native land during the reign of King James II. After the Battle of the Boyne, it was felt there should be some rejoicings; and popular vote decided upon a play, to be given at the Theatre free of charge. The choice was "Othello," and Wilks acted the Moor. He was a success and it turned his head—he was not the first and he will not be the last to take to the stage on so slender a foundation.

There being no scope in Dublin, he came to London and joined the company at Drury Lane, where the egregious Rich, seeing him a handsome and polite young gentleman, engaged him at a salary of 15/- per week, less ten shillings for "instruction." Wilks, blinded by the glamour of the

92

stage, accepted. His successor to his post under the Crown eventually made a fortune of £50,000 out of it. That is what Wilks sacrificed for 15/- per week and the glory of being an actor. But conditions at Drury Lane under Rich did not suit this eager young man, who had already met at a dancing school and fallen in love with Miss Elizabeth Knapton, whom a little later on he was to marry.

He went to Betterton, sought his advice, which was that he should return to Ireland, where he had friends, and make a start there. Wilks took the advice, which, like most things of Betterton's, was good. He left the Lane, went back to Ireland, got a job, and was so successful that he soon commanded £50 a year salary and an annual benefit. This got to the ears of Rich, who bit his fingers at finding he had made a mistake. He sent a special messenger to Wilks asking him to return and offering £4 a week as salary. This was top price—and here was his chance, not only for London but for Drury Lane. There is little surprise that Wilks " fell for it."

But Dublin valued him and was not going to let him escape so easily. The Duke of Ormond issued a warrant to prevent him leaving the country. It is doubtful if such an honour was ever paid to an actor before or since. With him in Dublin was George Farquhar, then actor himself, after his army career. He had, however, wounded a brother actor in a stage fight, which made him lose his nerve, and he determined to try his hand at writing plays.

Lovers of the great theatre have reason to be grateful for Wilks' decision. Had he not returned and taken the course he did, the history of Drury Lane might have been a very different one. And the theatrical history of Dublin, brilliant as it is, might have shone even more brightly. Wilks was a fine, handsome man with a sterling character. Though upon the stage he was the lightest, gayest and mirth-provoking light comedians, in private life he was serious and even sad, for his stage and business success was offset by domestic troubles and disasters. He was nearly always in mourning for one or other of his large family. Eleven of them died, and tragically his wife followed them in 1714. Yet he never complained, and he did good to all who appealed to him. He married again, a Mary Fell, widow.

On his return to the Lane, he clashed with Powel, the leading man and head cook and bottle washer for Rich. That slimy man was probably tired of Powel and his drunken ways, and saw in the gentlemanly Wilks a much better proposition. So he ordered Wilks to take over Powel's parts. That worthy had seized for himself all those lighter ones played by poor Mountford. Wilks, a gentleman, did not want to ride roughshod over Powel, so he approached him civilly to see if some friendly arrangement could be come to. Powel was civil in his turn and pretended to advise him as to the part for his debut, giving him one which he did not much like and which Mountford had never played. Wilks, a bit inexperienced, stiff and awkward, had the advantage of playing opposite to Mrs. Mountford, the actor's widow, and he gave a pretty good account of himself. Younger, more handsome and in every way more acceptable than Powel, his popularity with the audiences, and consequently with Rich, grew greater in every part he played.

Powel's almost contemptuous display of friendly help to a raw actor now changed to open jealousy. The two men contended for stage mastery, playing series of parts against each other, now one winning, now the other. But the good nature of Wilks was soon exhausted by the evil rancour of Powel, and the young actor began to try hard and put forth every effort, whereas previously he had, out of respect for Powel, rather held himself in. Powel knew he was beaten, got no support from Rich, and so walked himself in high dudgeon out of Drury Lane into Lincoln's Inn Fields, leaving the stage of the Lane in the hands of Wilks.

CHAPTER 12

FARQUHAR DISCOVERS ANNE OLDFIELD

RICH should have been now reaching a new flood tide of success. He had three good actors, who were all to become great, in Wilks, Cibber and Doggett.

He was, it is true, to lose the fascinating and brilliant Mrs. Mountford, for this poor woman lost her reason and went mad. Not raving mad, but quite out of her mind. She was quite harmless and they allowed her to wander about her house; but one night she escaped and got to the theatre.

94

They were playing "Hamlet" and she had been a famous "Ophelia." Before she could be stopped, she pushed aside the actress who was to appear that night, and went on to play for the last time, a mad woman playing a mad woman with melancholy but striking effect—a scene strange and unique in stage annals. She was a very fine actress indeed, and having overcome her objection to male attire, and worn it in "Oroonoko," she made many successes in "breeches" parts, as they were called. In "The Rehearsal," for example, she played "Bayes" as well if not better than any actor of her time.

Wilks, a determined man and one of a high character, now became a thorn in the side of Rich, whom he pestered. He began to demand better terms for himself and his associates. He wanted to see statements of account, to which he and the others were entitled, for their salaries depended on the way in which the theatre was conducted and the state of business. Rich never showed anyone accounts. He gave them rambling verbal statements of how things stood, which none of them could understand. He tricked them into sharing losses with him, on the vague promise that they should share in profits (if any were made). He saw to it that there never was a profit. Most of them were in debt to him for sums advanced "on note of hand alone," and he always held these trifling debts over their heads. The poor wretches had to submit. There was nowhere else for them to go. Anything in the nature of a "Trust" is extremely bad for the Drama, those who live by it, and consequently for the public too. The great days of the theatre have been those of widespread competition, with no Dictator to call the tune.

Rich had noted that the "best people" patronised the "booth" of Betterton rather than Theatre Royal, and to entice them back, he hit upon the expedient of letting their footmen have free access to the upper gallery on the off chance of their dropping a word to their masters of the excellent fare to be had at the senior theatre. This did not work well. No free list ever does. Something for nothing breeds contempt. The public are apt to assess a thing by what it costs them. And these footmen produced nothing but disturbances and riots, often serious ones.

Rich also instituted a charge for going back stage. Up to now it was the privilege of those who were known, and who tipped the doorkeeper. But that worthy knew enough to keep out the undesirables, unless their high standing blinded his eyes to their morals. Now everyone could get in, and the state of things behind the scenes was almost indescribable.

But Rich had a real "headache" in Wilks, who would not let him alone. In the outcome, Wilks prevailed, and became undisputed master of the stage at Drury Lane at a salary of £4 per week. His methods improved matters greatly. He made everyone work hard and set the example himself. Cibber, to some extent, suffered for his championship of Wilks against Powel, for when Wilks took over, he often cast Cibber for bad parts, which, however, he never refused to play. Nor did he once jib at playing second or even third fiddle to Wilks, whom he recognised as a great actor. And all the while his scheme of a Triumvirate revolved in his head. The two men, who were to become such excellent partners, were totally different. He reflects in late life that anxiety over his profession kept Wilks "lean" until the end of his days, whereas he (Cibber) was happy and comfortable. Also that when Wilks left the stage he said goodbye to life, whereas Cibber enjoyed life all the more after his retirement. Cibber was a first class psychologist and philosopher. Nor was he jealous of the friendship which sprang up between Mills, a good painstaking actor, and Wilks, whereby Mills got many parts which Cibber thought should be his. The careful, thinking Cibber merely bided his time—and watched points very carefully.

The opposition at Lincoln's Inn had to a large extent been worn down, but Drury Lane had become the "comedy" house, whereas Lincoln's Inn with Betterton at its head, upheld the flag of the more aristocratic tragedy. Congreve, who might have been Drury Lane's dramatist, belonged to the other house, but did not live long enough to enrich it beyond "The Mourning Bride" and "The Way of the World," after his astonishing "Love For Love." Betterton was getting old, so were his associates. There were long and constant disagreements.

At Drury Lane, the great drawback of Rich and his tricks persisted. But there were new actors like Wilks, new dramatists like Sir John Vanbrugh (who also wrote for Lincoln's Inn), George Farquhar and Colley Cibber. Nat Lee had gone; he had become a lunatic, but that did not prevent him from making a very sane reply to a wit who

Top left. Mrs. DAVID GARRICK, who before marriage to the great actor was a Drury Lane dancer name MADAME VIOLETTE.

Top right. CHARLES KEAN, the son of EDMUND KEAN. He made his debut at Drury Lane in 1827.

Bottom right. DOWTON, a Drury Lane star who refused to have his name billed in larger type than his fellow actors.

Mrs. ABINGTON, one of Old Drury's most famous actresses, in the character of " Sir Harry Wildair." She was the original " Lady Teazle " in *The School for Scandal*.

was tormenting him in Bedlam by jeering that it was a very easy thing to write like a madman. "No," riposted Lee, "it is not an easy thing to write like a madman, but it is very easy to write like a fool." No wonder he was released shortly after.

Southerne had given the King's company "Oroonoko," a famous play. And there were others. Here is a nice little picture of what a new dramatist had to endure in those days in order to get his play even heard. It is commended to that multitude who daily send their typed manuscripts to the offices of theatrical managers and complain of the treatment they get. This is the experience of a budding dramatist who sought the favour of Rich: "A gentleman carried a play to Drury Lane. A day was appointed for the reading. A dinner was bespoke at a tavern, to which only half the number of players came—as it seems each was presumed to pay his share of the score. In the reading of it (that is, after dinner) most of them dropped off, but two remained to hear it out and then they walked; so that there was but the gentleman and his friend left, and not a penny all this while paid towards the reckoning. The play was ordered to be licensed so that forty shillings for the dinner and forty more for the licence, made just £4, so much it cost him already. This happened to be in Lent, and the players having then the first day of a play given them this was bespoke; so the author had the mortification of having it acted in Lent, but the devil on't was, he was obliged to treat every one of the players whilst it was in rehearsal, to keep them in study, and in that exploit it cost him in coach hire and wine near £10. Well, his third day came, and a good appearance there was. I sat in the pit, and I think I never saw better boxes. The play came off pretty well and the poet was much exalted for so good an escape, for it was his first. His friends joyed him when it was over, and he thought he had now the Indies to receive. Pay day came and what do you think he received?" The addressee, after making certain enquiries, guesses that the dramatist gained £70. The shattering answer is that, full house notwithstanding, he got only £15. For "they brought him bills for gloves, for chocolate, for snuff; this singer begged a guinea, that dancer the same . . . " and in the end he lost by the production. That is how Mr. Rich conducted his theatre.

That good old English custom of taking drama and

nourishment at the same time flourished then, for we learn how the citizens had to hurry from their dinner to be in time, and that they took the remnants of the unfinished meal with them in a coloured handkerchief. And as soon as the plot really got going, they began to stuff with food, yawn and mutter "Lord, when will these tiresome people have done? I wish we had a dance, and were abed." One can see similar behaviour in any theatre to-day.

And did this long-suffering public—or the part of it which should have been intelligent, deserve much better? Jumping forward a very few years we find this comment delivered by a titled playgoer, considered to be a critic and a man of taste, delivered in a smart coffee house in response to enquiries as to how he liked the new play at Drury Lane. His reply was "Extremely well, sir, a mighty full house. Did Mrs. Oldfield's part become her? I never saw her look with better red and white in my life. Wilks, they say, appeared to great advantage in his part? Certainly, the greatest fancied suit of clothes he ever wore. Was not Mills prodigiously clapped? Oh, he spoke some fine things, but I must own the cock of his hat and the dangle of his cane were not amiss. But Cibber is sure the comicalest impudentest dog that ever was born." That was how a man of fashion observed the play. Anyhow Cibber got a good notice. Is it so very different nowadays?

Old Penkethman was one of those who knew his Rich. This hardened old gagster, who often perverted his lines for the amusement of the public once overdid it and was hissed. So he put in another gag to cover up. Glancing at the audience, his comic face bearing every sign of remorse, he said "Oddso, I seem to have overstepped the mark this time," which brought a roar of laughter and applause. When, however, he took his benefit, he took no chances, for he was a good business man. He issued a notice that "all persons coming behind the scenes are desired to pay their money to none but him"—he knew what would happen if Rich got his fingers on it, and he also stipulated that nobody could go into the pit or boxes without a subscriber's ticket."

Penkethman was a good actor and shone especially in "Adelazar or The Moor's Revenge" as Harlequin. So good was he that as the masked harlequin he enchanted people. They knew Penkethman's funny face and desired to see what he could do with the part when unmasked. But alas, his

98

face and his grimaces ruined everything—it was just Penkethman, no longer Harlequin. Penkethman made a great deal of money by his drama booths at the great fairs of Bartholomew, May Fair, Southwark and elsewhere. All the actors went in for this line of business and Doggett was another successful booth proprietor.

A word about Aphra Behn, the woman dramatist in whose pantomine Penkethman had played Harlequin. Her works were the most licentious of those written in a licentious age for a licentious public. She went much further than any of the men to supply filth. She was a curious character. She married a Dutchman and became an English spy in Amsterdam at the time when there was war between the two countries. On her return, she took to writing plays very successfully.

At this time everything was wrong internally at Drury Lane, and Cibber mentions that for one period of six weeks none of them received a penny of their salaries. When they did get some money, Rich gave out that he was paying them out of his own pocket, and some of the actors believed it, or pretended to, for they spoke a prologue referring to his sweetness, his wit and his good nature. This was either tact or stupidity.

The company then included Mr. Bagges (also Rich's accountant), Mr. Bullock, Mr. Bowman, Mr. Fairbank, Mr. Cibber, Captain Griffin, Mr. Huband, Mr. Hall, Mr. Johnson, Mr. Beveridge, Mr. Mills, Mr. Norris, Mr. Newman, Mr. Penkethman, Mr. Swiney and Mr. Wilks. The actresses were Mrs. Bicknell, Mrs. Campion, Senora Gasparini (a singer with perhaps a suitable name) Mrs. Kent, Mrs. Lucas, Mrs. Moore, Mrs. Rogers, Mrs. Shaw and Mrs. Verbruggen (about to have her mental breakdown).

More opposition loomed ahead. Sir John Vanbrugh was talking of building a new theatre, and in the Haymarket of all places. Rich made light of this, for it was almost in the country, and the district infested with footpads. With Betterton already in the field, this seemed to the thoughtful Cibber a portent of danger. He called upon Rich to ascertain that gentleman's views. Cibber was wondering where he came in, with all this going on, and turning over in his mind which attitude would pay him best if there were to be further desertions from Theatre Royal. Loyalty when Betterton seceded had paid him well enough; but here was the same problem again.

He mentioned to Rich that their ranks were sorely thinned, Rich replied "Don't trouble yourself. Come along and I'll show you." Then says Cibber: "He led me about all the by-places in the house, and showed me fifty little back doors, dark closets and narrow passages, in alterations and contrivances, of which kind he had busied his head most part of the vacation, for he was scarce ever without some notable joiner or a bricklayer extraordinary in pay for twenty years. And there are so many odd obscure places about a theatre, that his genius in mock building was never out of employment, nor could the most vain-headed author be more deaf to an interruption in reciting his works than our wise master was while entertaining me with the improvements he had made in his invisible architecture, all which, without thinking one part of it necessary, though I seemed to approve, I could not help now and then breaking in upon his delight with the impertinent question of ' But Master, where are your actors?' "

This little episode is slightly out of chronology, but goes in here to show the state of mind under which Rich ran what should have been a treasured possession. To-day there are theatre proprietors who boast of their fine refreshment rooms, their up-to-date bars, their exquisite stalls, their perfectly appointed cloakrooms. One is tempted to reply like Cibber and ask "Yes, masters, but where are your plays?" for without them, and the actors, the rest are mere nothing.

Also, it was in one of those dark closets in a narrow passage that the skeleton which supplies the ghost was found, bricked up during one of numerous visits by the builders. And although Drury Lane had been rebuilt, and burned down completely to be rebuilt again before the grim discovery, always some of the old fabric had remained, incorporated in the new.

One night in 1683, there was born to the wife of a Captain in the Royal Guards, a baby daughter. Her arrival occasioned no excitement, and probably very little pleasure, for her father was richer in ancestors than in guineas, and here was another mouth to feed.

Of that baby's early life little or nothing is known, save for the fact that she was christened Anne. Her childhood was probably spent in genteel poverty, than which nothing is worse, and as soon as she could go out to work, she was put to do so. Her father was dead and anything which added to the meagre family purse was welcome. So little Anne was found a job as sempstress. We don't know what sort of a needlewoman she was, probably not very good; for she devoted a lot of time to studying old plays, and those of the period, and in learning long passages in them by heart. She was a stage-struck girl, and without question, in her spare time or whilst on errands, hung about the stage door of Drury Lane and Lincoln's Inn to catch glimpses of the great ones. She often went to the inn kept by her aunt, Mrs. Voss (whom some say was her elder sister) and there lent a hand. Often she was to be found in the little parlour behind the bar, doing her sewing, and reciting as she sewed.

One afternoon, towards the end of the 17th century, a man stepped into the bar of the inn, which was the "Mitre" in St. James's Market, and on whose site to-day most aptly stands a famous theatre, The Criterion. The bar was empty at the moment, and there was nobody to serve him; yet he stood there silent, surprised and amazed at what he heard. For from the room behind the bar came a lovely voice, of delightful quality and perfect cadence, reciting, with every sign of full understanding, a scene from "The Scornful Lady."

Captain George Farquhar, for that was the identity of the eavesdropper, forgot his thirst, stood for a while; listening in amazement to the voice in the bar parlour. The recital went on, and he, with his professional curiosity aroused, went behind the bar and into the parlour. He saw a tall, lovely, well-formed girl; very elegant, with a fine shaped and expressive face, lit by great sparkling eyes (which in due course she learned to use so well); a girl full of birth and breeding, not at all in place in such surroundings, reciting to a small circle of admiring friends and relations. She was standing before a background of bottles, but so carried away by her art that in spirit she was in the centre of Old Drury's stage.

Surprised before, Farquhar was stupefied now. This was not what he had expected. He hardly knew what he had expected to see—some serving girl, maybe, who had a gift of mimicry—but certainly not this enchanting vision.

The girl caught the eye of the stranger, and stopped. The spell was broken. The little party turned round and stared; there was some confusion. But Farquhar, with his easy manners, soon ingratiated himself and put them

101

at their ease. It is possible that the hostess, Mrs. Voss knew him as a customer, for George was well known at the taverns in the town. Possibly the girl had seen him when watching Drury Lane, of which he was forever in and out. Farquhar hints that if she went on the stage there might be a great career for her, and her eyes light up and she glows with excitement, for her secret ambition seems about to take shape. Did she not tell Chetwode, of Drury Lane, long years after, that " I longed to be at it and only wanted a little decent entreaties?" She was very sure of herself even then.

Farquhar, good as his word, told Vanbrugh of his discovery, and the latter, who probably thought it was just another one of "those finds," was persuaded to go and see for himself.

The two captains went to the Mitre Tavern—it was a in a very different neighbourhood to the Piccadilly Circus we know to-day, and were shown into that historic little bar-parlour. No doubt Farquhar was just as excited as his little friend Anne, but perhaps Vanbrugh was very dubious and more than a little bored. He had seen, and heard, discoveries before. Most of them would have been better undiscovered, and were lost again as soon as possible.

Company was gathered for the occasion, the few relations and a handful of old friends being there to give moral support. There was quite a flutter as the two gentlemen entered, and Anne herself greeted them, beautiful to look at but decidedly nervous.

Mrs. Voss, the hostess, was delighted to welcome these two fine gentlemen, both as friends and customers, though doubtless, on this occasion, the drinks were "on the house." In her business woman's mind's eye was a vision of greatly increased custom if her "niece" became an actress at Drury Lane. Nobody could hazard what might come of it—there was Nell Gwynne—ah, but the Monarch was different to-day—still—there were Dukes, Earls—so she plied the gentry, who could do so much, with her best wine. Anne's mother was as excited as the girl herself. Could this be the turn of the tide, which had been running so strongly against her for the best part of her life? Could it be her little Anne's destiny to be famous and rich—and able to help her end her days in comfort? The atmosphere of the little room became electrical.

Vanbrugh gently kept them all calm. His good looks,

his stately manner impressed. He adopted a fatherly tone with Anne to gain her confidence, and asked her in what direction did her dramatic tastes lay. He got his first shock when the girl replied "In Comedy." This took his breath away, for everyone else he had ever seen had declared for Tragedy, the aristocrat of the Drama. So, must struck, he begged her to begin. When it was over, he was astounded. Farquhar had really found something. Not only did he shower congratulations upon her but immediately promised to use his influence with Christopher Rich on her behalf. He and Farquhar left behind them a group of people in the seventh heaven of delight.

And, so great was the impression made upon Vanbrugh that he did not forget. Indeed, he called on old Rich without delay and insisted that the girl should have a chance. He was too powerful a man to be disregarded, and Rich agreed readily.

In a very short space of time the girl was sent for and her name put on the Drury Lane roll as an actress to be in receipt of fifteen shillings a week. The year was 1699 when she signed the book as a member of the Royal Company at Theatre Royal, Drury Lane for the first time. The name inscribed, as she signed on, was . . . . Anne Oldfield.

CHAPTER 13.

LAST RIVALS DEFEATED.

IN 1699 George Farquhar was the only dramatist to write outstanding plays. His "Love and a Bottle" and "The Constant Couple," or "A Trip to the Jubilee," filled the house. The latter gave Wilks his famous part of "Sir Harry Wildair," afterwards a stock part for light comedians, and also a favourite one for actresses who liked to "wear the breeches." Peg Woffington gloried in it, and it was to be the cause of one of the best retorts that the great Quin, a master of caustic wit, ever made. Dashing off the stage in her male attire, during a performance of this play, she said to Quin, who was in the Green Room, "I have played this so many times that half the town thinks I am a man." "And the other half *knows* that you are not," was Quin's pointed comment.

The battle between the theatres was still raging, but

it was strange to see how things were now reversed. This was the second Battle of Drury Lane. The first had been fought with The Duke's Theatre. Then, Drury Lane had all the old actors, and the Duke's all the young ones. In this second battle, Drury Lane v. Lincoln's Inn Fields, Drury Lane, the senior theatre, had the young players and Lincoln's Inn the old stagers. Slowly but surely, in spite of all that Rich could do to prevent it in the way of bad management, the battle was going in favour of youth. Fortunately, the Lane has always risen superior to bad management, of which it has had more than its share.

One of the worst troubles at Lincoln's Inn was the smallness of the theatre, which meant that even when business was good the margin of profit was small. But now, as hinted before, a new venture was to rise. Vanbrugh decided to build another theatre, this time in the Haymarket. He got thirty important and wealthy people to subscribe one hundred guineas each to help him.

Italian opera was getting known in this country, and both houses, Drury Lane and Lincoln's Inn, cashed in on the idea, to the detriment of the true actors, who were now being crowded out by singers and dancers and consequently receiving less and less money. Rich also encouraged tumblers, rope dancers and acrobats to perform at Drury Lane, in preference to real actors and real acting. He was only deterred from engaging a very large elephant which had come over from abroad by the fact that his pet builder told him that the making of an entrance for the beast might endanger the structure of the whole theatre.

Anne Oldfield, the new recruit, had not set the Thames on fire, despite her romantic engagement. She was like everyone else, kept hanging about for over a twelvemonth, and when, by Vanbrugh's influence, she got a part in " The Pilgrim " ("Alinda "), Cibber thought little of her—" I thought she had little more than her person that appeared necessary to the forming of a good actress; for she set out with so extraordinary a diffidence that it kept her too despondingly down to a formal, plain, (not to say) flat manner of speaking." Nor could her lovely voice, at first, enchant him. Indeed Gildon, in 1702, wrote something in which he included this young actress amongst "the mere rubbish that ought to be swept off the stage with the filth and dust."

It may have been that Anne needed the hand of a

producer, an official then unknown, to set her going; it may be she had not yet gained confidence; or perhaps the clever brain behind that lovely face was just "foxing" and biding its time. Anyway, however small she was in public or theatre favour, she had a benefit, as they all had in turns, in 1702, and this occasion provided quite a lot of excitement and also another insight into what Drury Lane was like at this period.

For there was what was popularly referred to as a "rencounter" on the actual stage itself on this Benefit occasion. The play was "The Scornful Lady." We are told that "many people of distinction were behind the scenes." Amongst others Beau Fielding came and being always mighty ambitious of showing his fine make and shape, as he himself used vainly to talk, "he very closely pressed forward upon some gentlemen, but in particular upon Mr. Fulwood, a barrister of Gray's Inn, an acquaintance of Mrs. Oldfield's. Mr. Fulwood, being a gentleman of quick resentment, told Fielding he used him rudely. Upon which the other laid his hand upon his sword, Mr. Fulwood instantly drew, and gave Fielding a wound of twelve inches deep in the belly. This putting the audience into the greatest consternation, Mr. Fulwood was with much entreaty persuaded to leave the place. At length, out of respect to Mrs. Oldfield, he did so."

There's a pretty picture for you. The audience certainly got their money's worth at that benefit. No wonder they were in consternation, but it must have been as nothing to that of Fielding's, for twelve inches of cold steel in the stomach, with a crowded house looking on, is not most people's idea of an evening's enjoyment. It is charming, too, to find that they used entreaty to get Fulwood to go away. He wasn't thrown out, or even arrested, and only went at last to please Mrs. Oldfield herself. There is still a "Fulwood's Rents" in the neighbourhood of Gray's Inn. If it is named after this man, he evidently specialised in rents, for he made a good one in Fielding. Nobody knows how Fielding fared. But Fulwood hadn't finished his evening. He went straight up to Lincoln's Inn Theatre and there fell foul of a Captain Cusack, whom he challenged. Cusack and he repaired to the nearby Fields, and the Captain proved a better man of his hands than Fielding, for in less than half an hour they heard in the theatre that Fulwood was dead.

No wonder good Queen Anne, in 1704, issued a Command forbidding people other than the players to be on the stage; that no woman was to wear a vizard, and that nobody was to be allowed in unless they paid the proper price. Charles II tried to stop the abuse of the stage visitor, but he had no more success than Anne. However, all these things conspired to make the idea of a new theatre very popular, and Society gave it its blessing. And, as we have said, its money as well.

Vanbrugh, as might be expected of the architect of Blenheim House, designed a beautiful theatre, but when it was opened, the acoustics were found to be terrible.

Betterton now relinquished Lincoln's Inn and went over to Vanbrugh, and the house was opened on 9th April, 1705 under the joint management of Vanbrugh and Congreve, with an Italian Opera sung by an Italian company. The name of this work was "The Triumph of Love," but the only triumph was in the title. The music was bad, the company said to be the worst that ever came out of Italy, nobody could hear them, anyway, and the whole thing only ran for three nights. This was a setback, and no wonder old Rich was chuckling at Drury Lane and keeping on with his mixture of attractions.

Betterton was now a salaried actor and no longer in control. The new theatre was a failure, and Vanbrugh began to think the time had come for a reunion with Drury Lane.

Vanbrugh knew he must not seem anxious. He also knew that he had a slippery customer to deal with in Rich, particularly as just previously something had happened to strengthen his hand. The new young actress, Mistress Oldfield, had come into her own.

In 1703, after the London season, the Court, as usual, went to Bath. Thither also went Her Majesty's Company of Comedians from Drury Lane. The Queen signified her intention of coming to the theatre, so there was excitement in the little place, for she had not done much playgoing since her accession. The playhouse was crowded.

Wilks was in the cast, so was Cibber, and the play was to be "Sir Courtly Nice, or It Cannot Be." It was a favourite of Cibber's and gave him a good chance. No doubt he had persuaded the others to stage it on this occasion. There was a bit of trouble about who was to play "Leonora," the leading female role, which usually fell to Mrs. Verbruggen.

But that poor lady had been left in town, her mental condition being deranged. So they gave "Leonora" to Nance Oldfield. There was some tremor at this, especially from Cibber, who had to play opposite her. She "gave" him nothing, even at rehearsals. "Before she acted this part I had so cold an expectation from her abilities that she would scarce agree with me to rehearse with her the scenes she was chiefly concerned in with Sir Courtly, which I then acted. However, we ran over, with a mutual inadvertency of one another. I seemed careless, as concluding that any assistance I could give her would be to little or no purpose and she muttered out her words in a sort of misty manner, at my low opinion of her."

So things were not too happy backstage when the Queen took her seat in her Box, accompanied by that great friend Sarah Churchill. And just before the curtain rose a dull, heavy-looking man came in too, looking sleepy and overfed. It was the Royal Consort, George of Denmark.

The prologue over, the play began with the scene in which the two girls, Leonora and Violante discuss their lovers. Something came over the audience—they stopped gazing about them, and leaning forward, concentrated excited attention on the stage. It was the new girl who was the attraction. Even the Queen applauded, and Prince George, for once, did not go to sleep and snore. "Who is she?" everyone asked his or her neighbour. She held them more and more. It was her afternoon, her play: even Cibber's great comic scene went for very little—they were waiting for Leonora to appear again. It was a complete triumph. At the end she was acclaimed. And that afternoon—Anne Oldfield—Nance Oldfield—stood forth as a great actress. There were two Queen Annes in the house—one in the Royal Box and one on the stage. Cibber handsomely admitted his error. "But when the play came to be acted she had a just occasion to triumph over the error of my judgment, by the (almost) amazement that her unexpected performance awakened me to; so forward and sudden a leap into nature I had never seen; and what made her performance more valuable was that I knew it all proceeded from her own understanding, untaught and unassisted by any one more experienced actor."

So a new and very great actress weaved herself into the tapestry of Drury Lane, and Cibber hurried to his drawer to take out a play which he had started and laid aside,

called " The Careless Husband." He had put it away because he had despaired of finding an actress who could play
the part he had created therein of " Lady Betty Modish."
But here she was, the girl he had not believed in, and who
it had been recommended should be swept out of the theatre
with the filth and the rubbish.

He staged it at Drury Lane in 1704. Its cast is
memorable:—

Lord Morelove	Mr. Powel
Lord Foppington	Mr. Cibber
Sir Charles Easy	Mr. Wilks
Lady Betty Modish	Mrs. Oldfield
Lady East	Mrs. Knight
Lady Graveairs	Mrs. Moore
Mrs. Edging	Mrs. Lucas

It was what is now called " a smash hit "—and in the
very heart and centre of the " smash " was Anne Oldfield.
It was her great moment of triumph. Her first had been
at Bath, but this was at Drury Lane. The critics and the
public raved. Never had such an actress been seen in
comedy. Never had an actress displayed such gentility
as to the manner born. Never had anyone pointed
lines or got her laughs better or more easily. Here was the
real lady of fashion seen in her true colours. Here was a
tour de force. She was Queen Anne of Old Drury.

The accession of Oldfield to the throne of leading woman
of the stage did much for Drury Lane in the circumstances
in which it found itself, and was to do more as time went
on.

For Drury Lane v. Lincoln's Inn was over, and the
victory was to the Lane. Drury Lane v. Haymarket was
nearly over, and there was a tacit armistice whilst Vanbrugh steeled himself to make terms—or even to ask for
them. He went to work diplomatically.

He did not approach Rich himself. He got hold of
Swiney, one of the Drury Lane company who also acted as
Rich's manager. He probably pulled strings at Court, too,
for the Lord Chamberlain began to put pressure on Rich
to agree to an amalgamation. The suggestions were that
the Patentee and his adventurers should surrender or merge
their Patent and become sharers, by virtue of it, in the new
theatre and the company founded by the Queen; that the
previous liabilities of both sides should not come into the
bargain; that those put into power by the Queen could be
changed whenever she so directed and all details of the
merger to be left to the Lord Chamberlain.

No wonder Rich smiled. He now had a strong young company, a superb actress, and was doing well with his variety shows (personally, that is). He brought his legal knowledge and his capacity for splitting hairs into play. He pointed out that he was concerned with about forty persons as sharers with him in the Patent, whose trustee he was, and to take in other sharers now would be a breach of such trust and would tear him to pieces with law suits. He gave quite a lot of very pointed reasons and kept his thrust for the last. He was quite dignified in writing: "Sir, I am a purchaser under the Patent to above the value of £2,000 (a great part of which was under the marriage settlement of Dr. Davenant). After ten years' employment, expense and diligence, I have succeeded in pleasing the town, and the profits begin to reimburse, and the result must be the undoing of myself and others, to raise great estates to Mr. Vanbrugh." Nothing wrong with Rich. One admires his solicitude for his sharers, a rare event—much more tactical than real. No wonder Vanbrugh went to Swiney.

To this man Vanbrugh proposed the management and proprietorship of the theatre in the Haymarket at "the casual rent of £5 for every acting night, the whole not to exceed £700 a year." It looked easy. Swiney took the proposition to Rich, as Vanbrugh thought he would, who was not at all disinclined towards it, for it would really mean that. through Swiney, he would control both houses, and he loved power. He was basking in a moral glow over his rebuff to the Lord Chamberlain. Had he not protected his shareholders, and was not the great Vanbrugh preparing to throw over all those who had trusted him in the most shame-faced manner? But there was more to it than that. He would use Master Owen Swiney, and when he had got the better of him, out he should go.

So they talked terms, and here he had the whip hand (or thought so) for Swiney owed Rich over £200. They came to a verbal arrangement—Rich never put his name to paper if he could help it—and Swiney proved easy prey, flushed with the importance of the post and undertaking offered him. He did not realise that it was in Rich's power to hold him to the bargain, or call it off, whichever way it went. So Swiney took over from Vanbrugh, and under his verbal agreement with Rich, went off to the Haymarket with Wilks, Estcourt, Mills, Keen, Johnson, Bullock, Mrs.

Oldfield, Mrs. Rogers and some of the other lesser lights. The only important actor whom Rich insisted on keeping was Colley Cibber.

But Swiney was soon to do a little double crossing on his own, for Cibber got a letter from him, asking him to join the Haymarket Company. Our opportunist was in a quandary. He had profited by standing by Drury Lane once, he had little faith in the new venture, so he went to Rich to find out all about it.

Rich brushed his questions aside and enlarged upon his musical plans. Cibber's mind worked quickly. He could see no advantage to himself. So he came down to brass tacks. He reminded Rich that he had stood by him before when so many of his best had left him. He asked that if he did so again, he should not lose by it. He said that either his casual pay should be increased or his salary made certain for as many days as they had acted the year before. In other words, he wanted a guaranteed minimum. Rich was not to be drawn; this was too near a definite promise. All he would promise was that Cibber might choose any parts he liked. Cibber made up his mind. Looking Rich straight in the face he said " You know on what terms I am willing to serve you " and bowed himself out. He went to the Haymarket, where he found business better. They were getting full salaries, a thing none of them had known for a considerable time.

At the new house Anne Oldfield was going from success to success. She showed she could play tragedy as well as comedy. And she appeared there with Mrs. Bracegirdle, playing with this great actress for the first time. It was a meeting of the young queen and the old, and must have been an intriguing sight for the audience. But Mrs. Bracegirdle, with whom Mrs. Barry had refused to compete, knew that her own day was over. She in her fading years, was not going to compete with this lovely young thing, so full of beauty, ardour and supreme talent. Wise Mrs. Bracegirdle, well-to-do and happy. She retired gracefully, leaving behind her only fragment memories of her beauty and her powers. She lived for a long time, outliving indeed her successful rival—Anne Oldfield was now Queen of the Stage.

Swiney was now trying to get a proper agreement out of Rich and was finding out what he was up against. Rich knew all about procrastination. He was pursuing his own sweet way at the Lane, and things got so low that on one occasion when Rich introduced rope dancers into a little play Cibber had written some time before for the Lane, the outraged actor-dramatist went into the pit and addressed those about him, saying that he was sure they would not take it as a mark of disrespect from him for not appearing on that stage any more which had been brought to such a low point of disgrace. The audience agreed with him, and Rich thought it best to take no action.

The actors at the Haymarket were really in little better case than they had been at the Lane, for Swiney had no reserves in case of bad business. They had been " bounced " into the new order, but for the moment it was all right. There had apparently been some talk of pooling profits and sharing losses between Swiney and Rich, but the former could never get the latter to disclose his accounts. Nor could anyone else. And someone who had tried for years and failed now comes into the picture.

This was Sir Thomas Skipworth, introduced briefly before. He held the major number of shares, but could never get anything out of Rich at all. He got sick and tired of the whole thing. He met and took a fancy to one Colonel Brett. To him he confided that he had had no return out of Drury Lane for ten years, and if the Colonel like to take over his interest he was welcome. Now Brett liked the theatre. He had been to Oxford and studied the law but he preferred a sidebox at the play to any Court of Justice. He had an income of £2,000 a year, into which he had dipped considably. He liked acting and actors, and he was the first friend of any position that Colley Cibber had made. Brett had a tremendous regard for the enormous periwig which Cibber wore in " The Fool in Fashion," and this was what first drew him behind the scenes. So in reality it was his great fancy for a great wig which led to him becoming joint Patentee of the greatest theatre in the world. There are some curious reasons why people embark upon theatre ventures, but admiration for a periwig is surely the most curious of all.

He was popular backstage and friendship cemented by many a good bottle had grown up between him and Cibber, so even though Cibber was now not at Drury Lane but at the opposition house, Brett asked the actor's advice. Cibber freely gave it, and we may be certain that the likelihood of a powerful friend at court served to flavour it. So

111

Brett, having paid Skipworth the consideration of 10/- for his major share in the Patent of Drury Lane, that precious and unique document given old Killigrew by Charles II set up a new low-level record.

Cibber now gave him more good counsel. He advised him how to handle Rich, and to make it his purpose, for he had the power, of bringing back the actors to Drury Lane, to make it the pre-eminent home of the drama once more, and leave Swiney down at the Haymarket to concentrate on opera. Cibber's advice was not a little tinctured by his love and respect for the old Theatre, which it commands from all its true servants. Brett had power and friends at the Court. He pulled his strings. The result was an order from the Lord Chamberlain that the actors should at once return to Drury Lane and that opera only should be given at the Haymarket. This scared the actors. They had done pretty well under the new regime and had been paid quite regularly up to then. Now they were to be forced back under the tyranny of Rich. They sent in a remonstrance to his lordship begging to be left alone. Then entire company signed it, including Colley Cibber. But it was of no avail to them. Things had been fixed up, and back they had to go, whether they liked it or not.

And now Drury Lane, having won its battle, by somewhat curious means, but won it indeed, stood once more as the chief and only theatre in London—for the Haymarket went over to opera.

***

CHAPTER 14

RICH IS CHECKMATED

RICH was never pleased when business was good : it made it difficult for him to underpay people and cook his books. And Drury Lane was now prospering under Brett. Brett seems to have been a pleasant man with good business ability and, above all, to have understood how to handle the actors. No doubt Cibber and Wilks were always at his elbow, advising and guiding. The actors now regarded Brett as their master, deferred to him, did as he told them, and a time of peace and prosperity, to which this playhouse had long been a stranger, held sway.

None of this pleased Rich, who, resenting having his wings clipped, tried by every means in his power to make mischief and freeze Brett out. He did not succeed, so he took an extreme step. He called a meeting of the other members of the board—that is to say, the other holders of shares in the Patent. He had kept them out of his counsels for years, and had also kept them out of any profits. But now, by this cunning move, he got them together ostensibly to discuss their improving prospects. His object was to get a majority vote and with it the power to hamstring Brett's activities. He also went to the (for him) very extreme length of proposing a dividend. He recommended himself to them for the care which he had taken of all their interests for so many years, and represented that the improved position now in being was the result of a " long-term plan " of his own formulation. Simultaneously, he began to pay old debts, the idea being to swamp any chance of future profits being made by Brett and make him tired of working for nothing. He put his plan into action, but before it was apparent whether it would succeed or not, something happened which might have been an answer to his prayer.

Sir Thomas Skipworth and Brett had a quarrel. Skipworth alleged that he had not really parted with his share in the Patent to Brett but had merely left it with him in trust. The document which transferred the interest is in being, and is a clear conveyance for the consideration of 10/-. Brett put in a reply but did not let the matter come to Court. He did not want it to appear that he had indulged in any suggestion of sharp practice. Also, maybe. he found the job a pretty hard one, and was longing for a life of pleasure again. So he re-conveyed the share back again, but to the son and heir of Sir Thomas Skipworth.

So Rich, with characteristic luck, got rid of his enemy without the least trouble to himself. In power once again, his interest in his shareholders vanished. At once all talk of a dividend ceased : at once the creditors found themselves being asked to "call again."

Not only were the actors underpaid but Rich began monkeying with their benefits. It was really by these benefits that they were able not only to live in some sort of comfort but to make any sort of provision for sickness or old age. The benefit was a highly prized prerogative. The first to be given had gone to Mrs. Barry, in James II's time, in respect of her great personal success. In reality it was a spontaneous act of public appreciation. But the practice became general in 1695, when Rich seized upon it as an alternative for paying proper salaries, and as Cibber points out, paid the actors "half in cash and half in promises." This astute man noticed that the public rallied to a favourite actor or actress on a benefit occasion, and saw a chance of diverting some more into his own pocket. The provision of benefits became part of their articles, according to their standing, " a clear benefit," "half a clear benefit," and similar phrases being embodied in their agreements.

A clear benefit was one in which the actor took all the proceeds, after the management had deducted an agreed sum for expenses; half a clear benefit was where the player received half the proceeds after expenses had been deducted, and so on. On one or two very rare occasions the management threw in the expenses as their share of the benefit. The players who supported the beneficiary played for nothing, and had the compliment returned in their turn. The benefit was finally abolished by John Hollingshead when he was controlling the Gaiety Theatre.

Now written agreements meant little to Rich. We know that he always left clauses through which, as a lawyer, he could drive a coach and four. But when the actors all returned to Drury Lane there were no written agreements, only verbal ones. They had been driven back by the Lord Chamberlain. So there existed only words of honour and gentlemen's agreements, neither of which meant anything to Rich. He determined to get things his own way, and demanded that all his players signed agreements defining what their shares were to be. He laid down his own terms and conditions. Very naturally, the front rank flatly refused to sign—the agreements were much too one-sided. So Rich next tried it on the smaller people. These were tempted, for if they signed, they stood to get preference in selection of days and periods, very important factors in the yield to be expected, for some nights were much better than others, and the same was true of various periods of the year. Lent, for instance, was useless. When the leading people were made aware of this situation, they saw the danger.

In the end they were forced to sign under protest; but they determined to seize the first real chance of hitting back. Meanwhile they bided their time: wisely, as it turned out.

On April 7, 1709, old Thomas Betterton, who had virtually retired, had his benefit. This was right in the

114

middle of the battle of the benefits, and turned out to be a really terrific occasion. Everyone wished to do honour to the grand old veteran of stainless character. He was now seventy-four years of age, and he said he was just beginning to learn something about his business. The play chosen was "Love for Love," with which he had made such a brilliant start at Lincoln's Inn in his rebellion against Rich. Mrs. Barry and Mrs. Bracegirdle came out of their retirement to assist him. Doggett played "Ben," and every part was in the hands of somebody brilliant. Old Betterton himself played "Valentine." Let words written by an eye witness for the first number of "The Tatler" describe the scene:—

"On Thursday last was acted for the benefit of Mr. Betterton the celebrated comedy called 'Love for Love.' Those excellent players Mrs. Barry, Mrs. Bracegirdle, and Mr. Doggett though not at present concerned in the house, acted on that occasion. There has not been known so great a concourse of persons of distinction; the stage itself was covered with ladies and gentlemen, and when the curtain was drawn, there appeared also a very splendid audience. This unusual encouragement, which was given to a play for the advantage of so great an actor, gives an undeniable instance that the true relish for manly entertainment and rational pleasures is not wholly lost. All the parts were acted to perfection and there seemed a peculiar regard had to their behaviour on this occasion; no one was guilty of the affectation to insert witticisms of his own; but a due respect had to the audience, for encouraging this accomplished player. It is not now doubted but plays will revive, and take their usual place in the opinion of persons of wit and merit, notwithstanding their late apostacy in favour of dress and sound. This place is very much altered since Mr. Dryden frequented it. . . . But however the company is altered, all have shown a great respect for Mr. Betterton and the very gaming part of this house . . . in this gentleman have pitied Mark Antony, of Rome; Hamlet, of Denmark; Mithridates of Pontus; Theodosius of Greece; and Henry the Eighth of England. It is well known he has been in the condition of illustrious personages for several hours together, and behaved himself in those high stations, in all the changes of the scene with suitable dignity. For these reasons we intend to repeat this late favour to him on a proper occasion, lest he who can instruct us so well in personating feigned sorrows may not be lost to us in suffering under real ones."

It is pleasant to record that Betterton netted over £500, a very considerable amount in those days. The following year he enjoyed one more benefit, just as brilliant if not so big, at the Haymarket. He did well, although struggling with a serious attack of gout, but the repressive measures he took were too violent, and a few days afterwards he died —on 28th April, 1710. He was buried in Westminster Abbey.

The actors had now made up their minds for a decisive encounter with Rich. Having seen the damage done to their own benefits by Rich's chiselling, they laid their case before the Lord Chamberlain. That functionary considered the case, was more than sympathetic, and made a demand upon Rich to show why the players' benefits had been diminished by one-third—for that was what they were losing—against the custom of the profession. Rich pleaded that the actors had agreed, and produced their receipts in support of his case—a damning admission which one is surprised to find him making. These were easily shown to have been secured under duress.

Rich produced, at long last, his accounts, or accounts he had cooked up for the occasion. As an example of theatrical book-keeping as then practised, they are worth recording fully. He starts off with a preamble in which he states that they had, during the previous season, allowing for Royal Demise and other interferences, acted 135 days, which made 6 days a week for 22 weeks and 3 days. He says " In that time:

	£	s.	d.
To Mr. Wilks, for salary and taking care of the rehearsals, paid	168	6	8
By his benefit play	90	14	9
Total ...	259	1	5
To Mr. Betterton, by salary for acting, £4 per week for himself and £1 per week for his wife, although she does not act, paid	112	10	0
By a benefit at common prices, besides what he got by high prices and guineas, paid	76	4	5
	188	14	5
To Mr. Estcourt, at £5 per week salary paid	112	10	0
By a benefit, paid	51	8	6
	163	18	6
To Mr. Cibber, at £5 a week salary, paid	111	10	0
By a benefit paid	51	0	10
	162	10	10
To Mr. Mills at £4 a week for himself, and £1 for his wife, for little or nothing, paid	112	10	10
By a benefit paid to him (not including what therein she got by a benefit play)	58	1	4
	170	11	4
To Mrs. Oldfield, at £4 a week salary which for fourteen weeks and one day; she leaving off acting presently after her benefit (viz.) on the 17th March last, 1708, although the benefit was intended for the whole nine months acting, and she refused to assist others in the benefits; her salary for these fourteen weeks and one day came to and she was paid	56	13	4

In January she required, and was paid, ten guineas to wear on the stage in some plays, during the whole season, a mantua petticoat that was given her for the stage, and though she left off three months before she should yet she hath not returned any part of the ten guineas 10 15 0

And she had for wearing on the stage in some plays a suit of boys' clothes, paid 2 10 9

By a benefit paid 62 7 8

_____

132 6 9

Cortainties in all £1,077 3 8.

Besides which sums above mentioned the same actors got by their benefit plays as follows:

Note, that Mr. Betterton had £76 4 5 as above-mentioned for two thirds of the profits by a benefit play, reckoning his tickets for the boxes at 5/- apiece, the pit at 3/-, the first gallery at 2/- and the upper gallery at 1/-. But the boxes, pit and stage, laid together on his day, and no person admitted but by his tickets, the lowest at half a guinea a ticket; nay he had made much more, for one lady gave him ten guineas, and most one guinea, supposing that he desired not to act any more and he had delivered tickets out for more persons, than the boxes, pit and stage could hold it is thought he cleared at least £450 over and besides the £76 4 5 ... ... 450 0 0

'Tis thought that Mr. Estcourt cleared £200 besides the said £51 8 6 ... ... 200 0 0

That Mr. Wilks cleared by Guineas, as it is thought about £40 besides the said £90 14 9 ... ... 40 0 0

That Mr. Cibber got by Guineas, as it is thought about £50 besides the said £51 0 10 ... ... 50 0 0

That Mr. Mills got by guineas about £20, as it is thought, besides the said £58 1 0 ... ... 20 0 0

That Mrs. Oldfield, it is thought, got £120 by guineas over and above the said £62 7 8 ... ... 120 0 0

_____

In all ... 880 0 0

So that these six comedians, who are the unsatisfied people, have between the 12th October and the 4th June last, cleared in all the following sums:

	£.	s.	d.
Acted 16 times, Mr. Wilks certain	259	1	5
and more by computation	40	0	0
	299	1	5
Acted 16 times, Mr. Betterton certain	188	14	5
and more by computation	450	0	0
	638	14	5
Acted 52 times, Mr. Estcourt, certain	163	18	6
and more by computation	200	0	0
	363	18	6
Acted 71 times, Mr. Cibber, certain	162	10	10
and more by computation	50	0	0
	212	10	10

	£	s.	d.
Acted — times, Mr. Mills certain	170	11	4
and more by computation	20	0	0
	190	11	4
Acted 39 times, Mrs. Oldfield certain	132	6	7
and more by computation	120	0	3
	252	6	10

In all £1,957 3 2.

Had not acting been forbid seven weeks on the occasion of Prince George's death, and my Lord Chamberlain forbad acting for five weeks, before the tenth of July instant; each of these comedians would have had twelve weeks' salary more than is above mentioned.

As to the certainties expressed in this paper to be paid to the six actors, the same are positively true; And as to the sums they got over and above such certainties, I believe the same to be true, according to the best of my computation.

Witness my hand, who am Receiver and Treasurer at the Theatre Royal, Drury Lane.

ZACHARY BAGGS.

What we learn from this egregrious document is that the determined Cibber played more often than any of the others and that Mrs. Oldfield had temperaments as an answer to Rich's tricks, and stayed "off," as many others have done since. She appears, also, to have converted parts of her wardrobe to her own use. That has been done since, but with considerably less provocation than Oldfield's.

The Lord Chamberlain brought his own powers of computation to bear, and probably showed the accounts to the complaining actors, who would have plenty to say in criticism. Between them they came to an understanding. The final judgment was left in abeyance until the leading actors could see if they could form a body responsible enough to allow the Chamberlain to depose Rich from the Patent and transfer it to them and a responsible head with them. So Swiney at the Haymarket was to be allowed to take those of them he wanted to be sharers with him at the Haymarket, there to do plays (at the moment he was allowed opera only) until the matter was thrashed out. He chose Wilks, Doggett, Mrs. Oldfield and Cibber, whom we may be sure was the ringleader in all this, and who had by now, in all probability, decided with Wilks and Doggett that they should be the three who would in the near future run Drury Lane. Barry and Bracegirdle had retired before this little affair, and Betterton was too old.

Then there was the question of Mrs. Oldfield. Should she be made a fourth partner in the concern? She was the unrivalled actress of her day, and it looked the strongest combination possible. But Master Doggett spoke up. Not that he had the slightest objection to Mrs. Oldfield on the score of merit. She was first class. But, said the grim, determined Whig, their affairs would never be secure if more than one sex were admitted to the management of them. Doggett did not believe in petticoat government, or influence. But he did not want to lose the Oldfield. With a pretty shrewd idea of what he was talking about, he suggested offering *carte blanche* in the way of salary instead of a share, and when the others suggested that the lady might feel slighted, said he thought not. He was right, for Mrs. Oldfield took it as a favour and with some relief. She did not want to be involved in management, she knew what a bother it all was. She asked them £200 a year guarantee and a benefit clear of all charges. They signed her up at once on such reasonable terms.

All this had taken about a month to bring about. Nothing had happened during that time, and Rich began to think that once again he had triumphed. So he began to take action, launching a series of petty revenges against all who had complained. He gave parts to those who had kept out of the quarrel and ignored those who had been active in it. He began to favour and to promote those whom he thought were loyal to him.

But one day the Lord Chamberlain swooped. He sent for the spokesman of the aggrieved actors, (they had not yet left Drury Lane) and we can be pretty certain it was Colley Cibber, and showed him a document known as a "Silence Order" all drawn up and in proper form, which was to be served upon Rich. This "Silence Order" meant that under it the theatre would be closed and those in possession of it expelled and dismissed therefrom. It was the equivalent of the withdrawal of the Lord Chamberlain's licence of to-day. Cibber dashed back to the theatre and told his fellow conspirators the good news. They were all at a rehearsal, for which he too had been called. His absence had been duly noted by Rich, and that gentleman determined to make it an occasion for some of that petty tyranny which he so loved. He had Cibber called and began to bully him in front of all the others, for his insubordination and unprofessional behaviour in being absent from his duty. The actor broke in upon the tirade, standing erect in the centre of the Drury Lane stage and adopting the attitude and air of a hero of tragedy. His reply took the

119

breath out of Rich, for he said: " Sir, I have now no more business here than you have; in half an hour you will neither have actors to command nor authority to employ them." Rich could not quite get the hang of this, but must have smelt a rat and become a bit scared; for he now became very dignified and said with cold reproof and sternness: " If you do not do your work, you shall not be paid." Then he turned and bade the rehearsal proceed.

But proceed it did not, for a messenger from the Lord Chamberlain entered. In his hand was the dreaded Silence Order which was then duly served upon Rich, whilst all the company stood in silent excitement at the terrific event. But Cibber had not quite finished with him yet, for as Rich took the document and broke its seal, Cibber hurled at him a quotation from Henry the Eighth—" Read o'er that. And now to breakfast, with what appetite you may!"

To enforce the Silence Order, the Lord Chamberlain's representative fixed a silken cord across every entrance, sealing each with the official seal. The reign of Christopher Rich was over.

The actors trooped off to the Haymarket, where under the agreement already made with Swiney they set about doing their best. Opera had not proved a success, and the theatre, as we know, was far from perfect. They altered its structure, they altered its seating, and they reopened as soon as they could. They did not do very well, for if they drew in money for a play, the succeeding opera in which they had to share as well, lost that money.

The trial of Dr. Sacheverell was convulsing the town and putting people's minds off playgoing, and in addition, a new tenant of Drury Lane had arisen. He did not hold the Patent for he had not applied for it, but he got open nevertheless. He was William Collier, a lawyer of good business mind and genial manners, and as Member of Parliament for Truro and a man of means, he had considerable influence. He saw Drury Lane vacant and unable to open under Rich. So the other shareholders and proprietors in the Patent and Theatre were debarred from getting any income at all. Offering £4 a day instead of the £3 a day which Rich had paid, he applied for a licence to produce plays at Drury Lane, and got it.

The actors who had been left to Rich now signed on with Collier. They made a poor show for scenery and wardrobe were missing. But they had young Barton Booth amongst them and a girl, Miss Santlow, who was to become his wife. They produced a play called "The Fair Quaker of Deal," of which Cibber (in opposition) says "had some low strokes of natural humour in it, rightly calculated for the capacity of the actors who played in it and to the taste of the public, who were now more disposed and had leisure to see it." Miss Santlow was the draw, a beautiful woman who had up to then been a popular dancer and who now showed herself a good actress and a favourite one.

But fortune turned again to the ex-Drury Lane actors at the Haymarket. The more discerning playgoers, eschewing the somewhat ragged and inexperienced crew at Drury Lane, supported the stars. And Mr. Collier began to find the path of the theatre was edged with more thorns than roses.

CHAPTER 15

THE TRIUMVIRATE IN ACTION

COLLIER had no real love for the Theatre. He had seen it as a money making concern and as something which would give him publicity and bring him into the public eye.

Directly he found it was going to be an occasion of trouble and expense to him, he began to shift his ground. He pulled important strings at Court. He pleaded that his action in letting Swiney have the best actors (and their wardrobes) had placed him at a severe disadvantage and pecuniary loss. Therefore, he said, as he had given Swiney so much, he should have, with that operatic manager, an equal share in the Haymarket Theatre, and be made indeed Chief Director of Opera. Swiney was made to agree to this very unfair proposal, and an agreement to that effect was signed.

But there were two troublesome points in the agreement. It was considered that plays would be more profitable than operas, so it was laid down that Swiney and the actors should pay to Collier, whilst he remained Director of Opera, the sum of £200 a year, thus in actual fact, Drury Lane was subsidising opera. The second point was that Drury Lane should remain closed every Wednesday, on which night an opera should be performed at the Haymarket. This up-

121

set the bulk of the actors, for it meant that they were deprived of a sixth of their weekly income, payment in those days being made per acting day. But Cibber saw further than the others. He knew that because of the Wednesday closing, audiences would be better on the Thursday, forced abstinence increasing appetite.

Collier, having got what he wanted, sublet his interest in the Haymarket to Aaron Hill, (who had more practical experience than he had himself) at £600 per annum. But he took it back from Hill before the season was over. Hill was probably making it pay. Then, observing that Swiney and his actors were making a good thing of it at Drury Lane Collier decided to put his fingers back into that pie too. Once more he pulled strings. His idea was to change over again with Swiney, taking Drury Lane back in exchange for the Haymarket. Swiney did not see the fun of this, and who will blame him? But the only law which protected the theatre then was Royal favour, and Collier had this, whilst Swiney had not.

Sir John Vanbrugh, who was a friend of Swiney's, advised him to agree, pointing out that if he refused he would forfeit the regard in which he was held, and in respect of which he was allowed in the theatre at all. So poor Swiney had once more to go back to the Haymarket whilst Collier obtained a licence for himself, Wilks, Doggett and Cibber to take over and run Theatre Royal, Drury Lane. . Swiney's enforced move ruined him. He went smash owing to poor support. In 1711, it not being possible to make opera pay, he left the country.

Collier, having got power into his hands now drove a hard bargain with the real masters of Drury Lane, Wilks, Doggett and Cibber, who had to have him. A mere sleeping partner, he demanded of the three actors, the sum of £600 per annum, plus half of the £200 they had been forced to pay him under the old Drury Lane-Haymarket agreement. This meant a total of £700 a year for doing nothing except leaving them alone and not intriguing against them. They offered him an equal share with themselves. He refused it. So they had to accept his conditions.

Collier, being thus sterilised into a well paid but non-active member of the management, Wilks, Doggett and Colley Cibber became the actual actor-managers of Drury Lane Theatre. They were to write a chapter which is one of the best in its long history. For this was the first real instance of actor-management, and it was to show, as has been amply proved since, that it is under that form of government that the Theatre becomes important, glorious, and a real part of the life of the people. This was the beginning of the famous Triumvirate.

They were perhaps an ill-assorted trio, yet each provided something which the other two lacked, and this made for good business and direction. All three were at the height of their powers as actors and men of affairs. Things were prosperous. They were able to, and did, pay better salaries to actors and actresses than had ever been paid before, so they got good service and happy companions. The actors must have thought the Golden Age had come!

Doggett was the financial boss. He was an economist, and not only kept the accounts but regulated expenditure within the bounds of receipts. Wilks looked after the productions and the stage direction. In this he was apt to be extravagant, for he believed in doing things well. With Wilks, achievement was everything, financial gain nothing. He wanted the glory of the stage before the glory of personal profit. Applause meant more to him than guineas. At the beginning of every season he would order new clothes and new suits for the leading actors, not only for new plays but for the constant revival of old ones, so that they should all look fresh. He would also order some for himself although not in immediate need, and he would do this without consulting his partners. Then the bills would come in, and Cibber, who liked it as little as Doggett in actual fact, would have to smile and try to drive it into Doggett's head that the expense was a lesser evil than serious dissension, and that it was not improbable that credit for such good appearance of actors and production would show results by increase of popular favour. Old Doggett would grunt and say no more. Cibber was a great pourer of oil on troubled waters. He would agree with both sides when there was an argument, but not give way to either. He would give some credit to one, and then some to the other, with the result that friendly compromise was always effected. He was of the utmost value too, in his social contacts. He was actually a member of White's Club, the first actor to be so, and the only one until the late Arthur Bourchier was admitted to those exclusive portals.

In twenty years the Theatre never had a creditor who had to call twice for his bill; every Monday morning all liabilities were paid before they took one penny for themselves. And for twenty years they never asked an actor, or were asked by actors, for a written contract. That is something of which Drury Lane has reason to be proud.

Cibber himself thanks Heaven for the share of good fortune which made this possible, knowing full well the quick changes of which that fickle goddess Luck is capable in theatrical affairs. But, nevertheless, it was their sound judgment, honesty of purpose and practice, and by the fact that they worked themselves and took an active part in the affairs of the great playhouse they guided so successfully that is the bedrock of their achievement. During all this time their own incomes never dropped below a thousand pounds a year each. A lot of money in those days.

In the early days when success smiled upon them so continuously, things went very smoothly. Their excitement at getting power, the joy of putting their own long discussed ideas into practice, and the greater joy of finding that they worked, made their Board Meetings occasions for mutual congratulations. Their high spirits made their own performances full of that spontaniety and enthusiasm which early successes always engenders. Of the triumvirate, Wilks, however, was the weak spot. Once, at least, he nearly broke the partnership by being big and generous at their expense and without their consent first.

And now a great and important event took place in the production of a play which created a tremendous sensation, and which lived for many years in every theatre repertory.

Addison had written a play, or portion of a play, and as early as 1703 Cibber had been shown the first four acts. He read them privately to Sir Richard Steele with the greatest of joy, and was very dashed when Steele told him that he did not believe Addison would ever let the play be acted. Political considerations were the great stumbling block. Steele did not decry the play; on the contrary, he was delighted and excited by it and exclaimed, " Good God, what a part would Betterton make of Cato." For that was the name of the play as well as the title role. But Addison's " Cato," was destined to make stage history and be a yardstick and measure of theatrical reputations, a test part for every actor, by which he was tried, and passed or found wanting by the critical public of those days. It gave us some lines which have become a proverb to-day, and which the late Sir Oswald Stoll had emblazoned over the proscenium of many of his halls, and indeed took as his motto— lines which many people attribute to Shakespeare but which are the great Addison's:—

" Tis not in mortals to command success
But we'll do more, Sempronius, we'll deserve it."

It might well have been the motto of the Triumvirate, for they did indeed deserve — and receive it.

In 1712 a change had come over the political world. The Tories were out of power and the Whigs were in the ascendant. Now "Cato" was a play which pointed and adorned Whiggery, and Addison's friends besought him to finish it and have it "brought upon the stage." He did so, and he made a present of it to the Drury Lane Triumvirate.

This was too good a chance to miss: the times were absolutely ripe for it, and Wilks, Cibber and Doggett hurried on the production. Doggett must have given every assistance possible, for he was a staunch and inveterate Whig. He it was who hailed the accession of the House of Hanover by instituting a race for the Thames Watermen, a race which carried the blue riband of the river, and the prize for which was an ornate coat and badge, known then, as now, as Doggett's Coat and Badge. It is still competed for, and its origin, it should be remembered, was Drury Lane Theatre. So "Cato" was right up Doggett's street.

The month was April, a time when most of the benefits were taken; but the Triumvirate thought that such a work by such a man should take precedence of all else, and hurried to get it on. Because the author had given it to them, and asked for no share in profits, they decided that it must have every chance in the way of staging and casting. Even Doggett made no demur at this.

The question of the casting arose. The part of "Cato" was not one in which Wilks would shine and, he knew it. It was given to Booth, who had stood by Collier when the others went to the Haymarket, and who had now become a fine actor. A young man named Ryan, the son of a Westminster tailor, was given the part of Marcus, at the request of the author, which could not be disregarded. Wilks, Cibber and Oldfield played the other important parts. It was produced for the first time on 14th April, 1713 (1712 according to Cibber, who is often careless in his dates).

The time was doubly propitious. Marlborough had

turned Whig and had asked to be made "Commander-in-Chief" for life. Harley, Bolingbroke and other Tories were appalled at this, and went about yelling that it was an attempt at a dictatorship. At any rate on that April evening, expectation ran high. A play by Addison, reflecting through classical history the moods and political fortunes of the day. A comparatively new actor in the lead; Wilks, Cibber, and incomparable Anne in the cast, the the debut of a quite new actor (important and interesting events such debuts were then); and above all, a chance maybe to let off Party steam. These were the expectations, and all were fully realized. "Cato" was a vast and overwhelming success.

Booth was, perhaps, the great hit of the evening. He surpassed himself and all his previous promise. His dignity, his power, his pathos and his dramatic appeal were equal, in this particular part, to anything which Betterton had ever done. Yet there was no imitation, no striving for effect in the school and manner of the old Master. It was Barton Booth's own creation and his own ideas which triumphed. Ryan, too, who had been coached by Addison himself, made a big success, and there is no need to say that Wilks, Cibber and Oldfield were as fine as they could be. A veritable night of triumph for Drury Lane.

The play was watched with breathless interest and almost constant applause. The Whigs applauded to the echo every line which referred to Liberty (and they were many) as a reproof and defiance to the Tories. The Tories, in their turn, not to be outdone, applauded as well and as heartily, as if to make the impression that those were their sentiments as well, and to appear quite unconscious of the bitter satire upon them. It was one of those electrical nights when it is so wonderful to be in a theatre, and Old Drury has given more of them than any theatre in the world.

The pit was in a whirlwind of enthusiasm, the boxes could not contain their delight. It was a scene of continuous and indescribable frenzy of feeling and emotion.

When the curtain finally fell, and after innumerable calls had been taken, Lord Bolingbroke sent for Booth to his box. That night Booth had stepped into the premier position on the stage. But it was not only for that Bolingbroke wanted him. He presented the actor with a purse containing fifty guineas which had been collected from gentry present, who had experienced the greatest delight at the energy with which he had resisted dictatorship and maintained the cause of public liberty. This was rubbing in the political side with a vengeance, for Booth had only repeated the lines which Addison had given him, although he had been superb. The present was for the sentiments expressed, even more than the expression of them. Bolingbroke knew the gift would be the gossip of the town and desired to make capital out of it. For Bolingbroke was a Tory and this would be a nice comeback at the Whigs.

This triumph of Booth's and the public testimony to it made the Triumvirate think a bit. How long would Booth be content to remain a salaried actor? Was he going to turn into a rival? They remembered he had stayed with Collier. They thought of their own ideas in such a case and indeed of their own past actions.

Doggett, although staunchly unafraid of anyone, hit upon an expedient. He said that this present given by the Tories would redound to their great credit. As a Whig himself, he could not bear that. He therefore proposed that the management should make Booth a present of a similar amount. This, he said, would show the town what good people and generous masters they were, they would get much credit for it, and it would bind Booth more closely to them. For no actor had ever received such a big mark of esteem before.

Wilks, who only wanted as astute a mind to be as cunning as Doggett, thought it a grand idea, and was all for giving it to Booth then and there with his own hands. But they had not yet got Cibber's consent and this must be obtained. Cibber was playing a game of his own, to balance between Wilks and Doggett. He said coldly to Doggett that if indeed he could purchase Booth so cheaply it would be a triumph for his economic methods, but, personally, he thought Booth would shortly demand a share in the management and profits, and that by his success he had every justification to do so. Cibber also remarked that Booth had powerful friends and would be an awkward customer to deal with if it came to a tussle. But Doggett said that nobody could be offended by such a handsome gift as was projected, and, so far as the theatre went, it was theirs, as were all the scenery, costumes and clothes. They did not belong to the Crown, so he thought it would be all right. Anyway Booth got his fifty guineas that night, and the town rang with the news to the great glory of the Triumvirate and the greater glory of Booth. Yet Cibber in his prophecy was quite right, as they were soon to find.

But "Cato" continued a raging success. Private benefits were for the moment set aside, except for Monday nights, and Cato was performed every evening save Mondays. Cibber says it was acted for a month to immense audiences. Research disputes this : some say it was played twenty-five nights, others say twenty. But if you leave out the Mondays, old Cibber was not far out. Anyway he should have known, for he and his partners netted thirteen hundred and fifty pounds each out of it, even allowing for the fifty given to Booth.

But success usually costs something—and "Cato" was indeed going to bring a great change over them very shortly.

CHAPTER 16

A GALAXY OF GREAT PLAYERS

JUST as Cibber had foreseen, Booth soon demanded a share in the partnership and the profits.

His demand was fostered and backed by Lord Bolingbroke, a most influential man. It threw the Triumvirate into a state of acute embarrassment, if not confusion. Cibber having foreseen it, was not particularly upset, though perhaps in his heart he regretted those fifty guineas. Wilks, since Booth was an out-and-out tragedian, was not so put out as he might have been had Booth been likely to want the parts he played himself. But old Doggett was in dead opposition. It was not so much that he had any complaints against Booth as an actor, or even that there would be a further "cut" in the profits; but Booth was sponsored and backed by a Tory peer. To Doggett, the uncompromising old Whig, that was anathema.

Booth's demand placed the Triumvirate in an awkward position. Management of the theatre in those days was a very complicated business; and if the theatre happened to be Theatre Royal, crises were even more difficult to handle. Also, there was the sleeping partner Collier to be reckoned with.

128

A typical visitor to the Green Room of Drury Lane
in the Regency Period.

The THEATRICAL ATLAS.—

George Cruikshank.   May 7, 1814.

EDMUND KEAN AS RICHARD III., SUPPORTING DRURY LANE THEATRE (UNDER WHITBREAD'S MANAGEMENT)

A contemporary print of EDMUND KEAN, showing that great actor, in the
character of "Richard III," supporting the entire weight of Drury Lane
Theatre, which in fact he did.

Booth's noble friends got the Lord Chamberlain to issue a new licence for the theatre which included Booth's name in the management. Against this the present partners could do little. They had to swallow it, however much they disliked it from personal reasons. They knew they could not do without Booth (Doggett, of course, being a dissentient) but there were other considerations to be taken into account. Here was Booth made a partner by a few strokes of the all-powerful Lord Chamberlain's pen. But to what extent was he to share? Their trump card was the fact that all the scenery, wardrobe, properties and plays produced since they took over (excluding the old stock ones, of course) were their property. It was true that the Queen could cancel the licence if she so desired, but although the theatre was no use without the licence, the licence was no use without the wherewithal to produce plays. They owned all the things necessary for the business of the stage, they had three parts of the shares in the licence, the fourth being held by Collier, who still exacted his £700 a year, and with his power behind him, they knew there was no chance of getting it abated. How were things to be arranged, on the admission of Booth, so as to be fair to all concerned?

They laid it before the Lord Chamberlain. That dignitary, having got them into the mess, washed his hands of anything further. It was their affair, he told them, to be settled amongst themselves. So they met to discuss it. Wilks said they ought to set a good price on everything as it stood, and expect Booth to pay for his share proportionately to his earnings. Cibber, wanting the last word, turned to Doggett for his view. Doggett asserted flatly that he had no mind at all to dispose of any of his property, so the question of price did not arise.

It was crisis at Drury Lane. Here were the Triumvirate who had put Drury Lane on a pinnacle of glory, and here, maybe, was the end. Doggett's reply was characteristic. "You may both do as you please," he growled, "but nothing but the Law shall make me part with my property." And he walked out of the room, out of their councils, and out of Drury Lane, never to re-enter it as partner again. The remaining partners soon fixed up with Booth, who stood in on equality with them, in shares and liabilities. He was to be answerable equally with them to whatever claims Doggett made on them and any lawsuits arising therefrom, and to pay them £600 for a share in their theatrical properties etc., such sum to be paid out of his profits. They gave him no written guarantee on their part, but he gave them his written undertaking on his.

They all saw each other almost daily in Button's Coffee House, but whilst Wilks and Booth cut Doggett, the wiser Cibber never failed, however it was received, to raise his hat and say, "Your Servant." For years Doggett ignored him. Then a friend of Cibber's, when the actor was out of town, wrote and told him Doggett was dead. Cibber wrote in reply a carefully worded letter about Doggett, saying how sorry he was they had never made up their quarrel. He smelt a rat. Sure enough the friend showed it to Doggett and when the two next met things were different. They often sat at the same table, these men who had done so much for Drury Lane, behaving as strangers, but on this occasion, Doggett slowly extended his hand and accepted a pinch of snuff. They were friends again.

Barton Booth, the new member of the Triumvirate, was of gentle birth, born in Lancashire and related to the Earls of Warrington. Originally he was destined for the Church, and to that end was sent to Westminster School. There he was a good scholar, became proficient in Latin, and looked as if likely to do well in his future calling. But there was a school play, and he was cast for "Pamphilius " in Terence's " Andria." He was such a success and so loudly applauded that he determined to go on the stage. He ran away at the age of 17, joined some strolling players, and actually appeared with them in a booth at Bartholomew Fair. Later, he got to Dublin, whence Wilks had sprung into eminence. Here he was cast for " Oroonoko," the great Drury Lane play. This required a black face, which he duly assumed; but the evening of his first performance was so hot, that forgetting his make-up, he kept wiping his blackened face until he became piebald, to the intense delight of the audience. The next night he determined to take more care, so persuaded one of the women members to make a mask of crepe which he fastened over his face. In the intensity of his acting, he made half of it peel off and looked worse than ever. For the rest of the show they rubbed lampblack on him, and he had to be nearly flayed before they got him white again.

He came to London in 1701 with a letter of introduction

to Betterton. Thus he followed in the steps of Wilks. The grand old man gave him some instruction and his London début, for he appeared with him in Rochester's "Valentinian" at Lincoln's Inn Fields, in 1701, with Mrs. Barry in the same cast. He held his own with these two great ones. Booth had a failing, he was too fond of the bottle; but when he saw the way Powel was going down-hill, he swore off. So, indirectly, poor George Powel did one good thing for the stage. Booth played The Ghost to Betterton's Hamlet and shared the honours of the play. But it was his performance of "Pyrrhus" in "The Distressed Mother" which first showed the London playgoers that Betterton's successor had arrived. From that, with the short interval of the Haymarket-Drury Lane interregnum, he went to "Cato" and became the star tragedian of the day, and a sharer in Theatre Royal.

Booth was not a strong man. After his success in "Cato" he became the pet of Society, and kept late hours. The management tried to prevent this by keeping him very fully employed, but every night a coach and six would be waiting for him to convey him to some great house. Often as many as six of the nobility would compete for his company at once.

Cibber and Wilks both thought he would not last long. They brought over an actor to be ready to replace him, Tom Elrington. He made his début at the Lane in 1709 as "Oroonoko," the part that Booth had attempted in Dublin. He was as yet inexperienced. He was later allowed to challenge Booth in the latter's great part of "Bajazet" in "Tamerlaine," Booth playing the name part. The senior actor killed the junior, although playing an inferior part. Elrington admitted that he had never felt such a force before, and that Booth's acting made him shrink to nothing. Booth ended the battle by congratulating Elrington. The latter proved a good man, and in his own parts held his head up with the best.

There have been statements that Wilks and Booth were jealous of each other, but that is doubtful. Each had his own line. There may have been some rivalry however in the question of which drew the most applause.

Other Drury Lane players, and especially Anne Oldfield may now come into the picture. Oldfield was now at the height of her fame. She was the Queen of Old Drury. She had won her spurs in comedy, but could play tragedy too, although she said she did not like it. She had been seen in this first at Drury Lane in 1712 when she played in "The Distressed Mother." It so happened that in the company was a Mrs. Rogers, and she resented Oldfield getting this part. She considered herself better than Anne, and persuaded her friends that this was so. When Anne was cast for "Andromarche" in the above-mentioned play, Mrs. Rogers took it ill. She got her supporters to pack the house and make it hot for Oldfield. Hoots, boos, hisses, and catcalls arose. In vain did Oldfield struggle, pandemonium broke loose. Royal Guards had to be sent for to stop the riot, and the play abandoned, for that night, It nearly broke Cibber's heart. He moaned, "We have been forced to dismiss an audience of £150 from a disturbance spirited up by obscure people."

But Oldfield was not the one to take defeat lightly. She tried again, precautions were taken, and she triumphed. Yet whenever she played tragedy she complained, "I hate to have a page dragging my trains about. Why don't they give Mrs. Porter these parts? She can put on a much better tragedy face than I can." Which gives us an insight into how the heroines of tragedy dressed and what they endured. Mrs. Porter was very good indeed, but she had to play second fiddle to Oldfield by public demand.

The rivalry between Mrs. Rogers and Anne Oldfield blew up from time to time. Wilks put a stop to it, and artfully too. He let them both play "Lady Lurewell" in Farquhar's "Trip to the Jubilee" and left it to the public to judge. The public, of course, chose Oldfield. Mrs. Rogers left to join John Rich when he opened at Lincoln's Inn Fields.

Another challenger to Oldfield arose in the person of Mrs. Horton, a real barnstorming actress, but Oldfield defeated her signally. Anne had that talent which could save a bad play. There was a fairly deadly specimen in one called "Sophonisba" by James Thomson. Cibber put this on because he wanted to play "Scipio," a part in which he fancied he would shine. But he was wrong, the public would have none of him. They hissed him off the stage. In the ordinary way that play would have died, but whilst they hissed Cibber they cheered Oldfield. So it got a second chance. The next night Cibber stayed off and "Scipio" was played by Williams, quite a popular actor.

But he wore the same costume as Cibber and the house thought Cibber was at it again. Groans and hisses arose. They were told it was Williams and then they gave him applause. Once more Oldfield got an ovation and saved the play. Cibber's thoughts must have been grim, though there was comfort in the fact that anyway they were making money.

Oldfield's private life was not chaste like her predecessor, Mrs. Bracegirdle. She set up house with Arthur Maynwaring, but they were never married. She bore him a son. Dukes and Duchesses called on her and she received the smiles of Royalty. For she was witty, handsome, well dressed and smart—and very famous; a sure entrée into Society then—and now. Maynwaring died in 1712, with Anne by his side. Then came General Churchill, nephew of the great Duke of Marlborough.

Rumour spread to the effect that Anne Oldfield and General Churchill were married. Society was intrigued. The two parties most interested kept their own counsel. So no less a person that Caroline, Princess of Wales, put the question to Anne, who replied graciously: "So indeed they say, may it please Your Royal Highness, but the General is good at keeping secrets." She had a son by the General. She understood publicity and she indulged in it as much as was possible. She always went to the Theatre in great state, dressed in her most gorgeous gowns, in a sedan chair accompanied by two footmen. She is said to have kept herself aloof from her brother and sister players, but although she probably queened it in the Green Room, she remembered her own humble start too well to be unkind.

Of Mrs. Rogers, her rival, or would-be rival, there is not much to say. She was extremely handsome and was a great prude. She probably owed her advancement to the fact that Wilks fell passionately in love with her, that he swore if she did not yield he would kill himself before her very eyes. So she gave in—probably the prudery was assumed.

Mrs. Porter, on whom eventually Oldfield's mantle was to fall, was of a different stamp. Betterton had seen her act as a child and had encouraged her. She played second fiddle to Oldfield quite cheerfully. She lived a respectable married life, and was friendly with good families. She had her share of pluck, for, when one night she was driving home to Hendon, where she lived, a highwayman stopped her chaise, and demanded her money, she promptly presented a pair of pistols at his head, which she carried with her for just such an emergency. This overpowered the man, who assured her he had been driven to robbery by necessity and a starving family. His story moved her more than his threats, and she gave him her purse. She was tall, fair and of good figure, full of dignity and power and became a tragedy queen of the first rank.

And now as regards Cibber himself. We know his early start and his rise to fame and fortune. But there is much about this curious man which is of great interest. His was a many-sided character. His detractors can see little good in him, but he was one of the great men of the theatre and one of the great men of Drury Lane. Son of a man who made images and statues but was not a real sculptor, he rose by his own merit and his own brains. We know he starved at Drury Lane, but in him burned the fire of ambition and love of the theatre—especially that theatre, for which he did so much. We know how upright was the management in his days. We know that he and his partners did much to clean up affairs back-stage. He did not have the capacity for making friends, and all through his life, although his partners stuck to him, it was for his business and acting ability rather than from any sentiment. He had a bitter tongue and used it freely.

Cibber fell in love when he was penniless. He was visiting the house of a companion with whom he would often go drinking, one John Shore, a trumpet major. Outside the door he heard a lovely voice singing. He asked whose it was and was told it was the trumpet major's sister. He met her, fell in love, got engaged and married her, when hardly able to keep himself. So badly did the brother take it that he spent the money intended for his sister's dowry on building a house which became known as "Shore's Folly." In his wonderful autobiography, Cibber says little about his marriage except that "I did commit matrimony." They had a large family whilst he was a struggling actor and playwright, altering plays, writing prologues and epilogues for a few guineas. He remarked that his Muse and his Spouse were equally prolific; he never became father of a play without her becoming mother of a child. He seems very vague about his offspring, saying that he believes he had about a "dozen of each sort" presumably six children and six plays.

When he married he had but one pound a week as actor, very irregularly paid, and twenty pounds a year allowed him by his father, which was equally intermittent. Whenever he was very hard up he wrote a play. And he was much addicted to gambling, which did not help either. His first play of note succeeded. His second, "Xerxes" died after the first performance.

In the days of his greatness he was peacemaker in chief at the Lane, but he was never popular with his brother actors or the members of the company. It was probably his sarcastic tongue. Once when a young actor was rehearsing a part in "Love for Love," in which he had seen Booth play, he remarked to Cibber, who was taking the rehearsal, that Booth had omitted certain words from an important line. Cibber replied, "There was more beauty in his forgetfulness than in all you remember."

Cibber altered Shakespeare unblushingly to suit acting of his own calibre, and his versions held the stage for years. In all he was responsible for twenty-one plays, two operas and a masque and an interlude, also a dialogue. Most of them were performed at Drury Lane, one "Xerxes" at Lincoln's Inn Fields, which even Betterton and Barry could not save from disaster, and some at the Haymarket.

It fell to his lot, probably from choice, to be the reader and selector of plays for Drury Lane. He had a short way with would-be dramatists. He would command them to bring their plays to the theatre and they would be received by the three managers with Cibber sitting in the chair of state. The other two never ventured to object to his judgment. He would nod to the nervous author as a sign to commence, and that poor creature would start to read his work. If his reading did not please Cibber, and it seldom did, he would take the manuscript away and read it for him. If on the other hand the applicant read well, or perhaps if on listening Cibber saw a good part for himself, he would let the author read on, and then put down his pipe and say, "By God, there is something in this. I don't know but it may do; but I will play . . ." and select the part. Then he would begin to cut and alter the play so that it is probable the author would not recognise the child of his brain at the finish.

But his judgment was pretty sound, although like all of those who have the difficult and onerous task of reading plays, he made his mistakes. He turned down "The Fair

135

Quaker of Deal " which became a success and, alas for his sake and the sake of Drury Lane, he also refused " The Beggar's Opera." That was to have a repercussion. He had a real quarrel with Pope, the great poet, and that vitriolic writer flayed him in " The Dunciad."

He was, however, in the right parts, a grand actor. His natural line was comedy, so naturally when he got power he went in for tragedy. Whatever his faults, Cibber was a pillar of the English theatre and a great pillar of Drury Lane, which personified the English theatre in his day. And Drury Lane should, and does, cherish the memory of one who rose in it from the lowest rung of the ladder to the very highest, and died Poet Laureate as well.

CHAPTER 17

THE TRIUMVIRATE DIES

THE death of Queen Anne closed the theatre for six weeks; but as it occurred on 1st August, the opening of the vacation, the closure was not so serious as it might have been.

Now that the Tories were out and the Whigs in, the acute mind of Cibber conceived that it would be advantageous for them to ally themselves to somebody who stood well at Court, and who could get help in getting rid of the incubus Collier. He suggested Sir Richard Steele, and the others agreed.

Steele was zealous for the House of Hanover, with whom he stood well. The managers knew Steele's love for, and understanding of the Theatre (was he not a playwright?); and there was another reason, too. Here, for the first time, we see the beginning of the power of the Press in theatreland. Cibber says: " We knew, too, the obligations the stage had to his writings; there being scarce a comedian of merit in our whole company whom his *Tatlers* had not made better by his publick recommendations of them. And many days had our house been particularly filled by the influence and credit of his pen."

What the triumvirate really wanted was a new licence from George I which would cancel the old one and so edge Collier out of it. They did not mind Steele sharing. Steele agreed and went to the Duke of Marlborough, who at once responded by granting them a new licence, which included the three of them and Steele. Thus, the battening Collier was eliminated for ever.

The new Royal House and the prospect of settled times proved good for business. The newly rearranged firm did well. There were, however, still a certain number of snags. Rich, who had been expelled, still held the original Patent, and now wanted it applied to Lincoln's Inn. So a rival was to appear once more to Drury Lane, and the battle of the theatres to be resumed. If Queen Anne had been alive, Rich would never have dared apply, but things were different now.

Meanwhile Cibber, Wilks, Booth and Steele were in proud possession of their new Patent, and at once began to arrange with Steele about his share. They told him the danger that competition might bring, but also pointed out that although people might flock to the second playhouse to start with, they would return to the better run Drury Lane when the novelty was over. They told him how opposition might prevent them from paying the seven hundred a year to him, which Collier had enjoyed when they were without opposition. But Steele cut them short. He came amongst them, he said, at their own request. He would always be beholden to them, and had no desire to embarrass them. He told them that what would be agreeable to them would be agreeable to him.

Feeling secure, the management started off with a revival of Dryden's " All For Love " on which they expended no less than six hundred pounds, which made it the most expensive production ever staged until then. Thus they took the sound road towards meeting opposition by doing things better rather than by economising in the face of battle. They felt secure, and their prestige was very high.

Now wicked old Christopher had died, but his son John, an equally extraordinary character, had opened Lincoln's Inn Fields against them in 1714. But so far he had made no headway against the Triumvirate. So a rumour was put round the town, which they suspected came from him, that the structure of Drury Lane was unsafe and that it might collapse at any moment. This began to empty the house. Wilks was for offering a reward for the discovery of the slanderer and his immediate prosecution when found. But Cibber took a longer view. The first thing he realised, was to prove the rumour false. So they asked the King for the services of the State surveyor, Sir Thomas Hewat, and got him to come down and make a careful survey. His report that the Theatre was perfectly safe was printed at the management's expense in every newspaper. At once the public flocked back.

Now here is a second instance of the growing power of the Press. Although Steele's *Tatler* had been on the side of the Triumvirate, there was another paper which took delight in baiting them. This rejoiced in the name of *Mist's Journal*, which set about criticising them as if they were Ministers of State, and really tried to bring them down. Wilks and Booth were for reprisals. Again that clever calculating brain of Cibber overruled them. He pointed out that *Mist's Journal* hardly ever got things right, as it usually relied upon hearsay stories, thereby missing much which, had it been well informed, might have made real trouble. He said also that if they had not been successful and known to be successful, the criticisms would never have arisen, and the only effective way to silence them would be their failure as managers, and that was not likely. His considered opinion was that if the attacks were ignored they would eventually cease, and that in any circumstances the best plan was to go on pleasing the public. Cibber, of course, was quite right, and his method remains the best to-day, when such attacks are just the vicious stings of insignificance against popularity.

As might be expected when the theatre at Lincoln's Inn opened there was some desertion from Drury Lane. For the new playhouse, as Cibber had foreseen, started off by doing well out of public curiosity, and Drury Lane was losing a certain amount of business. The chief deserters were Keene, Bullock, Pack and Leigh (son of the famous Antony Leigh). But the Triumvirate did not bother much They had seen it all before, and knew that sooner or later the deserters would want to come back. Cibber's policy was "Give the Public the best and what they want, and you will succeed," and that was what Drury Lane did.

Lincoln's Inn had started concentrating on musical shows, so Cibber thought the Lane had better do some also. He therefore concocted a masque called " Venus and Adonis," which succeeded; and followed with " Myrtello," a Pastoral interlude. Old Cibber inveighs against the prostitution of the stage by this sort of entertainment, but he was powerless to stop the trend. It was what a large portion of the public wanted. It was also part of the pageant of pantomime.

138

which had, in a somewhat obscure way, lifted its head at Drury Lane in 1702, by means of a show called "The Tavern Bilkers," and been followed the next year by something even more like a pantomime in "The Libertine Displayed." This was a precedent of which Rich, at the opposition house, was to take full advantage. For this rough, illiterate man was to be a protagonist of pantomime, and a great Harlequin. He, perhaps more than anyone, fostered the seed which had been sown at the Theatre Royal, and by transplanting it to Lincoln's Inn and afterwards to Covent Garden, was to play a tremendous part in founding the British tradition of pantomime. Drury Lane had to answer back, and there was not only a battle of theatres but a battle of pantomime.

There was now hanging about Drury Lane, engaged at a small salary, a young man who, like Colley Cibber, felt greatness within him, and who also felt frustration, just as Master Colley had experienced. He was to learn the same lesson that his manager had learnt too. His name was James Quin, a well-born youth made illegitimate because his mother, thinking her first husband dead, had married again, with Quin as the result. The first husband turned up, and she had to return to him. Quin's father looked after his boy, but on his death, the relations seized the estate to which Quin, by reason of his illegitimacy, had no legal claim. He had not the money to fight an action. He loved the stage better than the law, to which his father had put him, and he went on the Dublin stage. There he met Chetwode, Drury Lane's prompter, who saw his value.

Quin, on his advice, came to London, met and made friends with Ryan, of Drury Lane, who got him a job there. Quin never forgot it and was grateful to Ryan all his life. Ryan, could not, at that time push his friend any further, and Quin became one of the numerous small part men who went on with banners, and hoped for the best. They were known as "faggots," which showed the esteem in which they were held.

But Quin had a remarkable memory. One night Mills was taken ill, when he was to play "Bajazet" in "Tamerlaine," a very big part. Quin volunteered to read the part. They let him do it, for it was a thankless job and nobody wanted it. He was a big success. The next night, Mills still being off, he offered to play it again, this time from memory. He did it so well, and was so word perfect, that

139

he got a lot of applause. Naturally Quin thought he was made for life, just as did Cibber in similar circumstances. But the coincidence does not seem to have occurred to Cibber's mind—or maybe Booth and Wilks thought the young man a bit too good. For Quin found he advanced no further. So he left and went to Rich at Lincoln's Inn Fields. In course of time he became the greatest star of his day, a fine actor, and a rich and many-sided personality whom we shall meet again. It was a pity Drury Lane let him go, for they lost a star of great brilliance. When Booth died, Quin became the foremost living actor, and Covent Garden had the glory, not Drury Lane. Perhaps Cibber had been too busy on his new play, one which was to cause a sensation, to worry about the ambitions, hopes and disappointments of a mere "faggott."

This new play of Cibber's was "The Non-Juror." Its author freely admits that he borrowed from "Tartuffe," of Moliere, and made the character into an English Popish priest hiding under the vestments of the Church of England. "The Non-Juror" was topical. It was bitter and brilliant. It was for the established monarchy and against the Jacobites. Produced on the 6th December 1717, its cast included Cibber himself, Booth and Mrs. Oldfield. It ran for eighteen consecutive performances, a great success then. The King gave Cibber a present of £200. The loyalists cheered and the Jacobites rushed off to throw mud, the most violent attack coming from Pope. Cibber was accused of plagairism, and did not deny it. He knew that all this controversy was good for business.

In spite of opposition, under the good management and care of the Triumvirate, the success and glory of Old Drury grew. They were in high favour with the King. They got command performances galore, and sometimes were sent for to play at Hampton Court Palace. There the favourite play of George I was "Henry VIII." The Drury Lane company did very well out of these performances, although they were prepared to lose money for the privilege of playing at Court, for the King gave them £200 out of his own pocket. That seems to have been his standard gratuity.

But although everything seemed fair to the outside public, there was trouble within Drury Lane itself. The cause was Sir Richard Steele. That gay, careless man was in distress all round. He had never taken his job at Drury Lane seriously, but had drawn his salary all right. As the result of debts and difficulties his affairs got into the hands of the lawyers and a law suit was instituted against Cibber, Wilks and Booth, who were required by the Duke of Newcastle, the new Lord Chamberlain, to surrender their old patent in return for a new one which he would give them. Meanwhile, he suspended Cibber.

In January, 1719, Newcastle had the licence revoked and shut the theatre, which was a most unjust act, but good was to come of it eventually, for Wilks, Cibber and Booth got their new Patent which made them entire masters, and excluded Steele.

Somehow or other Steele got back into Drury Lane, but his lawyers now started an action to make the managers account for all the money they had had, and to justify the amounts charged against Steele, who was in bad financial straits. The result was a big law suit. It came for trial in 1726. Cibber was put up by his own counsel to conduct the case and make the great speech. He says he was scared at first, but once having got into his stride, and feeling the eyes of the Court upon him, his genius as an actor came out on top, and he made such a fine speech, so perfectly delivered that he won the day; and in the final judgment won Drury Lane for himself and partners, and Steele ceased to have any more to do with it. It was one of Cibber's greatest triumphs.

In the same year there was another great success at Drury Lane, for the theatre and for Cibber, the production of his play "The Provoked Husband." The play was partly Vanbrugh's, but the core of it was supplied by Cibber—with his eye always on a first-class part for Oldfield. The enemies Cibber had made over "The Non-Juror" were lying in wait for him, although years had elapsed. They determined to wreck "The Provoked Husband." But they had reckoned without Anne Oldfield. Although there were many enemies in the house, so well was the play written, and so superbly played that there was unbounded applause. So the wreckers waited for the epilogue spoken by Oldfield. As she began: "Methinks I hear some powdered critic say . . . . a man in the front row of the pit began to hiss. Anne fixed him with her beautiful stare and paused. When she had focused the attention of the audience full upon him, she said, loudly enough to be heard by all and in terms of ineffable scorn, "Poor creature." And then went on with the Epilogue, to be greeted with repeated cheers.

It was a triumph for her, for the play, and for the management. "The Provoked Husband" was played for twenty-eight nights, and was "taken off" to a house of £140. Nothing like that had been known before.

But an end was coming to all this glory. For Death and ill-health were soon to break that combination, the like of which had not been seen before and rarely since, if we except the days of Garrick at the same theatre, of Irving at the Lyceum, of Charles Kean at the Princess's and Tree at His Majesty's Theatre. It shines and gleams in the story of the stage like a bright jewel.

Booth was the first to go, stricken down by ill-health. His never too strong frame had given way under his labours. He had struggled along for some time, but it was apparent to all that he was nearing the end of his short but glorious career. A friend of his and of the theatre's, a Mr. Theobald, beseeched him to act "Julio" in "The Double Falsehood" at a time when he should have been resting. It was too much for him, and broken down completely he left the Lane in 1728. He was then only forty-six. Five years later he died.

Another great pillar of the noble playhouse, Anne Oldfield, was the next to pass away. She had perhaps reached the culmination of her career in her performance of "Lady Townley" in "The Provoked Husband." She was then over forty, but her talent, her charm, her beauty and her figure, were all unimpaired. But a cruel disease seized her. She played on, however, and in "Sophonisba," gave a wonderful performance. One night in 1730 she left the theatre, never to return again. She died on the 23rd October, 1730. After her death, Mrs. Saunders, her maid, had the body of the actress dressed in a Holland shift, with tucker and double ruffles of fine lace, a Brussels lace headdress, and a pair of new kid gloves. A law, which enjoined that all corpses should be covered by a woollen shroud, had made Oldfield tremble in horror during her life, and Mrs. Saunders saved her from that dreaded indignity. So great was the respect in which she was universally held that, with her face made up to resemble life, she lay in state in the Jerusalem Chapel of Westminster Abbey, in which hallowed building she was buried.

Gay's famous "The Beggar's Opera" had been produced at Lincoln's Inn Fields. It was, as everyone knows, a smashing success; it ran for 62 days there, and was performed subsequently all over the kingdom. It brought money and fashion to the rival theatre and made them downcast at Drury Lane, especially as Cibber had refused it. It was an unprecedented rage of the town, and its leading lady married a Duke. Cibber tried a counterblast with an opera of his own called " Love in a Riddle."

There was opposition in advance. Before "Love in a Riddle" saw the stage, Gay had tried to produce a sequel to "The Beggar's Opera" called "Polly," but this had been suppressed, because of alleged political satire.

Society took sides about this and even the King and Court circles joined in. Supporters of Gay, and certainly Cibber's many enemies, sedulously spread reports that the manager of Drury Lane had pulled strings to stop the production, so when Cibber's effort came along, they were waiting for it—and for him. Cibber was warned but kept his course. He produced his opera. Although the Heir Apparent graced the house, there was such a terrible uproar that the show could hardly continue. Then a little-known actress tripped on, in the part of " Phillida." Such was her charm, so entreating her manner, so complete her talent, that she stilled the unruly house. A man in the stage box yelled to his companions : " Zounds, Tom, take care, or this charming little devil will save all "—a tribute to the actress, and an unanswerable proof of organised rioting. That actress, then called Katherine Raftor, we shall meet later as Kitty Clive.

The howling and booing broke out again. So Mr. Cibber, never one to shirk a fight, walked on to the stage himself. Always a fashionable man, he had excelled himself that night. He wore his periwig, his silks and satins, his ruffles and his diamond ring. He carried his snuff box, he was in every respect the fine gentleman they were wont to applaud on the stage and the fine gentleman they saw in all the best places in town. But to-night there was no applause. The catcalls and the hullabaloo continued. Cibber stood there unabashed. So collected and calm was he that at last they paused to hear what he had to say. Indeed, his courage pleased them, and the booing turned into applause. He waited just as calmly for this to subside. Then he spoke :

" Gentlemen, since you are not inclined that this play should go forward, I give you my word that after this night it shall never be acted again. But in the meantime (and he gave a glance at the Royal Box) I hope you will consider in whose presence you are, and for that reason at least, suspend what further marks of your displeasure you may imagine I deserve."

He bowed and walked off in dead silence, and the play went on. The next night the house was full again, but Cibber kept his word—another play was substituted. But some time afterwards all that was best in "Love in a Riddle" was reconstructed into an opera called "Damon and Phillida," which was a success—only Cibber did not put his name to it.

Now Cibber's last companion and partner was to pass on. Robert Wilks, the master of the stage, died on 27th September, 1732. He was buried in St. Paul's, Covent Garden, within hail of the theatre he had served so well and so long. Cibber, the last remaining branch of the Triumvirate, was a mourner and pall bearer, and the Gentlemen of the King's Chapel attended and sang the anthem. In spite of all that bad temper for which Cibber, Doggett and his other associates blamed him, in spite of his grumblings and his temperaments, his disregard of his partners' feelings, Wilks was in the main a magnificent character and an actor in his own parts without equal.

So now Colley Cibber was left alone at the Lane. At Booth's death his share had been sold to a man called John Highmore, who was to bring no luck to the Lane. Stage-struck because he had played "Lothario" as an amateur, Highmore flattered himself that he knew all about it. Wilks' widow appointed another amateur, Ellis, an artist, to control her late husband's share, and Cibber, very naturally, could not get on with either of them. He was getting old himself, so he appointed his son, Theophilus to act for him. Cibber junior, who was a thoroughly nasty young man, soon got at loggerheads with his two associates, and Highmore offered Cibber the tempting sum of three thousand guineas to be rid of the objectionable youngster.

And now the time has come for us to say farewell to Colley Cibber, that truly remarkable man. Practically all the great figures of his time had passed on. But Cibber remained—remained to be a man about town, a wit and a club member, and to be Poet Laureate. He wanted to enjoy himself, he wanted to write his autobiography; and this he did, leaving a treasure behind him, a chronicle of the stage of his time without which our knowledge would be poor indeed. The history of our drama would be very misty without Pepys and Cibber.

Whatever had been written about him, however much has been said to his detraction—and much of this sort

144

The Ruins of the Theatre from Bridges Street, after the Fire.

London Published August 7th 1811, by Robert Wilkinson, No 58, Cornhill.

All that remained of Theatre Royal after the disastrous fire of 1809.
From a contemporary print.

" Druriolanus," otherwise Sir AUGUSTUS HARRIS, one of the most famous managers of Theatre Royal.

of thing has been done—the fact remains that Colley Cibber loved the theatre. He spent the best years of his life labouring for it. He left it immeasurably better than he found it, in quality, in morals and in art. He lived in a great time and held his own with giants. Vain he was, but he never let his theatre down, nor his associates. Mistaken he often was, but only in small things and for the moment. A bad poet he may have been, but he was the only actor to become Poet Laureate. He was a good playwright, a magnificent comedian, and even in tragedy he sometimes did well. And he held that Triumvirate together with infinite patience and tact so that they could write a great chapter for the stage in the world's greatest theatre. He was alive at the coming of Garrick, and he could not—or would not—see the new order which was come upon him. Yet he acknowledged to old Mrs. Bracegirdle that "the fellow was clever." He was unhappy in his children. But he spent his last days as he wanted to spend them, and let us take our last glimpse of him, as faultlessly attired and diamond studded as ever, as he stands in White's Club at the age of eighty-four and acknowledges Horace Walpole's greeting, "I am glad to see you look so well, sir," with the quick riposte of "Egad, sir, at eighty-four it is well that I am able to look at all."

His end was peaceful. On the morning of 11th December, 1757, his servant found him awake and quite affable and chatty. At nine o'clock he brought the old man his customary chocolate, and saw him, as he thought, enjoying a peaceful sleep. It was a sleep from which he never awakened. For the greatest actor-manager of his time and one of the greatest of all time, who had elevated his calling and even his great playhouse, had gone from the stage of this world.

CHAPTER 18

NEW STARS ARISE

WHEN Cibber left Drury Lane the bad old times came back. Gone was the hand of experience, gone were the great names. The leadership of the stage passed to Quin; first at Lincoln's Inn Fields, and afterwards at Covent Garden. For John Rich had not been idle. Although he could hardly speak the King's English, never got anybody's name right, and shared his office with a number of cats, he was a pushing fellow and knew his business from a to z. He, however, had his troubles too. His Lincoln's Inn Theatre was in a bad state; moreover, it was too small. So he called for subscriptions, quickly raised the necessary money, and built a new playhouse in Bow Street. He transferred his patent to it and it became Theatre Royal, Covent Garden.

This new house at once became a serious rival to Drury Lane, against which it was to stand in competition and antagonism for centuries, sometimes one being in the ascendant, sometimes the other, until finally Covent Garden became an Opera House, leaving Drury Lane still supreme as a theatre. Here, with Quin as his leading man, John Rich started to do things well, for he had not the brains and talent of the Triumvirate to contend with.

There was another playhouse, too, which had sprung up in the Haymarket, just over the way from Vanbrugh's House, now known as the King's, and devoted to opera and to Handel. This small theatre was not given a licence and had therefore a very difficult start. Known then as " The Little Theatre in the Hay," we cherish it to-day as The Haymarket Theatre. It was destined to make stage history and play its part in the long drawn out battle for freedom in the theatre by challenging constantly the oppression and repressive powers of the Patent Theatres, Drury Lane and Covent Garden.

All that Drury Lane could muster against the varied opposition was Highmore, an amateur, and Theophilus Cibber, son of Colley, but unworthy son of a great man. Not that Theophilus was a bad actor, he was not. But he was a blackguard of the first and very dirty water. Indeed, Drury Lane was under a cloud.

Just as in the history of nations, so in the history of theatres; the hour so often produces the man. And, hovering on the verge of Drury Lane's story, were already two names which were to add much to its lustre. Those names are Charles Macklin and David Garrick. Macklin was to enter first. In the meanwhile, Theophilus had got to war with Highmore on his own account. Highmore had purchased Wilks' share in the Patent from his widow. He had paid old Cibber 3,000 guineas and wanted to get rid of Cibber junior, but Cibber junior was not to be shaken off. There was no real leadership at the Lane. Cibber, an opportunist like his father, but by no means such a clever one, led a revolt of the actors, who were now as badly off as they had been under Christopher Rich. The managers locked out the actors, who in their turn broke in and locked out the managers. The chief sufferers were the playgoers, and in self defiance, *they* flocked to Covent Garden.

A patched up peace lasted a very short while, for soon Theophilus was up in arms again. This time he not only revolted but left Drury Lane, taking the company with him. They opened at the little Haymarket Theatre, flouting the Patent, and started to do shows. Highmore struck back, and had one of them arrested as a rogue and a vagabond. He chose the wrong man, for the arrested actor was of good character, a householder in the Parish of St. Paul's, Covent Garden and a man of substance. He was released, a triumph for the rebels and for the many opponents of the new Licensing Act which had just come into force.

Over at the Haymarket, young Cibber produced "Romeo and Juliet," announcing it as being for the first time for 100 years. He was wrong. Pepys saw it in 1662, and it was now 1733. Theophilus evaded the Patent Law by advertising a concert at his "Academy" and then presenting the play as a rehearsal by his pupils, a trick upon which Samuel Foote was to improve later at the same house. The law, however, was on the side of the big Patents, and as a result of the combined efforts of both Drury Lane and Covent Garden, Cibber was turned out of the little playhouse and forced back to Drury Lane. But the trouble had ruined Highmore, and he left Drury Lane wiser and poorer. He had bought his theatrical experience dearly.

But before he left, and during the time of the revolt, another young actor, with his wife, had signed an engagement with him. This was Charles Macklin, destined to bulk largely and sensationally in the theatre's story. He was an Irishman whose real name was M'Laughlin. He had already made some small stir at Lincoln's Inn. When the revolt at Drury Lane took place which deprived Highmore of all of his best people except Bridgewater, Mrs. Horton and that little lady once known as Raftor but now billed as Kitty Clive, Macklin went there and was engaged. He made his first appearance as Captain Brazen in "The Recruiting Officer," and played a round of other good parts. Following Highmore's ruin, the Patent was sold to Charles Fleetwood, another amateur with money, and he and Macklin

147

got on well. Both were gamblers and both spent their nights at the gaming tables. But with the departure of Highmore came the return of the rebels, and there was no room then in the same theatre for young Cibber and the touchy, irate, quick-tempered Macklin. So the Irishman left and joined Fielding, who was again trying his luck at the Haymarket. And for a while, he ran it himself.

Fleetwood now had to rely almost exclusively on the judgment of Cibber, but finding that Cibber was no good, he soon recalled Macklin, who rose in power and prestige until he was Fleetwood's manager as well as leading man.

Macklin's rise from strolling player had been swift, and his acting ability was beyond question. But his gambling nights with his manager and his wild, uncontrollable and violent temper must have made Drury Lane a most uncomfortable place. He even got power over Fleetwood by backing a bill for him; but when it fell due it was found that he had shuffled it off on to another man, who went to prison. Business was not so bad at Drury Lane, for they had succeeded in getting Quin away from Rich and now had a strong company. Macklin, however, was as yet no real rival to Quin. The old school of acting was in the ascendancy still, and Quin was its arch exponent. Slow, mechanical, almost gestureless, he nevertheless rolled out his lines with magnificent elocutionary powers, and relied upon the music of the voice to compel his audience. He taught elocution to the young Royal Princes. He also indulged in very long pauses, and it was one of these, later on, which was to bring him the message that his day was done. But for twenty years he was England's leading actor.

Now Macklin belonged to the new school. He was its pioneer. He was not so far advanced at this time, for the more natural school did not begin in full force until Garrick made it. But still he was a more realistic actor than Quin. Macklin had three stock pauses, his short, his middle and his Grand Pause. Once there was a stand-by prompter at Drury Lane who, not knowing the actor's peculiarities, took it upon himself to prompt Macklin audibly in the middle of his greatest effort. The infuriated actor dashed off the stage, felled the prompter to the ground, and returning to the front, informed the audience that " the scoundrel had prompted him in the middle of his Grand Pause." He got a round of applause, and continued his part.

This, however, was a very mild example of Macklin's fury. A more serious and tragic one was to come. On May 10th, 1735, he was sitting in the Green Room of Drury Lane with a brother actor, Thomas Hallam. The play was "Trick for Trick." Macklin and Hallam started to quarrel about a wig, which both claimed and both wanted to wear. The more timid Hallam, when the dispute got very heated, gave up the wig to Macklin, who was his superior in prestige and position; but the raspy and ill-tempered Irishman continued to grumble at him, and when Hallam answered back, Macklin made a thrust at him with the stick he was carrying. The stick pierced Hallam's eye, and that unfortunate man fell to the ground. He died within twenty-four hours. Showing a remarkable spirit of forgiveness, before dying, he did what he could to absolve Macklin of the blame—a charity most people would consider wholly undeserved. Macklin was tried, and the jury found him guilty of manslaughter. But there is no record of any sentence or any punishment at all. The punishment for manslaughter then was branding on the hand with a hot iron. Sometimes, in mitigating circumstances, the executioner went through the motions with a cold iron. This may have been so in Macklin's case, for he certainly never had a brand mark, and he was back again at Drury Lane in no time, being received with great applause. Indeed, it is likely that the house was crowded to see the actor who had killed another in that very theatre.

All through his very long life—and he lived until he was 107—Macklin was a storm centre. He was always quarrelling, always fighting, always at odds with authority.

At this time Quin was receiving £500 a year from Fleetwood, and played there from 1734 until 1740-41, when he went to Ireland. At Macklin's trial he had given evidence in favour of a man who was to challenge and displace him during his absence, a man with whom he was on unfriendly terms for many years. But when the tragedy took place, Quin was securely on his high horse and Macklin had not yet taken the step which made him so famous. The two men were at loggerheads all their lives, and Quin's gift for quick, devastating phrase-making and cutting repartee gave Macklin plenty of offence. When he played Antonio to Macklin's Shylock, he told a brother actor that if God Almighty wrote a legible hand, Macklin must be a villain. Macklin had a strongly marked, gnarled face, and Quin

149

would never tire of jeering at it, for when another actor said he thought Macklin would make a good player, having such strong lines in his face, Quin remarked, "Lines, sir? I see nothing in the fellow's face but a damned deal of cordage."

No doubt all this got back to Macklin, for they had a serious quarrel. Macklin was playing a comedy part and made the audience roar. He scored too freely for Quin, who told him to leave off his "damned tricks," adding he could do without them. Macklin, angrily replied "You lie." Quin was chewing an apple, and spitting out the contents of his mouth, threw the stuff in Macklin's face. Macklin pushed Quin in a chair and punched him, good, hard and plenty, in the face. Quin's face swelled up so that he had difficulty in playing the rest of the show. But he challenged Macklin to meet him at the Obelisk in Covent Garden, a favourite spot for duels. But Macklin had to play in the after piece and Fleetwood interposed, gave Macklin supper and made him apologise to Quin, who was none too happy at cooling his heels whilst waiting for Macklin's blood.

That happened not long after Macklin's killing of Hallam, so Quin showed the pluck for which he was renowned. After that incident they observed the most studied cold courtesy to each other at rehearsals and whilst playing. The quarrel was not healed till many years afterwards, when they met at a funeral. There, after the obsequies, they made it up, and at six in the morning, after many bottles, Macklin carried Quin home on his shoulders, being not quite so drunk—though not very much more sober, than his old antagonist.

The year 1741 was fraught with greatness for the stage in general and Drury Lane in particular. Fleetwood was still at Drury Lane, but Giffard, who also had a theatre in Goodman's Fields, Whitechapel, had a share in the Patent. Giffard had got Booth's share but could not agree with Fleetwood and sold out. His theatre at Goodman's Fields prospered although it was unlicensed. It was too far away for the Patentee to trouble about, but Giffard, who was an honest and straight man, had his own troubles over Walpole's infamous licensing act. However, by resorting to the expedient of always having some music in his productions, he got along without running foul of the law.

Drury Lane, under Fleetwood, had sunk, despite all

Quin's efforts; and when that great actor left to go to Dublin, things got worse. But this was wild Macklin's chance, and he seized it. Macklin, who had power with Fleetwood, persuaded him to stage "The Merchant of Venice" with himself as Shylock. For years this play of Shakespeare had been defaced and degraded. The most popular version of it was called "The Jew of Venice," a travesty of the great original. It was customary to present Shylock as a comic character in a red wig and with a red beard. Doggett had so played it. Macklin now proposed to restore the Shakespearean text and play it as he thought it should be done. When the night of the performance came, on 14th February, 1741, there was a very crowded house. And they saw this truly remarkable company:

Antonio	Mr. Quin
Bassanio	Mr. Milward
Gratiano	Mr. Mills
Shylock	Mr. Macklin
Launcelot	Mr. Chapman
Gobbo	Mr. Johnson
Salarnio	Mr. Berry
Prince of Morocco	Mr. Cashel
Lorenzo	Mr. Harvard
Prince of Aragon	Mr. Turbutt
Duke of Venice	Mr. Winstone
Tubal	Mr. Taswell
Salarino	Mr. Ridout
Portia	Mrs. Clive
Nerissa	Mrs. Pritchard
Jessica	Mrs. Woodman

There was much excitement before and behind the curtain. Macklin was the coolest of them all there, but he admitted to feeling a bit nervous before his first entrance. When he stepped on the stage he got a thunderous reception. At the end it was a complete triumph, such a one as that character was not to receive again until another momentous occasion in Drury Lane's history. Macklin destroyed tradition that night and made a new one, and in so doing he drove the audience to wild flights of excitement, and the great building trembled at their tumult of cheers. It was such an evening as actors dream of but seldom achieve. He had also rocked the old school of acting to its foundations. Fleetwood met him with outstretched hands and said: "Macklin, you were right at last." His brother actors joined in the praise, but Macklin did not believe in their sincerity. But he did not care about this: he had played Shylock as it should be played, as now

151

we know this character. He had triumphed, he had tasted the intoxicating cup of success to the dregs and found it sweet. He felt above money and mundane affairs; he trod on air. He was an actor and acclaimed as a great one—visions were before his eyes—more and more achievements and greater and greater triumphs. It was his night of nights. Contemporary writers pay him tributes, and Pope enshrined his victory in an immortal couplet:

> This is the Jew
> That Shakespeare drew.

There is another little sidelight on this "Shylock" of Macklin's. George the Second, who did not think very highly of poets, plays, playhouses or actors, who in his own bastard English said he despised "blays and boetry," nevertheless came to see Macklin. He was frightened out of his life at the grim, tragic, stark intensity of the performance, and admitted later that he did not sleep that night.

In the morning, Sir Robert Walpole waited on him to say that he was a bit afraid the faithful Commons were going to oppose a measure of which the King was in favour. "I wish your Majesty," said Walpole, "would suggest some way of frightening the House of Commons." "Vot do you dink," replied the King, "of sending dem to see dat Irishman play Shylock?"

But that King, for all his dislike of "blays," was to figure in another historic scene at Drury Lane. It was a night in 1746. Rebellion and bloodshed were racking the land, but the King showed spirit by going to the play. He was in the Royal box when a dispatch rider, a mask of dust and mud, demanded audience with His Majesty. They took him to the retiring room and fetched the King. The rider, sinking to his knees, handed His Majesty the dispatches from the Duke of Cumberland, announcing the complete defeat and rout of the Young Pretender at Culloden Moor. The King, overjoyed and excited, rushed back into the box. He wanted to tell the world then and there. He wanted to announce the news to the assembled audience. The house gazed at him in amazement, even the players stopped and stared at the foreign gentleman who ruled over them, and now stood frantically waving papers in his hand. George wanted to tell them; but in his frenzy of excitement his little English played him false. All he could do was to yell "" Hey, hey, hey" An equerry came to the rescue. Gently taking the papers from the King, he read to the whole house, now standing on its feet, the news of the victorious battle, of the last battle actually fought on the soil of Britain. Then, indeed, the house went as mad as the King. There were cheers and counter-cheers and the company on the stage—His Majesty's Servants—lined up and sang the newly composed "God Save the King," which had been sung for the first time in public on that very stage on 28th September, 1745. So the news for which the nation was hoping and waiting, came to them from the Royal box in Theatre Royal, with the King himself amongst them, a romantic episode unique in theatrical annals.

CHAPTER 19

ENTER GARRICK

BEFORE Garrick, the Great Star, enters; before the man whose name is world famous takes the centre of the stage; let us take a glance at those who were to appear with him. For now so many great names throng Old Drury that celebrities tread on each other's heels as they crowd the scene; names that live to-day and will endure. The years which follow are star-spangled indeed.

At Drury Lane there was Charles Macklin, James Quin, Mills, Mrs. Clive and Mrs. Pritchard; and soon after came Delane, a tragedian to replace Quin, who, like Garrick, had graduated under Giffard at Goodman's Fields. It is desirable to sketch in the portraits of some of the women.

Katherine Raftor, who became Kitty Clive, we met in the time of old Cibber, when she nearly saved "Love in a Riddle" from planned disaster. Since then she had progressed as far as playing "Portia" to Macklin's Shylock. She came from Ireland, where so many of the stars were either born or trained. She first appeared at the Lane in 1728, when she was seventeen. She was a success and when she nearly saved "Love in a Riddle" she got into the front rank.

Kitty married George Clive, a barrister, but they did not get on too well together. There was nothing against Kitty's morals, but she was temperamental. She had received a very scanty education, her spelling was atrocious even for those days; but she could and did write amusing stage shows. She had a quick wit. When asked why she did not visit a certain nobleman of very doubtful reputation who had cast his eye upon her she replied: " Why, because, dear, I choose my company as I do my fruit; therefore I am not for damaged quality."

By 1741 she was an acknowledged star, earning fifteen guineas a week and a clear benefit. She probably made eight hundred a year. Sweet Kitty Clive dances through the annals of Drury Lane, good natured, helpful, always on the side of the under dog, pleading causes and fighting them even to her own loss.

She went to Drury Lane with Garrick when he took it over, and stayed there until her retirement twenty-two years later. She led Garrick a frightful life at times, but they were friends to the very end. He called her by a nickname, " Pivey," and gave her a great benefit on her retirement. She died in 1785 at the age of seventy-four.

Mrs. Pritchard was different altogether. She shone with virtue in an immoral age, and there is from first to last no word of scandal against her. She started as a strolling player and she won her position by hard work. Her husband had a small post at Drury Lane.

As a tragedy queen she was without equal in her prime; her Queen in "Hamlet" ranks with the Ophelia of Susannah Maria Cibber. She was a natural actress, and besides her tragic qualities could play comedy with the best of them. Her enunciation was perfection. Garrick as Benedict was overshadowed by her Beatrice, which did not please him. She played all the great parts and played them finely, but perhaps her greatest character of all was "Lady Macbeth." Rumour has it that she knew nothing of the play save her own part and never looked at the rest of the text. And remember that she played it in the clothes of her own period and in the height of the present mode, as did Garrick. There was no suitability of costume then. She wore, as did all tragediennes, long black gloves. Until Mrs. Siddons came, Mrs. Pritchard was supreme as Lady Macbeth, and when the former actress wanted to put in new business, we shall see what Sheridan did to try to prevent the departure from the Pritchard tradition. The latter's "Give me the dagger" froze the blood of the audience, and she "read" some lines quite differently from Siddons. For instance, in reply to Macbeth's query, "And if we fail?" instead of accepting the fact, Pritchard hurled the question back: "We fail? But screw up thy courage to the sticking point and *we'll* not *fail.*" She was much more versatile than Siddons, who could not tackle comedy. She had no claim to beauty, she had no claim to education—and some laughed when she referred to her "gownd"; she got very fat towards the end, but she never lost her deportment, her earnestness, her clearness of utterance, and at whatever speed she spoke, the audience never missed a syllable.

There is a good story of her stoutness. She was playing in "The Careless Husband" with Kitty Clive, who had also put on a good deal of weight. Pritchard played the mistress; Clive the maid. The business of the play called for a letter to be picked up off the ground. Neither of the two great actresses dared to bend down; here was a dilemma! But Mrs. Pritchard solved it. Said she to Clive, "Well, Madam Pert, since you won't pick up the letter, I must get one who will" and went through the motions of ringing the bell. The prompter had his wits about him and sent on an attendant. The scene was saved.

Of Mistress Peg Woffington so much has been written and so much said that little need be repeated here. This poor, ragged child of the Dublin streets, befriended and given a chance to shine on the stage by Violante the wire walker, started her London career at Covent Garden. Having quarrelled with Rich she went to Drury Lane. She varied between the two playhouses. Peg was a woman of many love affairs. In Garrick's early days she shared her favours between him and his friend Macklin. They all set up house together. And there were others; for we know how one night Garrick had to vacate her bed in a hurry to make room for a nobleman who also had a share of her affections. In his flight Garrick left his wig in her room, and Woffington had to explain its presence to her noble lover by saying it was part of the make-up of a character she was shortly to play, a "breeches part." He believed her, for she excelled in these.

Later Macklin left the *menage à trios* at 6 Bow Street, and Garrick and she carried on together elsewhere. But they often quarrelled on account of her extravagance. Garrick was a terribly careful man. They took it in turns to pay the weekly accounts, and once, when it was Garrick's week, and they were entertaining Doctor Johnson to tea, he went nearly mad with fury when she carelessly threw in another spoonful of this expensive luxury, then about twelve or thirteen shillings a pound, and seizing her hand said: "The tay, madam, is as red as blood."

But Garrick intended to marry her, and went as far as buying the ring. Then they quarrelled and parted. She sent him back all his presents, but he retained a pair of lovely diamond shoe buckles she had given him.

Yet one more name must be mentioned, Susannah Maria Arne, better known as Cibber, who made her first public appearance at the age of 18 at the King's House in the Haymarket in the opera "Amelia." Two years before that, Susannah had married Theophilus Cibber, the under-sized, vicious, and altogether rascally son of Colley Cibber. As a singer she was a great success. Handel thought much of her, wrote Galatea in Acis and Galatea especially for her, and also the contralto songs in "The Messiah," for the singing of which she received the astounding tribute of a Dr. Delany, who rose in his place when it was sung in Dublin and shouted: "Woman, for this be all thy sins forgiven thee." The sins to which he referred were rather those committed against her than by her. For in 1738 her marriage broke up in failure and she sought the protection of a worthy man called Sloper, whilst her husband fled the country to avoid his creditors. On his return the wretched Theophilus sued Sloper for "criminal conversion of his wife," despite the fact that he had deliberately thrown the girl at Sloper's head. He claimed £5,000 damages, and got £5. The following year he had another attempt at blackmailing Sloper. This time he wanted £10,000 and got £500. Susannah never returned to her husband but remained with faithful Sloper and was respected by everyone.

But Susannah had got tired of opera and wanted to be an actress. Her father-in-law trained her and made a good job of it; but in the old manner. It was left to Garrick to bring out the best in her. At Drury Lane in 1753, she played Juliet to Garrick's Romeo and he put her "opposite" to him at every opportunity. She threw herself into her parts with great vigour, and often wore herself out. "Oh that my nerves were made of cart-ropes" she exclaimed when exhausted, on one occasion. Garrick said she was the greatest actress at Drury Lane, but complained that she sometimes got the better of him and gained her own way despite his will. Be this as it may, they always remained friends.

Covent Garden had now become a bitter rival to Drury Lane. Rich, for all his quaintness and roughness, was a better manager than the reckless Fleetwood at Old Drury, where only Macklin could keep things within bounds. But once again in the history of Theatre Royal, necessity produced a man who was to restore the great days of the Triumvirate, and in many ways to transcend them.

On 2nd March, 1737, two men left Lichfield to try their luck in London. They were, David Garrick, a young man of twenty, and a slightly older but still young man of twenty-six, named Samuel Johnson. They lacked money but had plenty of brains. They reached the capital by the method now described as " hitch-hiking " or " thumbing."

Young Garrick had intended to study for the law, but a legacy of £1,000 put him into the wine trade, in partnership with his brother, in Durham Yard, Strand. They were not in a big way of business, and the bitter wit of Samuel Foote jeered later at Garrick for calling himself " a wine merchant on the strength of three quarts of vinegar in a cellar." But the wine trade did not attract young Garrick. He preferred the stage. As a boy he had played at Lichfield in an amateur performance of " The Humourous Lieutenant," and made a success. Those who look for omens will see one here, for it was with that play that Drury Lane Theatre first opened its doors. He frequented the theatre, went to the coffee houses the actors used, and made many acquaintances, among whom was Charles Macklin.

The theatre got right into Garrick's blood, for he now turned playwright and wrote his first play, " Lethe." He spent a lot of time at Goodman's Field Theatre, in Whitechapel, which was run by that excellent actor-manager Giffard, and where young David's friend Yates played regularly. One night, when Yates was to play Harlequin, he was suddenly taken ill, an awkward situation in those days of no understudies. Garrick, the lad from Lichfield of Irish-French ancestry and descent, stepped forward and volunteered to go on. He had watched the play so often that he knew every move. They gave him the chance, and he took it. He was a success. All he asked now was for opportunity, and that was to hand. But his innate caution asserted itself even as early as this. Confident of his powers, he as yet had no technique. Actually, he was one of those very rare things, a born and natural actor; still he thought some experience before attacking London would be valuable. So he went with Giffard and Dunstall to Ipswich in the summer of 1741. There, at the theatre in Tankard Street, he gave his first professional performance. Wisely he did not aspire to a lead, but took the character of " Aboan " in " Oroonoko." It was a black-faced part, and he thought that by this device he would not be recognised afterwards, if he failed. Cautious Garrick again. But he need not have worried. He was a success.

In the autumn they all returned to London to re-open Goodman's Fields. Garrick played " Richard III " for seven nights in succession. Each night his fame grew, and although the receipts for those performances totalled only £216 7s. 6d. Giffard knew he had a good thing and that more would soon roll in. It did.

It soon got around that this new man must be seen. To this end the two great theatres began to empty, and the coaches of the nobility and gentry blocked the way to Whitechapel. All the critics were there. Pope took old Lord Orrery, who had seen Betterton, to see that old champion's true successor arise. The veteran playgoer was impressed. So was Pope, who said he thought the new actor would soon be spoiled as he would have no rival. Garrick played other parts, and success piled on success. The Patent theatres grew uneasy. Quin, the leader of the profession, felt qualms as well. So he went along to see Garrick as Richard of Glo'ster. He professed himself disgusted. "If this young man be right," said he, " I and the rest of the players have been wrong."

Old Cibber, still alive and kicking, went to see him play " Bayes." He said he preferred his own son. But both Cibber and Quin, of course, belonged to the old school and the very slow school. Slowness was power to them. It is said that once an actor playing in a scene with Mrs. Brace-girdle went to sleep on the stage during a very long speech and fell up against her. Cibber found none of this tedious-ness in Garrick; and he did not like it. " I tell you that this character's manner is little, like his person " (he had just seen Garrick as Richard III, a part he fancied himself in). " It is all fuss and bustle. This is his idea of a tragic

158

scene: ' Give me another horse. Well, well, where is the horse? Don't you see I am waiting for him? Bind up my wounds. Look sharp now with those wounds! Have Mercy, Heaven, but be quick about it, for the old dog cannot wait for heaven.' Bustle, bustle, bustle." It was a most clever epitome of the new and wonderful style of Garrick. Cibber usually got laughs in Richard where he should have got thrills.

The management of the Patent theatres, Rich and Fleetwood, grew alarmed at the menace of Goodman's Fields. So they took steps to have it closed, as indeed was in their power. Then, for once, Fleetwood of the Lane stole a march over Rich, for he offered Garrick a job. Probably Macklin told him that was the way to profit out of evil. He offered Garrick £500 a year, the same salary as the great Quin was receiving at the Garden. Garrick took it, and Giffard and his wife, both good performers, their own house having been closed by the Patents, signed on with Fleetwood, too.

Garrick made his first appearance at Drury Lane at a Benefit performance for the widow of Harper, the comedian who had just died. His care was again manifest, for he played " Chaumont " in " The Orphan," by no means the leading part. But he gave a new reading of it, and so greatly did he play that he stole the show.

At Drury Lane, Garrick arranged with Fleetwood that he should play " Richard the Third," " Bayes " and " King Lear," all of which he had performed with marked success at Goodman's Fields. This series was outside the main agreement and consequently on a profit-sharing basis. So his first actual performance there was on 11th May, 1742. (Davies says April) when he played " Chaumont " in the Benefit. As usual on such occasions, he played for nothing. He then played his round of agreed parts and stepped at once to the leadership of the stage. It was a complete triumph for Garrick the actor, and for the new school of acting which he exemplified.

Sure of himself now, Garrick made some experiments. He had proved he could play comedy and tragedy with equal ease and success. He now played " Hamlet " with great brilliance, bringing out much that was new to playgoers. His meeting with the Ghost excited them so much that the applause on his exit continued right through the next scene until his reappearance. His delivery of the soliloquies as natural thought and not recitations amazed them, and "Oh, what a wretch and peasant slave am I" brought down the house. Everything he did was superb, and Drury Lane was rolling over Covent Garden like a steam roller.

Everything would have been splendid for that old playhouse had the management been sound. But it was not. Fleetwood was in ever-growing difficulty, and heading straight for disaster. He was in debt and in the hands of the money-lenders. Salaries were unpaid, a matter of urgency to the players and anxiety to the money-loving and parsimonious soul of Garrick. The brokers came in.

In this sorry pass, Garrick, Macklin, Clive and Pritchard, collectively and separately, brought the grievances before Fleetwood. He listened to them politely enough, whereas his treasurer treated their demands for arrears of salaries with every form of insolence. But politeness was all that Fleetwood could afford. He owned they had a just grievance, he admitted he owed them the money, he shouldered the blame, he reproached himself bitterly,—and he wheedled them into playing on. For Fleetwood had the gift of persuasion in the highest degree, as so many bogus managers have had since his time. His repeated promises were always broken. There seemed to be no hope. So the players conferred amongst themselves. Late in the summer of 1743, Garrick called them all to his lodgings in James Street, Covent Garden. He asked them all to secede from the Lane in a body, and no person to enter into negotiations with Fleetwood without the agreement of all the others. He said their case was the same as Betterton's in a similar predicament with old Rich, and that they should do as he did and place the matter before the Lord Chamberlain, who was then the Duke of Grafton, and in whom Garrick said he placed the greatest reliance. Macklin, whilst never averse to a fight, said he thought the best thing to do was to go once more to Fleetwood and tell him openly and straightforwardly what they proposed, before they struck. Garrick objected to this because he said the manager, if warned, could get to the Lord Chamberlain before them. All the others supported him, and Macklin, in a minority of one, was forced to agree and sign the document they drew up between themselves to stand all together, sink or swim. This was signed by Garrick, Macklin, Havard, Berry, Blakes, Mills, Mrs. Pritchard, Mrs. Clive and Mrs. Mills.

Their petition was duly and in proper form laid before the Duke of Grafton. To their horror, he refused to support them. He turned them down, and they were mutually bound not to return to Fleetwood. Fleetwood, on his part, could not get hold of another company worthy of Drury Lane. It was deadlock. Both sides appealed to the public. Nothing came of this, though probably the actors had the public sympathy.

Fleetwood determined by hook or by crook to get his theatre open in September with a production of " The Constant Couple." He actually billed it for 20th September. Although this was largely bluff it shook the players. Negotiations were opened between Garrick and Fleetwood, and the upshot was that Garrick agreed to bring the actors back to Drury Lane on terms to be strictly observed. But he did this without the knowledge or consent of Macklin, fearing probably that Macklin's violence would upset the prospect of peace. Macklin reproached him bitterly, but Garrick's mind was made up. He agreed terms with Fleetwood, and it must be admitted that Fleetwood won; for whilst Garrick got his own salary raised, and their old terms for the other stars, some of the smaller people found their salaries much reduced. One thing was insisted on by Fleetwood. Macklin must stay out.

CHAPTER 20

MANY REFORMS

MACKLIN had been hardly done by. Although heart and soul for the battle with Fleetwood, and rebellion if need be, he had wanted to have a last word with the manager before appealing to the powers that be : and he had been overruled by Garrick. The meeting between the two, when the Irishman discovered that Garrick had gone over to Fleetwood, must have been worth seeing. Garrick, of course, knew in his heart that he was in the wrong, and so offered to pay Macklin's salary out of his own pocket until such time as he could be reinstated. He also got Rich, of Covent Garden, to promise Mrs. Macklin a job at

£3 per week. Macklin rejected every offer, every overture. He had been betrayed and would not profit by the hand which had done it. Perhaps he knew that Garrick had raised his own terms to between £600 and £700 per season. Swearing revenge, Macklin got busy. He had friends. The story Garrick's behaviour got around town. It was quickly believed by many, for there are always plenty to believe anything against a successful man. Drury Lane reopened on the advertised date, and Garrick was there. The play was "The Rehearsal," and Garrick played "Bayes," one of his most successful roles. There was noise and disturbance as soon as the curtain rose. When Garrick entered there was an uproar. He bowed several times, and very submissively, asked to be heard. All he got were loud hisses, boos, and shouts of "Off, off, off." He attempted to speak, he attempted to pacify the unruly mob, but without success. But the riot was expected, and Fleetwood had taken precautions. He had brought to the theatre a lot of his friends from Hockley-in-the-Hole and the Bear Gardens, two of the lowest and roughest resorts in London. These, planted in various parts of the house, had orders to deal with Macklin's supporters, and the arguments they used were fists, sticks and bludgeons. Even so, little or nothing was heard of the play.

But the magic of Garrick triumphed. He had had his first taste of a hostile audience—and by no means his last—but he won through

During this eventful season Garrick played at the Lane seventy times. His biggest success was "Macbeth." Covent Garden did their best against him, but Garrick and Drury Lane triumphed, whilst Fleetwood squandered the admission money. Garrick played Richard III at the Lane, Ryan played it against him at the Garden; Garrick's round; Garrick and Peg Woffington played "Lord and Lady Townley" at the Lane, Ryan and Mrs. Horton played the same at the Garden: Garrick's round. Garrick and Peg Woffington played Hamlet and Ophelia at the Lane, against the same parts by Ryan and Kitty Clive. She had gone over to Covent Garden when the rebellion failed. She thought Macklin and the small people badly treated. Again it was Garrick's round. Not even Quin, and afterwards Sheridan of Dublin, could get points for Covent Garden when they played Macbeth, with Garrick and Mrs. Gifford piling up the points for the senior theatre. The Garden

tried a distinguished amateur as " Lothario," they turned
on Quin as Lear, but Garrick beat them every time. Not
even Charlotte Charke, Colley Cibber's queer daughter, in
breeches, could win them anything. It was a terrific series
of victories for Garrick and for Old Drury.

By this time Fleetwood had come to the end of his
tether, despite the money which Garrick made to roll into
the coffers of the Lane. He had to get out. The Patent
came up for sale. It was purchased by two City men,
who bore names redolent of traffic lights to-day, and
admirably suited for theatrical management,—Green and
Amber. Their knowledge of the theatre was limited, but
they had a man on whom they could rely, James Lacy. He
had a good record of success though always overshadowed
by Garrick. One regrets to record that in the end Green
and Amber were broken completely. It was not Lacy's
fault, or the fault of Drury Lane. The cause lay in
the 1745 Rebellion and the bad finance of the bankers'
subsequent ventures.

There is no doubt that Lacy had held out the hope that
he could secure Garrick, and that the new actor was the
sheet anchor on whom all had staked their hopes. But he
had reckoned without Garrick's notorious caution. Garrick
did not like the look of things in England. To the fury
of Lacy, he accepted Sheridan's offer for Dublin and remained there all through the trouble of '45.

The end of the war coincided with Garrick's return.
Lacy was after him at once. In Dublin, Garrick had been
a huge success. His rival Quin came over to oppose him,
but returned beaten completely. But during this visit of
Garrick's a new genius had flared up in the Irish capital,
which seemed to have a faculty for raising theatrical stars.
This was a young man called Spranger Barry. He made a
tremendous impression in " Othello." Garrick himself was
full of his praises, and wrote letters on his behalf to friends
at home. Lacy had come over to survey the field for Drury
Lane, and promptly secured Barry for that theatre. He
thought he had a card wherewith to force Garrick's hand,
for negotiations were still going on. But nothing was
settled when Garrick returned to town in May 1746.

Strangely enough to the outside world, but probably in
pursuance of his policy of playing up Lacy for terms,
Garrick engaged himself with Rich at Covent Garden. Or
it may have been that he wanted to kill the rivalry of Quin

once and for all. The two men met now for a final duel on the stage at Covent Garden. The encounter was to be more than a *duel a outrance* between two actors for the leadership of the stage: it was a decisive battle between the old and new styles of acting. Quin was obviously worried, and Garrick whispered: " Faith, I believe Quin is as much frightened as myself."

The play was " The Fair Penitent." " Horatio " was Quin, "Lothario " was Garrick. The scene in the play arrived when Garrick hurled a challenge at Quin. The latter in his old-fashioned heavy style made a long pause before accepting it. A voice from the gallery interposed with the deadly remark, " Why don't you answer the gentleman?" Quin knew his hour had come. At the end of that season he withdrew from the stage.

This short season was the only time Garrick played at Covent Garden. It was very prosperous for Rich—and for the actor. Lacy now made his final offer to Garrick of complete partnership in Drury Lane, and Garrick accepted. A deed of partnership was signed on 9th April, 1747, between the two men. Lacy undertook to obtain a new—or renewed—patent, made out in their joint names for a period of 21 years. There were mortgages, debts and what were called " encumbrances " on the theatre (one of them was an annuity of £500 to Fleetwood) which were computed at £12,000. These the two new partners shouldered equally, and Lacy agreed to be responsible for anything over that amount. Each was to draw £500 a year as manager, but Garrick was also to have a like sum as actor, plus a clear benefit.

Lacy and Garrick divided the running of the theatre between them, and they never trod on each other's toes. Lacy looked after the wardrobe, the scenery and the front of the house and business affairs. Garrick was supreme in stage matters. He cast the plays, treated with authors, engaged the actors, took rehearsals and controlled all behind the curtain. He got Mrs. Pritchard and Mrs. Cibber over from the Garden.

The new management opened on 15th September 1747. The play was " The Merchant of Venice," which seemed destined to make Drury Lane history. Garrick's great friend, the colossus of learning, Dr. Samuel Johnson, himself wrote a prologue, which Garrick spoke on this momentous occasion. It contains some lines which have become almost a proverb in our language and which admirably sum up the whole essence and being of the " Profession."

> " Hard is his lot, that here by fortune plac'd
> Must watch the wild vicissitude of taste
> With every meteor of caprice must play
> And chance the new blown bubbles of the day
> Ah, let not censure term our fate our choice
> The stage but echoes back the public voice
> The drama's laws, the drama's patrons give
> For we that live to please, must please to live
> Then prompt no more the follies you decry,
> As tyrants doom their tools of guilt to die;
> 'Tis yours, this night, to bid the reign commence
> Of rescu'd nature, and reviving sense;
> To chace the charm of sound, the pomp of show
> For useful mirth and salutory woe
> Bid scenic virtue form the rising age
> And truth diffuse her radiance from the stage."

This appeal of the worthy Doctor's through the mouth of Garrick found its echo in the hearts of the public. And that night was the beginning of the most golden age of Drury Lane. One might imagine that the building itself, now approaching fast to its centenary, might have glowed with pride, had it been, as one sometimes thinks it is, a sentient being.

It was a brilliant start made by a brilliant company imbued with the highest ideals. But before they opened they had done much spade work, and Lacy had so rearranged the seating that the theatre now held £40 per performance more than before. They abolished the bad old custom of " tasting a play ": admission was by ticket only. And they made a determined effort to stop the custom of the audience coming up on the stage, for at the bottom of all their bills for a month there is a statement

> " As the admittance of persons behind the scenes has occasioned a general complaint on account of the frequent interruptions to the performances, it is hoped gentlemen will not be offended that no money will be taken for the future."

They were not successful then, but in the end it was Garrick and Lacy who killed this pernicious system. When we read that at a benefit performance " the stage will be formed into an amphitheatre, where servants will be allowed to keep places " we know the play and the players could have little chance. At Quin's last performance, when he did " Falstaff " (his most famous part), so great was the crowd in the stage entrances that the poor man, padded out as he was, could not make his entrance for several minutes, and

was out of breath with fighting his way through the concourse of overflow audience. No wonder Garrick decided
to fight this system tooth and nail.

But this was only one of his attempted reforms. He
insisted on order, decency and decorum back-stage, and he
himself set an example in this respect. He insisted as
strongly, maybe more so, on punctuality at rehearsals. In
this he was implacable. He made the cast rehearse just as
if an audience were present. And he insisted on them all
becoming word perfect, too. He burst wide open the old
idea that certain parts belonged to certain actors by right
of seniority and custom. He cast the plays according to
merit and talent. It is said that his production of Ben
Jonson's "Every Man in his Humour" was the most perfect that play ever received. It made a success of something which had never " got over " properly before.

One of his best and wisest actions was to restore
Shakespeare's own text to his mutilated plays. Though
Cibber's versions—or certain parts of them—lasted for
some time, Garrick threw overboard all the "improvers."
Garrick's production of " Macbeth " was an example. This
play had been overlaid with alterations since the days of the
Restoration, when Davenant had turned it into an opera
and added a lot more spectres because he thought that
Shakespeare had given short weight in this respect. This
version had held the stage right up to the time of Garrick's
revival in this period. He did not go the whole hog in
a revival of "Romeo and Juliet," in which Woodward, an
excellent actor whom he had now engaged, and Mrs. Cibber
excelled themselves. But still, his version was on the right
lines. As regards Macbeth, actors had raised Macduff into
the leading role, but Garrick put the Thane back in his
right position. So great was his intensity in this role,
always a test part for actors, that when he exclaimed to
the First Murderer " There's blood upon thy face," the
horrified actor put his hand to his visage and stammered
" Is there, by God? "

Quin jeered at his Othello and said he looked like the
little black boy in Hogarth's picture, " The Harlot's
Progress." In his retirement, although the sneer stung
him at the time, Garrick admitted the resemblance — in
looks, maybe, but not in execution. He had the supreme
gift of living the parts he played, of identifying himself
with them completely. So he reversed the usual procedure

166

of those days. You were not looking at Mr. Quin—or Mr. Garrick—playing King Lear or Macbeth—you were looking at Lear or Macbeth themselves, as portrayed by Garrick.

Parts calling for strong expression suited him best, he was a character, not a romantic actor. His style, which embodied quickness of utterance, speed, swift change of intonation was all against romance. Yet he was better at romance than practically all the others of his day; and when challenged, he would call forth his utmost and win. He was conscious of his lack of height—had he possessed a few more inches, there is no knowing what he might have achieved. He wore high shoes to give him extra stature. His facial expression and his ease of gesture were his great assets, his size and his restlessness, of which George II complained, were his greatest defects.

Garrick suffered much from stage nerves, as all good actors should, and first performances were ordeals to him. They are ordeals still, but just consider the orderly conduct of a first nighter to-day with Garrick's time. Then these gentry expressed themselves loudly, heartily and continuously, and he always feared them. He hated any interruption in his scenes—and neither he nor anyone else appreciated the missiles which were so often hurled at the stage.

As a rule, however, he could hold them quiet. His expression, rapt and tense, when he entered, or gay and jovial, seemed to express the whole character he played and the whole spirit of the play, and it usually gripped the house. He could play a silent scene as well as a strong and vehement one. When David Garrick was on the stage, nobody else counted for much. Dr. Johnson summed him up to Mrs. Siddons, who always bore Garrick a grudge, for which there is little justification. Said the Doctor: " Garrick, madam, was the only actor I ever saw whom I could call a master both in tragedy and comedy, though I liked him best in comedy." That was probably the whole thing in a nutshell.

He did not rely entirely on inspiration and his own ideas. He studied life and character around him. He always said that his " Lear " was founded on something he once saw in Leman Street, near Goodman's Fields Theatre. A man was leaning out of a window with his little daughter in his arms. He dropped the child, who was killed. The unhappy father went out of his mind. Garrick watched

167

it all and often went to the poor man in Bedlam. It was his model for Lear's madness studied first hand. They gave Garrick the title of Sovereign of the Theatre, King of Theatre Royal. He accepted it, he earned it and he adorned it.

In Drury Lane, in his day, the boxes were still the best seats, and their price was 5/-. They were the equivalent of our dress circle. Of stalls, of course, there were none. It was all pit on the ground floor. The pit still extended right from the back wall to the orchestra rail itself, and this was covered with spikes, on which the public hung things. It was still the popular part of the house and the haunt of the noisy, would-be smart and self-appointed critics of the coffee houses. Besides the Royal box there were other private boxes, and the stage boxes were literally right on the stage itself. There was another box in Garrick's time which was of importance. It was called "Burton's Box," after the name of the numberer or the counter who checked the figures of the box office. It held that name for generations after Burton had joined the Drury Lane ghosts.

Garrick introduced many other reforms. He tried to do away with half-price admissions after the third act. Plays began at six o'clock and it was still customary to send along servants to keep places, for they opened the doors in the early afternoon. Later on Garrick made the hour of opening at five o'clock, play to begin at six. His attempt to abolish the half price business led to riots in 1763, but he insisted on—and got—full prices all the time for new pantomimes: Oh yes, Garrick did pantomimes, and wrote them too. Is not Old Drury the original home of that kind of entertainment?

It has been said that Garrick invented footlights. He did not, but he improved those in existence and also altered the whole idea of stage lighting after his visit to the Continent.

He improved the musical side of the theatre—the great Dr. Arne became the musical chief—and for some time acted in this capacity to both Drury Lane and Covent Garden. Eventually, too, Garrick was to bring about reform in costume. Indeed, on January 6th, 1750, was produced " Edward the Black Prince, or The Battle of Poitiers " (attempted after the manner of Chapman) with Garrick in the cast, and the English characters were dressed in the habit of those days and made an elegant figure."

Some of the bills and some of the happenings are very quaint reading to-day. From the actual prompter's book of Drury Lane for the seasons 1746 to 1750, there are some curious entries and records. On 4th October 1746 appears a very human touch:

> "The Widow Turbutt begs to inform her friends that she has removed from the Swan in Smithfield to the Foundling Hospital Coffee House in Red Lion Street Holborn where she begs the continuance of their favours. She has provided herself with the best of liquors of all sorts, and Punch is made immediately as good and as reasonable as anywhere in London."

That was also in the bills, and one suspects Macklin's influence, for the actor Turbutt was the man who befriended him when he killed Hallam, and to whom he entrusted money for the doctor's fees.

There is a record of Spranger Barry's first appearance, which reads:

> "6th October 1746. 'On Saturday night last Mr. Barry from the theatre in Dublin perform'd the part of 'Othello' at the Theatre Royal in Drury Lane before a numerous and polite audience and met with as great applause as could be expected.'"

Volumes speak in those few words.

There is a very interesting entry on Monday 3rd November 1746, which says: "No play. A man in the gallery was carried before a Justice of the Peace on Saturday for throwing an apple on the stage with the intention of hitting some person who was peeping through the curtain but by mistake struck a lady of quality in the face who was sitting in a stage box. On his begging pardon and promising not to repeat the offence he was discharged."

There was a terrific affair for the Freemasons on 16th May 1747, with an array of talent including Mills speaking a prologue as a Freemason and Mrs. Mills speaking an epilogue as a Freemason's wife. At the particular desire of the Grand Master, a Mr. Custos sang a song. He, it appears, was "long confined in the Inquisition in Portugal, upon the account of Freemasonry; and with the greatest resolution nine times underwent torture without either renouncing his religion, or having the secret of Freemasonry extorted from him." We may be sure Mr. Custos stole the show. The proceedings closed with "Long Live Great George Our King"—the first version of the National Anthem. Three rows of the pit were specially railed off for the Masons, and it is added : " Those Brethren who intend accompanying the Grand Master to the Play are desired to meet His Lordship cloath'd at the Rose Tavern, the corner of Bridges Street, Covent Garden."

In addition to the players' routine benefits, Garrick gave one for the Lock Hospital, and one for the sufferers in a great fire in Cornhill, handing over to the Lord Mayor (and advertising it as well), the sum of £208 1s. 0d. One of the most extraordinary of these special benefits was given for the benefit of " A Young Lady distressed by the bankruptcy of her Guardian."

This was the man and these his times. His system and style were the beginning of something new, not only in Drury Lane but in the Theatre of the whole world. For Garrick was not only famous in his own country; his renown spread all over Europe. When he visited France he was made free of the Comedie Francaise. He never played in Paris, but he would " Oblige " after dinner with some of his talent, and the critical French were amazed. Wherever he went it was the same story. He was an internationally great man.

CHAPTER 21

NEW PLAYS

AN early act of Garrick, as actor-manager, was to produce the tragedy of " Irene," written by his friend Dr. Johnson. This was done on Monday 6th February 1749. It was billed as " Mahomet and Irene." Garrick played Demetrius and Barry " Mahomet "; Berry, Havard, Burton, Sowdon, Blakes, Usher, King, Mrs. Pritchard (" Irene ") and Mrs. Cibber (" Aspasia ") were in the cast. The boxes were five shillings and the pit 3/-. Nobody was allowed on the stage.

Garrick took the greatest pains over his friend's one and only play. The dresses were rich and magnificent, the scenery splendid, and the interior of a Turkish harem was a dream of Eastern elegance. It was only a moderate success. Some of the critics fell foul of Garrick's strangling the heroine in full view of the audience. But it got a run of nine nights. Aaron Hill praised Garrick and Mrs. Cibber to the skies, but slated Barry as Mahomet. Doctor Johnson, sitting in a box, was not perturbed at all. It is probable he expected little. That it was not to the town's taste is shown by a steady decrease in receipts. Its third night realised £177 1s. 6d. its sixth £106 4s. 0d. and the last £101 11s. 6d. Garrick had done his best, and Drury Lane had the honour of producing Johnson's play.

But trouble was going on back-stage all the same. Barry was forever complaining that he was given the bad nights on which to play; though actually Garrick was looking after his interests in every way possible. To please him, Garrick let him choose his own nights. To his mortification, his own choice led to no better results. Mrs. Cibber, too, was troublesome. She had Clive and Woffington and Pritchard to contend with. Eventually, she and Barry both left Garrick for Covent Garden. So did Woffington. Rich called Quin back, paying him £1,000 a year, the record price then that an actor had ever received.

War to the knife was now declared between the two theatres. Barry and Mrs. Cibber put up " Romeo and Juliet," expecting to do damage to Drury Lane. Garrick replied by rehearsing Miss Bellamy, a charming and clever young actress, as " Juliet," while he himself took " Romeo," which at the Lane he had given to the very man who now fought him. It was a risk. Silver-voiced Spranger Barry, handsome, romantic and celebrated, was a very " Romeo " and Mrs. Cibber was the ideal Juliet. But—Garrick was Garrick. So he played " Romeo and Juliet " at the Lane against the Garden. There was, in consequence, only the one play to be seen in town. At first, naturally, it caused excitement and comment. Both places were crowded to compare the rivals, both male and female. Some inclined one way, some the other. For nearly a fortnight the battle raged. Those who came to town and hoped to see a show complained bitterly that their only choice was Shakespeare's tragedy. An epigram circulated :

" Well, what's to-night, says angry Ned
As up from bed he rises
Romeo again! And shakes his head
A Pox on both your houses."

That might well have expressed the spirit of the whole town after the first flutter of excitement. But when actors challenge each other, the public, for once, is disregarded. Garrick and Barry fought it out. It was more than a clash of stars, it was a battle of planets. Yet in spite of his physical unsuitability and Barry's natural gifts, it would seem that Garrick's Romeo was the best. It was a contrast in styles not only of the Romeos but the " Juliets " as well. Susannah Maria was the best " Juliet "; she had more experience. But the little Bellamy also put up a good show. Cibber's " Juliet " was a modest girl lost in an ecstasy of love; Bellamy's, a girl impatient for her lover's arms, with adoration and passion radiating from her. A critic said that at Covent Garden he saw " Juliet and Romeo " but at Drury Lane he saw " Romeo and Juliet," which seems to sum it up. Garrick was better than Barry and Mrs. Cibber better than Miss Bellamy. At last the Garden withdrew the play under the pretext of Mrs. Cibber's indisposition. Garrick played one night more to establish his holding the field, and was then very glad to give up. So he won his first duel with Barry — on points.

Both houses lost money by the fight, but Garrick was not worrying. He knew there would be reductions at the Garden, and he had not long to wait. Quin hated Barry and Barry would not bow to Quin. Mrs. Woffington and Mrs. Cibber behaved to each other like the leading ladies they were. Faction was rife and so was strife. Garrick went on filling Drury Lane. With Woodward's assistance he did a pantomime called " Queen Mab." It ran for forty nights and closed Covent Garden.

Garrick always encouraged new talent. He had given the ungrateful Barry every chance, and now he presented others, including Dexter, Mossop and Ross. Yet it had always been laid at the doors of the actor-managers that they must be all in all and the rest nowhere.

Dexter made his début in " Oroonoko " and seems to have been an off-hand sort of fellow, for half an hour before curtain rise, when the second music started, he decided he had better leave the pit where he was chatting with friends and dress and make up for the part. He was a big success, however, and Garrick was delighted. But Dexter was a good beginner and bad finisher. He never played again so well as on his début and gradually waned in public esteem.

Ross was given " Bevil " in " The Conscious Lovers " for his entrée, and took full advantage of it. He seemed

172

to be the ideal stage fine gentleman. But he preferred social life and the bottle; he soon became what is known in stage circles as "unreliable."

Mossop, a man of great power but with an ungainly awkward manner, chose "Richard III" to challenge fortune, and as his defects were disguised in this part and his voice was magnificent, he triumphed. He was a success for some time, but he made a melancholy end, which is no part of our story.

Garrick now took another step. He undertook a new role, that of husband. He married the delightful and charming Violette, the Austrian dancer, and theirs was a happy marriage. He brought her to his home in 27 Southampton Street, where they lived for years. They moved to the Adelphi later, where the river flooded them out. They had their villa at Hampton—still there to-day—where the wits and great ones of stage, arts and literature, delighted to visit them.

At Drury Lane Garrick was always looking for new plays and new authors. He produced "The Gamester" by Edward More, but it was considered too strong meat. But despite these small set-backs, the success of Drury Lane was complete. Garrick sometimes feared the public might get tired of him, and constantly kept up the flow of new blood. He knew that the Christmas pantomimes were certain means of keeping the exchequer well replenished, but all the same, he was always casting about for new ideas. In pursuit of this laudable design he engaged Noverre, the great ballet master, to provide novelties. This man was famous all over Europe. He had devised a stage entertainment which he called "The Chinese Festival." It was a gorgeous affair in which all the stage arts combined. Garrick had Europe scoured for dancers and announced them as French. Noverre was actually Swiss.

Unfortunately for Garrick, war was declared on France, just before the date of production and naturally there was a great public outcry about the employment of all these (alleged) French people whilst the two countries were at war. It was alleged also that all the dresses had been made in France, to the exclusion of English dressmakers. Actually the whole lot had been made in London. As eighteen months had been spent in getting ready, Garrick decided to stick to his guns, and despite all public outcry, produced on 12th November, 1755. The King came to the aid of Old Drury and was present at the opening performance. But even his presence could not curb his loving subjects. They were out for trouble. All the time there was pandemonium. Garrick tried to placate the rioters, but they would not listen. He struggled on. The old King was much amused at the scene and laughed heartily all the while.

Garrick had little to laugh about, but he tried a second night, whereupon the audience began to take sides. The young men of fashion quarrelled with the more plebeian members of the audience who were causing the uproar. Garrick himself appeared in the first piece of the evening and regularly " got the bird." The support of the more expensive part of the playhouse only incensed the cheaper parts the more, and for six nights the battle raged. At first the ladies in the boxes helped their menfolk by pointing out the noisiest of the rioters. The men jumped into the pit to seize them and ascended the stairs to the gallery. Still the fight raged on. On the sixth night swords were drawn and blood shed; the help of the ladies turned to screams of horror and the mob got out of hand. They fought all over the place, tore up the benches, broke up the scenes, smashed the candelbra and did terrific damage. Then a section declared they were going to Garrick's house in Southampton Street to burn it down. Garrick sent for the military, and after his windows had been well and truly broken, the soldiers dispersed the mob. But from that night, until 1895 or 1896, a squad of soldiers regularly mounted guard at Theatre Royal, as at the Bank of England. The failure of the " Chinese Festival " cost Garrick and Lacy £4,000.

Even after the shouting and tumult of " The Chinese Festival " had been put down by force, the more turbulent element of the public seemed still disposed to persecute Garrick. When he reappeared as " Archer " they started to hoot him. He tackled them firmly. He acknowledged all past favours received but stated clearly that unless he was allowed to play in peace that evening, and do his best as he had always done, he would leave the stage forever. Whilst he was speaking the opposition was stilled and the whole house hushed, and when he ended, there was a great burst of sympathetic and friendly applause. It rocked the theatre. In a moment of clear vision these citizens of London realised that they could not do without their own Davy Garrick, and all was harmony and peace again.

Indeed, Garrick was no coward: he had defeated many rivals, in particular Barry in the battle of the Romeos when the odds were against him. He was to beat this same rival once again when the odds were on his side. For Barry challenged him again, this time as "Lear." Once more there was only one play in town. Once again the public compared and chattered; but the result was a foregone conclusion. The Press of the time made the matter beyond doubt.

> "The town has found out different ways
> To praise the rival Lears
> To Barry they give loud Huzzas
> To Garrick they give tears."

But an epigram settled it:

> "A King and every inch a King
> So Barry doth appear
> But Garrick's quite a different thing
> He's every inch King Lear."

Once again, Drury Lane had won a battle of the theatres: Barry was beaten, and Woffington had died in 1757. Garrick did all he could for her at the end despite her bad temper and her continued opposition. They had once been lovers and he had never forgotten.

Samuel Foote was now a considerable figure in theatrical circles. He had made the little theatre in the Haymarket a paying concern, and by his extraordinary gift of authorship and still more extraordinary mimicry had drawn the whole town. So cruel were his impressions of others that people feared him, and it is likely that Garrick did likewise, for he took care to keep on his right side and frequently lent him money. Foote only sneered and took advantage. In 1754, after a trip to Paris, Foote produced a play called "The Englishman in Paris," and had it done at Drury Lane, playing "The Englishman" himself. Garrick wrote a prologue.

In 1755 and 1756, Garrick himself produced two plays by Dr. Browne: "Barbarossa" was a fair success but its successor, "Athelstan" failed.

About this time Garrick started a war on his own account. He decided to produce a play called "The Busybody," which he had written himself. He waited for Covent

Garden's announcement of " Douglas," and then announced
" The Busybody " for the same night. Covent Garden postponed. So did Garrick. They dodged about like this for
a long time, and the jockeying for position is reminiscent of
the game which Powel played with Betterton when Drury
Lane fought Lincoln's Inn Fields. At last there was nothing
for it but for both to produce at once. Fashion split into
two camps : some went to Garrick's first night, some to the
Garden. In the end " Douglas " triumphed over " The
Busybody." That famous school recitation commencing
" My name in Norval " comes from " Douglas."

Garrick did not often lose a battle. He refused at
first a play called " The Orphan of China," but Murphy, the
author, was persistent. Garrick produced it at last, and the
author rehearsed secretly with Mrs. Yates, who had got the
lead owing to Mrs. Cibber, who had rejoined Garrick, being
ill. It was a great success and Mrs. Yates stepped into the
front rank.

In 1760, Macklin, friend, foe and now friend again of
Garrick's, offered him his play " Love a La Mode." This
satire on the Scots succeeded. Macklin was magnificent as
" Sir Archie M'Sarcasm." Moody, a good actor of Irish
parts played and Mr. King, to cut a distinguished figure at
the Lane, was Squire Groom. Some Scottish gentlemen protested, but this only got the play more publicity. George II.
then 77, did not go to the theatre now, but heard so much
about the play that he asked to read it. This he accomplished
in eleven weeks, rather less time than the average theatre
manager takes to read a play to-day. Seeing that the King's
knowledge of English was never great, one wonders what
he made of it all.

Thomas Sheridan, the Irish manager, came to London,
and nothwithstanding a coolness between himself and
Garrick, appeared at Drury Lane. His success was considerable and there is no doubt that he aroused Garrick's
jealousy. There was again a battle in the theatre. Sheridan
scored heavily in " The Earl of Essex," a new version
of " The Unhappy Favourite." Sometimes he and Garrick
played together and packed the playhouse.

In March 1761, the poet Churchill launched his
" Rosciad." Not since Pope's " Dunciad " against Cibber
had such an attack been made upon the stage. Churchill
knew what he was talking about. He was a regular and
observant playgoer. He praised Mrs. Cibber, Mrs. Clive and

176

At left. GRIMALDI, the great clown.

Top. GEORGE GROSSMITH, manager of Drury Lane in 1931, and a star of musical comedy.

Bottom. A great pantomime combination. JOHNNY DANVERS, DAN LENO (seated) and HERBERT CAMPBELL.

At right.
MARIE GEORGE, a Principal Girl in Drury Lane's pantomime in the 1900's.

Below.
MABEL LOVE played in Drury Lane pantomime in the nineties.

Above.
WALTER PASSMORE, in Drury Lane pantomime, *Babes in the Wood*, in 1907.

Mrs. Pritchard, but slashed to ribbons every actor of the lot—except Garrick, whom he overloaded with compliments. The players howled, the public laughed—and bought the poem. The great praise made Garrick uneasy. It was laid on far too thick and had the natural effect of making him unpopular with his friends and brother professionals. It seems that he denounced it publicly and that some of his words got back to Churchill. Churchill wrote an Apology in which he not only made matters worse for the theatrical profession in general, but made a bitter attack on Garrick as well.

King George II had passed on, and George III now reigned,—poor old Farmer George. To celebrate the Coronation, both the Theatres Royal staged their Coronation shows. Garrick knew that Rich would spread himself with his love of spectacle. At Drury Lane, therefore, he did not trouble much. He used the old dresses which had served their turn before—since 1727 in point of fact. He showed the Coronation spectacle, as an after-piece, for 40 nights, and it was said to have been the worst thing he ever did.

It is of interest to record here that John Rich, of Covent Garden, who was Garrick's only real rival in management—Foote having only a nuisance value—died in 1761.

In 1762, Garrick and Lacy enlarged the theatre by some clever work which did away with the necessity for seats on the stage, and in 1775 it received its front designed by the Brothers Adam.

If we have witnessed a few Garrick defeats, it is well to remember that there were many victories to counterbalance them. The sparkling comedy "High Life Below Stairs," done in 1759, was one. Garrick had a large hand in the writing of this, as he had also in "The Clandestine Marriage," in which he collaborated with George Colman. He should also have played in this piece, but left it to King, that excellent and sound actor, who created the part of "Lord Ogleby." "The Jealous Wife" was another success. Colman wrote this alone, although Garrick had much to do with the construction.

"High Life Below Stairs" had brought a new actress as a recruit to Drury Lane. This was Frances Barton (later Mrs. Abington), destined to be a great star. Hers is another romantic story. This lady claimed that she was descended from a family distinguished in the reign of William III. So she may have been; but her father was a private in the Guards, and when off duty worked in a cobbler's in Windmill Street, while her brother was an ostler who watered the horses of the Hampstead Coach at the Halfway point in Hanway Street, Tottenham Court Road. Nothing at all is known about her mother. So little Frances Barton had to support herself to a large extent, and to that end she sold flowers in St. James's Park, being known as "Nosegay Fan." Her intelligence and good looks brought her many customers. She also sang in the streets, and sometimes in the better class coffee houses like the Bedford and the Shakespeare. She became a servant for a French milliner in Cockspur Street, for whom she ran errands, and probably learnt a good deal about life. She seems to have been a cook maid as well. She had determination as well as beauty, charm and personality, and she taught herself French and Italian.

Frances got her first stage chance at the Haymarket, and did well. Then she went to Bath, and then to Richmond, where Lacy saw her and engaged her for Drury Lane. She made her first appearance there in 1756, playing a round of parts, but was kept well under by Mrs. Pritchard, Mrs. Macklin and Kitty Clive. In 1759 she married James Abington, who was a trumpeter in the King's Service. From then on she played under her married name of Mrs. Abington. The couple set up house in St. Martin's Lane, then a fashionable street, and it is a mystery how they did it, for her husband's pays was small and her salary was thirty shillings a week. But shortly afterwards Abington disappeared. It is said that when she grew popular she pensioned him off to keep him away from her. In 1759 she left Drury Lane and went to Dublin where she made a sensation. Repeated offers were made her to go to Drury Lane, but it was not until Garrick returned in 1765 from a visit to Italy that she condescended to join his company.

Ten years before this, another girl, destined to be a Drury Lane leading lady, had played her first part. Her name was Jane Pope and she had appeared as a child in Garrick's pantomime "Lilliput." She also played in "Lethe," "Miss in Her Teens" etc. But on 27th September 1759, she made her real début, announced as a "Young Lady" as "Corinna" in "The Confederacy." She made very great success, and on the second night, whilst waiting to go on the stage, Kitty Clive called her over and gave her some advice which, with Colley Cibber's dictum, should be in the memory of every actor and actress.

Seated in the Green Room, the old actress made the young one listen to her and said: " My dear Pope, you played particularly well on Saturday night considering that you are, as yet, but a novice in the profession. Now take a piece of advice from me. You acted on Saturday with great and merited approbation, yet be not surprised when I tell you that to-night you must endeavour to act better, and yet at the same time make up your mind to receive less applause; for if you suffer your young heart to be too sanguine and place too much dependence on the caprice of public commendation and should find your hopes disappointed, you will foolishly let it cast a damp over your spirits and thus, instead of improving, you will sink beneath yourself. Therefore, take my advice for your future progress. The violent thunder of applause which crowned your first appearance last Saturday was not in strict justice deserved. It was only benevolently bestowed by the audience, to give you the pleasing information that they were well satisfied by your efforts. You must therefore consider it as an earnest of their wishes that you will, by your future exertions, merit the distinguished kindness they have manifested towards you." That was some of the soundest sense ever uttered in the Drury Lane Green Room, and Jane Pope took that advice and always remembered it. It stood her in good stead.

She played many parts, and was good in all. She stayed on after Garrick left, and created " Mrs. Candour " in " The School for Scandal." She never married, but was at Drury Lane for fifty years before she retired full of honours.

CHAPTER 22

A FAMOUS FAREWELL

THERE is no question that Mrs. Abington plagued Garrick almost to death. His description of her was: " She is as silly as she is false and treacherous," and he called her " that most worthless creature " and " the worst of bad women." Yet, on the stage, she was inimitable. She got on the right side of Dr. Johnson, too, and once he came to her benefit. But he chose to sit behind Sir Joshua Reynolds and a party of forty wits, where he could neither hear well nor see anything, and spent his time discussing with Boswell the question of prologues, saying that Dryden had written better prologues than Garrick, but Garrick had written more good ones than Dryden. On that occasion, commenting on Dr. Johnson's choice of a seat, one of the wits asked him: "Why, sir, did you go to Mrs. Abington's benefit? Did you see?" Johnson replied: "No, sir." "Did you hear?" "No sir." "Why then did you go?" "Because sir," came the crushing retort, "she is a favourite of the public; and when the public cares the thousandth part for you that it does for her, I will go to your benefit, too."

Some of Garrick's young actors were real discoveries. There was Smith, called "Gentleman Smith," partly because he had the air and deportment of one and partly because he married a lady of title. And Palmer, who excelled in such parts as "The Lord's Footman" in "High Life Below Stairs." In his everyday life, he acted the gentleman off the stage. Dodd, another, was the perfect presenter of the fop of the time, a successor to Colley Cibber; whilst King, already mentioned, was a very fine actor indeed. Had he not been a contemporary of Garrick, he might have led the stage. Parsons was a first-class character actor. All these men, who were to carry on the tradition of Drury Lane after the great master left it, had been trained by Garrick. And, indeed, the time of his departure was drawing near, for Garrick was getting very weary and wanted a rest. Historians have said that the fiasco and rioting at "The Chinese Festival" was the first thing to turn his thoughts to retirement.

In 1763, Garrick got another jolt, and a serious one, in the form of another riot. This was occasioned by his complete abolition of the half-price admission at the end of the third act and insistence on full prices. Garrick and Lacy had been contemplating this reform for years. It was now introduced as a regular rule, but a champion of half prices arose: Mr. Fitzpatrick by name. He and his friends circulated pamphlets around the coffee-houses in Covent Garden, protesting against this managerial action, claiming that Garrick had no right to exact full price for a revived play, and protesting that they proposed to have the matter settled in a decent and orthodox manner.

The orthodox manner of their choice was to riot, and they chose for it a night when a new version of "Two Gentlemen of Verona" was to be presented, a night when half price should not have operated, anyway. Fitzpatrick and his friends went down to Drury Lane in force. The ringleader harangued the audience from a box, set forth the wickedness of the grasping managers, and told the public that it was their right to fix what prices they should pay. Garrick at once came forward to speak against him but was howled down. Fitzpatrick further inflamed the mob in the theatre and they started once again to tear up the benches and to wreck the theatre. The house was closed, the play called off, and the money returned.

Next night the play was "Elvira," another new tragedy, and a fair occasion for full prices. But rioting began at once. Again Garrick faced them. They yelled their ultimatum: "Will you, or will you not, give admittance for half price, after the third act of a play, except during the first winter a pantomime is performed?" So bad and threatening did things look that Garrick capitulated and gave in to such a display of force. Even then the audience were not placated. They demanded apologies from the players who had struggled with them the previous night, calling especially for Moody, who had actually dared to restrain forcibly a man who was trying to set fire to the playhouse. Moody, a man of spirit, tried to laugh it off. He declared from the stage that he was very sorry that he had displeased them by saving their lives in putting out the fire. The joke was very ill received, and they demanded that Moody should go down on his knees and apologise to them. This was too much for plucky Moody. "I will not, by God!" he exclaimed, and strode off. Another account is that his actual words were: "I will not. I bow my knee to two beings only—my God and my King. You are neither." One hopes this was the correct version—it is far more dramatic.

Another Drury Lane success which had already been garnered in but which must be mentioned, was "Alfred." It had been done originally as a masque at Clieveden in the open air. Garrick altered it for the stage and produced it in 1750-51. It contained a song, "Rule, Britannia," composed by Dr. Arne, then at Drury Lane Theatre. Thus, Drury Lane can claim to be the first theatre in which this, our second National Anthem, was sung.

Theatrical finance is always intriguing. Here are some

figures of Garrick's in 1763. The salaries are charged per
night.

	£	s.	d.
Garrick	2	15	6
Mr. and Mrs. Yates	3	6	8
Mr. and Mrs. Palmer	2	0	0
King	1	6	8
Parsons		6	8
Mrs. Cibber	2	10	0
Mrs. Pritchard	2	6	8
Mrs. Clive	1	15	0
Miss Pope		12	4
Italian dancer	1	3	4
Second Italian dancer	1	13	4

There are also allocations of 3s. 8d. for the "nightly
charity" and of £1 15s. for "The Fund." It does not
look much!

There was always bickering as to who should find the
clothes—the artists or the management. Mrs. Yates
demanded from Garrick £700 a year and £200 for her
dresses. Mrs. Cibber had £200 a year and her dresses,
except her head dresses. Miss Bellamy appears to have
beaten the lot in the quality and appearance of her clothes
and petticoats, and that captious critic, George II, said that
her hoops were too large. The men groused about their
costumes, and Garrick was once so resplendent that he
suffered a rebuke from the irrepressible Clive. He appeared
in a glittering silver-spangled tissue shape which drew from
the actress, to the delight of the Green Room, the shout of
"Oh, my God, room, room, make room for the Royal Lamp-
lighter."

But to return to finance, probably the low record for the
house in Garrick's time was £3 15s. 6d. with himself and
Mrs. Cibber in the bill; £200 was a good average house.
They could take as much as £335. It cost about £522 7s. 6d.
a week to run the theatre. Here is their salary list, 13th
February, 1773, at £87 1s. 3d. per day or £522 7s. 6d. a week:

	Men	£	s.	d.
James Lacy, Esq.		16	13	0
David Garrick, Esq.		16	13	0
" "		17	10	0
Mr. S. Barry & wife		50	0	0
Mr. King		8	0	0
Mr. Reddish		8	0	0
Mr. Jefferson		8	0	0
Mr. Dame & wife		8	0	0
Mr. Didbin		6	0	0
Mr. Bannister & wife		6	0	0
Mr. Clinch		2	10	0

	Women								
Mrs. Abington	...	...	...	...	...	...	...	8 0 0
Miss Pope	...	...	...	...	...	...	...	8 0 0
Miss Young	...	...	...	...	...	...	...	7 0 0
	Singers								
Mr. Vernon	...	...	...	...	...	...	...	8 0 0
Mrs. Smith	...	...	...	...	...	...	...	6 6 0
Miss Venables	...	...	...	...	...	...	...	6 6 0
	Dancers								
Mr. Daigville & wife	...	...	...	...	...	...	...	6 0 0
Signora Vidini	...	...	...	...	...	...	...	5 0 0
Mrs. Sutton	...	...	...	...	...	...	...	5 0 0
Mr. Grimaldi & wife	...	...	...	...	...	...	...	5 0 0

The Jefferson in the list was the ancestor of the famous American actor, and the Grimaldi and wife were the parents of the famous "Joe" Grimaldi. There were other performers of lesser rank, dressers, property men and carpenters; the band cost £49, the soldiers £4 4s. (probably the permanent guard), numbers £1 10s., house barber £1 4s., candlewoman 12s., a pensioner Mr. Waldgrave 10s. 6d, and the sinking fund £21. Expenses were mounting, for in 1765 the nightly expenses were only £70 with a company 160 strong. To-day it costs over £3,000 a week to run Drury Lane.

One more Green Room story of the time is worth repetition. Stone, the prompter, thrust a note into Garrick's hand which read: "Stone, to Mr. Garrick: Sir,— The Bishop of Winchester is getting drunk at the Bear and swears Damn his eyes if he'll play to-night. I am Yours, W. Stone."

It was indeed time he had a holiday; and on 15th September, 1763, he crossed the Channel to Calais en route for Paris and Italy. With him went Mrs. Garrick, who from the day of her marriage to the death of Garrick was never separated from him for twenty-four hours.

Covent Garden, under Beard, was now giving musical plays and doing very well indeed. For the moment public taste was running that way.

Garrick had made provision for his absence. He left his brother George in his place to direct affairs with Lacy, and recommended light entertainment. He also counselled "spectacle" and told them to let the machinists have a turn. To counteract the advance of the Garden he had engaged Pompeio, a noted Italian singer. Garrick had also specially trained a young actor, named Powell, to appear in his absence. Powell's début was a big success, although Foote, the implacable enemy, was in the boxes and tried to deride him.

183

There was some internal dissension caused by Holland, another of Garrick's trainees, who was jealous of Powell and refused to appear with him. This Holland was a bad man, and nearly broke the faithful Miss Pope's heart. She was much in love with him and found him faithless. But Holland could not stop Powell, who went from success to success. Later on, Powell became manager of the Bristol theatre.

Garrick was away for eighteen months. He returned at the end of April, 1765, to find that, as he had reckoned, the public were eager to see him. You never miss a good thing until you have not got it, and they missed him. He elected to open in "Much Ado About Nothing." The King honoured him by coming to see the performance.

In the following year, 1766, Mrs. Cibber died, and Garrick's old friend and rival Quin passed away too. Garrick, however, went from strength to strength. He did not now appear so often. He knew that this abstention would increase business when he did. He spent more time directing and writing plays. His version of Wycherley's "The Country Girl" was a real winner. He produced "False Delicacy" by Kelly, probably the first English sentimental comedy. His friend, Oliver Goldsmith, offered him his comedy, "The Good Natured Man," but Garrick declined it. On the other hand, he did not neglect musical plays.

There was now at Drury Lane that turbulent genius and great writer of sea songs, Charles Dibdin, who, like the Captain of the Pinafore, hardly ever went to sea. This man's meteoric rise had made him resident composer at Covent Garden. He quarrelled with the management there and came to Drury Lane. Here, in company with Isaac Bickerstaffe, he composed "The Padlock" and played the leading part. Bannister sang the part of Diego. "The Padlock" was a great success, but later on Dibdin quarrelled with Garrick, as he quarrelled with everyone else, and left the Lane.

In a new version of Cibber's "The Non-Juror" (which in turn was a rehash of Moliere's "Tartuffe"), Mrs. Abington made a great hit, as she did in "Beatrice" and in Kelly's "The Way to Keep Him." In private life these days she was very much the fine lady, and the nobility called on her. She was having an easier time of it, for the old stars were going, among them Mrs. Pritchard, who retired in 1768.

Kitty Clive, her old rival and Garrick's tormentor—and also the greatest comedienne of her age—hinted at retirement in the following year. Garrick, on hearing this, sent Hopkins, the prompter, to know if it was true. Clive's spirit flared up. She disdained to answer an underling. So the faithful George Garrick was sent as ambassador. He received little better treatment, and was sent away with a flea in his ear and the message that if his distinguished brother really wanted to know he could come and enquire himself. He came.

After paying her many compliments, Garrick enquired if she really meant to retire, and said he hoped she would continue on the stage for some years. Clive replied with a contemptuous look and a decided negative. The actor-manager ventured to ask how much she was worth. The actress replied: " As much as yourself." Garrick smiled indulgently, so she added that " she knew when she had enough but that he never would." Though he did not want her to go, Garrick now saw her mind was made up. She made her farewell performance on 24th April, 1769, as " Flora " in " The Wonder," and " The Fine Lady " in " Lethe." Horace Walpole wrote her epilogue. She retired to Strawberry Hill, where she lived happily for many years in constant touch with the Garricks and her friends. She came up to town, an old lady, in 1784, to see Mrs. Siddons act. At the end they asked her opinion. She showed them she was still Kitty Clive, for in answer to what she thought of it, she said: " Think? I think it's all truth and daylight."

Havard, a very useful actor, dropped out in 1769 and died in 1778. Meanwhile, Jane Pope was Kitty Clive's successor. In 1768, Garrick produced Arne's "Artaxerxes " at Drury Lane. He had previously done his " King Arthur " and there had been some trouble over that.

But on his return from abroad Garrick had done another thing to rank highly in Drury Lane history. This was the foundation of the famous Drury Lane Fund. There had been universal horror a short time before at the discovery that Mrs. Hamilton, a good actress of Covent Garden, had fallen upon evil days and was in dire distress. Thomas Hull of that theatre formed a scheme whereby all players there should pay 6d. a week and that there should be an annual benefit and subscriptions invited to make a fund for the relief of such people, and further that this should be exclusive to Covent Garden.

When Garrick heard of it he was furious. As head of the stage he considered he should have been consulted. So he founded a special fund for Drury Lane. He gave it an annual benefit, played for it himself and got for it in all £4,500. In May, 1776, both Funds got a charter from Parliament. Garrick paid the necessary expenses for the Drury Lane Fund. When the power of the Patents was broken it was obvious that more liberty of choice should be given to actors, and The Royal General Theatrical Fund arose, in 1838, which absorbed the Covent Garden Fund. The Royal General Fund still flourishes, an excellently run species of insurance society. But the Drury Lane Fund remains in being, independent and self-administered. Only Drury Lane actors, actresses, and stage officials can be members. Certain modifications have been introduced to meet altered circumstances since Garrick founded it, but the object remains the same. Its present secretary is William Abingdon, the splendid stage director of the Lane, and under him the Fund flourishes. But the foundation was Garrick's.

To return to the fortunes of the great theatre, we are now confronted with the personality of a figure almost the equal of Garrick in stature, and certainly the greatest actress we have ever had—Mrs. Sarah Siddons.

She had been brought to Garrick's notice, this young daughter of a strolling actor, and he sent King to Cheltenham to see her. King did not give a good report; so Garrick sent Dr. Bate, a vigorous example of muscular Christianity, to Worcester to have a look and give him his opinion. Bate saw the young Siddons play Rosalind for the first time, in a theatre which was little more than a barn, with a stage a few feet wide. Although she was shortly to be confined, he noted her excellent figure. Her face he considered very beautiful, but he thought little of her deportment, her action, or her voice. He heard that she had made a hit at Worcester as Hamlet, and concluded that she would play breeches-parts very well.

Bate heard also that Covent Garden was after her, so he got into touch with her husband, whom he describes as a damned rascally player but a civil fellow, and found the two of them very humble and very willing to leave everything to Mr. Garrick. Mr. Siddons begged to be included, if his wife got a job; he was absolutely servile about it. "You can station him," wrote Bate, "so as to satisfy the man without disturbing the property." Matters were fixed up on very low terms. There was a delay because of the birth of the baby, and so Garrick could not open the season with his new actress as he had wished. He appears to have sent the couple £20 to cover expenses. Mrs. Siddons' first salary was £5 per week.

Mrs. Siddons made her Drury Lane début on December 29th, 1775, as "Portia," billed as "A Young Lady" to King's "Shylock." She repeated it, billed as Mrs. Siddons, on 2nd January, 1776. She failed. She played "Epicene" on 18th January, but failed again. On 2nd February she played "Julia" in a poor farce, "The Blackamoor Washed White." Again she failed. On 15th February she was "Emily" in "Runaway." Still a failure. She did no better as "Maria" in "Love's Metamorphosis." Then she appeared with Garrick himself as "Mrs. Strickland." Once again the same result. Her second appearance with Garrick was as "Lady Anne" in "Richard III," which she played twice, the last time on 5th June at a command performance before the Royal Family. It was no good. She got one Press notice which said: "In the part of Lady Anne, Mrs. Siddons was lamentable." She had also appeared in the non-speaking part of Venus, when Garrick staged his Jubilee pageant.

Meanwhile, the theatre had been enlarged again, taking in the Rose Tavern, and a new entrance had been made in Bridges Street. The work was done by The Brothers Adam, and a lovely playhouse was the result. But the old guard of stage favourites was thinning out; already old Mossop had gone, and in 1773 Lacy died, and although Willoughby Lacy took over the Lacy part of the Patent, it left the whole business of the theatre on Garrick's shoulders.

Another new candidate for Drury Lane honours had arisen in Richard Brinsley Sheridan, and at the beginning of January, 1776, Garrick arranged to sell to Sheridan, Thomas Linley and Richard Ford, his half of the Patent for £35,000. The sale was completed on 24th June, 1776. He then announced his own retirement.

The news shocked everyone. They did not want him to go, could not believe he was going. But he was adamant. He announced his farewell programmes. People came from all over the country for a last glimpse of Garrick's greatness. Never had the Lane seen such audiences, never had there been such sentiment, such feeling, such applause, such love expressed and shown. At last the night came when he must leave the theatre and that great stage on which he had done so much. It was a melancholy occasion. All of his last performances had been given with the fire of youth lit by the golden light of experience. Never had he played so well as Hamlet, Lear, Richard III, or any of the great and favourite rôles. He determined to leave an imperishable memory behind him. He succeeded. He had done so much for the stage, for Drury Lane. He had filled it with great plays and great acting by himself and his company. He had given many chances, he had made new stars. He had found and made playwrights, he had revolutionised stage methods, he had cleared the audiences from the stage, he had employed great scenic artists, amongst them Loutherbourg, to whom he paid £500 a year. He had gone far towards dressing plays in their proper periods and types of costumes. He had done so much, and it was at Drury Lane he had done it. He had written plays, prologues, epilogues and songs—one of them "Hearts of Oak" (the words are his) to obtain immortality. Against all this there was no scandal. He was an ideal husband of an ideal wife.

He chose, for his farewell performance, to appear as "Don Felix" in "The Wonder." He played for the last time on 10th June, 1776.

The vast theatre could not accommodate all who wished to be present. Great personalities fought to get in, and were content with any corner. It was a night without parallel in theatre history. Garrick, who had played the part so many times, gave yet his finest performance; but it was noted that he did not join in the gay Country Dance which ended the show. The curtain fell; and to a hushed and tremulous audience the great actor advanced alone on that beloved stage to speak his last lines, to say farewell. For the first time he betrayed emotion, he was near to tears. He mastered himself with a visible effort; and amidst a deep hush, he commenced to say the last words he would ever utter from the boards which he knew so well:

"Ladies and Gentlemen,

"It has been customary with persons under my circumstances to address you in a farewell epilogue. I had the same intention and turned my thoughts that way; but indeed I found myself then as incapable of writing such an epilogue as I should be now of speaking it. The jingle of rhyme and the language of fiction would but ill suit my present feelings. This is to me a very awful moment; it

188

is no less than parting forever with those from whom I have received the greatest kindness and favours and upon the spot where those favours were enjoyed. (Here he broke down and shed tears and the audience joined him.)

"Whatever may be the changes of my future life, the deepest impression of your kindness will always remain here (he touched his breast) fixed and unalterable. I will readily agree to my successors having more skill and ability for their station than I have; but I defy them all to take more sincere, more uninterrupted pains for your favour or to be more truly sensible of it, than is your humble servant."

CHAPTER 23

SHERIDAN'S MASTERPIECE

RICHARD BRINSLEY SHERIDAN, who now became Patentee of Theatre Royal, Drury Lane, was the son of Thomas Sheridan, manager of the Dublin theatre, who had employed Garrick over there, and in turn appeared at Drury Lane under Garrick's banner. He was a good actor, good enough to make Garrick jealous.

He went to Harrow School, where he was despised as the son of a poor player, though since then his name has been remembered in one of Harrow's famous school songs. He spent a somewhat riotous youth, eloping in the end with Elizabeth Linley, daughter of a celebrated musician, and herself a fine singer. He was received back into the bosom of the Linley family in due course, and although Sheridan could never agree with his own father, he appears to have gained complete control over his father-in-law. Sheridan had no money and no profession, but eked out a precarious livelihood by writing for the newspapers. He also showed himself something of a poet, and incidentally fought two duels previous to his marriage, both for the honour of his fiancée.

It was in 1775 that he really found his vocation. Then he commenced to write for the theatre, and his first play, "The Rivals," was produced at Covent Garden on the 17th of January of that year. It still lives. It had a bad reception on the opening night, but he made quick alterations which ensured its triumph. He was now the hero of the family into which he had married. He had made good. He had done a good deal more, for, following on the heels of Goldsmith, whose " She Stoops to Conquer " and " The Good Natured Man," had laid down fresh lines for English comedy, the wit and genius of Sheridan showed that there were men who could write as well, if not better, than many of the Restoration dramatists whose works still held the stage. Sheridan's next play was " St. Patrick's Day," also produced at Covent Garden, on 2nd May, 1775; and on 21st November of the same year came " The Duenna." He was now the sensation of the time, his name on every lip and the cup of success held firmly in his grasp. Only twenty-four, his ambition soared and he flew at the highest game attainable—Drury Lane.

It was in the October of 1775, that Sheridan got wind of Garrick's impending retirement, and that the Patent had been valued at £70,000. That meant that Garrick must receive £35,000 and interest amounting to £3,500 per annum, a nice little ten per cent. for Davy. This to Sheridan, seemed a bagatelle.

" While this is cleared the proprietors are safe, but I think it must be infernal bad management indeed that one does not double it." Thus airily spoke the budding and in-experienced manager.

They took a Doctor Ford in with them, and by some means, nobody quite knows how, they raised the money to buy Garrick's share. Apparently they borrowed £20,000 at five per cent., Sheridan raked up £1,300 with his wife and the rest came no one knows whence. So they started pretty heavily burdened.

The Garrick share, acquired in June 1776, was then divided into seven shares, of which Sheridan held two, Linley two, and Ford three. This James Ford was a fashionable doctor and an accoucheur of great repute amongst the highest circles. This led to an amusing letter from Kitty Clive to Garrick about his successors. " What a strange jumble of people they have put in the papers as the purchasers of the Patent. I thought I should have died with laughing when I saw a man-midwife amongst them : I suppose they have taken him in to prevent miscarriages."

The new partners invited Sheridan pére to be acting manager, but he refused. He did not like his son, and he did not like the terms. Richard made himself business manager, about the worst move that could have been made. Linley was musical director. But Sheridan's enthusiasm and energy was such that he had no doubts at all of his being able to beat Garrick's record—not of acting, of course, but of management and production. He was on top of the world, going up like a rocket. So he took risks with the greatest confidence.

Sheridan, very fittingly, opened his new theatre on September 21st, 1776, with a play of his own, a revival of " The Rivals." It was followed by Congreve's " The Old Bachelor," Betterton's famous part; then by " Jane Shore." These were followed by a round of old plays. The hopeful Sheridan was finding that a manager's life was not the primrose path he had imagined. He was now getting the full brunt of leading lady tantrums. Managers who to-day have to cope with but one at a time will feel for poor Sherry who had to deal with three all at once—Mrs. Abington, Mrs. Yates and Mrs. Younge. They bullied him, badgered him, they threw up parts, went into temperaments. But probably it was still fun, whilst the freshness lasted.

At any rate he had plenty of energy, for in a single week in December he produced a musical dramatic romance, sponsored by Linley with music by his son, entitled " Selima and Azor." Sheridan spread himself over this production, to show the public what they might expect. He spent a lot of money on the scenery by Loutherbourg and dressed it well. Mrs. Baddeley played in this, and we are told "looked like an angel and sang the flower song like a syren." This was the wife of Robert Baddeley, the pastry-cook actor. That she looked like an angel is true, but there the resemblance ended. That she sang like a syren is true also, and there the resemblance continued. For this good lady was a thoroughly bad lot, and flagrantly faithless to her husband. He got accustomed to her lapses and used them to get himself a bit of publicity, of which he was very fond. He would always challenge his rivals and prepare to fight a duel. On one occasion he challenged George Garrick, and the two men met at dawn in Hyde Park. As their swords crossed, Mrs. Baddeley dashed from some adjoining bushes and threw herself between them. Thus interrupted, explanations took the place of bloodshed, and there were mutual reconciliations. The whole affair would get into the public prints coupled with the name of Baddeley, which suited both of them.

Mrs. Baddeley sang much at Vauxhall as well as at Drury Lane, and had numerous admirers, many of them of title. On one of the many reopenings of the Pantheon, she was told that if she tried to get in she would not be admitted. She told her " boy friends " about this, and fifty of the smartest and most notable men about town, coming from the most exclusive clubs, escorted her sedan chair through the streets. On arrival at the Pantheon, they drew their swords and forced admission for her. More, they compelled the two society hostesses—both duchesses—to receive her, and she passed in under a canopy of crossed, glittering blades. News of this was taken back to Drury Lane, where there was much rejoicing.

Then on 10th December, Sheridan staged " Romeo and Juliet," Juliet being " a young gentlewoman making her first appearance on the stage." Her name was Mrs. Robinson, and she was the wife of a man who had been a friend of Sheridan's at Harrow. Now we find that Garrick, although right out of Drury Lane, could not keep away and would come down to see how Sheridan was getting on, and lend a hand. The great actor rehearsed this young lady himself, and took the most unremitting pains over it all, playing Romeo at rehearsals until he was worn out. The " Romeo " of the actual performance was William Brereton. On the night, Sheridan stood in the wings to encourage Mrs. Robinson, and Garrick sat in the orchestra to watch events. One wonders if this allayed the young lady's very reasonable nervousness. The house was brilliant, and according to the lady herself, " there were peals of clamorous approbations." The " pros " in the company probably murmured about " friends in front."

On December 11th, Sheridan presented " Semiramis," a poor sort of tragedy by Ayscough. This play must not be laid at Sheridan's door; it was one he took over from Garrick, who had been coerced into buying it. He did " Love for Love " and also " The Way of the World," taking out some of their salacity. But he had not yet got the knack of management; his presentation and his casting were definitely faulty.

Garrick's advice to Sheridan was to write some more plays, so the new manager set to work. But he did not call upon his own inventive wit to any great extent. He re-wrote " The Relapse," Sir John Vanbrugh's old success, and called it " A Trip to Scarborough." At first the

The Drinking Fountain in memory of Sir Augustus Harris, erected in the front of the theatre by public subscription out of gratitude from playgoers.

Portion of the Rotunda at Theatre Royal, Drury Lane, showing statues of GARRICK (*left*),

audience rejected it. It was not pure Sheridan. They wanted some more plays like "The Rivals" or "The Duenna."

All these semi-successes and failures upset Linley, but Sheridan kept on encouraging him. If only Sheridan had been as good a man of action and business as he was of words! Anyway, he was working hard now, in his own happy-go-lucky, slipshod manner, in fits and starts. He was writing a new play. It was growing in his head, it was being committed to paper, it was being altered and re-altered, and polished all the while. It was awaited with anxiety by the players, by Garrick, who was worried about the state of his beloved theatre, and above all by Sheridan's partners. For something big was wanted in the way of success to counteract the bad management which had already resulted in many of the actors "subbing" their salaries and getting heavily into debt.

The three leading ladies continued to be perpetually troublesome. Let us take a glimpse at one of them, that Mrs. Robinson who had played "Juliet," and whom Garrick had rehearsed with such care because her voice reminded him of Mrs. Cibber's. Her maiden name was Darby, and she was a native of Bristol. Her father dissipated his fortune, also a legacy of hers, in an attempt to civilise the Esquimaux, surely one of the most hair-brained schemes ever embarked upon.

She played on after her success and became a leading lady. Her stage career was destined to be short but glorious. Such grace and beauty had not been seen since Woffington first appeared. The critics praised her, the gilded youth besieged her with offerings and protestations of love, and even the Drury Lane company admitted her wonderful taste in dress. There came a night when she was to bring Romance, and Royal Romance, into Drury Lane Theatre. On 3rd December, 1779, there was a Royal Command for "A Winter's Tale." Robinson, who was to play "Perdita," entered the Green Room amidst a murmur of admiration, so lovely did she look. "You will make a conquest of the Prince to-night," laughed Gentleman Smith, "I never saw you look more lovely."

The Royal Family were in the box, the King, the Queen, the Prince, all of them. "Perdita" made her entrance, and a hum of admiration went round the house. The young Prince leant forward, spellbound . . . A letter came to her that night, the first of many, a letter of impassioned love signed " Florizel." It was brought, as were its numerous successors, by the Earl of Essex, who wooed her passionately by proxy for the man who signed himself " Florizel" and who was the Prince of Wales. He gave her the Prince's portrait and a heart made of paper which bore two inscriptions, one in French, for the sake of romance, " Je ne change qu'en mourant " and the other in English " Unalterable to my Perdita through life."

No wonder the young woman was flattered. She had shown her mettle by sticking to her husband when he was a prisoner for debt, and he was repaying it by spending her salary which he drew himself from the treasury at Drury Lane. No wonder she listened to what she afterwards described as a " magic of wooing she could never forget." She met her Royal lover secretly, in a boat moored off Kew. The wooing culminated by moonlight in Kew Gardens.

" Perdita " was true and helpful to the Prince. He swore his affection would overcome the grave and that his generosity would exceed even that. Poor Perdita, she put her trust in Princes as so many have done. He gave her a bond for £20,000 in earnest of what was to be hers, and to be payable on his attaining his majority. That majority came, but no £20,000. For when he reached man's estate, he discovered that his love had passed with his minority. He repudiated his bond, he repudiated the lady, he cut her dead in the Park, and when she hurled an insult at him, affected not to hear. She was abandoned—her little hour of romance finished. To the credit of Charles James Fox, the great Whig, it must be recorded that he got her a pension of £300 for life—but the money came out of the pockets of the taxpayers and not her Royal lover's. She thought of returning to the stage, but was dissuaded. A wave of morality was passing over the country, and the reaction of the public could not be foretold. Her stage career had lasted only four years.

At the Lane things were going badly once more. Gone was the strict discipline of Garrick, gone was his severe example, for although he was about the house, he had no power. Weston was to have a benefit. He owed the management so much that they informed him they would repay themselves out of the takings. He refused to appear, indeed he said he could not, because he had been arrested. He asked that no falsehood should be told about ill-health, but the stark truth, so that everyone should know. A perfectly fair and straightforward apology was made from the stage, but the artful actor was in the upper gallery sitting with the bailiff who was in charge of him, and angry that his money was to be impounded, rose to his feet and announced that it was all untrue. He was in the house and ready to appear. There was a riot lasting an hour, and then he was allowed to play, and the management had to pay the bailiff. This kind of incident shows the conditions ruling at that time. Something big was wanted at Drury Lane, urgently and at once. As always in the famous playhouse, that something was to turn up.

Whilst playing revivals at night, the company were rehearsing a new play by day, rehearsing under difficulties, for they were getting the play page by page, with long and increasing intervals, from the brilliant but unreliable manager-author, Richard Brinsley Sheridan. He was working, but in fits and starts, as the fancy took him. Yet what they had got was so good, and promised such a triumph, that they worked hard and hoped on. Again Garrick came to the rescue. He read the play as it came haltingly from the pen of its erratic author. He undertook the supervision of rehearsals, what we should now call the " production." Down on the stage, there were frequent stoppages because there was no more to learn; messages of entreaty, of sarcasm, of abuse, went up to Sheridan by the prompter from Miss Pope, Mrs. Abington, and the rest of them.

But Sheridan had envisaged a perfect cast for his idea, and was writing each part for the right person and in the manner they could best perform it. He was determined on success. He would not, or could not hurry. Meanwhile confusion and unrest grew. At last one day, with the prompter Hopkins standing at his elbow in his big room at Drury Lane (in spite of fire and rebuilding, it is still there, and his portrait gazes down from over the huge fireplace) he scribbled the last dashing lines, leaned back with a sigh of relief, and then penned a few more words as afterthought. They were:

" Finished at last, Thank God. R.B.S."

He handed the pages to Hopkins, who hurried downstairs, read them through, and added a P.S. in his own handwriting,—" Amen."

" The School for Scandal " was finished. Now it had

to be produced. Sheridan, and probably Garrick with him,
had given it a wonderful cast:

Sir Peter Teazle	Mr. King
Sir Oliver Surface	Mr. Yates
Joseph Surface	Mr. Palmer
Charles	Mr. Smith
Crabtree	Mr. Parsons
Sir Benjamin Backbite	Mr. Dodd
Rowley	Mr. Aickin
Moses	Mr. Baddeley
Trip	Mr. Lamash
Snake	Mr. Packer
Careless	Mr. Farren
Sir Harry Bumper	Mr. Cawdry
Lady Teazle	Mrs. Abington
Maria	Miss P. Hopkins
Lady Sneerwell	Miss Sherry
Mrs. Candour	Miss Pope

It was shown on the stage of Drury Lane Theatre, on
8th May, 1777, this play written especially for that playhouse and the pick of the company.

The whole thing glittered and shone as a work of art,
a perfect jewel of a play. Of its success there is little need
to speak. It has become a world classic. It ran for twenty
nights on its first production; it held the stage of Drury
Lane three nights a week for several years; it brought to
the box office nearly twice as much as any other play
had ever done. It was a supreme example of team work,
and of an author understanding and writing for his cast.
For Palmer had the very manner of " Joseph " in his private
life, Gentleman Smith had been in trouble at Eton and
King's College, Cambridge for over indulgence in festivities
and matters of ill-balanced finance, King was the fine old
gentleman in his own person and very like Sir Peter, Miss
Pope was the real " Mrs. Candour " of the Green Room,
and Mrs. Abington had the brilliant caprice and tantalising
manner of Lady Teazle. Right down the bill each of them
was fitted like a glove, even to Lamash, who played "Trip"
and was in reality just as much of a gentleman as a Gentlemen's gentleman could ever hope to be. The bluffness of
Sir Oliver was the bluffness of Yates.

It was a perfect play, perfectly played by a perfect
cast. This greatest of all original plays ever performed at
Drury Lane, came at the moment when it was most needed.
Garrick had polished the jewel until it blazed with lustre,
and the bedazzled and excited audience cheered it again and

again. "The School for Scandal" was a landmark in Old Drury's progress. It was also the beginning of a new school of dramatic thought.

Had there been a press representative at Drury Lane in those days, how he would have rejoiced at sending out the paragraph which appeared in a newspaper:—

"Yesterday morning Mrs. Sheridan was delivered of a son. In the evening of the same day, Mr. Sheridan's muse was delivered of a bantling which is likely to live for ever."

And whilst we linger on "The School for Scandal," we may recall the story of Robert Baddeley. He has already made his bow. He shone as a good actor, and on that night in 1777 he put the finishing touch on his career with a fine performance of "Moses." Thereafter he always played it whenever "The School for Scandal" was performed. He was on the Committee of the Drury Lane Fund, and was held in deep respect in the theatre, this ex-pastry cook who had proved that he could create a part as well as he could mix a cake. Above all he loved the theatre in which he played, in which he was one of His Majesty's Servants. He always wore the Royal Livery off the stage, and was indeed the last actor to do so. One night in 1794, making up in his dressing room for the part of "Moses" he was stricken down with sudden illness. He was carried to his nearby lodgings but died the same night.

And then his will was found. It was a lengthy document, but it proved him a man of property and it testified to his adoration of Drury Lane Theatre. He directed that his house at East Molesey should be used as a home for old actors in connection with the Fund — the house was finally merged into the Fund's property. He also directed that certain trees on his little estate should be cut down and the timber used somewhere in his beloved theatre. That, too, was done, and the timber survived the Fire and the rebuilding and is there to this day. And he did something more. He left the sum of £100 in trust, invested in 3 per cent. funds. The interest was to be used for making and baking a cake to be eaten in Drury Lane Theatre every Twelfth Night by the company of His Majesty's Comedians appearing there, so that his memory, in Shakespeare's words, should be kept fresh and lasting.

And this unique custom, peculiar to Drury Lane alone in the world's theatres, is still observed. It has been faithfully carried out every Twelfth Night since 1794, except for eight years. Two of these occurred during the last war, owing to sugar shortage, and the custom has been in abeyance since 1939, (the last time the Baddeley Cake was cut), because since then, owing to the occupation of ENSA, there has been no Company of His Majesty's Comedians to carry out the old actor's bequest.

CHAPTER 24

TRIUMPH OF MRS. SIDDONS

BUT whilst Drury Lane had been basking in the glory of "The School for Scandal," a new star had risen in the theatrical firmament, a man whom only a few years previously that great theatre had spurned and cast out without even the courtesy of a proper trial. This star was John Henderson, considered by all who saw him to be, in acting, the true successor to David Garrick.

He was born in Goldsmith Street, Cheapside, of an Irish factor of Scottish descent, who died within a year of the boy's birth. His mother, whom he adored all of his life, took her sons to Newport Pagnell, and brought them up well on almost no money at all. She taught them to read and inspired in them a taste for literature. Young John's marvellous memory showed at once, and he soon had long speeches—nay, whole pages—of Shakespeare by heart.

He was always stage-struck, and decided early to become an actor. At a performance in a barn in Islington he gave so wonderful an impersonation of Garrick that the audience remarked it was either the great actor himself or "Antichrist." That mimicry of Henderson was destined to lead him into trouble. He followed up his impersonations of Garrick by trying to obtain a job at Drury Lane from the Patentee. He got no further than one of the lieutenants of the actor, who produced a foot rule, solemnly measured him and told him he was an inch and a quarter too short to become an actor. This from an employee of little Garrick was pretty good.

Everywhere Henderson went he met rebuffs, but although he was fighting and beating consumption, he struggled on. At last the august star of Drury Lane granted him an audition, listened fairly, told him his voice was neither good nor strong enough for Drury Lane, but gave him a letter to Palmer, the manager of the Bath Theatre. There he got his chance and took it. He was called the Bath Roscius, and although very grateful to Garrick, he could not resist gaining applause by giving public imitations of him, which were so good that they reached the ears of the mighty man and displeased him seriously. At length, when Foote had left the Haymarket to die, George Colman, its new manager and Garrick's friend, gave Henderson his long-desired London opportunity. He played Shylock and was an immediate success. Old Macklin came to see him and complimented him. This was in 1777. Garrick, who had just retired, came too, but all he would say was that he thought the actor who played Tubal was very good, a most deadly snub for Henderson's ill-timed imitations.

But by now he was acclaimed, and in the winter of 1778, when an attraction was badly needed at Drury Lane, Sheridan at last engaged Henderson to play in the theatre of his ambitions. He was to have £10 a week and a benefit. But old Palmer of Bath had a contract and was for calling Henderson back there. So highly did Sheridan esteem the new actor that he gave Palmer the Bath rights of " The School for Scandal," a very considerable solatium indeed for the release of Henderson. For two years he was the star of Drury Lane.

In the Lent of 1785, whilst the theatres were closed, Sheridan wanted to make some money, which he always needed so sorely, and which he always squandered so readily. He suggested to Henderson that they gave public readings at the Freemasons' Hall. Henderson had come across a poem which was a drug on the market. He read it and made it; for so vivid was his reading that the public flocked to buy the poem of " John Gilpin," and one bookseller sold 6,000 copies that had collected the dust for years. Henderson and Sheridan made a profit of £800 by these readings.

But despite the triumph of " The School of Scandal," the takings at Drury Lane could not compete with the expenses. On July 13, 1777, Garrick wrote to King: " Poor old Drury, it will, I fear, soon be in the hands of the Philistines." Sheridan had, however, bought out Lacy, if indeed the money really passed, only to find that Garrick had a mortgage on Lacy's moiety of the Patent, and expected the interest due.

On 6th May the theatre treasurer, Benjamin Victor, wrote to him to say that "I am directed by the proprietors to inform you that it will not be in their power to pay the interest on Mr. Lacy's mortgage until the debts and expenses of the theatre are discharged." Garrick replied, very rightly, that this interest was as just a debt and expense as any other, and told them he should expect the interest and eventually the redemption of the mortgage or they must suffer penalty, but he also wrote to Lacy to say he would do nothing to embarrass him. Now Lacy had just sold out, the price being £45,000, so Sheridan now held one half, whilst Linley and Ford had a quarter each. In 1778 the Patentees persuaded Sheridan's father to take charge of the stage. But the son, now master, would never let his father act, and a deep bitterness grew between them.

Sheridan was now writing again. He delivered himself of a satirical comedy called "The Camp," with songs and music. This ridiculed the big camp which had been opened at Coxheath in Kent the previous June, when there was fear of a French invasion. This was an ill-fated play, for Garrick, attending a rehearsal of it (it was produced in November, 1778), caught a bad cold. That rehearsal was his last visit to his old home. His cold got worse, he became seriously ill, and on 20th January, 1779, he died. He was buried with much ceremony in Westminster Abbey. Sheridan, his friend and successor to the Drury Lane patent, was chief mourner, for Garrick had no children.

Sheridan now had to bestir himself. Things were bad. He started to write again, but owing to his leisurely methods, all the hold-ups and delays of "The School for Scandal" repeated themselves. Bit by bit the script dribbled down to the anxious company, and two days before the advertised date, the last scene had not even been written. King and Linley resorted to strategy. They lured the errant author down to the theatre (he was supposed to be writing at home), they got him in the Green Room, gave him pens, paper and ink and the prompter's copy of the play as far as it went: and they left him two bottles of claret and some anchovy sandwiches, and then locked him in. They called through the door that he was to finish the wine, and the farce, before they would let him out. The joke of it appealed to Sheridan, and he finished all three—the wine, the sandwiches and " The Critic."

It is possible that this play was written to pay out the

rival playwright, Cumberland, who was also a critic, for his bad behaviour at the first performance of "The School for Scandal," when he reproved his children for laughing, telling them there was nothing to laugh at whatsoever. This was duly reported to Sheridan, whose reply was characteristic. "Devilish ungrateful, that, for I sat out his play last week and laughed the whole time." As Cumberland was a writer of tragedy, the satire is barbed. "The Critic" was Sheridan's last play of note; the rest of his contributions were of no great interest.

But Sheridan ably kept up Drury Lane's tradition of pantomime. In 1779 he had revived "Harlequin Fortunatus" or "The Wishing Cap" (and here it may be pointed out that at this time and for many years afterwards the title of every pantomime was prefixed by the word "Harlequin"). He put in a new interlude, straight out of dispatches from the Spanish war, showing a scene where a British Tar, having scaled the wall of the enemy's fort, and having, for some reason best known to himself, two cutlasses in his possession, gallantly presents one of them to a Spanish officer whom he encounters, scorning to slay an unarmed man. Needless to say, in the ensuing contest, he beat the Spaniard and spared his life. This was the sort of thing the public liked then. At the last rehearsal it was found that no time had been allowed for the stage hands to change an elaborate scene. Sheridan at once sat down at the prompter's table and then and there wrote a song to fill in the gap. Called "The Midnight Watch," and set to music by father-in-law Linley, it passed into the national repertory.

In 1781 he wrote a pantomime himself, the subject being "Robinson Crusoe." It seems to have been very rambling and incoherent, but it is notable because it gave rise to the legend, the truth of which is still in doubt, that at the first performance Richard Brinsley Sheridan himself played "Harlequin Friday." If so, it was a remarkable thing, but quite in keeping with the mercurial genius who had by that time become Member of Parliament for Stafford. To play a leading and active part at two such places of national entertainment as The House of Commons and Theatre Royal, Drury Lane, might be a labour of Hercules for any man! Something, it would seem, would have to go. We do not know what his stage performances were like (if indeed he did play Man Friday), but his performances at Westminster belong to British history.

Once again something with terrible impact was wanted at Drury Lane. And once again that something was rapidly approaching. This time it was an actress. It was a woman who had been there before and had failed—Mrs. Sarah Siddons.

There were rumours of her coming in the very early autumn of 1782. She had now got what she wanted—experience of a better kind than she had possessed at her last visit. And she was the possessor of a great provincial reputation based on a long series of triumphs.

Sarah Siddons had worked hard and well. She had one steadfast ambition always before her—to conquer London and to win where she had lost her first battle, on the stage at Drury Lane. So when she got a note from Sheridan, whilst she was playing at Bath, to revisit the great theatre, she wrote: "That was to me a triumphant moment." Perhaps she remembered that it was at Bath, too, where Anne Oldfield, then despised at Drury Lane, had her great moment of triumph, and as a sequel returned to be Queen of the Theatre. Henderson was another who had gone from there to don Garrick's shed mantle of Old Drury. She had precedent enough to make her spirits rise. And she had spirit enough of her own, too.

The Drury Lane bills announced that "Mrs. Siddons from the Theatre Royal, Bath, would shortly make her appearance in this theatre in a capital character in Tragedy." The actress and her family came up to town, and took lodgings at 149 Strand.

She had absolutely paralysed provincial audiences as "Isabella" in "The Fatal Marriage." Sheridan urged her to play this, and after consideration she consented. She was duly billed to appear on 10th October, 1782.

When she got on the stage at rehearsal she was in a state of panic. She had been told her voice was too loud and piercing, so she held herself in. But gradually, as the play took hold of her and the actress triumphed over the woman, she began to let herself go. As the play went on, she herself observed that many of the company were in tears.

She awoke enthusiasm in old Tom King, who had reported badly on her but who was now manager for Sheridan. So realistic was she in the deathbed scene that her own little eight-year-old son Henry, who was playing himself in the play as her little son, was so deceived by her realism that he thought his mother had really passed away and howled the place down until she finished the scene and comforted him.

On the night of the production, almost in a trance she went into the wings, passing her father on the way. He was trembling with agitation. Her cue was spoken and Mrs. Siddons stepped on to the stage of Theatre Royal, Drury Lane—the real Mrs. Siddons this time. She faced her audience, she forgot to be Mrs. Siddons and became "Isabella." That first appearance of hers was comparable only to those of Garrick and, later, to Kean.

She made such a deep impression on the packed house that the audience "were nearly drowned in tears." One emotional woman tried to repress her feelings and drove herself into convulsions. In "The Fatal Marriage," that play of undiluted grief, and innocence betrayed, Mrs. Siddons took all the many chances it gave her, and played upon her audience as a great pianist does on his keyboard. She was brilliantly supported by Gentleman Smith, Palmer, Farmer and Wrighton. Long before the final scene there was frenzied applause. When the final curtain fell the ovation was unprecedented. Mrs. Siddons was too overcome to speak the epilogue. She could only bow to the storm of cheers.

Her family were naturally all agog to see the papers. The critics had gone to the Lane that night very much on their guard, for there had been a lot of advance publicity about Mrs. Siddons—much more, indeed, than was usual at that time. This was the work of her husband. The more experienced and careful father had been dead against it. He knew what preliminary over-praise could do. But they need not have worried. She who had received only one Press notice on her previous appearance at Drury Lane, in which she was described as "lamentable," now received columns of approbation. The "Morning Chronicle" and "The Morning Post," the two great papers, spread themselves about her. The latter, indeed, rated her above Mrs. Cibber, and its critic ended by saying: "The late hour prevents us from dwelling on the merits of this accomplished woman, who beyond all comparison is the first tragic actress now on the English stage." There was only one dissentient voice in the whole of London, that of Horace Walpole, who loved to be in a noisy minority, and would decry anything the majority praised.

At that time Sarah's salary was ten guineas a week. She was in the prime of her life and at the height of her classical beauty. Even off the stage she caused people to stare at her, so great was her personality, so striking her appearance. On the stage her movements were perfection, even her stage "falls" were miracles of the right way to do it. She was news—unwittingly she set fashions. At her first benefit, which was a great occasion, she received amongst other things a purse of one hundred guineas, subscribed by one hundred gentlemen of the Bar of England.

She played "Euphrasia" in "The Grecian Daughter" on 30th October. She herself had inclined to this part for her début. It was not such a good play as "The Fatal Marriage" and up to then had been the great vehicle for a tragedienne called Mrs. Crawford. But when Sarah Siddons rushed on the stage with her eyes shooting fire, and her veil streaming behind her and in a great speech stirred on the Greeks to war, veteran playgoers forgot their old heroine and all beholders had a new memory to cherish. Her climax that season was "Jane Shore." She transcended all her previous efforts, and the death scene when Jane expires from starvation caused hardened men playgoers to weep unashamedly, while women in faints were found in every part of the house.

Meanwhile, Mrs. Yates had left Drury Lane and was the Garden's counter-attraction. Once again the rivalry between the two theatres was aflame. Yates had played "Calista" in Rowe's old play, "The Fair Penitent." So Mrs. Siddons played "Calista" too. It revolutionised the play, which took on new glories from her acting. She had driven the fame of Mrs. Cibber, Mrs. Crawford, Mrs. Yates, and Peg Woffington into minor places. Drury Lane was itself again, it was once more the home of great acting, its vast auditorium was packed each night.

But the greatest event of the season was still to come— the benefit night of the 100 guineas purse. The date was 14th December, 1782, the play "Venice Preserv'd." Mrs. Siddons was "Belvidera." Unprecedented scenes were witnessed. Fights and struggles at the pit entrances caused many casualties. It is a wonder that anyone got into the theatre at all. A modern gallery first-nighter, with his boast of a forty-eight-hour wait, has "nothing on" the pittites of the eighteenth century.

In 1783 the King and Queen came to see Siddons, and

having seen her, they wanted more. She played all her great rôles for them at the Lane. King George III wept heartily, and good Queen Charlotte was so overcome as to be forced to turn away her face. "Farmer George," who considered himself a bit of a judge on theatrical matters, sent for Siddons and told her that although he had tried, he had failed to catch her out in a single wrong emphasis. He contrasted her great repose with the acting of Garrick. "He was a great fidget, he could never stand still," said the King. Mrs. Siddons received a Court post from King George and Queen Charlotte. She was made "Preceptress in English Reading to the Princesses."

CHAPTER 25

COMMAND PERFORMANCE

IF the success of Siddons' first season had been great, the ensuing season was to add even fresh lustre to her reputation. The King and Queen ordered a "Command Performance," and with the Royal Family, attended in state.

The front of the Royal Box was built out for this occasion, so that His Majesty's subjects might have a a chance of feasting their loyal and dazzled eyes on the glory of Royalty. A canopy was extended over the Royal heads. It had a dome of crimson velvet, adorned with carved and gilded decorations, and the draping valances were also enriched with cords of gold. Its furniture was almost overpowering in its regal splendour. The Monarch had determined to show his people what he could do when he wished, and for one to whom he wished well. He himself wore a plain quaker coloured suit, although it had gold buttons; but the Queen literally gleamed in white satin and diamonds. One Princess wore a blue and white and the other a rose and white dress of figured silk. They had a canopy of their own, of blue satin. His Royal Highness the Prince of Wales, (to be the First Gentleman in Europe and the very form and mould of fashion and "nobility") sat in solitary state under a canopy of blue velvet trimmed with silver and put his plainly attired father quite in the

205

shade by sporting a suit of dark blue Geneva velvet smothered in gold lace. That is how Royalty went to the show when the show was Siddons.

Mrs. Siddons had avoided Shakespeare in her first Drury Lane season, but now she had confidence enough to take the plunge. She startled the town with her " Isabella " in " Measure for Measure."

Soon after, like all eminent people of her time, especially the servants of Drury Lane, she paid a call on Dr. Johnson. He was short of chairs and there was nowhere for the Queen of Tragedy to sit. Was the Doctor put about? No, his greatness shone at once. " Madam," he said, " you who so often occasion a want of seats to other people will the more readily excuse the want of one yourself."

Siddons had got her brother, John Philip Kemble, engaged for Drury Lane. He made his first appearance with his sister in an old favourite, " The Gamester." It was another triumph for " Sarah." As " Mrs. Beverley," her sacrifices plunged the house into tears, and nobody cried harder than the Prince of Wales and the Duke of Cumberland. One old playgoer was so upset and overcome that he could not bring himself to listen any longer, but watched the rest of the play through the glass panels of the box. She so played upon the feelings of her audience that they were roused to anger against poor Palmer who played the villain. Villains gloried in being hissed, but this was real hatred and he retired hastily.

Kemble was allowed to " play himself in," which he did as " Hamlet." His moody Dane had not the genius of Garrick's, nor the mystic spell of Kean's, but Kemble, who had not yet assumed the mannerisms which later did so much to spoil him, acquitted himself very well. He had a noble appearance and he wore his clothes with grace. But he only occasioned any excitement when he appeared with his sister.

It was Sarah they wanted to see. The King commanded " King John," with Kemble as the King and Sarah as " Constance." When she was not on the stage the thing missed fire. Whilst she was there, tragedy stalked the stage with wild, unruly locks and black velvet. Such was the dominance of Sarah Siddons at Theatre Royal. But very naturally the comedians, who felt slighted, began to whisper and complain.

Covent Garden, down in the dumps because of the success of the great actress at the Lane, now threw down a challenge. They put up Mrs. Crawford, whom Mrs. Siddons had already routed, to oust the newcomer. It was the old tragedienne against the new. Mrs. Crawford had been Mrs. Dancer, and then Mrs. Spranger Barry. She was now an old woman and it was on her name and the memory of her greatness that her backers staked their fortunes. The old war-horse sniffed the air and gave battle. Her husband had challenged Garrick in the same way on the same stage, and although beaten, had put up a good fight in " Romeo." She might do better. So "Douglas " was staged and she played " Lady Randolph," one of her best parts. The gauntlet was thrown down with a flourish. Mrs. Siddons picked it up. She played "' Lady Randolph " at Drury Lane, and outshone poor old Mrs. Crawford like the sun outshines a candlelight.

The history of Drury Lane at this time is manifestly the history of Siddons. When the Lane was closed she went to Ireland and played there. Here she found trouble. An actor called Daly had a grudge against her. Never strong, she fell ill, (she was taking no rest) and he spread the tale that she was shamming. She had barely recovered when an old scoundrel of an actor—but a popular scoundrel— one Digges, had a paralytic stroke. A benefit was arranged. He asked Mrs. Siddons to play. She had only one spare night and that was promised to the Imprisoned Debtors whom she had disappointed on her previous visit. Daly was the emissary, and he told Digges that Siddons had refused point blank. He put the story all over the town. But Siddons had done nothing of the kind. She made a night possible somehow, but when she came to play, found nothing but a handful of third-rate actors, and the whole show was a bad flop. Siddons' fame had brought her enemies, and the story spread like wild-fire. It got into the London papers. She reappeared at the Lane on 5th October, 1784, and the moment she went on the stage there was a demonstration. They booed and hissed, they shouted the dreaded "Off, off, off." She faced the angry crowd and tried to get a hearing. Unable either to play or speak, she stood until Kemble led her off. Once in the wings, she fainted. On the stage, they continued the play. Sheridan, Kemble, her husband, all helped to revive her and encourage her. On returning to consciousness one thing only was

207

clear to her. London had refused her once, now it had done so again. She would leave it for ever. But the three men argued and strove with her until the curtain fell on the first act. In the interval, they prevailed. She had courage enough and would fight it out. She went on the stage and they took up the curtain.

There stood Sarah Siddons alone, gazing at the audience in the theatre which meant so much to her. Taken by surprise, the audience stared back at her in silence. They, actress and audience, gazed long at each other. Then she spoke. It was an impromptu speech and like all real impromptu worth all the carefully prepared orations in the world.

These are the words she spoke:

"Ladies and Gentlemen, the kind and flattering partiality which I have uniformly experienced in this place would make the present interruption distressing to me indeed were I, in the slightest degree, conscious of having deserved your censure. I feel no such consciousness. The stories which have been circulated against me are calumnies. When they shall be proved true my aspersors will be justified. But, till then, my respect for the public leads me to be confident that I shall be protected from unmerited insult."

This short speech went home. One can guess how she dwelt on the words "calumnies" and "aspersors" in the true Siddons manner. The house swung over and although a small contingent refused to be quiet, the majority were for Siddons again.

Continuing her career of smashing the old idols, she played "Margaret of Anjou," the famous part of Mrs. Yates, in "The Earl of Warwick," so much better than the older actress that Mrs. Yates was routed like the rest, and she was a very good actress indeed.

About this time Sheridan was getting into deeper and deeper water. He was spending the money which Siddons drew in, and giving hardly any time to his wonderful theatre. He was in debt all round. But the danger sign and the storm signal were not yet on the mast. Indeed, he had found another star—Dorothy Jordan,—who made her first appearance at Drury Lane in 1785.

Jordan had put about a history of herself as being the granddaughter of a dignitary of the Welsh Church, while her father was an Army Colonel. She wove a most romantic tale, but it is much more probable that her mother, Grace Phillips, was an actress at the Smock Alley Theatre,

Dublin, and her father perhaps a stage hand. Dorothy Jordan herself was born in Waterford. She graduated to the stage from a milliner's shop. That same Daly who had made trouble for Mrs. Siddons was running the theatre. He was a theatrical manager of the kind often pictured in novels but seldom encountered in real life. He used to lend small sums to small part actresses and then make them live with him. He tried this on with Mistress Dorothy, but she would not look at him. Then, determined to have his way, he abducted her to a lonely house and raped her. It was a colourful story, and she told it well. At any rate, she had a child by him and then, with her mother, brother and sister she ran away to England. At Leeds they met Tate Wilkinson, now of some importance. She asked him for a job. He in turn asked her whether she could play tragedy, comedy or farce. Her answer was " all of them." He gave her a job. The year was 1782 and she was twenty. Wilkinson took the risk. Financially, it was not a great one, for he paid her fifteen shillings a week. She played in a tragedy and then, afterwards, would sing a lively song. She succeeded in both. She now called herself Mrs. Jordan; her condition demanded the matrimonial prefix.

Wilkinson took her to Cornelius Swan of York, for her education to be completed before she tried London. Swan found he had little or nothing to teach her. " Gentleman " Smith, on holiday at York Races, saw her play and sent in a good report. She had an offer from the Lane of £4 per week, and accepted it.

After a poor start due to nervousness, she soon found her feet and pleased everybody, audience, critics and management alike. She got a rise, and in her first season, that of 1785, she became a leading lady (and with Mrs. Siddons there, too), and in receipt of a salary of £12 a week and two benefits. The Bar which had given Mrs. Siddons One Hundred Guineas, was outdone by the gentlemen of Brooks's Club who sent Dorothy Jordan a purse of Three Hundred Guineas.

She grew steadily in favour and popularity, playing all sorts of comedy, including the famous " Sir Harry Wildair " in breeches. She was also excellent in Shakespeare. Lamb speaks of her wonderful " Viola." Hazlitt praises her and Genest says she " had the best leg ever seen on the stage." Yet she was by no means a raging beauty. It was verve and charm that got her to the top.

Even Mrs. Siddons was very much aware of her. In a letter she says: "We have a great comic actress now, called Mrs. Jordan. She has a vast deal of merit but to my mind, is not perfection." But on the stage they were not rivals. Their lines were different. They came into competition once only, when both played "Rosalind." On that occasion the victory was not Mrs. Siddons'.

She reached the height of her beauty and fame in 1790. Then Royal romance once again breathed o'er Theatre Royal. The Duke of Clarence had begun to take notice of Dorothy Jordan and soon she became his mistress. He was made Ranger of Bushey Park, and there she lived with him in the intervals of playing at Drury Lane and bearing her Royal lover his children, who were named Fitzclarence. There were ten of them.

One little cloud had drifted across the princely romance. Old King George expressed himself shocked when he heard of his son's mistress, and still more horrified when that young hopeful told his Royal father that he was allowing the actress £1,000 a year. "What, what, what?" gasped the Farmer King, "it's too much, too much. Give her five hundred." The Duke told his beloved about this, and the story goes that she fetched a playbill and drew his attention to the notice: "No Money Returned After the Rising of the Curtain." She was not called "The Little Pickle" for nothing.

But like many Royal Romances of its kind, it was not to endure. When it became apparent that George IV would have no heir, the Duke of Clarence was groomed for the throne, which he afterwards ascended as William IV. So there must be an end of scandals and Mrs. Jordan must go. The children had been provided for. The elder became the Earl of Munster. All got good jobs around the Court. Mrs. Jordan was retired to France, where she died, at St. Cloud.

Harriet Mellon who had understudied Mrs. Jordan at the Lane left the theatre to marry Thomas Coutts, the banker. She inherited his money and later married the Duke of St. Albans.

But now the spotlight swings back from the lesser though brilliant stars to the great Siddons herself.

She was now meditating the part of "Lady Macbeth," studying it with the greatest care and concentration. She knew what it meant, she knew what she was up against, —that the greatest obstacle in her path was tradition. She must live down the memory of Mrs. Pritchard, up to then the supreme "Lady Macbeth," and whose business in the part and whose inflexions as well, were taken as the standard. But it was in Mrs. Siddons' mind that she might create a tradition of her own.

She decided to take the plunge and play the part, which she fixed for her benefit on February 2nd 1785. As always before playing a great part she remained in complete solitude, in her dressing room. But Sheridan came in and broke the train of her thoughts as she was trying, as she always did, to project herself into the character she was about to act. His business, he said, was urgent. He had been told that at rehearsals she had introduced some new business in the sleep-walking scene. He understood she put down the candlestick at the top of the stairs to leave her hands free for the business she had introduced of seeming to wash them. Sarah replied that she considered this absolutely necessary. He told her the public would resent her departing from the Pritchard tradition, but she insisted on taking the risk. They argued until her cue came, but she stuck to her guns. Right through the play she scored and when the disputed scene arrived she had her greatest triumph of all. She put down the candlestick as she had said she would, and when she went through the hand-washing business she had the audience entranced. She had added Mrs. Pritchard to her collection of scalps and had become the greatest "Lady Macbeth" of all time. Characteristically Sheridan was the first to congratulate her. Her hand-washing tradition remains to-day. No other Siddons has arisen to break it.

Kemble was progressing. He had chosen as wife the widow of Brereton the actor, and daughter of the old prompter Hopkins—a woman of the theatre indeed. There was no glamorous honeymoon for them. They had dinner at the Bannisters' house in Frith Street, Soho, and then the bride went back to the Lane to play. Kemble had the evening off but he called for her after the show and took her to their new home in Caroline Street, Bedford Square. They were very happy.

But things were getting worse with Sheridan. He would never give anyone proper authority to act for him, and he expected them to know what he was thinking without being told. In 1785, he took to having many consultations with his old friend King. The upshot was a new pantomime and a new opera. They commissioned Cobb to write the latter. Sheridan had high hopes of the pantomime, in which two Harlequins were to appear, one speaking and one dumb. He began to tinker with General Burgoyne's comedy " The Heiress," and also arranged for a French company to bring over plays by Beaumarchais. The pantomime was called ": Hurly Burly, or The Fairy of the Well." It was an utter flop.

General Burgoyne's play, however, succeeded. Sheridan promised to write an epilogue but forgot all about it. Most people remember Burgoyne for his unfortunate defeats in America, which were no fault of his but of home mismanagement. How many remember that he was a victor as playwright at Drury Lane?

Sheridan was finding the mortgage on the Lane a millstone about his neck. He had got rid of Ford, and taken over his share. He was supreme, but he was neglecting the great playhouse and dabbling at the Opera House in the Haymarket and at the Pantheon. He would soon have to pay dearly.

As to the theatre itself, which was shortly to undergo a great change, Fops Alley had gone, and Garrick had driven the people from the stage. But on a Siddons' night, anything between five hundred to a thousand people, representing box office receipts of about £365, would shove and push and battle outside the pit entrance for an hour before the doors opened. Men used their weight and their fists. Weak men and women went to the wall or underfoot. Pickpockets reaped a rich harvest. Often the force with which those first at the doors were shot into the theatre was so great that many were hurled past the payboxes and so got in for nothing. Seats went to the most muscular of the first comers, and they held them by brute force. The acoustics were bad. Unless the audience was quiet it was difficult to hear the actors and there never was silence save when some great actor or actress compelled it. The gallery were particularly rowdy.

Behind the scenes there was intrigue. The old combination of Sheridan, Linley and Ford had broken up. King, the actor, tried to get hold of Ford's share of the patent but could not raise the money before Sheridan took it over. King had to be content to manage. He had never been pro-Siddons. He pinned his faith to comedy, to Mrs. Jordan, and to Miss Farren, in whom Lord Derby was taking more than a general interest, and King perhaps thought he saw a way there. But Mrs. Siddons was an irresistible force. She knew King did not like her and already she had planted seeds in the mind of Sheridan for his dismissal. Was there not John Philip Kemble ready to do all and more, and much better than the old actor? Sheridan had a chat with Kemble about it. He could not afford to lose Siddons.

So Kemble took over the reins,—or took them over as far as he could. He established discipline, he got law and order. He ran the stage more like Garrick did, and developed team work. He had considerable knowledge and he dressed plays correctly. He threw overboard out-worn traditions, he overhauled the prompt books. Smith retired and Kemble took over the parts he had played. He became Drury Lane's leading man, while his sister was its great star.

But he battled against the tide of Sheridan's excesses. Moreover, a tragedy was impending over the nation. Mrs. Siddons had the first whisper. She had been to Windsor in her official capacity to instruct the Princesses. She met the King who seemed to her to be behaving in an odd way. With a great show of mystery he led her on one side and gave her a blank sheet of paper with his name signed at the bottom. She could make nothing of this and took it to the Queen. It was the first sign of insanity in the King. Every day he grew worse. That was bad for the country and what is bad for the country is bad for theatrical business.

And now Sheridan was faced with another problem: He had to rebuild Drury Lane Theatre.

CHAPTER 26

THE THEATRE REBUILT

OLD DRURY was by now in a shocking state of disrepair. It had stood since 1674, a period of 117 years It had seen Betterton, the Triumvirate, and Garrick, and all who had come between. No doubt the constant tinkering to which Rich had subjected the building had not helped, for t was surveyed and condemned. Sheridan faced this crisis as he had faced others. He decided to go one better and one bigger. He not only conceived grandiose schemes but put them into action. He commissioned Holland to build a new theatre of vast scale of magnificence, with seating accommodation beyond anything previously imagined. Sheridan's was the common managerial mistake of thinking that capacity means everything. What really matters is the capacity of the stage to fill the capacity of the house. The only thing which really counts in any theatre is what happens when the curtain goes up. It is no good having rows of seats you cannot fill.

But Sheridan was nothing if not big. And it is to be feared that Kemble encouraged him. The estimated cost was £150,000, and they began to demolish the old theatre, which had stood so nobly through six reigns. The second Drury Lane was going, the third was arising.

The last play in the old house was " The Country Girl," followed by the farce, " No Song, No Supper." Palmer spoke a farewell address on that night of 4th June, 1791. Orders were given that at least one plank of the old stage should be preserved and incorporated with the new, so that they could still say these were the boards which " Roscius " trod. During the rebuilding, the Drury Lane company played at the Haymarket.

Troubles now came upon Sheridan thick and fast. His wife died, after giving birth to a daughter. It was a terrible blow to him and deprived him of his last prop of stability.

Then it was found that the building estimates were exceeded by £70,000, and this additional sum had to be raised somehow. The ground landlord, the Duke of Bedford, made trouble over the lease. He pointed out that Sheridan did not in fact hold the Charles II Patent, which had been suspended by the malfeasance of Rich; all he had was the licence granted by Queen Anne. So Sheridan had to unearth the document from the people who held it, and buy it back at a considerable price. Actually, it was still in possession of the Rich family. All this cost much money and there was some curious legal procedure. In the end, the Duke gave them a lease, on condition that the Crown guaranteed the existing Patent for a further 21 years, and also that the Duke of Bedford had a private box for himself and his descendants. That box is still there. It has the Bedford arms on its face, and boasts its own private entrance and retiring room; and every night an attendant appointed by

214

the Duke waits there to look after His Grace's family or guests. The box could not be sold for profit by the Duke, nor could the proprietors of Drury Lane have any control over it. A somewhat different arrangement has recently been made with the present holder of the title.

Sheridan raised the money by issuing shares at £100 each, which entitled the holders, amongst other things, to 2s. 6d. per day for every day the theatre was open for performances, and giving the Renter the right of free admission everywhere except behind the scenes. The shares were valid for one hundred years. Sheridan carried on in his slipshod way, creating for himself many difficulties which were, before long, to bring him down.

But the new theatre was ready at last, and a noble playhouse it was indeed. Whilst retaining much of Wren's structural work, Holland had spread himself on height and loftiness. There were four tiers, and the box tiers were made on the lines of an opera house. It was found that the fronts of them were too low. The gallery was so high and far away that its occupants had difficulty in hearing unless the declamation was loud; moreover, the line of sight was very bad. There were eight boxes on the stage itself, and eight " slips " on either side of the pit which were no good at all—in wet weather people hung their coats and hats in them, and these dripped on the pittites below. The boxes held 1,828 people, the pit 800, the 2s. gallery 675, and the upper gallery 308. Its total capacity in people was 3,611, and in money £826 6s.

The exterior was very different from the one we know to-day. To begin with, it fronted Russell Street, and had so many rows of windows that it looked like a barracks. There was a colonnade, and above it a great central block, crowned with a pillar which carried a statue of Apollo with his lyre. The length from east to west was 320 ft.; breadth from north to south 155 ft.; and the width of the roof was 118 ft.

Sheridan thought it was all very fine; and as a piece of architecture of the time, it certainly was. Inside there were many modern features. The builders anticipated the present-day L.C.C. requirements, and had a fire-resisting curtain made of iron.

The opening play, on April 21, 1794, was " Macbeth," with Mrs. Siddons reviving all former thrills, and a very good performance of the Thane from Kemble, with Charles

Kemble as "Malcolm." For the first time the Ghost of Banquo was played invisibly, with much effect, and the setting of the Banqueting Hall aroused the wonder of all beholders. Drury Lane was now going in for lavishness in mounting and spectacle.

But the star attraction of the evening was undoubtedly the fire curtain. Miss Farren had the honour of the opening address and drew attention to this phenomenon. The address was written by Colman, and amongst other things it said:

> " The very ravages of fire we scout
> For we have wherewithal to put it out
> In ample reservoirs our firm reliance
> When streams set conflagrations at defiance."

The iron curtain was then lowered, and someone struck it heavily with a large hammer to show its strength and solidity. Its clangour echoed through the house and aroused the excited audience to enthusiasm. Then it was raised, and the audience were thrilled at the sight of the exhibition of a cascade of water rushing down from tanks with which the roof had been supplied, roaring into a huge basin which had been prepared for its reception; dashing, splashing, tumbling over artificial rocks. Then a man appeared in a boat on the artificial lake and rowed about. The audience could scarcely contain themselves with excitement and approbation. In spite of all this endeavour, the theatre was destined to be burned down a mere fourteen years later.

Sheridan called it his Grand National Theatre, but it was an unlucky house almost from the beginning. With never enough money for his own wants let alone those of other people, Sheridan's finance was dreadful. Peake, the treasurer, was always receiving notes from him to send money at once. Somehow or other he had to get it. There were crises with bankers which Sheridan somehow tided over by bluff and charm. But at the Lane itself it was a sorry spectacle. Kemble put up a great fight, but he had no ammunition. Not even under Rich or Fleetwood had things been worse. From the highest to the lowest, no one was paid. There were constant strikes. Good players would be sacked because they demanded what was justly due to them, and their places were filled with inferior people. On Saturday mornings they would besiege Sheridan's room. "For God's sake, Mr. Sheridan," they would say, "pay us our salaries. For heaven's sake let us have something this week." He would again—if he were there—turn on his charm, faithfully promise them payment, go to the treasury, draw out whatever money there was, slip it in his own pocket and vanish by another door.

The poor actors and staff were penniless. Kemble had to bear the brunt of it all. It got so bad that he resigned and handed his job over to Wrighton, a good actor, but Sheridan blarneyed him back again.

In 1796 a strange thing happened at Drury Lane. On 2nd April of that year, a play was put on which missed what could have been its correct production date by twenty-four hours. This was "Vortigern and Rowena." It had been brought to Sheridan by a lad of nineteen named William Ireland, who claimed that it was a hitherto undiscovered play by William Shakespeare. In reality Ireland, who fancied himself as a poet, and who could get no sort of recognition, forged the whole thing. Yet it bluffed such Shakespearean experts as Malone and Porson. Boswell, at the sight of the manuscript, went down on his knees and kissed it as something sacred. Sheridan and Kemble snatched it up for Drury Lane. Nobody knows if Sheridan was really sincere or not. He was at this time in a pretty fix, and here was a chance of making some money. He was thinking of writing again, and had started talking once more about his play, "The Foresters"—the play which never materialised. Meanwhile, he took "Vortigern." The announcement was a great thrill for all. It was eagerly discussed. Kemble was to play "Vortigern" and Mrs. Jordan "Rowena." As rehearsals progressed, Kemble began to have his doubts.

At its production, the house was packed from floor to ceiling. Kemble played "Vortigern" on true Shakespearean lines, and perhaps this showed up the fraud. But as the play progressed, it became clear to everyone that this was no work of Shakespeare's. The audience realised that, and moment by moment got more and more restless. When Kemble spoke a line in the fifth act, "*And when this solemn mockery is over* . . . ." it was too much for them. They saw to it that it *was* over. There were howls of rage, of disdain, of anger from everybody, and the play died its rightful death. Sheridan had promised to pay Ireland £300 down besides agreeing to his having half the profits for the first sixty performances. Actually Ireland received only £90 in cash. And that was £90 too much.

But here we must pause a moment, for an old friend

has left us. Old Charles Macklin passed away in 1799. He was then said to be 107. He had bade farewell to the stage in February, 1789, at the age of 97, when he tried to play "Shylock," for the last time, at Covent Garden. But the old man's memory had gone, and Mrs. Pope, his "Portia" on that occasion, had a rough passage. Not the least of Macklin's peculiarities was to wash himself all over every night in brandy and then sleep in his clothes. When he died the last link with the great old days was snapped.

But a new source of drama had been found by Sheridan —Germany. In 1798 Sheridan produced "The Stranger, or Misanthropy and Repentance," by Kotzebue. Its theme, the repentance of an adultress, gave rise to violent controversy, but provided one of Mrs. Siddons' greatest rôles. Lawrence went into ecstacies over her as "Mrs. Haller." Immoral or not, the play filled Drury Lane to overflowing at a time when success was badly wanted. "The Castle Spectre," a real piece of clap-trap, also drew big business. But the greatest success of all those adaptations from the German was "Pizarro." So well did Sheridan adapt it that his version was retranslated back into German and played to the disregard of Kotzebus's original script.

Sheridan, by the by, had repeated his tricks of "The School for Scandal" all over again. He delivered the script page by page, keeping the actors waiting because he said it was good for them and kept them on their toes with excitement. A dramatist who died recently, Walter Hackett, adopted the same method and made the same remark. "Pizarro" was a great success, it being said that all London saw it, from the King and Queen to the crossing-sweepers.

In the following year, when the eighteenth century turned into the nineteenth, there was an unrehearsed but exceedingly thrilling drama provided at Theatre Royal, Drury Lane, a drama no less startling than the attempted assassination of King George the Third of blessed memory and length of reign. The theatre had already seen some notable sights. From it a King had carried off a player. In it one actor had murdered another; it had been the scene of riots, duels, arrests. Announcements had been made in it of Royal victories. Bailiffs had been in possession, mistresses chosen by Princes from the ranks of its actresses; highwaymen had swaggered on its stage.

But now Theatre Royal was to see the life of its own master, the reigning monarch, threatened within its own walls. It happened on Thursday, 15th May, 1800. The King had commanded a play, or rather two plays: "She Would and She Wouldn't" and "The Humourist." The house was crowded as it always was when Royalty was present, and there came that sudden hush which falls, as if by instinct, on an auditorium just before the Sovereign enters. Then into the Royal Box came the King. The audience rose as one man and applauded lustily. The King bowed and the applause increased. He bowed his bewigged head again—and above the noise of the clapping and cheering rang the sharp report of a pistol shot.

A shower of plaster flew from the Royal Box, and pieces fell on the Royal wig, which was only just about a foot or fourteen inches from where the bullet had embedded itself in a pillar. It was a very narrow squeak. The King stepped back a pace, and turned a little pale, as well he might, whilst those in his company crowded round him. And down below, in the pit, at the end of the front row farthest from the box and therefore possessing the best view and field of fire, there was a swirl and a struggle. Amid the noise of panting, and scuffling, a torn, breathless figure was flung over the orchestra rail, to be seized and run to the music room below. The play went on. The prisoner and would-be regicide was one James Hadfield, a discharged soldier who had been orderly to the Duke of York himself.

At the trial, the Judge (Lord Kenyon) stopped the case. It was clearly a case of insanity. Hadfield was sent back to Newgate and from there to Bedlam, where he died.

The shooting produced an enormous sensation and much talk. A medal was struck to celebrate the King's escape. The following night " The School for Scandal " was billed for the benefit of the worthy Miss Pope, and one is sure that " Popie," as she was always called, did well out of it. She was playing when the attempted assassination took place.

The success of " Pizarro " brought Kemble back in favour as manager. Pitt said he was the noblest actor he ever saw. There was talk of a partnership between him and Sheridan. Lucky for Kemble he avoided it. For despite the fact that " Pizarro " drew £15,000, the business of the theatre was worse than ever. Peake could not get his hands on a penny for "Treasury Nights." The actors did not know how to live. Sheridan owed Mrs. Siddons so much that her hoped-for retirement looked far off indeed.

Although a tragedienne who always failed when she tried comedy, Mrs. Siddons made a Drury Lane audience laugh uproariously one night in 1801. She was playing in "Julian and Agnes," a pretty bad play. In it she had to rush on to the stage carrying a baby in her arms. The usual dressed wooden doll was provided. But as she entered she caught the pretended baby's head a sound smack against the scenery and the good hard ring of wood meeting wood sent the house into hysterics.

Sarah Siddons' reign at Drury Lane was drawing to a close. She played one more new part there, "Hermione" in "A Winter's Tale"; and it was very nearly her last part in this world, for, whilst standing on the pedestal as the statue, her draperies caught fire. The draught blew the filmy stuff over some lamps at the back and flames enveloped her. A stage hand crawled on and put the flames out with his bare hands. He saved the actress and the theatre. Siddons rewarded him handsomely.

But breaking-point had come for both brother and sister. Owed money, fobbed off with promises, they could neither stand nor afford it any longer. After a performance of "Twelfth Night," her last appearance at the Lane, they both left the theatre where they had done so much and earned such fame. She was its greatest daughter and he one of its greatest sons.

But to stay on was hopeless. She wanted a rest, and he went abroad and returned to buy a share in Covent Garden. There they reopened, to add a page to the glory of the Garden and to oppose the playhouse which had been the birthplace of their fame.

Now indeed were things bad at Old Drury. The two great aces of the pack were gone. Well might Sheridan worry. But the Theatre is a strange place. Like Scipio's Africa, there is always something new in it. One door closes and another opens. The inspiration of the actress who had left it was to provide something to fill the old playhouse again. This time it was an infant prodigy, Master Betty, the Young Roscius. This remarkable youth was born at Shrewsbury and taken to Ireland as child. Master Betty was a star in his nursery. He was taken to see Mrs. Siddons act in Dublin and that settled his career. He informed his parents he would die if he did not become an actor, and was so vehement about it that they gave him the necessary training. He studied for two years, this precocious child, especially the part of "Osman" in "Zara." At the ripe age of eleven he made his début and astounded everyone. He was a handsome child with a lovely voice, and the ease, power and assurance of a Garrick. Billed as "The Infant Roscius," he went from success to success. After Ireland he came to conquer England. Macready's father engaged him at Birmingham. There he was seen by an official of Drury Lane who made him an offer of £100 for seven nights and half a benefit. Wily old Macready, who was handling the business, stuck out for a clear benefit. There was demur at Drury Lane and Covent Garden slipped in and got him for 12 nights at 50 guineas a night and a clear benefit—amazing terms. Drury Lane complained to its rival, who rightly replied that a better offer should have been made. Eventually he was to play at both houses.

On December 10, 1804, he played "Young Norval" at Drury Lane and his death scene brought down the house. When he died with the whispered word of "Mother" on his lips, there was not a dry eye in the theatre. He played Hamlet, and Mr. Pitt adjourned the House of Commons to give the Members a chance to see him. But like so many infant prodigies, his talent died with his youth.

Just before the Infant Roscius, another small child edged his way into the Drury Lane tapestry, a child of a different kind, but a child whose name was to become at once legendary and immortal.

We have seen the name of his parents—Grimaldi—in Garrick's salary lists. Poor little Joe Grimaldi had a long start on Master Betty, for he began his stage career at the age of three at Sadler's Wells. But he was soon at Drury Lane as "The Little Clown," in which he mimicked everything done by his father, with whom he appeared. He played regularly at Drury Lane up to 1788, and was a great favourite. He married Miss Hughes, daughter of the Sadler's Wells manager, and they were very happy. It nearly killed him when she died in childbirth. In 1800 he was again in the Drury Lane panto, and this time a man called Byrne produced it. It was Byrne who gave us the costume of the Harlequin as we know it now. Previous to him, Harlequin had worn the loose trousers of Italian convention. Byrne gave us the skin-tight clothes of to-day.

221

In this show Grimaldi played Punch, and at the end changed to Clown. The title was Bluebeard.

A revival of the same show in 1803 brought a severance between Joe Grimaldi and the Lane. This was not in Joe's contract, for it was billed for a time when he had to appear at Sadler's Wells. Very politely he waited upon Kemble and drew that august person's attention to the position. Kemble received him with his usual pomp. Grimaldi stated his case humbly but firmly. Kemble listened with dignity and then said: "Joe, one word here, sir, is as good as a thousand. Joe, you MUST come." Now Joe, although respectful, was proud, He did not like that "must." His answer was: "In reply to Must, there is only one thing that can very well be said. I will NOT come, sir." "Will Not, eh, Joe?" said Kemble. "I will not, sir," said Joe. "NOT?" said Kemble with emphasis. "NOT," replied Joe with as much force as Kemble. "Then," said Kemble, taking off his hat and bowing, "I wish you a very good morning." Grimaldi bowed in return and walked out. His name was taken off the bills and replaced by an unknown. That is how Kemble conducted business—and Joe Grimaldi, too.

CHAPTER 27

FIRE AND A SECOND REBUILDING

GRIMALDI'S greatest popular hit was known as a "terrific broadsword combat." This was a highly prized item always put on to fill out time whilst a heavy scene change in the pantomime was effected. Grimaldi had arranged it all, and nobody but he knew the business; so in the "Blue Beard" production, Kemble ordered the combat to be cut out.

For the opening night there was a very big house, and all went well until the change of scene occurred where the combat normally took place. The audience were eagerly awaiting the fight. Instead, there was a very long weary wait, whilst the stage hands bumped about in darkness. The house grew restive. It wanted its broadsword bout. Everybody began to hiss, to hoot, to yell. Kemble went on

222

to explain, but to no purpose. The Drury Lane audience wanted tradition, they wanted the fight. They told Kemble not to talk but to do the fight himself.

It so happened that Sheridan was in a box. He had been congratulating himself on the excellent business and the way the show was going. The sudden change of front of the audience scared him. He rushed on the stage, where the players were lining up for the final call. "Let no one stir," he shouted, and took the centre of the stage. The curtain was kept down, whilst on the other side the hooting continued. He spoke solemnly. "In this affair" he said, "I am determined to be satisfied. I call upon someone to answer me one question. What is the meaning of this infernal clamour?"

There was a pause, for no one liked to tell him. Then Barrymore, who was playing "Blue Beard," informed him that the reason for the row was that a broadsword combat between Roffey and Joe Grimaldi had been cut out. "And why was it not done, sir?" bellowed Sheridan. "Why was it not done? Where is Joe, sir?" Barrymore got a bit rattled, it was not his fault anyway. "It is impossible for me to say where he is, Mr. Sheridan," he replied. "Our old friend Joe was dismissed at the end of last season by the stage manager." Sheridan raged, as only he could. He sent a messenger straight up to Joe's house to tell him to be on the stage the next day at noon precisely. Then with a flourishing bow to the scared company he walked off. The next day he received Joe in person, and very kindly. He not only reinstated Joe, but gave him £1 per week rise in salary, and called a rehearsal for the next day.

One night, in 1803, Joe was amazed on entering the Green Room to be greeted heartily by a well-dressed stanger. To his joy, the man turned out to be his long-lost brother John, who had run away to sea, Fortune had favoured John, and here he was, with £600 in his pocket, come to congratulate his famous brother, the Clown. Joe eagerly introduced him to others in the Green Room. But he found time to warn his brother of the danger of carrying so much money about with him. Then he had to go on the stage.

His brother waited in the Green Room, chatting excitedly with them all, and sailor-like flashing his money all round. When Joe had finished on the stage, he told his brother to wait for him and they would go to see their mother. But when he came down, after changing, there was no sign of brother John. Joe searched high and low, but there was no trace. He waited a long time, then searched the streets and the adjoining taverns. His brother John was never seen again. It was another unsolved mystery of Drury Lane. What became of Joe's brother after Joe left him, why he left the theatre, if leave it alive he did, and why and whence he vanished, nobody will ever know.

When Kemble left the Lane, in 1805, Joe was saving a very bad pantomime called "Harlequin Fireside." So good was he, however, that it ran, on his name, until Easter. Wroughton succeeded as stage manager. Joe, his mother and his wife were all playing there. When the Lane reopened in the autumn, "The Country Girl" was put up, with Mrs. Jordan in the cast. This was on 14th September 1805. For the next night, "The Honeymoon" was billed, and the name of Byrne, the Harlequin, appeared thereon. So queerly was the business of the Lane conducted at this time that nobody remembered Byrne had left long ago! There was in consequence nobody to arrange the dances. Wroughton asked Grimaldi to do it, and offered him £2 extra. Grimaldi agreed if the £2 was made a weekly increase for the whole season. To this Wroughton readily assented. Joe, who had learned to be cautions, had this arrangement confirmed in writing by Graham, a magistrate and a chief shareholder in the Lane. A few days later, a man named d'Egville was appointed Ballet Master. To his surprise, next Treasury Day, Joe found his salary had reverted to the old figure. He spoke to Peake, the treasurer, who was amazed. He spoke to Wroughton, who was off-hand and said he could do nothing about it. Grimaldi consulted with his wife, who suggested that, as he was so badly treated at Drury Lane, he should approach Covent Garden.

Although Kemble was in charge of the stage over there, and he and Joe had already crossed swords, he got a warm welcome and an offer of £6 per week for the first season, rising to £8, and also permission to appear at Sadler's Wells. He accepted the offer. His salary at Drury Lane was £4.

Joe left the Lane on 9th November, 1805. We shall meet him there once more only, on the occasion of his last public performance.

Poor old Drury Lane was now rushing fast downhill. Sheridan preferred Parliament. His debts increased. The theatre suffered; it could not meet its liabilities. It had reached a low level of show and prestige. Horses dis-

Above.
ᴏɢᴇ Lᴇssɪɴɢ, Drury Lane Principal
Girl of the early 1900's.

Above.
Vᴇsᴛᴀ Tɪʟʟᴇʏ, a great Drury Lane
Principal Boy of the eighties.

At left.
Aʀᴛʜᴜʀ Rᴏʙᴇʀᴛs, the great " gagster,"
a pillar of Drury Lane pantomime in
the eighties.

Top left.

Villain and Adventuress of t
famous drama *The Whip*
Drury Lane in 1909. CYR
KEIGHTLEY as "Capta
Sartorys" and NANCY PRI
as "Mrs. D'Acquilar."

Bottom left.

JAMES WELCH, famous actor w
was chief comedian in T
White Cat, the Drury La
pantomime which failed in 190

Below.

QUEENIE LEIGHTON, a typi
and famous Principal Boy
Drury Lane pantomimes
1904, 1905 and 1906.

placed actors, and shows only fitted for a circus occupied its hallowed stage.

Then as in so many previous crises, something happened. That very danger which had been so gaily derided at its opening, when water flowed, iron curtains clanged and people cheered,—that very danger which had been so flouted, was now to show its power. Fire was to take the stage, not only the centre, but all of it, and, for the second time in Drury Lane's history, to prove that it was stronger than any Royal patent.

On February 24th, 1809, Sheridan was in the House of Commons. He was waiting to speak in a debate on the Spanish War. Through the window suddenly came the glow of a great conflagration, and cries of "Fire" were raised in the House itself. The news spread that Drury Lane was burning. It was a crisis for Sheridan. One of his biographers, Rae, says that whilst an offer was made to adjourn the House out of sympathy for Sheridan, he refused it, saying that "whatever might be the extent of the individual calamity, he did not consider it of a nature to interrupt their proceedings on so great a national question," and he remained in the House until three o'clock in the morning.

The most accepted version, however, is that Sheridan, when he heard the news, was almost paralysed with anxiety. He hurried to the Piazza Coffee House, in Covent Garden, where he watched the destruction of the theatre and all that it meant to him. The Duke of York went with him. By now he was master of himself, and sat in a window watching the blaze whilst drinking a bottle of wine. To the remarks on his seeming fortitude which arose from his friends, he replied: "May not a man be allowed to drink a glass of wine by his own fireside?"

The blaze of Drury Lane lit all London. It was seen for miles. It was a calamity of the first magnitude; not merely the burning of a theatre but of *the* Theatre, the oldest in the town in tradition and glory, the original holder of the title Theatre Royal. Destructive as the fire was, some of the Wren building survived it, for eyes to see to-day. Otherwise little was rescued. Peake and his assistants managed, at great personal risk, to save the iron box which contained the Charter and other important documents. An organ valued at £800, and once the property of Handel, perished in the flames: so did Garrick's clock, which was only wound once a year, on the day the annual balances were struck. Sheridan lost a bust of the Prince of Wales, a personal gift, and his beloved wife's harpsichord.

Everyone connected with the theatre lost much, but Sheridan was faced with complete ruin. For the building which had cost well over a quarter of a million, had been insured by him for only £35,000. The loss was staggering. Only a few months before it was burned down, its employees had been busy on its roof putting out the burning sparks which fell on it from the fire which was consuming its rival, Covent Garden. Besides the charter, a few costumes, including some of Mrs. Jordan's, were also got out, and some wigs which had been Garrick's. Nothing else was saved.

A lesser man than Richard Brinsley Sheridan would have collapsed with the walls of his playhouse. Characteristically, he started all over again. His chances were slender, for few would trust him, and he was all but submerged by a vast accumulation of debt.

To get things going, he put himself in the hands of Samuel Whitbread, a brewer and a relation of his second wife. But for that move there might have been no more Drury Lane Theatre. But by that move, too, there was to be no more Richard Brinsley Sheridan at Theatre Royal, Drury Lane. Whitbread appears to have had a great sentimental regard for Old Drury. His name should be emblazoned on the walls in gold. Needless to say, it is not, and the average playgoer or man in the street knows nothing of what he did for the playhouse. In the end it was to cost him his life.

Whitbread got busy at once, by means of that honoured British institution, a Committee. He persuaded celebrities who mattered to serve on that Committee, and, more important still, to work for it. These included Lord Holland, the Hon. Douglas Kinnaird, Lord Byron and others. He told the people that Drury Lane was their concern, it was a theatre of which the nation should be proud. He was a curious man, this brewer, a mixture of over-cautiousness and great enthusiasm, but somehow the mixture showed results.

First there was the company to think of; it must be kept together. This was solved by taking over the Lyceum Theatre, then in possession of one Lingham, a breeches maker in the Strand. But Arnold, son of the man who had tried to make the Lyceum an English Opera House and a licensed theatre, and who had failed because the Patentees of Drury Lane and Covent Garden stepped in and prevented him, did his own share of stepping in now. He was beforehand with Sheridan, never a difficult matter. He took over the Lyceum. And he made the Drury Lane Patentee get a licence for the Lyceum, which now became a theatre at the request of its former opponent. It also got Arnold a footing with the powers-to-be at Drury Lane, which was just what he wanted.

Whitbread was an M.P., and often opposed Sheridan in Parliament. That worthy eventually laid his defeat at Whitbread's door, but it would seem that only Sheridan could defeat Sheridan, and Sheridan succeeded.

One thing Whitbread had quite made up his mind about. There was to be no more Sheridan at Drury Lane. He had a scheme and he carried it through. So great were his, and his Committee's exertions, that he raised £400,000 for the rebuilding of the theatre. But there was a mass of complications to resolve. There was the complex system of the Patent and its sharers, the debts, which Sheridan had amassed, a new lease, new terms, all sorts of troubles. But Whitbread went to work with a will. He nearly broke the heart of Sheridan by excluding him from the Committee right from the very beginning.

He discovered that the debts on the theatre amounted to £436,971. The Duke of Bedford, for instance, was owed £4,250 for rent. It says much for His Grace that he waived his claim. A lot of others followed suit, so high did Drury Lane stand in their regard. Next, the new shareholders whom Sheridan had created had to be dealt with. On the whole they were pretty reasonable. Settlements were made with practically all the creditors. Then Whitbread had to buy out the Patentees. He proposed to give Sheridan £24,000 for his half share, £12,000 to Tom Sheridan for his quarter, and £6,000 to a Mrs. Richardson for her quarter, for which she had not fully paid.

The Committee had now regularised the affairs of Drury Lane. They decided that £300,000 would build a new theatre, stock it with all it required and liquidate the debts. There were certain side issues of income, such as rent of a tavern, houses belonging to the theatre, vaults under the playhouse which were let out as storage, rent of private boxes, etc. They expected by way of straightforward theatre revenue, to earn £49,000 per season.

The next step was to get a new licence, by means of an Act of Parliament. They got it in 1811, and Whitbread, Peter Moore and Harvey Christian Coombe were appointed trustees. The old Patent was to be considered dormant, and they were to run under the new one. But one cannot keep a good Patent down. It cropped up later, under the reign of Bunn.

The new Committee wasted no time anywhere. They contracted with Rowles for the building and with Wyatt for the plans. Both were under penalties for failure to complete within a certain time. The first stone was laid on 29th October, 1811, and the theatre was completed and opened on 10th October, 1812. This was—and is—the Drury Lane we know to-day. Details, of course, have been added since. The portico in front and the colonnade at the side were added later, the portico coming from Nash's quadrant in Regent Street; the auditorium has been re-created; but that Theatre which stands to day, is substantially the Theatre of Edmund Kean, of Elliston, of Macready, of Augustus Harris, of Arthur Collins, of Alfred Butt and of Ivor Novello.

There is no need to describe the fourth Drury Lane Theatre, it is there for all to see. Benjamin Wyatt had built it on the lines of what was then considered the finest theatre in Europe—the one at Bordeaux. Its exterior is somewhat plain, but that was because it was never completed : the ornate garniture with which it was to be embellished never went into place. That matters not one whit. Drury Lane looks what it is, a stronghold of the Drama, a theatre built to resist and withstand the encroachment of time and opposition—and this it does and has always done.

Benjamin Wyatt, the architect, was accused of stealing his idea for the theatre from another architect of the same name, George Wyatt. He wrote a book rebutting this charge.

Its first manager was that Samuel James Arnold, of Lyceum fame. He was under the control of a committee which included the Earls of Essex and Dudley, Lord Holland, Lord Byron, William Adam, Harvey Coombe, John Dent, Richard Ironmonger, Hon. Douglas Kinnaird, Colonel John MacMahon, Peter Moore, Charles Ward and Samuel Whitbread. With the exception of their manager, all were amateurs.

The company included William Elliston, a new star to blaze later at Drury Lane as Lessee as well as actor, Ellis, Dowton, Robert Palmer, Wewitzer (the last survivor of Garrick's company there), Lawson, Wrighton, Jack Bannister, Wrench, Mrs. Glover, Mrs. Edwin, Miss Duncan, Miss Kelly and Miss Mellon. Dowton was a fine old actor, who had one great peculiarity. He would not allow his name to be printed on the bills larger than those of the other players, and that although he was leading man. His sort are seldom met with.

The theatre was magnificent, the company the best possible, but the management was very bad. It was amateurish and therefore doomed to failure. Lord Byron said that when he was a member of the Committe of Management, there were five hundred plays on the shelves awaiting production. He had them looked through and in his opinion there was not one worthy of putting before the public. The great unacted have existed as long as the theatre has been in the world. ,

Lord Byron said he had little trouble with the players, despite their reputation as vexatious people. He used to protect Miss Smith because she resembled Lady Jane Harley, and resemblances went a long way with him. Among further glimpses of what went on, he said: " My new function consists of listening to the despair of Cavendish Bradshaw, the hopes of Kinnaird, the wishes of Lord Essex, the complaints of Whitbread, and the calculations of Peter Moore, all of which and whom seem totally at variance. C. Bradshaw wants to light the theatre with gas, which may perhaps (if the vulgar be believed) poison half the audience and all the *dramatis personae* . . . . To crown all, Robins the auctioneer, has the impudence to be displeased because he has no dividend."

Nothing good can be said about the place for some years. They produced a play called " Remorse," by Coleridge, but although it played twenty times, all that can be advanced in its favour is that it was the best of a bad bunch.

Yet this collection of amateurs, mostly by luck and partly by the guidance of the only professional amongst them, Arnold the manager, were to bring something to Drury Lane Theatre which was to create such a blaze of glory that its memory is not dimmed to-day. And that blaze of glory was a new actor, named Edmund Kean.

CHAPTER 28

THE MAN WHO WAITED

EDMUND KEAN! The mere name sends a thrill through every lover of the Theatre. Many books have been written about him, many more will be written: but even then, some of his secrets will remain forever unsolved.

The mystery of his origin is no concern of ours; our affair is with Edmund Kean at Old Drury. " Muster " Richardson, the great showman, believed that he knew the true story of this strange man's parentage. Be that as it may, and whoever his progenitors were, there came into the world a creature of storm, the like of whom had never been seen before in the Theatre and has never been seen since. Kean was born to smoulder, to glow and to blaze with such an intensity of glory that he consumed himself in the white-hot fire of his own genius. His whole life was one of combat, of seemingly insurmountable obstacles dared and conquered. Even at the highest peak of his amazing success, there was still battle, there was still an adversary with whom to grapple and struggle, the one adversary he could never overcome—himself.

In his comparatively short life and career, Kean did such marvels, he made such an impact, that the purple patch he wove in the tapestry of Drury Lane, highly coloured as that tapestry is, glows to-day with a brilliance which time can never dim. The greatest actor of his day, he was also, in his own particular sphere, the greatest actor of all ages. His whole story is one long fanfare, and his page at Drury Lane is truly written in fire. It is strange, exciting, almost overpowering, drama in the story of drama, and it is real " theatre " throughout.

Ignoring the vexed question of paternity — whether his father was Carey, Kean or, perhaps some sprig of nobility— it is on record that from his very earliest childhood, the aura of Drury Lane was over Kean's life; and the love for it, the desire to conquer and shine in it, must always have been in the heart of this curious, precocious child.

His "Uncle" Moses, no mean performer, had played there; so had Charlotte Tidswell, who brought him up from the age of two. His early years were spent in and around the Lane. He then lived with his "Aunt" Tidswell. According to Molloy, he made his first appearance at the age of four, when he portrayed Cupid in Noverré's ballet opera "Cymon." His anxiety to be chosen, his remarkable dark eyes, his arresting little gestures, all brought him to the attention of the stage manager, who gave him the part; and he sat at the feet of "Sylvia" and "Cymon" in an "enchanted car." So much did he please, that he was engaged to play demons, apes and fairies in subsequent pantomimes.

Kean had reached the age of six when he made his first notable, if unfortunate stage gesture. This was on an important occasion—the opening of the rebuilt Drury Lane Theatre in 1793. The play was "Macbeth," with Mrs. Siddons and Kemble. On the stage too was Edmund Kean, then known as Edmund Carey. He was one of the evil sprites in attendance on the Three Witches. He played it for that evening only. For whilst he and other attendant sprites stood in a line, at the mouth of a cave waiting to dash on, Edmund slipped and fell against the boy in front, who in his turn knocked over the boy in line ahead, and so on, until the whole line of them rolled over like so many toy soldiers. It was an awkward situation and caused something more than a titter.

Kemble, as "Macbeth," naturally took a gloomy view of the mishap, and was in no forgiving mood when Edmund was brought before him. The boy excused himself by saying that "it was the first time he had appeared in tragedy." He was sacked. He appeared again later in pantomimes, where such peccadilloes would not matter. He himself claimed to have appeared as a "Page" in "The Merry Wives of Windsor," but there is not usually much reliance to be placed on his later recollections. There is also a story that he upset Kemble by mimicry of him, and that as a result of a push given him by the angry actor, he fell down a trap and was lamed for some time.

Over the period of his early adventures, his appearances with Richardson in his great portable theatre, his days as stroller and as obscure provincial actor, his marriage and his children's birth, we have not space to linger. We start when those struggling amateurs now running Theatre

Royal heard of a new actor who was said to be remarkable, and sent down their manager Arnold to have a look at him. That visit came about through the recommendation of one of Kean's few friends, Dr. Joseph Drury, who had been headmaster of Harrow and was therefore a man of influence. Drury had seen him at Exeter, and had admired him. So to him he appealed. Drury mentioned him to Pascoe Grenfell, one of the Drury Lane Committee. They needed a tragedian. In comedy they were strong; but in their day it was the tragedians who pulled in the money. Nowadays the reverse is true.

Edmund was wretchedly poor, and his little boy Howard was ill. He had applied personally to Arnold, at Drury Lane for an engagement, but had received no answer. Yet London called insistently. So next he wrote to Elliston, who had been a Drury Lane actor, but had now left and was running the Olympic Theatre, in Wych Street, which with his customary effrontery he called Little Drury Lane. It was just around the corner. Kean got his Aunt "Tid" to tackle Elliston as well.

After a long interval he heard from Aunt Tid that Elliston would have him; but to Kean's chagrin, the terms offered were for stage management and principal parts at a salary of only Three Guineas a week. Kean wrote Elliston one of his rambling, pompous letters—he was always writing them—accepting this roundabout offer of an engagement, and concluded in his own mind that the matter was settled. He had no scrap of writing from Elliston himself. However, as still no letter came from Elliston, Kean wrote and put his case to Dr. Drury, asking for help and advice.

At this moment Kean was with the company in Dorchester. His boy Howard was now very ill; yet, although there was no word from London, and still no definite answer from Elliston, he could not believe in the possibility of failure, or that the chance he knew he could take would be denied him. His present great need was money, wanted urgently and desperately if he was to save his Howard's life. So once more, clutching at his only straw, he wrote to Elliston again, confirming the one-sided contract of his engagement. Again came no answer. That was in November 1813.

Four nights later, he was playing in the Dorchester Theatre in "The Mountaineers" to a very small audience.

But in a box, paying the greatest attention to everything on the stage, sat a distinguished stranger.

The main play of the evening over, Kean went to change for his part in the ballet. For he was an expert dancer and a fine Harlequin. Whilst doing so he heard Lee, the manager, discussing him with the mysterious stranger. Lee was saying that he considered Kean a very clever fellow, and informed him that the actor was going to London. The stranger expressed polite surprise at this, but agreed that Kean was clever. He remarked also that he was very small. Kean wanted to hear more, and hurried onto the stage. He began boasting of his forthcoming engagement. He told the man that he had a contract with the management of Drury Lane and was shortly to go there. Again the man expressed polite surprise. He told Kean his name—Arnold, manager of Theatre Royal! Kean admitted afterwards that he felt as though he had been shot. But at the end of the show Arnold saw him again, and told him to come to his hotel in the morning when they would settle everything.

Arnold received him kindly, complimented him on his performance of the previous night, and told him that he thought he had every chance of success. He pointed out to Kean the difficulties of the theatrical profession, and the especial difficulty of gauging the taste of London playgoers. Therefore he made Kean two propositions. The first was an engagement, successful or unsuccessful, for three seasons, at eight guineas a week for the first, nine guineas for the second and ten guineas for the third season; or alternatively, the management would pay his expenses to London and his expenses whilst there, until he played, and then judging by his success, he could make his own terms with the Committee, while if he failed, his return expenses would be paid. Kean, hardly able to believe his own ears, embraced the first proposal. With starvation staring him in the face, eight guineas a week seemed absolute wealth. The deal was fixed up verbally. Hands were shaken.

Arnold returned to Drury Lane to report that he had seen the man and thought he had made a very good bargain. But Kean either because of his excitement or for other reasons, had unfortunately neglected to mention to Arnold his dealings with Elliston.

Kean rushed home in a state of ecstacy. Their struggles were over! He was to play leads at the greatest

233

theatre in the world. No more tramping the country, no more hardships, no more hungry days and nights for himself and his family. Success was his at last. He wrote off to Dr. Drury, one of his long letters peppered with Latin phrases, expressing his great gratitude. He painted the future in rosy colours. He could now get the best medical aid for poor little Howard. At last, at last, luck for them all, and his just due, were in their possession. Then came a bolt from the blue.

Elliston wrote to Kean, saying that the Olympic Theatre was to open in Christmas week, and he would be glad to see Kean. Here was a complication indeed. Kean tried to find a way out of the impasse. He wrote to Elliston that, since their correspondence, he had been made and had accepted an offer from Drury Lane. In these circumstances, he hoped that Elliston would understand why he could not possibly accept his offer, and he hoped that they might treat together another time.

Elliston hit back at once. The mere fact that Drury Lane wanted a man, whom he had considered worth only £3 3s. a week, made him quite decided that he would have Kean himself, and spite the Lane into the bargain. He wrote Kean promptly saying that a bargain was a bargain. And then poor little Howard died. If this struck a blow at Mary, his wife, it shattered Kean. He was heartbroken. True, there was little Charles, but Howard, the elder, had been the apple of his eye.

Yet even this blow did not mark the end of his troubles. Under the agreement with Arnold, he had to find his own travelling expenses to London. He relied for this on his benefit: but the benefit failed. So he had to borrow five pounds from Lee, the manager—and leave the bulk of it to keep his poor wife and the boy Charles. With only a few shillings over and above his fare, he set forth alone to conquer London. But his overwhelming troubles had driven Elliston quite out of his head.

He was twenty-six years old, when he reached London in November, 1813. He got lodgings at 21 Cecil Street, Strand. Arnold gave him a warm welcome and told him that he would at once commence to draw his salary, irrespective of when his début was to be. Kean was again in Heaven. His first act was to send for his wife Mary and Little Charles.

Arnold himself wasted no time. He put out some

paragraphs to the Press, giving Kean a boost. He appears, in his capacity as Manager-Press Agent—to Drury Lane, to have given his fancy a little rein, for he spelt Kean's name as Kain, and suggested a connection with Le Kain, the great French actor of English ancestry. Elliston, who did a great deal of this kind of thing himself, soon saw the paragraph, and it gave him the cue he wanted.

He did not really want Kean. Really, he had little use for a tragedian at all,·because the Drury Lane patent barred direct competition at the Olympic; but here was an opportunity of being "big,": and that was right up his street. He made a terrific fuss; he issued statements; he wrote letters. He defied the Lane to take actors away from him, especially actors who were under contract. All this quite apart from the fact that until he knew Kean was going to Old Drury, he had never written to him at all. But Elliston presented such a picture of injured innocence, and breathed such fire and threats that Arnold took fright. More, he took deep umbrage. Kean, he complained justly, had never breathed a word to him about the Elliston negotiations. Accordingly, when the actor presented himself at the Drury Lane treasury to draw his second week's salary, he was informed bluntly that he was not entitled to a penny.

Edmund rushed off to find Elliston, but that wily individual avoided him. Day after day Kean chased Elliston all over London, but he never got a sight of him. Day after day he besought an interview with Arnold—that great man was inaccessible. At last he sent one of his English-Latin letters to Elliston, beseeching for his release. The reply was pure Elliston, a curt note, a sneer at the bad Latin, and a mention of honour.

Kean did not know—how could he—that Arnold had made up his mind that he should play at the Lane. Having boasted of his capture to his Board, he could not let himself down. Nor did Kean realise that Elliston did not want him either.

By now, the condition of the Keans was pitiable. They had no means, no friends, no resources of any kind. And outside the weather was terrible, for the coldest winter for hundreds of years gripped London. One person only showed them feeling, their own landlady. For some reason she had come to believe in Kean. She did not press for the rent; she did not turn them out of her house.

At this time, Kean probably endured greater degradation and sorrow than he had ever known before. His proud, indomitable spirit was tried to the utmost limit. He would endeavour to see Elliston, then he would return to the Lane to seek an interview with Arnold. He was never admitted by either. He sat hopelessly at the stage door, the scorn of the whole place. Stage hands and mechanics brushed by him, the actors and actresses going in to the daily rehearsals looked at him in scorn. Who was he? this dark, undersized little man, poorly and meanly clad, huddled in his huge ill-fitting, many-caped coat, whose bright eyes seemed so full of fire, and who gazed back at them so defiantly. Some clod from the provinces trying to compete with His Majesty's servants. All this he had to endure. Rae, the leading man, who had played with him in small provincial companies now passed him by as a complete stranger. Munden, the great comedian, condescended to suggest that he should spend his evenings in the front, watching good actors. Maybe he would learn something. He became known as " Arnold's hard bargain."

At last Arnold and Elliston got together, for Arnold had to keep faith with his Committee. Kean was called in before the two of them. Both men dressed him down, and conducted their own talk together as if he were a criminal in the dock whose fate they were deciding. Elliston, who could see that the game was played out, then made his " grand " gesture. He would release Kean, but the actor must pay him, as consolation, two pounds a week out of his eight guineas. Although this proposal put Kean hopelessly in the wrong, he could do nothing else than accept it. Elliston rushed off saying he would give Kean a letter which would make it all right, but Kean must come and get it. Arnold then informed him, in stately tones, that when that letter was in his possession, then, and not until then, would his salary be resumed.

It was Christmas Eve next day, and a Friday. If Kean was to get money, he must at all costs get that letter. Once more he trailed Elliston around the town and after three o'clock, he got him at the Surrey Theatre. What is more, he got the letter. Hungry, tired and worn out, he hurried to Drury Lane. But there he waited, having the mortification of seeing everyone, even stage hands, have access to Arnold before his name was called. Then, after Arnold had read the letter, he informed Kean that his engagement would really only start from that moment, and, therefore, he could draw no salary that week.

Kean had made up his mind to play "Shylock" as his opening role. He had told Arnold of this, but now he found another actor put up in that part to make a début. This was Huddart from Dublin, who failed miserably. Kean now thought it was his turn, but again he was put off, and a trial given to Sowerby, who also failed.

Eventually, Kean was summoned before the Committee. His short stature—only five feet five inches—and his curious appearance with his big head, did not give them confidence in this choice of Arnold's. They endeavoured to persuade him to appear in a secondary character. His reply was that he would play lead or nothing. He reminded them that by his agreement, proposed by their own manager, he had choice of characters, and that his choice was "Shylock." Something about him silenced them; they had become conscious of the force of the man. The date was fixed for 26th January, 1814.

Arnold had dropped his puffs preliminary. Just one solitary advertisement in the *Times* announced the fact that on Wednesday, January 26th, 1814, Mr. Kean of Theatre Royal, Exeter, would make his first appearance at Theatre Royal, Drury Lane in the part of "Shylock." This attracted little attention, for he was quite unknown.

But before describing that memorable day of his début, let us take a glimpse at the state of things in the theatre which now bore the name of Kean outside it.

Despite the shortness of the time since its re-opening, the Committee was already foundering in hopeless muddle. The officials were indeed a queer lot. Arnold himself was all right, and Tom Dibdin, a kindly and efficient soul, at least knew his theatre, and could write good plays—he turned out nearly 200 of them. In the box office was Billy Dunn, who never saw one of the plays during his tenure of office, but who always, when asked his opinion, would make a long pause, take a pinch of snuff and say : " Wants cutting." One day Planché, the great writer of burlesques, asked if there was any objection to his sending a couple of friends down for a box? Dunn made no reply, so Planché left him. Four hours later he came back. Dunn was still there. He looked at Planché, took his snuff, and said, " No, I don't think so."

An incident involving Royalty may be related here.

George III and his son, afterwards George IV, were both playgoers. Old King George disliked his son heartily. One night, shortly after the new building was opened, the King and the Prince, in separate parties, both visited Drury Lane. The Rotunda, then as now, the crush room of the theatre, was crowded with nobility and gentry. The Royal father and the Royal son met face to face. Before he could be prevented, and before anyone knew what he was about, old King George got hold of his son, set about him, and soundly smacked his face and boxed his ears.

The management decided that such a thing must never happen again. So over the left hand door went up the words "King's Side," and over that on the right "Prince's Side." The rotunda was made no man's land for the Royal parties, who were tactfully persuaded to keep in future to the territory allotted to them. And there to-day you may read those signs, one of Drury Lane's unique curiosities.

CHAPTER 29

KEAN'S AMAZING TRIUMPHS

ONLY one rehearsal did Kean have for his first appearance at Drury Lane. No more were necessary: he knew precisely what he was going to do.

The company, scandalised at being asked to play with such an unknown quantity, such an odd, shabby little man, resented Kean to a degree. Most of them were late, and several did not turn up at all. One lady wrote her excuse "that she had such a headache as never was." Decent little Dibdin apologised, but Kean seemed quite indifferent. When the company did condescend to turn up, they walked through the scenes, some sneering, some just muttering. Kean kept his temper; he knew what he was about. Once, however, he showed them something they had never seen before. Busy George Raymond, the prompter, at once stopped him. "That will never do," he said, "it is an innovation, and totally different from anything that has been done on these boards." Kean gazed calmly at him and replied: "Sir, I wish it to be so." "But," said Raymond, "it will not do. Be assured at that." Kean's reply was final. "Well, sir, perhaps I may be wrong, but if so, the public will set me right."

Came the night of Friday, January 26th. Before setting forth, Kean said: "To-day I must dine." And, somehow, he did.

That day, as if it were an omen, the bitter frost, which had lasted over a month, had broken. At every corner, shovelled snow stood almost breast high and was now beginning to melt. Underfoot was a thick paste of black and biting slush. A wet chilling sleet was falling. And through this trudged the small figure in its great caped coat, the figure of Kean setting out to fight his greatest battle. Under his arm he carried in a parcel his stage clothes, his Jewish gabardine, his wigs.

In the theatre, nobody spoke to Kean, nobody wished him luck; they watched him go past them in silence. He had elected to dress downstairs below the stage, with the supers. He began to change for the part. The only human voice to address him before he stepped upon the stage was that of the call boy. To him Kean replied gravely, "I thank you."

He had heard the others speak of the House as being wretched, of one saying, "What can you expect? Look at the weather, there will be nothing until half price." By this the insinuation was that Jack Bannister in the farce called "The Apprentice" could be the only possible attraction that evening!

Kean finished dressing, and went into the wings to await his cue. He looked through the peephole at the audience. It was indeed a bad house, only a third full; and nothing looks so empty as a thin Drury Lane. But his eye lightened. He saw his friend, Dr. Drury, there. He saw also his kind landlady, Miss Williams, and he saw one great critic. It was enough.

The company gazed at him curiously. Then they stared in amazement. What was this dreadful little man up to? He was wearing a black wig and beard. Such a thing was unprecedented — why, even the great Macklin, who had revolutionised the character, had worn the traditional red wig and beard. This was iconoclasm. Well, they were in for a pretty evening, to be sure.

The play started, the curtain was up. His cue came, and Kean stepped on to the stage. He received the usual round of applause always accorded to those making a début.

He responded with a grave, courteous bow. Then he spoke his first lines. His voice had something which at once arrested attention. "Three thousand ducats," said Kean-Shylock, "well . . ." The audience were already alert, they were waiting. His "Signor Antonio, many a time and oft" stirred them, and when on Bassanio's exit he gave them a taste of his quality in the lines:

> "If I can but catch him once upon the hip
> I will feed fat the ancient grudge I bear him"

the applause began to come. By now he was dominating his audience. Everything he did, everything he said, brought volleys of applause. Each burst of applause was a spur to greater effort. The actor was inspired and the meagre audience enthralled.

The curtain fell on the first act amid wild enthusiasm. Back stage Kean did not go to his room, but walked quietly up and down at the side of the stage. Now it was the others who felt uneasy, now they began to wonder at this strange little man. They had been wrong, they had been foolish. Kean took no notice and spoke to none. The positions now were reversed. In front, the audience were seething with excitement. In the crush room there was hot debate about this new man. Others ran to the coffee rooms to bring in their friends. Some slipped over to the Garden, where the play was poor, and many of the playgoers there, on hearing what was happening over the way, flocked to Drury Lane. Surely no other actor in the world has ever changed a bad house into a good one in the course of a performance!

Kean, in the wings, stood by for his cue. When he stepped on to the stage it was as a conqueror. The applause rose to a crescendo. Kean gave forth his best. All his genius was aglow. And when the Trial Scene came, he surpassed himself. He took his bow to thunderous applause and excited shouts. He made his obeissance to the only master he acknowledged—the audience of Drury Lane. Only Dr. Drury caught him before he left, the man who had recommended him and shared his triumph.

Then Kean sped home. The slush, the sleet, the damp numbing cold had no power to touch him. He had won. The warmth of success, the burning glow of triumph, kept the elements at bay. He burst into his room. There the faithful Mary, anxious-eyed, sprang to her feet—agog to hear the news. He caught her in his arms, in a frenzy of

Above.
HENRY NEVILLE, celebrated actor and star of Drury Lane dramas, notably *White Heather*.

Above.
Sir JOHNSTONE FORBES-ROBERTSON, who made his farewell to the stage at Drury Lane in 1913.

At right.
Sir HENRY IRVING, who presented *Dante* at Drury Lane in 1903.

The Historic Ceremony of THE BADDELEY CAKE.

Cut in memory of ROBERT BADDELEY every Twelfth Night since 1795, the illustration shows the ceremony on Twelfth Night, 1935, the company being that of *Cinderella*.

JUNE and PHYLLIS NEILSON-TERRY sit behind the Cake.

At extreme right is C. M. LOWNE, then the President of the Fund.

delight and high spirits. "You shall ride in your carriage, Mary," he shouted, and then turning to lift little Charles out of his cot, "and you, Charlie, shall go to Eton." The only shadow on that night was the fact that young Howard was not there to share the happiness.

Next morning the whole town was talking. Hazlitt had been present. He had been told to be kind, but there was no need for charity. He gave Kean a magnificent notice. "His style of acting is, if we may use the expression, more significant, more pregnant with meaning, more varied and alive in every part, than any we have almost ever witnessed. The character never stands still; there is no vacant pause in the action; the eye is never silent. It is not saying too much of Mr. Kean, though it is saying a great deal, that he is all that Mr. Kemble wants of perfection." Other papers were not less laudatory. It was a complete triumph for Kean. He had not only conquered Drury Lane, but also John Philip Kemble, who for so long had reigned at Covent Garden.

Queerly enough the management of the Lane did not appreciate the gift that had been handed to them. They let a whole week go by before they allowed Kean to play again. Dibdin recommended his speedy appearance, so Arnold informed Raymond that Kean was to play Shylock on the first, third and fifth of February.

And each time his power grew, and so did the audiences. At his first performance the takings were £164. That was doubled at his second playing. During the first season he played Shylock fourteen times, and the gross receipts were £4,921 3s. 0d.

Among the real critics, Douglas Jerrold wrote that Kean "impressed the audience like a chapter from Genesis." Indeed, everyone was raving about him except the actors. In the Green Room they chattered that it was a passing craze: he could not last. "God renounce me," grumbled old Dowton, "'tis only necessary nowadays to be under four feet high, have bandy legs and a hoarseness, and mince my liver, but you'll be thought a great tragedian." "Nay," countered Munden, "no doubt the little man has great powers of entertainment, for I hear he is a wonderful tumbler." Jack Bannister had the last word: "Of that there can be no doubt, for he has jumped over the heads of us all."

Miss Mellon was constructive. She got Oxberry to

introduce them, and asked if Kean had yet signed his contract. He said he had not. She advised him to wait; he would get better terms.

But the management soon became wide awake. All doors were wide open; there were no more insults, no more waiting, no more hanging about. Arnold was all smiles. He came in person to see Kean. " You have exceeded our expectations, sir," he said. He requested him, not commanded him, to meet the Committee. And Kean went. It was a very different meeting from the last. This time Kean was in command. The Committee was bitterly conscious that they held no written contract. They knew also that maybe the fate of the great theatre lay in the hands of this young and extraordinary actor. They feared that he might take revenge for their scurvy treatment of him.

The usual compliments passed and then came the awkward pause whilst each side waited for the other to broach the business which had brought them together. They were wondering what he would ask them. Kean, remembering the terms he had originally accepted, was fighting a silent battle between his idea of honour and Miss Mellon's advice.

Arnold handed him a contract for the agreed amounts as settled at Dorchester. Kean took it and read it through. The Committee shifted in their seats, some appearing indifferent, some leaning forward to watch Kean's face. Having finished his reading, he lifted his piercing dark eyes and gazed at them each in turn round the table. Without a word, he then took a pen, dipped it in the ink, and signed the contract. There was a rustle of relief. Kean handed the document back to Arnold. Arnold took it—and to the eternal credit of Drury Lane, tore it into small pieces. He then handed Kean another, which was soon signed amidst smiles. It was for twenty pounds a week—to which they added fifty guineas as a token of their esteem.

After Kean had played Shylock six times, the Committee pressed him to undertake another character. He needed no persuasion. He plumped for his favourite rôle, " Richard III." The announcement excited the greatest public expectation. After Shylock, what would Crookback be like? Could the new man keep it up? This time the Committee took a deep personal interest in the production. New and historically correct scenery was painted. The date was announced—Saturday, 12th February, 1814.

For more than a week before the performance every box was engaged, and early in the afternoon every door was besieged. By six o'clock the roads to Drury Lane were jammed with the carriages of the illustrious.

Excitement in the theatre was at fever pitch when the curtain music was played. But the curtain stayed down. Then Wroughton appeared before it. The audience gasped. Was Kean not to play? No, it was only that he had a cold and begged to be excused for his hoarseness. Applause broke out first half-way through the opening soliloquy, and at the end of the first speech all knew that Shylock had been no fluke. They were in the presence of a great—a very great—actor. All through the play he held them entranced, save when their pent-up feelings burst into deafening plaudits. His dramatic powers knew no bounds. In the fight, his skill as a fencer stood him in great stead. He chased Rae, who played Richmond, all round Bosworth Field, and roused the house to frantic enthusiasm. He played swordless and disarmed, yet still thrusting at his antagonist with his empty hand as if, whilst breath lasted, he would fight on. At the end, the demonstration was amazing. Not even Garrick as "Richard" had savoured anything like this.

Over at the Garden, Kemble was shaken. Here was a challenger indeed. Was this new actor whom he now remembered as a boy, and a nasty boy, at the Lane, to dispute the great John Philip's male mastery of the stage? This would never do. He would show them there was another Richard in the field. So he played it himself a few nights before Kean. But Kean's "Richard" eclipsed Kemble's, and the critics awarded Kean the diadem of Garrick.

He was now king indeed, and almost at one bound the leader of his profession. He had turned the tide at Drury Lane, and on his own account was paying off a few old scores. Rae wanted to be friendly, so did Raymond, who had been very uncivil to him at first. One night there was "a scene" in the Green Room. Kean ordered a bowl of punch and invited the company to a drink. Rae partook, and Kean gave not the slightest inkling that they had ever met as fellow strollers. But when Raymond, the stage manager, pressed forward for a glass and some notice, Kean poured the remains of the liquor in the bowl over his head.

Next Kean played Hamlet, which he liked best of all;

243

but it was not quite his greatest part. He restored the Gravediggers, whom Garrick had cut out, and his scene with Ophelia burned an impression on the memory. He had some new business, too — after the command, "Get thee to a nunnery," he suddenly turned, and kissed her hand with great tenderness.

In front, at this performance, was an old—a very old—lady, whose entry had caused a flutter, for she in her time had been Queen Consort of Drury Lane. It was Mrs. David Garrick, come to see the only man who had challenged her beloved husband's memory. She found only one defect in Kean as compared with her David. He was not severe enough on the Queen in the Closet scene. She was nearing ninety, but invited Kean to come and visit her — a great honour. And when he came, very reverently, to her home near Regent's Park, she conferred on him the greatest privilege in her power to give. She made him sit in Garrick's favourite chair, kept until then as a guarded relic. She made much of him, she gave him flowers and fruit, and what pleased him mightily, some of Garrick's stage jewels.

On May 5th Kean scored another and perhaps his greatest triumph. He played "Othello." Prophets of doom had forecast failure. Kean was too small, they said, and the performance would be absurd. But his Othello is claimed to be the most perfect of all the Moors of Venice. He transcended all he had done hitherto. "By God, he is a Soul," cried out Lord Byron. Such a meteoric rise had not been seen since Garrick's, nor had such power, such acting, such genius.

The receipts for Kean's nights were now £600. Gifts were showered upon him, and at his benefit the takings touched £1,150. His first season closed on July 16th. He had played Shylock fifteen times, Richard twenty, Othello ten, Hamlet and Iago eight, and the Duke in "Riches" four times. The profits amounted to £20,000.

The Committee met to examine the accounts. Up to Kean's appearance there had been 139 nights of continuous loss. He had changed all that. They voted him £500. Four shareholders each presented him with a share in the Lane. Lord Jersey gave him £100, Whitbread called round at his house and slipped a £50 note into the hand of little Charles.

Kean did not forget his old friends. A surprising number turned up to claim him, and he helped them all. The once belligerent actors were now fawning on him. But he responded to two of them only, Oxberry and Pope, both of whom had shown him small kindnesses in the early days. And Pope, besides playing opposite to him, became his great friend. This actor, one of the family to which Jane Pope belonged—she who had only just retired—was second rank in tragedy as compared with Kean, but front rank when compared with others. He had, when playing Hastings in "Jane Shore," delivered his great speech so magnificently that the audience had fetched him back and made him do it all over again, so he shared with Quin the honour of being one of the only two tragedians ever to get an encore—and take it.

Kean, in his second season, played Macbeth, but he did not look so noble or imposing as Kemble. His Romeo was also a bad choice because of his figure. Spranger Barry and Garrick had the lead of him there. But his "Zanga" beat Kemble's hollow, and his "Richard II" was one of his most polished performances. He even tried "Abel Drugger," Garrick's old masterpiece of comedy. Mrs. Garrick told him he could not do it, and he told her that he knew he could not. But he tried all the same. In this period he could do no wrong. His nearest approach to a failure was his Romeo, but even that had something new from his genius.

But as Kean rode on the crest of the wave, tragedy came to another figure who had done much for Drury Lane. Samuel Whitbread, M.P., brewer, man of business and gentleman, became ill. His great labours had told upon him, not the least those connected with Drury Lane. Things were all right now that Kean had come, but the strain had been great. He had created the latest Drury Lane, he had borne the weight, he was no longer young. His mind snapped. For weeks on end he had not slept, and reason gave way. He took his own life, mourned and regretted by all. At the inquest it was disclosed that a fragment of his skull had been pressing on his brain.

A sad change now comes into the picture. In Kean's character there were two sides, that of genius—and the other. The other now called for an ally, and that ally was drink. Kean had tried to drown his sorrows in brandy the night poor Howard died, but there was not enough in the world for that. Now, however, he had unlimited means; he could have what he liked and when he liked. Between seasons at the Lane he went to Dublin, where his success was phenomenal. But one night he got so drunk that he was carried home helpless. This failing began to accentuate itself. Dr. Drury tried to remonstrate with him; Lord Essex reasoned with him. Kean spent more and more time with low pothouse companions, drinking in taverns, squandering money, and brawling. He who, when a struggler, had longed for the company of the best in the land, now that that was obtainable, turned again to the lowest he could find. So drink took hold of him with both hands. He brawled in the streets, and it is certain that he spent at least one night in the cells of Bow Street. Kean, who had been so great in failure, could not carry success. It went to his head. In Oxberry, too, he had a bad companion, who encouraged his wild excesses and then laughed at him behind his back.

Kean now acquired a tame lion cub, which he took everywhere with him. He became a leading light of "The Wolf Club," which should have been a gay Bohemian affair, but which became a kind of Thieves' Kitchen, and it was said hatched plots to keep anyone who might show signs of rivalling Kean well out of the way. The aristocracy were barred, but Kean took Byron to a meeting, and his Lordship came away shocked. To have shocked Byron was something indeed. Kean sparred with Mendoza, the pugilist, he rowed on the river, and tried to establish a rival race to Dogget's Coat and Badge. He founded a club called "The Screaming Lunatics," which met at the Harp. He offended Byron and Douglas Kinnaird by leaving a party of theirs to rush off and preside over a supper for pugilists. Kean did not love a lord. And he was spending money like water. Yet all the while it must be remembered he was carrying the full weight of Drury Lane Theatre on his shoulders.

His third season at Drury Lane opened on 6th October, 1815. He gave them the never failing "Richard III." On November 6th he appeared as "Bajazet" to the "Tamerlane" of Pope. His chief success in this seems to have been his dancing. Otherwise there was little of note. But that burning force which was Edmund Kean was soon to show them all that it was not spent—far from it. He had the field to himself, it was perhaps a pity that no rival had as yet appeared. But he could still, as actor, beat what he had done before.

On January 12th, 1816, Drury Lane presented Philip Massinger's "A New Way to Pay Old Debts." Kean played "Sir Giles Overreach." Many had tried before, but Kean proved there was only one "Sir Giles" who mattered. It required a terrific actor to play this terrific part, and Kean was to show them how terrific he could be. He reached heights never scaled before and certainly never scaled since. He had his audience entranced—spellbound. Lord Byron admits that he was frightened out of his life, and all over the house women screamed and fainted. Even the Drury Lane actors, hardened old professionals and experts, jealously upholding their own reputations against the flood of Kean, had never seen or experienced anything like this. If the playgoers were frightened, so were they. Mrs. Glover, the leading lady, fainted on the stage.

At the end of the play the stunned audience, when it regained its mental balance and the tension was relieved, yelled and roared for Kean, giving him an ovation such as Drury Lane had never seen.

Kean rushed back to Clarges Street, back to his wife. His frame of mind that night was much the same as on his first appearance at the Lane as Shylock. "I've done it again, Mary," he exclaimed. "And what did Lord Essex think of it?" demanded Mary. "Damn Lord Essex," shouted Kean. "THE PIT ROSE AT ME!" There spoke the true actor.

CHAPTER 30

DUELS FOR SUPREMACY

KEAN'S further success was a big blow to Kemble at Covent Garden. He was losing his position as leading actor, if he had not already lost it, and Covent Garden itself, which had taken the lead in the battle of theatres, was again well underneath.

Kemble was so ill-advised as to play "Sir Giles Overreach" himself, thus reviving the duels of Garrick's days between the Lane and the Garden. It was a deplorable failure, and after it, Kean's reputation stood higher than ever. Lord Byron gave him a handsome sword with a Damascus blade, and subscribed £50 at his benefit. The Committee and Company 'at Drury Lane collected £300, and gave him a gold cup made by Hamlet the jeweller in Leicester Square.

The success of "A New Way to Pay Debts" made the Committee risk Massinger again, and Kean appeared as "Sforza" in "The Duke of Milan." This was only given for seven nights, but it led to some trouble. Just over the horizon was peeping another personality destined later to reign at Drury Lane. This was William Charles Macready. Probably in their efforts to keep Kean within reason, the Committee had often invoked the name of this rapidly rising young actor. Kean did not fear him as a rival, but the name stuck in his mind nevertheless.

Kean had taken a day off at Greenwich, and on his way back he met some old friends at Deptford, then still in the country, and got drunk. When the time came to ring up the curtain at Drury Lane, Kean was not there. After the prologue had been spoken, Rae, who was at this time stage manager, went on the stage and told the audience that Mr. Kean had not yet arrived, and begged their indulgence. He got it, for they all wanted to see Kean. Some time passed by, and still there was no sign of Kean. Rae went on again, told them that Kean had that morning gone to the country in his one-horse chaise, and nothing had been heard since. He expressed regret, also the hope that nothing had happened to the actor. He substituted another play, which was naturally very badly acted, and the audience, who had come to see Kean, went away grumbling. Next day Rae received a characteristic letter from Kean.

"Dear Mr. Rae,
    I shall be quite unable to play in ' The Duke of Milan ' this evening. I met with a damned accident yesterday, being thrown out of a gig, and besides being stunned and bruised have dislocated an arm. Hoping soon to recover and with apologies to the public.
                                        I am, Yours in pain,
                                            EDMUND KEAN.
N.B. Perhaps the great W.C.M. may be got."

Kean enclosed a doctor's certificate, but the sting of the letter lay in its tail.

This statement of Kean's was made public, and the Press just did not believe it. They knew all about him. They printed stories comparing him with George Frederick Cooke, the great actor who was often unable to appear because he was insensible in a tavern. Mary Kean dashed down to Deptford. He even acted to her and bluffed her, but later, off his guard, began to gesticulate with the supposedly dislocated arm. Only Hazlitt stood his champion in the Press.

Kean was now to learn what happens when an actor upsets his master, the public. When he made his next appearance, an unruly house was waiting for him. There had been ominous rumblings before the curtain went up, but the playing of the National Anthem to welcome the Duke of Gloucester and Princess Sophia quietened things down for the moment. As soon as Kean entered, however, resentment broke loose. The cry arose, " Off, off, apology, apology." There was a counter-demonstration in his favour, but the " Apologists " won. Kean tried to continue his part—he was playing " Shylock "—but could not be heard. So he took off his hat and came down to the footlights. He got silence—trust him to get that—and he said:

"It is the first time in my life that I have been the unwilling cause of disappointment. That, in this theatre, it is the first instance out of the hundred and sixty-nine performances, I appeal to your recollection and the testimony of the managers. It is to your favour I owe whatever reputation I enjoy. It is upon your candour I throw myself when prejudice would deprive me of what you have bestowed."

Thus he fought them, and won. His enemies, and by now he had plenty, bided their time. They knew he would slip again, and they had not long to wait.

Kean went on frequenting the taverns, and over at the Harp he once threw a glass of wine in the face of an actor, one Fuller, who dared to imitate him. He followed it with a pint pot, which missed Fuller but made such a dent in the wall that it was shown, until the inn was pulled down, as a relic of Kean.

So far Kean had been unchallenged, save by Kemble. Now, however, new claimants to the first place of the stage began to arise. And Kean was to fight the first of many single combats in the art of acting. Kemble had retired after his failure as " Overreach," but for Covent Garden he found a young actor from Worthing who had once deputised for Kean at Brighton, when that gentleman had failed to turn up. Madame Storace, a star of the time, tipped off Kinnaird of Drury Lane to the value of this new man, but whilst the Drury Lane Committee were debating, Kemble slipped in and secured for Covent Garden the services of Junius Brutus Booth.

This young actor had founded his style on that of Edmund Kean. Kemble presented him at the Garden in " Richard III," and he had a great success. The public, always after something new, began now to flock to the junior theatre to see the junior actor. Naturally enough he soon asked for more money, but Covent Garden would not pay it. Now was Kinnaird's chance. He secured Booth and engaged him for Drury Lane before the Garden management knew what was happening.

By public acclamation, Booth was now a rival to Kean. The two met in Drury Lane to fight it out, the champion and the challenger. It was the night of February 20th, 1817, and the atmosphere was like that of a prize fight. It was made the more dramatic by the fact that Kinniard had got Kean to convey the invitation to Booth and invite his own antagonist to do battle with him. Everyone was there, every inch of space was packed. It was like old times again, when Garrick had challenged and defeated Quin.

Kean was to play "Othello," and Booth "Iago." There was breathless excitement. The curtain rose and the two contestants duly entered the ring. The physical resemblance between them was most marked, but Booth was the younger man by some years—at this time he was not twenty-one. He seemed nervous, whereas Kean showed all his self-command and firmness of demeanour. Booth warmed up and got applause. Both had the same mannerisms, both had the same odd stage tricks. But it was experience and ring-craft against the enthusiasm of youth. Kean gave his genius free rein. He seemed to grow in stature and Booth to diminish. Kean towered over him in every way, and after a while there was only one man in it—Edmund Kean. He even moved the other actors to emotion. At the end, he led Booth forward himself to receive his meed of applause, and then led him off, returning alone to receive the victor's overwhelming ovation.

So great had been the success of the duel financially that the Committee decided to stage it again. Consequently, it was billed for Saturday evening, February 22nd. The house was again packed to suffocation. But there was a delay in the start, which audiences of those days would not stand. What was the matter? An uproar began, which brought Rae before the curtain. He read them a letter from Booth, which he explained he had not received until late in the afternoon. The letter ran as follows:

"Mr Booth presents his compliments to Mr. Rae and begs to inform him that from the excessive anxiety of mind which he had experienced during the past week, he finds himself so extremely unwell, that he shall not be able to perform this evening, and he had gone out of town to recruit himself."

Booth had had enough, and had flung in the towel.

Kean went on from triumph to triumph, and from excess to excess. Conway was the next challenger and the next sufferer of defeat. Kean slew them all. Nevertheless, Kean was getting disliked at Drury Lane. He was misusing his power. He was acting the tyrant over the other members of the company and treading down all who might impede his way.

Financially, things at Drury Lane were not so good. The first flush of the Kean excitement had worn off. The amateur Committee, who had not known how to manage success when it came their way, were already in difficulties. Despite the enormous revenue from the early seasons of Kean, bad management showed a deficit.

In 1817 they had installed gas in the theatre as illuminant. This wise and progressive move led only to trouble. Some badly disposed soul spread a rumour that the gas was made on the premises and was likely to blow up at any moment and cause death and disaster. This had to be contradicted on an issue of special bills. Then the majority of the playgoers decided they preferred the old-fashioned candles. *The Times* commented that " after having sat through a whole evening in the theatre, playgoers felt a burning and prickling sensation in their eyes, a soreness in the throat, and a headache which lasted for several days afterwards."

In an attempt to make the place attractive, the Committee redecorated the foyer in the Chinese fashion, installing little alcoves hung round with lanterns. Again criticism arose. This was likely to attract undesirable characters, and it surely did. Within a few days, two ladies of the town indulged in a stand-up fight in the Chinese pavilion, and were dragged off to jail.

Kean had also struck a bad patch, his performance as " King John " failing badly. In his next appearance in " The Dwarf of Naples," he was soundly hissed and hooted. Once again he appealed to the audience and once again he won them over.

Everybody now began to blame everybody else, with Kean as the general scapegoat. On June 4th, 1819, the amateur Committee of Drury Lane resigned. They had managed to run up a deficit of £80,000, whilst the greatest actor in the world was actually their chief attraction. At the time Kean was away on tour. He wrote offering £100 towards the liabilities, for the Committee had opened a public subscription to get the Theatre Royal out of the mud. The Prince Regent gave £1,000; he knew something about debt himself. A Mrs. Butler, hearing that the place was to be let to the highest bidder, said that she cared not a bit what was done so long as it was for the honour of Old Drury. Mrs. Butler was the proprietress of a nearby brothel.

Drury Lane was acquired, much to Kean's disgust, by Robert William Elliston, his old oppressor. But Elliston wanted Kean, and in a most friendly letter said that he would esteem it a favour to play " Cassio " to Kean's " Othello." In reply, Kean said he was off to America, and would willingly pay £1,000 to break his engagement. But Mrs. Kean took a hand and brought the two men together.

Elliston now proceeded to do what he most delighted in—to make a big splash. Being the lessee of the world's greatest theatre, he decided everything must be of the very best. After having the house redecorated in the " best " style by the " best firms," he gave a great reception to three hundred of the " best " people, who had to watch a display on the stage of the new scenery. He announced that everything would be done under his own personal direction, and then Braham, the best tenor, and the entire strength of the company sang the National Anthem. After that the best people adjourned to the Foyer, had the best possible food and wines and danced to the best possible band.

Elliston was boosting Kean for all he was worth, printing his name in enormous type on the bills and playing up to his inordinate vanity.

Elliston put up Kean as " Lear."

"The Great Lessee," as he liked to be called, was accustomed to purveying drama to the transpontine patrons of the Surrey Theatre. And he had seen a version of "King Lear" played at Vauxhall with various queer effects. He decided to give Drury Lane audiences sensations of storm and hurricane, but this proved unworkable on the stage, so he got Loutherburg to paint some wonderful scenery and make it " practicable." Trees bent to the tempest, great canvas billows reared, rolled and crashed. Boughs creaked and swayed, leaves rustled and moaned in the wind. Everybody concerned was impressed to make thunder, lightning, and hail and rain. The result was that poor Lear was seen sometimes in a blue glare, some-

252

times in a green one, and sometimes in a purple hue. Everyone expected much of Kean as "Lear," and they were not disappointed. He triumphed even over Elliston's stagecraft, and the Press acclaimed it as his culminating glory. So he set the seal on his career by playing the part so often called unactable—by Hazlitt, for example.

Kean was yearning for other worlds to conquer, and at the end of that season he left Drury Lane to go to America. Before his departure, however, he played a round of parts at the Lane, and finally, after giving them "Richard III," made a long and flowery speech of farewell. Back-stage there was a ceremony, too. Kean presented the theatre with a plaster bust of himself to be installed in the Green Room. Elliston, as always, made the most of the occasion. The entire company, headed by himself and Kean, walked in procession to the Green Room, where the bust was placed in position. This was an unprecedented thing, and raised some comment amongst the actors. Dowton, who loathed Kean, spat in Elliston's face, but even that was smoothed over, and everyone drank solidly until it was time for rehearsal next morning. The offending bust was broken up long ago.

Elliston next set about the management of Drury Lane. His flamboyancy was soon evident in the quality of his presentations. The type of thing in which he revelled was shown in "The Cataract of the Ganges," a trashy drama which had for its main attraction a real waterfall. Yet, so much was public taste declining, that it drew money.

Just before Kean's departure, Elliston had met Madame Vestris. She had been in the audience, and was waiting for her carriage after the show was over. As the weather was very bad she remained in the theatre with a friend. Lord William Lennox suggested that they should drive home with him, but Vestris said she wanted very much to meet the great Elliston. The Lessee, hearing voices, came bustling up to find out what was going on, for everyone else had left. Now Elliston, unlike Kean, dearly loved a lord, and was more than delighted when Lennox presented Madame Vestris, and immediately offered her an engagement.

It was one of his lucky moves. Vestris, a clever and beautiful woman, was a great success. She and Braham appeared in "The Siege of Belgrade," a poor sort of song-show which then passed as English opera. The public liked her. Next, with Braham, Incledon and Miss Carew, she appeared in Arne's "Artaxerxes." Again success. "Shakespeare versus Harlequin," an old show of Garrick's was then staged, and Vestris played Pope's part of Dolly Snip with great gusto, to greater acclamation. In the May of 1820 came a real winner, a burlesque version of Mozart's "Don Giovanni," with Vestris, in male attire, as the rake. Some pretended to be shocked, but multitudes flocked to see her. So Elliston put her up as "Macheath" in "The Beggar's Opera," and once again the famous old opera scored : so did Vestris, again in breeches.

It was now Coronation Year, and Elliston was not the man to let this slip. He decided, according to custom, to stage a Coronation Spectacle. He was invited to the Coronation himself, but never went. He got too drunk the night before. However, he staged the show and played King George IV himself. He was so carried away by his own acting that he came right down stage and extending his hands over the heads of his astonished audiences proclaimed "Bless you, bless you, my people."

Kean had made a great success in America and arrived home on Coronation Day. Elliston had received a note from him announcing his arrival but had misread it and muddled up the dates. Kean had wanted to open some days later, but Elliston had plastered the town with bills announcing the great actor's return, in the part of "Richard III" on 23rd July, 1821.

Finding that he had to play that very night amazed Kean, but after a few drinks and a good deal of flattery from Elliston, he ceased complaining, and a full house cheered him heartily on his return. Next he played "Othello," and the enthusiasm recalled the good old days. But on July 27th, the Lane was closed, and a doctor's certificate was exhibited saying that Kean was ill.

Kean was away a long time, until November, in fact, and Elliston could find nothing to please the public. What made matters worse was that Kean was busy with the bottle and with Charlotte Cox, a flighty, emotional woman, certainly oversexed, who played a big part in his impending downfall. She was the wife of a City Alderman, connected with Drury Lane, who was beginning to suspect the relationship between his wife and Kean.

Kean went on tour, so that his inamorata could meet him

away from London. The Alderman caught them in Birmingham, and the fat was properly in the fire.

Elliston angered Kean too, by enticing Charles Mayne Young from Covent Garden to star at the Lane. Kean was apprised of this by letter, and immediately sent a wrathful reply, starting very curtly with the brief word "Elliston" and giving that worthy the rough side of his pen. He was disinclined to fight another opponent when his mind was preoccupied with the Charlotte Cox imbroglio. Nevertheless, he accepted the challenge, and in due course met Young as "Iago," he, of course, playing Othello.

Young had been warned what was in store for him. He was reminded of Junius Brutus Booth, whose noble Roman names had not saved him. *The London Magazine* warned Young publicly what he might expect from a roused and enraged Kean. But Young went on with it. He scored points in the first two acts from a very crowded house. But his wily antagonist was playing a waiting game, and from the opening of the third act, Kean proceeded to wipe the floor with him. There was the usual result at the end. Kean had won again.

But if Kean was "on to" Elliston, the Great Lessee was also "on to" the great actor. He saw that the way to get the best out of Kean was to make him defend his title. So he took a daring step and engaged the young and rising tragedian Macready at the salary of £20 a night.

Elliston explained to Kean that he wanted him to play with Macready. The public looked forward to another duel *à outrance*. But for the first time the old warhorse refused battle. Kean refused to meet his younger rival. They appeared separately and although Macready did not set the Thames on fire, nevertheless he steadily gained ground. Kean went off to his new house on the Isle of Bute— Achilles sulking in his Scottish tent whilst Hector held the field of Drury Lane. He was waiting for Macready to fail, but in vain. Not until Macready arranged a provincial tour did Kean return to the Lane. Charlotte Cox was becoming a bit troublesome, and unbeknown to Kean, had also taken another lover. At this juncture, the Alderman decided to intervene. He denounced his wife, said he would live with her no longer, and left the house. Mrs. Cox rushed off to some friends, which was just what Mr. Cox wanted. He came back, searched the house, and found all Kean's love letters. He took immediate action, issuing a writ against

255

Kean for criminal conversion of his wife. He began to persecute Kean too, for when the actor was in the chair at a public meeting, the irate Alderman appeared flourishing a pistol. The case was the talk of the town, a real, red-hot scandal. Kean went to France, then to Bute for Christmas, taking young Charles—now an Eton boy, for Edmund had kept his promise—and Mrs. Kean with him. His eyes were opened now to Charlotte's worthlessness and he turned to his family.

The day of the trial dawned, and Kean's impassioned letters drew laughter in Court. He lost the case, and the outraged husband got damages. The financial loss was small, but now Kean had both public and Press arrayed against him. They had both made up their minds to drive him from the stage altogether. His return had been announced for January 23rd, but Elliston thought that in the circumstances it had better be postponed. He went down to Croydon, to talk it over, and found Kean sitting up in bed smoking a cigar, being entertained by tumblers, and making inroads on the bottles of brandy surrounding his bed. Kean would listen to no postponement. He said he was ready to face the world. As a result of this interview, Elliston announced that he would reappear on January 24th, 1825, in the character of " Richard III."

CHAPTER 31

KEAN'S LAST VICTORY

ON that January night when Kean decided to face London after his defeat and loss of reputation over Mrs. Cox, the doors of Drury Lane were besieged all day. By six o'clock, all approaches to the theatre were completely blocked by masses of people, fainting and struggling. When the doors were opened, there was a battle royal. The pit and gallery were filled to overflowing in a few moments, but the doorkeepers could not control the spate of would-be spectators. The overflow crashed into the boxes and prepared to hold them against all comers. Hoots, groans, hisses, cheers and counter-cheers filled the air; there was a pro-Kean party and an anti-Kean party; a grand display of fireworks was in the making.

The orchestra played an overture which they could not even hear themselves. It was as if the moral reputation of England was to be fought for in Drury Lane Theatre. Everyone in charge feared the worst.

At length Kean walked on to the stage. On his appearance a very tempest of contending sound arose which brought even him to a standstill. He bowed and essayed to speak, but this time he was not to be heard. If possible, his presence and desire to be heard drove the mob to even greater violence. He and the rest went on with the play, but for all that could be heard, it might have been dumb show. By now the warring factions had come to blows. The Keans and anti-Keans in the pit and gallery were pummelling each other, and the more orderly antagonists in the boxes were exchanging cards. It had come to that.

Kean tried once again to address the audience, but this only resulted in renewed clamour. Keeping his head, he again went on with the show—but still nothing could be heard above the uproar. Once more he tried to speak to the audience, but this time, besides hard words, they hurled oranges and orange peel at him. Quite calmly and without interrupting his attempt to play the part, Kean removed some of it from the stage with the point of his sword. And so it continued to the end. Then Kean and Elliston were called, but both had the good sense to lie low.

Four days later, Kean tried again, as " Othello." A general fight was the result. Elliston came forward but was not allowed to speak. The play and the hullabaloo went on. Various members of the public tried to address the audience, to be howled at and pelted for their pains. At length " Othello " was over and the pantomime began. This in turn was interrupted by yells for Elliston. The Great Lessee came on and faced them. Somewhat to his surprise he was allowed to speak, and what he had to say surprised the audience. He informed them that he had engaged Kean to play that season for twenty nights at £50 per night, and that the engagement was made long before the domestic trouble arose. Having made the engagement he was going to keep his contract both to his actor and his public. He would not take Kean's name out of the bills. Such pluck and plain speaking made the mob pause. Elliston then asked for a hearing for Kean, went to fetch him and led

him on. There were again cheers and hisses, but they let
Kean speak. He made perhaps the most dramatic speech
of his whole career.

"If it is supposed," he said, "by those whom I address,
that I stand before you for the purpose of explaining or
justifying my private conduct, I must beg leave to state
they will be disappointed, for I am quite unable to do so.

"I stand before you, ladies and gentlemen, as the representative of Shakespeare's heroes, and by the public voice
I must stand or fall. My private conduct has been investi-
gated before a legal tribunal, and decency forbade my
publishing letters and giving evidence that would inculpate
others, though such a course would have in a great degree
exculpated me. I will not submit to be trampled upon by
a hostile Press; but if the public is of opinion that my
conduct merits exclusion from the stage, I am ready to bow
to its decision and take my farewell."

These plain words carried weight. There were cries of
"No, NO!", "Kean for ever!" and the people dispersed.
He had broken the back of the resistance. And night by
night he wore them down until it was obvious that only
personal prejudice was against him. Nevertheless, he
finished his season with the determination to go to America
and stay there. And after a provincial tour he did indeed
go to the States.

But in 1826 Elliston, the Great Lessee, foundered.
Heavily in debt, he was suddenly stricken down with
paralysis. He then found out how much help a man can
expect in adversity. He had spent over £30,000 on improvements in Drury Lane; he had paid the shareholders £66,000
in rent. He owed them only £5,500, and for this he offered
ample security. But they thought he was finished, and
they turned him out.

News of this had reached Kean in America and he tried
to get hold of the theatre. But an American manager,
Stephen Price, who had met him in the States, stepped in
and secured it, for a rent of £10,000 per annum. He had
the satisfaction of starting off with a Royal visit, for
George IV attended in state.

Early in 1827, Kean returned to England and Price
engaged him for the Lane. Whilst in America, he had been
made Chief of a Red Indian tribe. He thought mistakenly
that this would impress Londoners. Kean felt that he was
now beginning all over again, so very wisely he chose

"Shylock" for his reappearance at Drury Lane. He stepped on the stage on January 8th, 1827, and immediately the old spell worked. All the bad feelings were forgotten; the public received him with joy and acclamation.

He had never acted so well. At the end, the calls were so prolonged and insistent that he had to respond even after he had changed his clothes and removed his make-up. Then it was noticed how old, ill and worn he looked. At succeeding performances, too, he seemed much slower and largely bereft of the old-time fire and fury; but still he was Kean, and still they applauded him. He made no public speeches, but he worked, for the moment, regularly and well, for all his money was gone and he needed to earn his salary.

A friend of his, named Grattan, offered him a play, "Ben Nazir." Kean sent for Grattan, who called on the tragedian. At Hummum's Hotel, Covent Garden, he found Kean sitting up in bed, wrapped in a buffalo skin and wearing his Indian feathered headdress, a scalping knife in his belt and a tomahawk in his hand. An assistant was painting him up in the character of a Red Indian Chief. He decided to get Drury Lane to do "Ben Nazir" and said he was learning the part.

Rehearsals began, and everyone knew their lines except Kean, who was still reading from the script. He stayed away from the last few rehearsals, saying he was impressing points on his memory, and was best left alone. He expressed the highest hopes for the success of the play, even bought more expensive costumes for himself than the management had allowed. He said he would have his portrait engraved in the character when the show was produced. But so far nobody had any idea how he was going to play it.

The first night arrived, and the house was, as usual, a bumper one. As his cue neared they looked for Kean but he was not in the Green Room nor in the wings. They dashed to his room. Kean was there, and had collapsed in floods of tears. He was a picture of horror and despair. He now admitted he had been totally unable to learn his lines. What was to be done? It was too late to postpone. He must go on and do the best thing possible. They hoped against hope that with his audience before him the old war-horse would rear into life again. He did as they told him.

He was to be "discovered" on the stage at the beginning of the second scene. They got him on, and the curtain rose, disclosing him to the audience in a most brilliant and colourful costume. His arms were folded, his appearance one of great solemnity. The house thundered its applause. Then he spoke. Not the author's words nor anything like them, but short, incoherent sentences hastily uttered, barely heard, and certainly not understood. Somehow the scene was got through with Kean standing like a statue, expressionless and immovable, as one in a trance. The curtain fell on the act.

It was evident to everyone that something was wrong. They stumbled through what remained, Kean uttering a jumble of sounds, none of which made any sense at all. And at last the curtain fell on that most tragic of tragedies. There was a bad reception and it was some time before the manager could get a hearing. When he did so, he said he was commissioned by Mr. Kean to apologise for his ignorance of his part. Mental anxiety and bodily illness had impaired his memory and rendered him unable to do the author justice. To Grattan, Kean apologised humbly. It was the mere wreck of a genius who spoke.

To understand the next act in this drama within the Drury Lane drama, it is necessary to know that Kean and his wife now lived apart. He allowed her £200 a year. Young Charles was still at Eton, but Kean had determined to get him into the East India Company's service, for his schooling was nearly over. Mrs. Kean besought the boy not to leave her alone and friendless, so he promised his mother not to go. He went to his father and told him of his decision. Edmund asked coldly how he proposed to earn his living. If he would not do as his father wished, he told Charles, his father would disown him. Then Charles threw his bombshell. He told his father he intended to become an actor. Kean the elder was furious. He said he would be the first and last actor of his name; and on his son standing his ground, sent him away vowing never to see him again.

Even before his tragic failure in "Ben Nazir," Kean had quarrelled with Price. He now made overtures to Covent Garden. So Price had to think up some counter-move. He soon had a brain-wave. It was to play Kean against Kean, to trump the father by his son. Thereupon he engaged young Charles, a mere lad of sixteen, at ten pounds a week, to rise to eleven and twelve pounds if successful. He billed him to open as "Young Norval" in "Douglas." Edmund Kean was beside himself with fury, but the Town was vastly intrigued.

Naturally, the house was full to see Charles Kean when he made his début. He got a fine reception, which unnerved him at first; but he made a recovery and played on. Just a stripling of five feet seven inches, there was something in his face which recalled his father; but he had no experience, no vocal power or command, nothing save the grace and appeal of youth. He got his applause from a sympathetic audience, and had an excellent reception at the end. But his "Press" was poor. Most unfairly they contrasted him with his great father—a stupid, not to say disgraceful, thing to do. Price stood by and encouraged him, but he played the rest of the season to houses, however, which got thinner and thinner as the novelty wore off. He went from Drury Lane to Dublin, where he gained experience and success. Edmund went over to Covent Garden, which had even more trouble with the failing King of the Stage than Drury Lane had ever had. But he made it up with his son, and in the fullness of time the two of them played at the Garden together.

In December, 1828, Charles Kean reappeared at Drury Lane for Price, and had as his leading lady Miss Ellen Tree, whom he was to marry. He was, however, still too immature to be a real success. His determination to succeed was fixed, and back he went to the provinces to learn more. There was also a reconciliation between Edmund and Price, and he went back to the Lane again, but only as a shadow of his former self. He was utterly unreliable now, and the brandy bottle was his constant companion.

There was further tragedy in 1830. The tragedian now tried once more to learn a part he had never appeared in before, and they took the risk with "Henry V." He was to play it on February 22nd, 1830, but just before the doors of the theatre opened, his dresser found him lying in his room, dressed and made up as King Harry but in a kind of trance or coma, unable to speak, unable to recognise anyone. Notices were posted outside the theatre and the crowd sent away. He tried to pull himself together and on March 8th another attempt was made.

Everyone was anxious to see Kean, or rather what remained of Kean, in a new rôle, especially one so likely to suit him. The great theatre was filled. The orchestra played the overture, but the curtain remained down. The audience became restive. Were they once again to be fooled? The overture was played all over again, and this time the curtain went up. In the second scene, there was Kean, arrayed in regal magnificence and getting the welcome of a King, too, from his playgoing subjects. But that was as far as it got. It was "Ben Nazir" all over again. He mumbled, he jumbled, he made great cuts, he struggled; he tried vainly to recollect and pull himself together. It was a pitiable sight. There was a half-hour wait between the fourth and fifth acts, during which time the patience of the audience gave way. There seems to have been very little sympathy for the failing actor; the public did not seem to have been touched by the spectacle of the blind Titan fighting for his very life.

When the curtain did go up, he was received with hoots and hisses. He stood still, he waited, then came forward and bared his head, the traditional sign that he wished to address them. For some minutes he could not get a hearing. Then he spoke, interrupted often by the interjections from the crowd: "Ladies and gentlemen, it is now many years since I have had the honour to enjoy a large share of your approbation. You may conceive therefore how deeply I deplore this moment, when for the first time I incur your displeasure (cries of " No, No, not the first time "). If you wish that I should proceed, I must request your silence. For many years, give me leave to say, I have worked hard for your entertainment (here a voice was heard, " You have been well paid for it "). That very labour and the lapse of time and circumstances have no doubt had their effects upon my mind (here another voice demanded "Why do you drink so hard?" and Kean nearly broke down). Ladies and gentlemen, I feel that I stand before you in a most degraded situation (shouts of "Why did you put yourself into it?" and a few "No, no's "). You are my countrymen, and I appeal with confidence to that liberality which has always distinguished Englishmen." He bowed low, he tried to continue, but so badly was the whole thing done and so hopeless was he that the whole act did not last ten minutes. The final curtain fell amidst tumult.

There had been another sad sight on the stage at Drury Lane. Poor Joe Grimaldi, worn out with weariness and overwork, had broken down. He would never clown again.

He suffered a double tragedy, the loss of his money and the loss of the use of his limbs. He had for years been at Covent Garden, and asked them for a benefit, which was refused. He was prostrate and did not know where to turn. Drury Lane crossed his mind, but he had not played there for years, he had no sort of claim upon it, but the kindly old Theatre remembered its needy son. Stephen Price, for whom he had never worked, sent for him and told him that Drury Lane was at his disposal on the night of June 28th, 1828.

Joe played one scene out of "Harlequin Hoax" and also sang a song; but he did both from a chair, in which he was carried on to the stage, for he could no longer stand. Yet the old spirit flashed out, for he made them laugh uproariously. The curtain fell to terrific enthusiasm.

A benefit for Grimaldi realised £580, but in addition the Secretary of the Drury Lane Fund, that excellent foundation of Garrick's which carries on its good work to-day, called on Joe to tell him that he would receive from the Fund £100 a year for life. He paid him for the first quarter on the spot. So the old Clown's last anxiety was gone. Drury Lane, which he had served, now paid its debt of gratitude.

It is good to chronicle that generous action of Stephen Price's, for he was not to be in command of Drury Lane much longer. The constant troubles with Kean, the fall in public interest, had beaten him. He was behind with his rent, and so complicated had the situation become that the shareholders' representatives had to pay him to get out of the theatre.

A composer and publisher, Alexander Lee, stepped into his shoes, backed by a Captain Polhill, Member of Parliament for Bedford. Alfred Bunn was in command of the stage and was to have a good deal to say and do. He had been stage manager since the time of Elliston. He was a curious man, this Bunn, whom Thackeray has immortalised as "Dolphin" in "Pendennis." That great author paints him thus: "A tall, portly gentleman, with a hooked nose and a profusion of curling brown hair and whiskers; his coat was covered with the richest frog-braiding and velvet. He had under-waistcoats, many splendid rings and jewelled pins and neck-chains."

One evening Tom Cooke, the popular leader of the orchestra, had asked Bunn for an interview. He wanted an evening off and brought with him another young Irish lad who would, he said, deputise for him very efficiently. Bunn was amazed at this, for the boy was only fifteen. However, so confident did he appear, and so highly did Cooke recommend him, that he asked the boy his name. The reply was " Michael Balfe." It was the first meeting between two people destined to have many dealings together. After much hesitation Bunn gave the necessary permission and young Balfe deputised very well indeed.

Things were at a sorry pass with Lee and Polhill. Lee had an actress-wife, who played as Mrs. Waylett; Polhill had a lady whom he wished to see a star. No doubt that was his reason for entering into management. There were ceaseless disputes and recriminations, fanned by the wily Bunn, who wanted to get power himself.

Lee got out in 1833, and Polhill made Bunn manager, relieving himself of running responsibilities. That was exactly what Bunn wanted. He had watched and waited carefully for just such a moment. Things were bad in the world of the theatre; the prestige of the drama had never been so low. And here was Drury Lane without a real guiding hand, and Covent Garden in exactly the same position. Later on Bunn swooped. He startled the theatrical world by becoming at one and the same time Lessee of both Theatres Royal, Drury Lane and Covent Garden.

Alfred Bunn was a theatrical jack-of-all-trades. He was the most talked-of man of his day (he saw to that) and the most decried and criticised. He was actor, stage-manager, manager, librettist, impresario and poet (of sorts), and it was the last title which gave him the most pleasure. He wrote for the papers, he had a hand in everything. Withal, he had pluck, courage, enterprise, showmanship, optimism, and an indominable will to triumph over difficulties. In other words, he was a typical theatrical manager. More, he was the undisputed chief of the theatrical world of London,

Kean, now touring the provinces, made another attempt to return to Drury Lane. He and Macready were billed to appear together at Drury Lane, the old lion and the young one. Kean was to play, in 1832, fourteen times at Drury Lane, and in eight of these performances he was also to face the challenge of Macready. He chose Othello, with the young star as Iago. It was a time of strain and stress for everyone. Both contestants had a contempt for each other.

Failing in health and memory, a mere shadow of his former self, still the undaunted Kean would not admit that Macready was his master. The younger, sober and steadier man despised the vices of the elder, although admitting his great acting powers. So they met on Drury Lane stage and they fought it out.

Macready was tall, Kean short. Kean knew all the tricks, and Macready was often outwitted. Every night there was a row, every night the incensed Macready would appeal to stage manager Bunn. Kean always managed to get up-stage of him, so that half Macready's efforts were lost. Kean always manoeuvred him into positions where his facial expression could not reach the audience. It was the old hand against the new.

Thus, wracked with gout, and so ill that he could hardly hobble, Kean summoned up all his last resources, and played with such power and fire that once again he seemed to tower above the taller man, and he made the audience thrill and sob with those last flashes of his genius. He was nearly done. He must have gazed at himself in the glass and known that the race was nearly over. In defeating Macready he had used up his last reserves of strength but he had won.

CHAPTER 32

THE REMARKABLE MR. BUNN

MR. BUNN was a most remarkable man; and those who are curious to read his full career may do so in his own book, called " The Stage; Both Before and Behind the Curtain, from Observations Taken on the Spot." They will find a wealth of amusement, and a perfect picture of the theatrical times in which he lived—as seen through his eyes. In the present volume, it is possible only to relate what he actually did in Drury Lane.

Having got full power Bunn started off with a grandiloquent announcement that he would keep up the glories of both theatres and make them very temples of the drama. In fact, he had no such intention at any time. His real policy at all times was to purvey light entertainment and light opera, which he was perfectly correct in believing to be what the public of his day wanted.

In his new position of unique power, the actors and actresses soon realised that he was a completely ruthless dictator; for one of his first acts was to make all of them interchange between both theatres, and compelled to run from one to the other as time and schedule demanded. The public passing up Bow Street were treated to the nightly spectacle of actors in full make-up hurrying along with their costumes and props, having played at Covent Garden and now dashing off to be in time to appear at the second show at Drury Lane. Actresses were treated in just the same way, and whatever the weather, the dancers were compelled to face the elements in their flimsy costumes. Bunn's idea was that by owning both theatres, he could wash one hand with the other, make up on the swings what he lost on the roundabouts, and run the two practically for the price of one. He described his dual management as "The Grand Junction of the two Patent Theatres."

But there were hitches. He took over control in May, 1833, and opened in Drury Lane, on October 5th, 1833, with "The Tempest" and Milton's "Comus." His public announcement stated: "I throw myself on the candour and liberality of the profession, and also on that of the public and the Press, to aid and uphold me in my humble endeavours to restore the prosperity of that long neglected but national source of amusement — THE NATIONAL DRAMA."

The free list soon came under his eye for revision, and he was much criticised in consequence. In this matter, he was of course right, the system of free admission ruling at the time being perfectly outrageous. As a concrete instance, Bunn once had some legal business with a solicitor, and gave that gentleman a box for himself, his wife and family at Drury Lane. The attorney came with all his brood, occupied the box, slipped out in the interval to speak to Bunn on business for a few moments—and then sent in a bill, on which one of the items was " To attending you in your room at the theatre—6s. 8d."

Bunn scored an early success at Covent Garden in an opera "Gustavus the Third," but he could not do much good at Drury Lane. As a bait, he tried popular prices; but this failed, as for some reason people imagined the reduction meant they were not getting their money's worth. The Grand Junction was not enjoying an easy passage. Nor, indeed, were the artists. Templeton, for instance,

266

the finest tenor of his day, in common with all the rest, had to play nightly at both theatres. Once this caused a serious breakdown. " Masaniello " was being done at Drury Lane (already Bunn was plunging into opera) with Templeton singing in it after he had finished at the Garden. But the show at the Garden did not run to time. At the Lane they were all ready. The overture duly finished, but there was no sign of Templeton. Cooper, the stage manager, was in despair. Then a boy whom he had sent to Covent Garden to make enquiries rushed in to say Templeton was on his way.

Cooper at once gave orders for the singer's costume to be brought into the wings so he could jump into it in the least possible time. In the orchestra pit, Tom Cooke, guessing what had happened, started the overture all over again. Then Templeton arrived, breathless and cross. Cooper at once began bundling the unfortunate singer into his costume whilst he panted and perspired. The overture finished again, but still the curtain did not go up. The audience naturally began to stamp, clap and whistle, and Cooper had to go on in front of the curtain and explain that Templeton had been kept late at Covent Garden. There were cries of "Shame." Begging their indulgence, Cooper ordered the orchestra to play the overture for the third time. This was done amidst derisive laughter. Finally poor Templeton was pushed onto the stage and gasped out the opening bars, only to be interrupted by a burst of hearty laughter from the audience. Improperly fixed, Templeton's false moustache had blown off, got caught on the point of Cooke's violin, and that jolly Irishman was waving it in the air in triumph.

Incidents like this were common. Polhill was in despair and threw in his hand. He had lost £50,000. Without any backer, and almost destitute of ready money, Bunn was forced to desperate expedients. A natural gambler, he plunged by engaging the great singer Malibran to come to Covent Garden, at £125 per performance. She was to sing also at Drury Lane, though not on the same nights.

Malibran came, sang and conquered. She sang in " Fidelio " and in " La Somnambula." The season was a blaze of glory to packed houses. The only friction between Bunn and Malibran had been over an extra pair of silk stockings. He allowed her three pairs per costume. She wanted four. Bunn won. He might, and did, give her presents of rubies and diamonds, but he drew the line at extra stockings.

But that blaze of glory had been too costly for Bunn. He could not pay the rents, and his contracts terminated. But, at the moment, there were no other Richmonds in the field to take over. So Bunn offered both theatres reduced rentals. Covent Garden refused a diminution of £1,500 but the Lane accepted. As a result, the Grand Junction was finished, but Bunn retained control of the senior theatre, Drury Lane.

Charles Kemble opened Covent Garden against him, and tried reduced prices. At Drury Lane, Bunn was giving them Shakespeare. He was playing to £1,427, but as soon as cheap prices started over the way, the figure dropped to £814. Then they played opera against each other, both doing " The Bronze Horse." Bunn used Auber's music, but at the Garden they had a version by Rodwell. The battle of the theatres was on again. Bunn won by producing Planche's version of " The Jewess." It was a big success.

Next, as a big attraction, he engaged Macready. That great actor was anything but anxious to sign up with Bunn, but there was nowhere else for him to play in London with any real dignity. The agreement was that Bunn should, pay Macready £30 per week, play or no play, for 30 weeks, beginning on Thursday, October 1st, 1835. Macready was also guaranteed a clear half benefit.

Bunn was again in low water at the time, and had been forced to make a cut in salaries; but on the success of " The Jewess," he paid up in full, and got a letter of thanks from the company. But at last he had a stroke of real luck. If Macready should fulminate against being alternated with opera he did not care. " Masaniello " balanced " Hamlet," " The Cosair " (" Zampa ") balanced " Macbeth," " Fra Diavolo " made it possible to play " Lear," and " Der Freischutz " paid for the losses on " Othello." Shakespeare and Macready were at a discount. It was the lighter entertainment which kept the Lane open, so Bunn was forced always to be on the look-out for novelties. And then, one day, Tom Cooke brought him some news.

Our old Drury Lane friend Arnold was running the Lyceum as an opera house. He had a new English opera, entitled " The Siege of Rochelle," all ready for production, but the money was not there. This was the information which Cooke brought to Bunn. The Poet's eyes gleamed. "Whose composition is it?" he asked. And the delighted Cooke told him none other than Michael Balfe, the boy Bunn had once allowed to lead the orchestra at Drury Lane. Bunn remembered, and told Cooke to get the opera quickly. It was produced with great success at Drury Lane on October 29th, 1835.

All this was bad for Macready. It was his misfortune to be living at the time of great theatrical change. Ever since there had been drama, certainly ever since drama had been contained within the walls of a theatre, either roofed or unroofed, tragedy had been the aristocrat of entertainment. The tragedians had been the top-notchers, trailing clouds of their own glory, despising the lowly comedians and clowns—whilst a singer was just a thing apart, not really belonging to the theatre. Here now, at the National Theatre, at Drury Lane itself, under Bunn, opera shoved tragedy to the wall. Not only opera, but divertissements of every kind, musical entertainments, even semi-circuses with equine actors, were the public's choice. Thus, Drury Lane's vast auditorium was packed for Balfe, and packed again for "The Jewess," whilst Mr. Macready, "the eminent tragedian," as he always described himself, was playing to dismally poor houses.

First and foremost, Bunn was a commercial manager: the box office was his main objective. He had no time for Art for Art's sake. He was out to make money, to keep his theatre open. Having no backer, this was his only possible course. He was shrewd enough to observe the change in taste on the part of the public, and to give them what they wanted. Not what he wanted, and certainly not what Macready wanted, though those two aims were poles apart.

However, a new play was found in "The Provost of Bruges," in which Macready played with Ellen Tree as his leading lady. He got much praise for his performance but the tragedy just "failed to attract": It was played eight times only. Meanwhile, "The Jewess" filled the bill —and the house—on certain nights of the week, and so did "The Bronze Horse." A loss of £90 per night on straight plays was compensated by the musical productions.

Bunn now began to play Macready only in the afterpieces, making the main dish a musical one. The two men were not on speaking terms. This was pretty grim for Macready, it was tantamount to an admission that he could not fill the house, that he was only good to play at half time. Sometimes Macready played first and the opera followed, sometimes the other way round. The natural antipathy between the two men reached boiling point when Bunn announced, for the night of April 29th, 1836, a programme of Macready in the first three acts of "Richard III"; "The Jewess," and as a conclusion, the first act of "Chevy Chase," which was described as a "Grand Chivalric Entertainment." Such a bill is a fair indication of the mind of Bunn, and also of the popular taste of the time.

Macready, full of anger and rising rage, played the truncated tragedy. He left the stage and strode towards his dressing room. Alas, his path lay past the door of Alfred Bunn's office. The time was nine p.m. The poet was sitting at his desk, examining bills for payment. The only light was that of a reading lamp which reflected on the desk and left the rest of the room dim. Bunn gives us a lively, if one-sided, description of the scene which followed, a scene unique in the annals of Drury Lane.

The door opened suddenly, Bunn heard a voice say: "There, you villain, take that—and that." He received a violent blow in one eye, which closed it at once; he fell off his chair, and as he had the habit of twisting his left ankle round his chair leg, he sprained it in the fall; he rolled on the ground, covered in blood, ink, lamp oil and papers from the table; and on top of him was "Richard the Third"—in the person of Macready—holding him down. Recovering from his surprise, Bunn fought back, and when finally the pair were torn apart by Willmott the prompter, Bunn was found to have got Macready's little finger in his mouth and was viciously chewing it. Bunn took to his bed, and went to law. Macready allowed judgment to go by default, and Bunn got £150 damages.

Bunn made the most of the incident. He had got damages, he had got rid of Macready, and he was preparing Balfe's new opera, "The Maid of Artois," for production at Drury Lane with the one and only Malibran in the leading part. He hobbled to rehearsal on unnecessary crutches.

Bunn had written the libretto. Thanks chiefly to Balfe's score, but most of all to Malibran, the opera was

a big hit. There was a long and difficult finale which Bunn
knew would be encored. He asked Malibran to accede to
this. She said it would be impossible; she would be too
tired. Bunn besought her to do it, reminding her that
although he paid her a vast salary, she was always sneaking
off to give extra concerts in which he did not participate.
Malibran said she would do it, on one condition only, that
he gave her a pint of porter to drink before the encore.
" It is good for the voice," she said. The question was how
to get the porter to her, for she did not leave the stage.
Bunn was not beaten. It was solved by her pretending
to fall asleep on a heap of sand, rolling behind it, whilst
a stage hand, through a specially cut trap in the stage,
handed her the drink she thought so good for the voice.
And that is how it was done. She got her drink, and
Bunn got his encore. The audience were delighted, but
never knew how much it was indebted to that timely pint
of porter.

Bunn was in and out of the Lane like a jack-in-the-box.
And in and out of the Bankruptcy Courts too. Each season
he brought Drury Lane's prestige lower and lower. He
gave German opera, he brought in Ducrow and his performing horses, who did a show called " St. George and the
Dragon, or The Seven Champions of Christendom." When
excoriated for debasing Drury Lane, he reminded his critics
of how Kemble and Mrs. Siddons had presented " Blue
Beard " and " Timour the Tartar " supported by a whole
stud of Astley's horses. Also he reminded his critics that
before his time there had been a production at the Lane
called " Hyder Ali, or The Lions of Mysore," with elephants,
boa constrictors and a whole menagerie on the stage.

- He even went one better than all these things. He
engaged Van Ambergh's famous performing animals. The
Lane was now just a vast circus, another Astley's, a titanic
booth. But the highest in the land came to see those wild
beasts. The show was discussed in the clubs, in the nursery,
in the drawing rooms, in Court—and eventually the
Greatest Light of All shone on Bunn and his Beasts. For
Her Majesty Queen Victoria herself paid a visit to Theatre
Royal, Drury Lane, to see them. This was in 1839. And
she did not come once only, she came on January 10th,
January 17th, and January 24th; and on that last evening
she not only saw the show, but went behind the scenes on to
the stage and watched the animals being fed. Incidentally,

271

they had been starved for thirty-six hours so that the young Queen should see a nice refined jungle supper party.

Bunn was in the seventh heaven. The takings for the Command Performance were £712 7s. 6d. Where was Macready now? Where was tragedy? Where indeed was Shakespeare? Everybody was flocking to Drury Lane. The Duke of Wellington came twice, and talked to Van Ambergh for half an hour on each occasion. Came also the Marquis of Anglesey, Lord Brougham, all the glass of fashion, the mould of form, the high and the low, the nobility and the *hoi polloi*. It became the fashion to drop in at the Lane at 9 a.m. and see the beasts fed. Van Ambergh, a remarkable personality, was a lion of the season himself. The public went to the animals and Shakespeare and the Drama went to the dogs!

It has become the custom to look upon the early Victorian period as a most staid, solemn and respectable one, with propriety in the ascendant and amusement dull and slow. But the tale of Drury Lane, with Bunn and his German opera, his Weber, his Rossini, his Balfe, his promenade concerts by Jullien (with *tableaux vivants* as an extra), his Ducrow with "St. George and Charlemagne," his ballets and above all his Malibran, is quite sufficient to prove the contrary.

Bunn himself was always a storm centre. He had aroused trouble when he made the actors " double " at two theatres, thereby instituting something worse than two houses a night for the price of one; he had been in bad odour when he made a rule that nobody should receive more than £20 per week. He squabbled with the Lord Chamberlain, and even had a difference of opinion with old William IV, who knew a good deal about Drury Lane through Mrs. Jordan. He disliked actors, whom he referred to as " performers."

Kean, when pulling in £400 per night, drew £20 a week. Young had £20; Munden, Fawcett and Edwin Johnstone received £14; Dowton varied between £12 and £20, Liston started at £17 per week and rose to £20 per night. It was the nightly scale which annoyed Bunn, for Macready, who had started at £20 a week, was asking him in 1839 £30 per night.

He had troubles with authors too. Macready, a bad introduction, recommended a play by Bulwer Lytton. That worthy man demanded its acceptance unread. Very naturally

At right.

GEORGE ALEXANDER, who appeared
Drury Lane in *The Prodigal Son*
1905.

Below.

ELLEN TERRY, who at Drury Lane in
1903 acted with Sir HENRY IRVING for
the last time. It was at a special
performance.

RTRAM WALLIS, one of the Male
ncipal Boys in Drury Lane panto-
me, when, in 1914 the old tradition
s altered.

At left.
JULIAN WYLIE
who brought panto.
back to Drury La.
1929, after ten y
absence.

At right.
IVOR NOVELLO as
Henry V.
TOM ARNOLD'S presentation of Shakespeare in
1938.

Bunn declined. It was not all honey for him in management. Another trouble was the Drury Lane Free List, which was enormous. There were six hundred shareholders, all of whom considered themselves free of the theatre. So did everyone who had ever had a song sung there, or who had had a word of theirs spoken from the stage. As we have seen, he put an abrupt end to this abuse. Another of his reforms was to cut down the Press list.

It is with Bunn that we get our first glimpse of the theatre ticket agencies. He refers to Andrews, Sams, Mitchell, Ebers and Hookham. He had a fight with them, but like a wise manager, made it up and gave them a Reconciliation Dinner.

Yet although Bunn made money sometimes with opera, the expenses of the productions and the temperaments of the singers wore him down in the end. He engaged Albertuzzi for the Auber ballet "The Fairy Lake." She was to appear for two months. She kept him waiting, and caused costly postponements. When she did reach London, she said she was too ill to rehearse. The public got tired of waiting, and her appearance, when she did at last make it, was a flop.

The final blow was when Albertuzzi told him that now she could not appear because she was about to have a baby. The infuriated Bunn sent for the lady's husband, who had made the contract. That gentleman calmly declared that he had not the slightest idea of his wife's condition. It was the knock-out for Bunn. He had, for the moment, to give up. The Drury Lane Committee met and decided to put up the lease to public tender—they had to take this course by their recent Act of Parliament. The last thing Bunn did was to give a benefit performance for the widow and children of Thomas Haynes Bayley, a brother poet. Then he went bankrupt.

The lease of Drury Lane was taken in 1840 by W. H. Hammond. He was a comedian who had been connected with the unlicensed Strand Theatre, and evidently one of those who had not observed the change in public taste. Or else he was a true-blue upholder of the dignity of his profession—or else he had no right to be in management at all. He engaged Macready, who now returned to what had been in every sense The Lion's Den. He engaged that magnificent actor Samuel Phelps and Mrs. Warner. They opened with "Macbeth," which seemed to be Macready's usual opening at the Lane. He played the Thane, Phelps played Macduff and Mrs. Warner was Lady Macbeth. That was on January 20th, 1840. On January 22nd, a play by James Haynes, of course a tragedy, entitled " Mary Stuart," was presented. Macready was " Ruthven," Elton was " Rizzio," and Mrs. Warner, the ill-fated Queen—two tragic Queens of Scotland in the same week was good going for one actress. This was kept on for 20 nights, but it lost much money. At the end of February, Hammond. too went bankrupt for £8,000.

Drury Lane was now in a parlous state. Nobody wanted to take it on with the failures of the original committee, Elliston, Bunn, and now Hammond, fresh in memory.

But, as usual there was a man to fill the breach. It was one who had played there and suffered there,.one upheld by the dignity of the Drama which he believed it was his duty to support. So far he had met with little success as a salaried actor—now he was to become actor-manager and lessee. That man was William Charles Macready.

CHAPTER 33

HOME OF OPERA

MACREADY had always wanted to be manager of Drury Lane Theatre. He had controlled Covent Garden, but to him that was never quite the same thing. It is true that up to that time his associations with the Lane had not been of the happiest, but with Bunn's fall, the luck changed, and he was able to conclude an agreement with the Committee practically on his own terms. To such a depth had the great place fallen it could be leased with but one day's notice to terminate.

Macready was forty-eight years of age and his theatrical position was assured. He was the leading tragedian of his time, the acknowledged head of his profession. He was also something of a figure in Society. His friends were Charles Dickens, Landseer, Bulwer Lytton, Forster, and all the leading lights of Art, Literature and the social world.

Although he got the Lane cheaply enough, he inherited a lot of trouble with it. Apart from the bad state of repair backstage, there were gross deficiencies in equipment, and, at any rate in his opinion, the staff were incompetent. He took over for the Christmas season of 1841, and started off with that Drury Lane mascot, "The Merchant of Venice." His company included Mrs. Warner, Miss Faucit, Phelps, Elton, Anderson, Henry Marston, George Bennett. The comedians were Mr. and Mrs. Keeley, then at the height of their power, Henry Compton, and James Hudson, a Dublin discovery of Macready's and a good one. On the musical side (he was not going to neglect this) he had Phillips, Allen, Miss Romer, Miss Gould, Miss Poole and Miss P. Horton. Anderson was stage-manager, Serle acting-manager, and our old friend Tom Cooke was the musical director. Following the lead of Kemble and the example of Madame Vestris, he decided to develop the scenic side of the productions. This department was in the hands of Marshall and Telbin, masters of their art.

Even with this list of able lieutenants, he himself supervised everything with the greatest care. He issued the most meticulous instructions. He cleaned the theatre up, and shot out the rubbish—among it the ladies of the town, who made it their headquarters. He wanted a theatre the "family" could frequent.

On the day of his opening Drury Lane, he writes in his diary: "On this day I enter upon the lease and management of Drury Lane Theatre. I humbly implore the blessing of Almighty God upon my efforts, praying His gracious Spirit may influence me in adopting and carrying through all wise measures in a discreet, equable and honourable course, and only pursuing such a line of conduct as may benefit my blessed children, may be of service to the cause of good, and benevolent to those dependent upon me."

Later he records of the same day: "Saw my darling babes and, imploring the blessing of God on my undertaking, went to Drury Lane Theatre. Rehearsed the 'Merchant of Venice.' My room very uncomfortable. Lay down but got very little rest. Was much disturbed by being called for as the play began; resisted for a long while but was at last obliged to go forward. My reception was most enthusiastic. I acted Shylock very nervously, not to please myself. I saw the pantomime afterwards." By being "called" Macready meant that the public wanted him in front of the curtain to give him their best wishes. He always protested that he did not like this, but was very restive if other actors were called for too.

The pantomime which rounded off the entertainment was called "Harlequin and Duke Humphrey's Dinner, or Jack Cade, the Lord of London Stone." Nice compact little titles, the Drury Lane pantos had in those days. The mounting of his "Merchant of Venice" was superb, and it also made history, for it was the first time that a synopsis of scenery was printed on the bills of a Shakespearean production.

On January 2nd, 1842, Macready got his first managerial shock. He had imagined that he had no liabilities. His accountant, Brydone, now informed him casually that nothing had been paid for. Eventually he found that the total of debt was £2,500. Declaring that this was "very cruel," he gave instructions that nothing in future must be ordered without his written instructions. He was so shaken by the spectre of the £2,500 that he could not control his mind for anything else.

Business was not very good either, for he was giving them old stuff. It was probably against his heart's desire that he gave them opera in February, 1842—Gay's "Acis and Galatea," with the music of Handel and a truly wonderful scenic setting by Stansfield. This was a terrific success. Even that most captious critic, Edward Fitzgerald, was charmed. "Never in this country is the illusion which scenic art permits of been so completely and triumphantly displayed." Despite its success Macready took it off. Anderson, the stage manager, is brutally frank about its withdrawal. "It ought to have run 200 nights and brought thousands of pounds to the Treasury had the manager been so inclined."

Mr. Macready treated the public much as he did his own children—reared them on vegetarian diet and physicked them with homeopathic doses. Macready said he knew what probity was. He had promised variety, and he would be conscientious. He had his own way, but he lost his money. There is another good reason for the withdrawal which Anderson overlooks. Macready was not appearing in "Acis and Galatea."

At Easter Macready revived "Macbeth." Then he did a play by Darley, an Elizabethan tragedy called "Plighted Troth." This was a most unlucky venture. It happened that the name of the character he played, "Gabriel Grimwood," was also that of a man involved in a recent notorious murder. This led to facetious remarks from the gallery, to

Macready's great discomfiture. Nor was this the worst that happened to him in this ill-fated effort. Towards the end of the tragedy, he was stabbed with a bread-knife (and this did not overawe the audience). Whilst he lay on the stage "dead," an actor trod on his hand and hurt him. The infuriated if eminent tragedian, forgetting that he was "dead," sat up and cursed the actor soundly for his clumsiness and inefficiency. This was too much for the audience. They had begun their booing and cat-calling but the sight of the revived and angry "corpse" sent them into fits of uncontrollable laughter.

He came back on October 1st, 1842, with Mrs. Nisbet, a good comedy actress, and John Ryder added to his company. The opening attraction was "As You Like It," with Macready as Jacques. Once more the audience called for him before the play began, for he was very popular.

Remembering the success of "Acis and Galatea," Macready decided to produce "King Arthur." The production was memorable for one thing. Tom Cooke was the musical director, and during rehearsals he could not find anyone to do justice to the solo tenor part. Anderson, the stage manager, suggested a young man with a good voice in the chorus. After a brief audition Cooke rushed up to Anderson in his excitable Irish way, threw his arms round him, and said they must change places; Anderson should be the musical director and he, Cooke, would do the stage management. So the young man got the job, a small part. And far from being overcome by his opportunity, he showed a good deal of temperament and determination. He refused flatly to sing side face to the audience. His determination —and his voice—beat all opposition. He sang it his way and with overwhelming success. The singer was Sims Reeves.

On February 11th, 1843, Macready produced a play by Robert Browning called "The Blot on the 'Scutcheon." There had been stormy scenes between Browning and Macready, who had insisted on a lot of cuts and alterations. He thought the play was bad and the poet a very conceited man. He refused to appear in it.

But a few days before production, Phelps was so ill that Macready had to learn his part. But Phelps played after all and triumphed. A farce followed which Macready liked —"The Thumping Legacy." Although the farce pleased the tragedy only played three times.

A trial of opera in the shape of "Sapho" by Puccini, with Clara Novello as "Sapho" and Mrs. Shaw as "Climene," was a failure; but a burlesque by Planche, which followed, succeeded. An unexpected failure was Sheridan Knowles's last play, "The Secretary." Macready now made up his mind to leave the theatre. Despite his mannerisms and his peculiarities, his company did not want him to disband them. They offered to work at greatly reduced salaries.

Then came what he hoped was a gleam of sunshine. He received a command from the Queen. He suggested playing "Much Ado About Nothing" and "The Thumping Legacy." But the Queen chose "As You Like It" and "The Thumping Legacy." This upset Macready. "I was much annoyed by the selection," he wrote, "which does me no good." Yet he declared that he played "Jacques" very well on the actual night (June 12th, 1843). The Queen and the Prince Consort sent for him, and she thanked him and said she was very pleased. The Prince enquired if this was the real Shakespearean version, and Macready replied that they had restored the original text. He assisted in "lighting" the Royal Visitors out of the theatre in the old-fashioned manner.

There was an expression of general disappointment when Macready announced his retirement from the management of Drury Lane. There is no doubt that the true play-goers were sympathetic about his defeat, for defeat it really was. At Theatre Royal he had fought a good fight, he had done his best, he had struck a blow for good and distinctive productions, but the Fates were against him.

There was another factor which probably weighed greatly with Macready. In 1843, the monopolistic rights of the two Patent Theatres, Drury Lane and Covent Garden, had been definitely broken by Act of Parliament. There had been battles about this for a long time. As early as 1831 the Lyceum had made a determined effort to break free by petitioning the King. The Patent Theatre had lodged a counter-petition, and old Sailor William had referred the whole question to the Lord Chancellor, Lord Brougham. Three judges were called in to help. Their decision was that, by a Licence from the King, any theatre could be free to play any sort of play, Patent or no Patent. The Lyceum got its Licence, as also did the Haymarket—and the Patent Theatres now had two legitimate rivals. It was then only a question of time, and that time came when, after an

278

exhaustive enquiry by a committee, Bulwer Lytton got an Act through Parliament in 1843 which gave all theatres the right to perform any sort of attraction they pleased, from Shakespeare downwards. This brought liberty to the Theatre, and all monopoly ceased.

Macready arranged to go to America to recoup himself for his losses. His name stood higher than ever before, if his balance at the bank was lower. There was a distinction and a réclamé about being in his company which always got him support.

He had a nasty jolt just before he sailed, when he learned that his position at Drury Lane was again to be filled by his old enemy, Alfred Bunn. Bunn came back, bumptious and smiling as ever. And with him he brought Charles Kean, now thoroughly experienced and relieved from the competitive greatness of his father, now dead. His inferiority complex was gone, and he was signed up at £50 a week. He gave Drury Lane a production of "Richard III" which was a foretaste of the history he made later at the Princess's Theatre, a landmark in the story of the Drama.

But Bunn was again hankering after opera. He handed Balfe a libretto of another opera he had prepared, and Balfe set to work on it. There were repeated arguments and battles about the title, which was eventually fixed as "The Bohemian Girl." Bunn, who believed in the work, was ill all through this period, but struggled down to the theatre for rehearsals. Finally it was presented on the night of November 27th, 1843. It was a terrific first-night success, but then unaccountably hung fire, and Balfe, who had been conducting, got depressed and went to Paris. But Bunn hung on, and the tide turned. The piece ran for 100 nights. Actually, it started a fashion, and went all over the world. It is the only English opera whose music still retains its popularity to-day. Moreover, it gave old Alfred Bunn his "blaze of glory" at long last; and to Balfe it gave a marble statue in the Rotunda at Drury Lane.

During his last flutter at the Lane, Bunn made it a home of opera. Besides his Balfe, he produced many others, Benedict's "Bride of Venice," Wallace's "Maritana," etc. In 1848, remembering Van Ambergh's lions, Bunn imported The Cirque National from Paris, and made a success. Emboldened by this French experiment, he tried another dodge. He brought over a French company and put on "serial plays." They presented "Monte Cristo," and the action occupied two nights' playgoing. This caused a serious riot, for the public of 1848 would not stand tricks of that kind. They regarded it, and rightly, as an attempt to make them pay twice for one play.

This French flutter brought Bunn down with a bang. He went bankrupt again.

And once again Old Drury was in the dumps too. Then James Anderson, Macready's stage manager, decided to try his luck. He took over the theatre on December 26th, 1849. He had a good but by no means outstanding company. He produced "Ingomar," making a personal success himself. Drury Lane was now the home of spectacular drama, and Anderson kept up this reputation with two finely-done plays, "Azael" and "The Temple of Isis."

Theatre managers looked forward to a golden harvest from the flood of visitors who would surge to London for the 1850 Great Exhibition. But Anderson was to learn, as many have learnt to their cost since, that periods of national rejoicing and extraneous attractions do not spell prosperity for the theatre; rather the reverse. Everyone went to the Crystal Palace, but few came to see the plays at Drury Lane. Anderson was ruined. To crown his misery, a vast American Circus came to Town, took Drury Lane over and packed it to suffocation. That was the sort of thing the Exhibition visitors wanted.

CHAPTER 34

THE GREAT "GUS"

ANOTHER of those Farewells to the Stage which adorn the story of Drury Lane was to be witnessed on February 26th, 1851. This time it was in honour of Macready. It was a memorable occasion, and for once the great actor himself was deeply moved by the public applause —though not by the fact that he was saying goodbye to the stage.

His retirement made a sad gap at Drury Lane, which then fell on evil days. Gye, of Covent Garden, took it over, and called it The Grand National Opera House. He staged opera and drama. But the public found the Grand National prices a bit too high, and Gye came a cropper and left the Lane.

In July, 1852, a Mr. Sheridan Smith—much more Smith than Sheridan — reigned for one week, followed by Mr. George Bolton, who lasted for a similar pediod, whilst their successor, a Mr. De Vere, held the reins for only six days. None of them was able to meet the first week's expenses. A publican, ex-policeman and showman, E. T. Smith, took over at the end of 1852. This strange man was a manager of the lower-Bunn order. But he kept the theatre open for seven years. He started on Boxing Night with a huge success in " Uncle Tom's Cabin." The whole nation was reading Harriet Beecher Stowe's book, and Smith cashed in. Then he scored with Charles Reade's drama, " Gold," a version of " It's Never Too Late To Mend." He brought Drury Lane Gustavus Brooke, a fine actor who had never had the full meed of recognition due to him, but whose story belongs more to the Olympic Theatre than Drury Lane. He held the stage during 1853 and 1854. Then Smith got the opera craze. He gave Italian opera at popular prices, 4s. stalls, 2s. 6d. dress circle, pit and second circle 1s., and 6d. in both of the galleries. The price of a box was one guinea.

Smith featured Gassier, Lucy Escott, Miss Huddart, Hamilton Braham, Bettini, and many other good artistes. Like Bunn, he alternated opera with Shakespeare, with Charles Mathews, with Chinese conjurors, and with a " human fly," a man who walked on the ceiling of the theatre. He staged tragedy for the great Rachel and followed on with a circus. Indeed, it was now Booth-Royal, Drury Lane. Smith might have got away with it, but he put too many eggs into too many baskets. He ran Drury Lane, The Alhambra, Her Majesty's Opera House in the Haymarket, and a travelling circus. He even had a shot at Highbury Barn as a theatre-cum-pleasure garden. He was the landlord of the Radnor Tavern, Chancery Lane, a wine merchant, an auctioneer, a picture dealer, a land agent, a bill discounter and a newspaper proprietor.

Next came Dion Boucicault, to stage " The Colleen Bawn " with himself, his wife and Madame Celeste in the autumn of 1862. He followed this with a great military and topical drama " The Relief of Lucknow."

Then from the Lyceum, where he had made £13,000, came Edmund Falconer. What he had won at the Lyceum, out of a show called " Peep O'Day," he lost at Drury Lane. He produced a drama called " Bonnie Dundee," but whatever may have happened in the way of bonnet throwing in Scotland, the public refused to throw up their bonnets in Drury Lane, and the curtain rang down on a dire failure. Falconer had, as his acting manager, a man of very different type, F. B. Chatterton. Chatterton knew his business. He believed in quality, and did his best to persuade Falconer to provide it. So on Chatterton's advice they staged " King John," " Henry IV," " Manfred," " Faust," " Comus," and similar productions with really first class casts. They had Phelps, Walter Montgomery, Mrs. Herman Vezin, and good support. Samuel Phelps' performance in " Manfred " was one of the best things this great actor ever did.

But Falconer was a bad business man, and ignored much of Chatterton's good advice. So he lost all his money. Chatterton, meanwhile, had been watching points, and on Falconer's departure, he proposed himself to the Committee of Drury Lane as lessee of the theatre and they accepted him. He paid a rental of £6,000 a year, with an additional £10 for every night the theatre was open in excess of 200.

Under Chatterton's astute and upright guidance, the Drury Lane we know to-day began to take shape. He made a very great feature of the annual pantomime, and from 1866, when he took over, the Drury Lane panto became one of the premier annual events of London. He had observed that tastes were changing, and he was intelligent enough to anticipate the public demands. It was F. B. Chatterton who conceived and presented the big, panoramic dramas and the spectacular pantomimes with which Drury Lane's name has become indelibly associated. And he did them well. Beverley, one of the best scenic artists who ever lived, did the decor, and his transformation scenes were sheer marvels to stagecraft. In one of Chatterton's big dramas, " The Great City," be brought a hansom cab and horse onto the stage. The audience hailed it as a triumph of realism. They applauded to the echo a sight they could observe free in the street outside. The extraordinary thing is that stunts like these still pull the place down.

In 1869, Chatterton engaged the famous Vokes family, who monopolised the pantomimes for years to come. They were an extraordinary combination. Old Vokes had been a theatrical costumier, and as soon as his children could walk, he put them on the stage. They played in Shakespeare and anything in which children were required. The eldest son, Fred Vokes, had been call boy to Phelps, and assistant to Professor Anderson, the Wizard of the North. He developed an amazing strain of acrobatic dancing, and was known as "The Man with the Elastic Legs." Jessie Vokes, on the stage at the age of four, taught dancing as well at the Surrey Theatre, one of her pupils being Flexmore, the famous clown. She looked after business affairs for the whole family. Victoria Vokes made her stage début at the age of two, but Rosina Vokes beat them all for she was carried on the stage as a baby in long clothes. She subsequently married Cecil Clay, the composer of "Songs of Araby."

But clever as they were, the Lane was to get a bit too much of the multitudinous Vokes. In 1874, they were playing all the principal parts in "Aladdin." They even took a call as a family, and did a special dance whilst taking it. In 1875, they were the entire show of "Dick Whittington," with yet another member of the clan, Walter Vokes, cropping up to play the cat. In 1877, they were all in "The White Cat." Nobody else got a chance. Their dancing was the great attraction.

Eventually the public wearied of the Vokes and honest, genial, generous Chatterton failed. He had staked all on the pantomime, and the public were tired of undiluted Vokes. On February 4th, 1879, Drury Lane suddenly closed its doors, right in the middle of the season. Salaries were not immediately forthcoming, and the Vokes, who owed so much to Chatterton, went on strike.

The poor man was £36,000 on the wrong side. He had run Drury Lane for seventeen years. and richly deserves his corner of fame in the Drury Lane pantheon as a noble tryer, a champion of the drama and an honest man. It was he who enriched the proverbs of the theatre by his dictum— "Shakespeare spells ruin and Byron bankruptcy." He died in 1886, and left an untarnished name for kindness, good deeds and great work for charity.

The notice of the closure of Drury Lane posted up at the doors of the theatre caught the eye of a young man passing by. His heart gave a bound, for it had been his ambition to run Theatre Royal, Drury Lane, and to run it successfully. Here was the chance. But the total worldly

-wealth of that young aspirant to Drury Lane fame was £3 15s.

He was not a man to be daunted. Straight to the stage door he went and asked to see the Committee. Giving his name as Augustus Harris, he declared his business was "Drury Lane Theatre." Already he had the promise of a friend to back him if ever he got control of the Lane. On this the young Harris relied. The Committee considered his enquiry. They had one or two offers of which they did not think very much, but they wanted urgently to get the theatre open.

They decided to see him. He spoke confidently of his plans. The Committee were impressed by his enthusiasm but he looked rather young for the job. He admitted he was only 27. They said they would talk it over, and let him know. He waited. The young man was certainly full of self-confidence but the Committee wanted no more fiascos. So they had him in again and told him he had spoken well but that money was the best talker. He could have Drury Lane on reasonable terms if he would put down £1,000 as guarantee of bona-fides. Harris replied it was a deal and they parted with mutual esteem.

Highly elated, the young capitalist of less than four pounds rushed round to his moneyed friend. But that potential backer politely backed out. To soften the blow, he took young Augustus to dinner at the London Aquarium. There they ran into a Mr. Rendle, to whom his friend introduced Harris, as follows: "Allow me to introduce Mr. Augustus Harris, the new lessee of Drury Lane." Mr. Rendle stared. The friend added artfully; "I believe you were one of the unsuccessful proposers for the Theatre," and turning to Harris he added: "Mr. Rendle wanted to give the Vokes family another chance at Drury Lane." This was probably what had cooked Rendle's goose with the Committee.

The idea that this young Harris had got Drury Lane intrigued Rendle vastly. Noting this, Harris promptly proposed that they should join forces. Rendle was wary, but Harris gave him no peace. He kept calling in. He unfolded marvellous plans for spectacular drama and big pantomimes. He said that if he could raise only £3,000, he could stage his first big show, and after that it would be dead easy.

He so besieged Rendle that at length the harassed man

284

said, "Look here, Harris, I will find £2,000 if you will find the rest." "Agreed," cried Harris the optimist. And immediately he went in search of this £1,000. If he had no money, he had plenty of brains and drive. The first £250 was raised from a refreshment contractor of his acquaintance, probably on account of bar rent. This was to be payable on the signing of the lease. He next called on a kindly relative, and after a good deal of persuasion got him to back a bill for £250. Here was half the amount raised already. Finally, he went for a walk in the park to cool off, and to think. There, he met a couple of friends, who invited him to dinner. Over the cigars and wine, he asked for the loan of £250, and got it. And that was the limit of his borrowing capacity: he knew of no more available sources, and was still £250 short. But Rendle came in.

Two thousand seven hundred and fifty pounds was little enough to start Drury Lane with but Harris did it. He became the most successful manager there since the time of David Garrick.

Ignoring Chatterton's dictum, Harris started with Shakespeare. He put up George Rignold in a production of "Henry V," and it filled the theatre until Harris was ready with the Christmas pantomime. The piece was "Bluebeard," and it was far and away the most spectacular pantomime that London had ever seen. Harris had to engage the Vokes family, for he was late in the field. But he stopped their artistic tyranny, and at the end of the pantomime he got rid of them. They thought they had become an indispensable tradition at Drury Lane, but Harris made a new tradition in which they had no part.

The next year he launched the series of Drury Lane dramas which became so famous, with "The World," written by Merritt, Henry Pettitt and Augustus Harris. He always got in as part author on dramas and on the earlier pantomimes. It gave him more power.

When pantomime time came round again, Harris was ready with an up-to-the-minute show. He had Kate Santley as Principal Boy, and James Fawn and Arthur Roberts as chief comedians. Going thus to the music halls for his pantomime comedians was an entirely new departure. For the first time the "halls" invaded pantomime and the sacred precincts of Drury Lane—and they were welcome. The indignant Vokes family went to Covent Garden in opposition. Harris routed them completely with his music hall people in "Mother Goose." The book was by that master of the art, E. L. Blanchard, who wrote so many great pantomimes for Drury Lane.

One day Harris's stage manager announced he had found a young man who could do more with his legs than Vokes could. He could use both. Vokes, like so many others, tricked his public, really using only one leg in his dances. An audition was given, the young man was engaged. He was Fred Storey, destined to make a big name, and to live to see his daughter marry into the peerage from the Gaiety. That second pantomime, besides Kate Stantley, James Fawn and the great Arthur Roberts, had John D'Auban, Frank Wyatt, Fred Storey, Mark Kinghorne, Emma D'Auban, Julian Girard and Ada Blanche in the cast.

Harris always took his pantomime seriously. Although the result was laughter and joy, the preparation was a matter of urgent painstaking labour. He spent months in planning. His shows cost, in those days of easy money, between £5,000 and £6,000—unheard-of expenditure then. And those pantomimes made money, although one way and another he employed between 700 and 800 people.

Augustus "Druriolanus" Harris, as he loved to be called, supervised everything personally. His working day began at breakfast table. He would send for Charlie Alias, the great costumier, and draw pictures on the table-cloth of what he wanted. His breakfasts were " occasions " with secretaries in attendance, auditions going on and authors and scenic artists milling around. He worked every moment of his days, did many things at once, as the true theatrical magnate indeed must.

Not only did he help to write the pantomimes and the dramas, but he often played in them. In 1881, the autumn drama (for that was the formula, a drama every autumn, and a panto every Christmas, with all sorts of things in between), was called " Youth," written by Paul Merritt and Augustus Harris. A contemporary criticism says that " as a literary work it cannot take a very high place, but as a drama which interests the spectator and wins the sympathy of the auditor, it is unsurpassed."

There was indeed variety in the fare at Drury Lane under the Harris regime. There were light operas like " La Fille de Madame Angot," and dramas like " Lady Audley's Secret " in 1880, not to mention Miss Litton playing in " As You Like It." In 1881, besides " Othello " and' " Virginius," he gave a season of the Ducal Court Company of Saxe-Meiningen. In 1882, opera under the direction of Franks and Pollini got a turn and in addition, a German season of Wagner, Beethoven and Weber. Later he presented Madame Ristori. In 1883, the Carl Rosa Opera Company did a season, and repeated it during the following year. In the same year, 1884, Haverley's Minstrels from America played at Drury Lane. Black-faced minstrels, but nobody accused Harris of lowering the prestige of Drury Lane. His own prestige was too strong for that. He had made Drury Lane the National Theatre in fact; whereas his predecessors had achieved it in name at most.

In 1885 Harris gave a benefit to F. B. Chatterton, which was richly deserved. That year, Carl Rosa did another season, and William Creswick, a first-class actor, bade farewell to the stage. Another Carl Rosa season, " Frivoli " by W. Beatty-Kingston, a benefit to Lionel Brough, and Slavinsky's Russian Choir, were features of his varied presentations in 1886. In 1887, there was more opera by Carl Rosa and an Italian opera company, while Charles Warner had a well-earned benefit.

In 1888, a revival of " A Run of Luck," the previous autumn drama, filled the theatre from March to May; and the autumn drama was " The Armada." In 1889, Harris took things more quietly, there being only the autumn drama and the pantomime; but in 1890 the Carl Rosa were back again, and there was a production of the drama " Paul Kauvar " in the spring and a benefit to Blanchard's widow. The next year saw a revival of " It's Never Too Late to Mend," " Formosa " (Dion Boucicault's drama) and " Drink." There was a German-Italian opera season in 1892, additional to that at Covent Garden (Harris by this time controlled both theatres, as had Bunn). The attractions in 1893 were a spring season of English opera, a season by the Comedie Francaise, more overflow of opera from Covent Garden, and a special matinée to celebrate the 50th anniversary of " The Bohemian Girl." In 1894 there was English opera again.

In 1895, the indefatigable Harris gave English opera in the spring, followed by Eleanora Duse, a great attraction. After a spring season of English opera, Sir Augustus Harris died of a wasting disease, on 22nd June, 1896. He was only 45. His activities had been dynamic and wore him out. He controlled six or seven theatres in all, many touring companies, and business speculations. He once owned *The Sunday Times* and wrote a series of articles for it.

His eccentricities were many. He had been known to go to sleep and snore in the stalls on a Henry Irving first night. Once he took off his boots in a box at the Comedy Theatre. He also slumbered peacefully during a play in which Charles Hawtrey appeared. He must have been worn out, because that delightful actor would have kept anyone awake. He barred a facetious critic who described his portrayal of " Icilius." as " a cheap, cold performance, quite a penny-icilius." He gave generous presents; cigars for the stage hands at Christmas. Once he made it " pâté-de-foie-gras " and an unappreciative recipient complained he had never used such bad brown boot polish in his life!

Every year he gave a matinée for the Royal General Theatrical Fund at Drury Lane.

He was knighted not because of his services to the theatre but because he was an Under Sheriff of London during a visit of the German Emperor. But "Druriolanus," the title the Theatre itself conferred upon him, gave him the most pride and joy.

CHAPTER 35

PEERLESS PANTOMIME

THE pantomimes and dramas of Augustus Harris made so great an impression that nothing is likely to erase their memory. Harris did things in a big way in a big theatre. In pantomime he always gave overweight—and that was a good fault. Blanchard wrote the first nine scripts, but after that Harris joined in as collaborator in the story as well as in production.

The pantomimes were the real thing — great, solid, massive affairs, with huge crowds of performers, masses of colour, bewildering movement, a strong dash of magic, a transformation scene, and, of course, a procession. The fun-making was the job of the comedians. Harris would sit himself in the stalls and challenge them to make him laugh. And make him laugh they had to, or . . . .

Harris cast on a lavish scale. What a cavalcade of

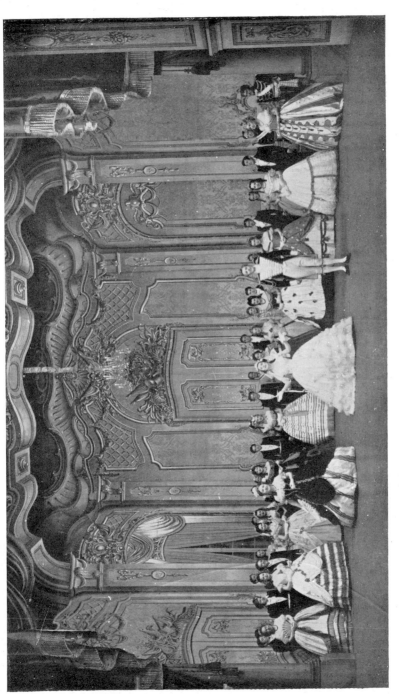

A scene from *The Dancing Years*, TOM ARNOLD and IVOR NOVELLO's record success. MARY ELLIS is in the centre. Produced in 1939, it was Old Drury's last pre-war show.

Members of the Drury Lane staff amongst whom the nosecap of the bomb fell when an H.E. hit the theatre in 1940. These men were actually sleeping in the wrecked room

handsome, dashing if monumental Principal Boys, enchanting Principal Girls, and top-notch music-hall comedians he assembled. There were Kate Santley, Ada Blanche, Arthur Roberts, James Fawn, Fanny Leslie, Harry Nicholls, Nellie Power, Constance Loseby, Vesta Tilley, Herbert Campbell, Kate Vaughan, Fred Storey, Charles Lauri (a wonderful animal impersonator), Grace Huntley, Nelly and Kate Leamar, and, continuing the list, Victor Stevens (who once played that traditional and legendary figure, Ally Sloper), Edith Bruce, Connie Gilchrist, Robert Pateman, Miss Wadman, Letty Lind, Charles Danby, Lionel Rignold, Harriet Vernon, Florence Dysart, Maggie Duggan, Belle Bilton, Agnes Hewitt, Little Tich, Marie Lloyd (always principal girl, never principal boy at the Lane), Mabel Love, Marie Loftus, Arthur Williams, Isa Bowman, Alexandra Dagmar, Sophie Larkin, Emily Miller, Decima Moore, Clara Jacks, and Paul Cinquevalli. It is a marvellous array of talent.

Harris's dramas were of the same calibre. He rang all the changes; he engaged all the best people. Their titles are as exciting as were the shows themselves: they sound a fanfare of melodrama. "The World" (1880); "Youth" (1881), "Pluck" (1882), "A Sailor and His Lass (1883), "Human Nature" (1885), "A Run of Luck" (1886), "Pleasure" (1887), "The Armada" (1888), "The Royal Oak" (1889), "A Million of Money" (1890), "A Sailor's Knot" (1891), "The Prodigal Daughter" (1892), "A Life of Pleasure" (1893), "The Derby Winner" (1894), "Cheer, Boys, Cheer" (1895). Where there are gaps in the list, there were revivals. The chief authors, with whom Harris insisted on collaboration, were Paul Merritt, Henry Pettitt, Robert Buchanan, and Henry Hamilton. "The Armada" and "The Royal Oak" were something more than melodrama, they were romantic plays of a high order.

There are two very great people in the Drury Lane story who demand special notice, and both of them belong to pantomime — Dan Leno and Herbert Campbell, the greatest combination of comedians ever known.

Dan Leno had Drury Lane in his destiny. As a very young man, when he was once passing the theatre with his partner, Johnny Danvers, he stopped and gazed long and earnestly at the vast pile. Then he walked up the outside steps and knelt for a short time at the top. After a few seconds he rose and rejoined the astonished Danvers. "Johnnie," he said quietly, "one day I shall play there."

If whilst kneeling, Leno had offered up a short prayer, that prayer was surely answered.

He was really the discovery of George Conquest, who told Harris about him. Harris engaged Dan for the Lane pantomime in 1888. This was " The Babes in the Wood," and one of the best things Harris ever staged. Leno, as " The Wicked Aunt," did not have a very big part, as the older hands, Herbert Campbell and Harry Nicholls, playing " The Babes," took the " fat " in every sense of the word. But Leno was a success, and Drury Lane became his Christmas venue for the rest of his life.

The following year Leno played a Dame in " Jack and the Beanstalk" and this time he was paired off with Herbert Campbell. The combination proved to be the ideal pantomime couple, each being a perfect foil to the other. Campbell was huge, ponderous, jolly and beaming; Leno small, quick, flashing, quaint, and, like all true clowns, able to turn on pathos when required.

Sir Augustus Harris's last pantomime production was in 1895-6. He died with the phrase " Harris had surpassed himself " ringing in his ears.

He was one of the giants of Drury Lane. In the Board Room is his picture, frock-coated, bearded, and looking very like King Edward VII; outside the theatre is his bust over a drinking fountain erected by public inscription. Bomb fragments and blast damaged it during the war, but Harris is untouched, as firm and enduring as his memory. Inside the theatre in the old store-rooms are many of the props he made for his pantomimes, as good as ever, and many of the baskets he used still bearing his name.

And with the end of Harris there nearly came the end of Drury Lane. His widow carried on the next year. A sinister rumour was abroad that the Duke of Bedford did not mean to renew the lease, that the great old playhouse was to be destroyed and the site merged into Covent Garden Market. And once again, in Drury Lane's hour of need, the man arose to save the situation.

Arthur Collins, who was not only to carry on the Harris tradition but to improve upon it and write a glorious chapter of his own, started life as a seedsman with Carters. But he had a gift for drawing and painting which interested him far more than seeds. He joined the staff of Harry Emden, the great scenic artist, and worked in the scene painting room—the Paint Frame—at Drury Lane. He entered it humbly in 1881. He was to remain in the Theatre for 43 years. He worked, watched, and studied. Beverley, the great artist, was still there. Collins, bitten by the theatre, hankered after the stage. He asked Harris to let him act and he was sent on tour in " A Run of Luck " at 30s. a week. One night, when Harris arrived at a provincial theatre so late that the show was over, he found Collins repainting the scenery. He made Collins stage manager of Drury Lane as a result of that voluntary overtime. Harris's sad death came soon after, and Collins helped the widow and her brother to carry on for a season.

Then the news got about of the pending destruction of Drury Lane. Collins conceived the idea of saving the theatre, but Rendle, an executor of Harris, said he could not transfer the lease without a payment of £1,000. The lease had about ten years to run. Collins had neither the money nor the means to find it. He sat alone in Romano's, the famous restaurant in the Strand, depressed and brooding. He had less than a week's respite if he were to achieve his ambition, and his position was curiously similar to that of his famous chief years before.

But a kindly fate watches over the destiny of Drury Lane, and manifested on this occasion in the form of an Australian merchant who loved theatre-going. This man asked Collins what was the cause of his gloom. Collins told him, adding that unless he could get the £1,000 he and the Lane were sunk. The man smiled and told Collins to send round to his office in the morning and collect.

Scarcely able to believe his luck, Collins rushed to the agent of the Duke of Bedford, the ground landlord. The agent demurred, but a great public outcry arose in the Press over the threat to Theatre Royal, and Collins got the remainder of the lease, with a renewal, for eighty years.

On May 28th, 1897, for the first time in its history, Theatre Royal, Drury Lane, became a Limited Liability Company, with Arthur Collins as its Managing Director.

Collins carried on at the Lane as Harris had done. He knew better than to upset the perfect formula. His first drama was " White Heather," produced in the Diamond Jubilee year. And it was a Jubilee play and a diamond itself. His first pantomime was " Babes in the Wood," in which, again following the Harris tradition, he collaborated as author with Arthur Sturgess. Ada Blanche was Principal

Boy, Violet Robinson Principal Girl, and the "Babes" were Dan Leno (boy) and Herbert Campbell (girl).

These were the first of many. Arthur Collins loved the Lane, respected its conditions and never let it down. His reign is not only comparable to Harris's, but in some ways transcends it.

His dramas were mostly written by Cecil Raleigh and Henry Hamilton in collaboration. These two men became the Gilbert and Sullivan of melodrama. They were utterly unlike each other. Raleigh was brimful of vivacity and wit, and had a tremendously high regard for his own work. Hamilton, a precise, cultured man, wrote the more dramatic parts of the shows. He was an epicure, though he lacked the senses of taste and smell. The mere fact that the food he ate, the wines he drank and the cigars he smoked were the best, gave him the feeling of the utmost satisfaction. The two men were never on very friendly terms with each other, and, at rehearsals, each would carry on loud conversations whilst his collaborator's work was being played.

Collins's pantomimes were speedier and less cumbersome than those of Harris, but still inordinately long. He always took his call at the end of the first half—it would have been too late at the final curtain. Pungent was Herman Finck's "wisecrack" when he and his wife staggered out one Boxing Night. "I wonder what time it is," said Mrs. Finck. "You mean you wonder what day it is," rejoined Herman the wit.

Arthur Collins dealt the Harlequinade its death-blow, despite the clowning of Whimsical Walker. It got shorter and shorter until a mere ten minutes sufficed, and that ten minutes was nearly all given over to advertising.

In the spring of 1898 "White Heather" was revived, and the autumn drama was "The Great Ruby." In this production Collins staged a Bond Street jeweller's, Lord's Cricket Ground, Hampstead Heath with all its glories, and a secret balloon ascent by night. That year's pantomime was "The Forty Thieves," with Nellie Stewart from Australia, whom Collins always said was the best "Boy" of them all, Leno and Campbell and Johnny Danvers, Leno's old partner.

Collins banished the old-time transformation scene and did his pantomimes in two halves, which annoyed Bernard Shaw but pleased the public.

In 1899 the drama was "Hearts are Trumps." Once

again Collins staged familiar sights, including the Botanical Gardens in Regent's Park and the Private View at the Royal Academy. There was a terrific curtain to the Academy scene. The villain, by some device of his own, had a picture painted of the heroine, in the nude. It was hung on the Line. Crowds, including the villain, stood before it, whispering, nudging, scandalised and amused. The solitary figure of a woman approached and the startled spectators fell back as she moved slowly towards the picture. Then suddenly she whipped out a knife and slashed the picture to ribbons. Angry attendants leapt upon her. " By what right have you done this deed? " they demanded. She shook them off and faced the audience. " By the greatest right that God or man ever gave a woman. I am—her Mother." Curtain and overwhelming enthusiasm. The actress who spoke those words was Violet Vanbrugh.

In the year the Boer War broke out, the pantomime was " Jack and the Beanstalk." In it, of course, were Leno and Campbell, and Nellie Stewart. In the last scene a huge recumbent Giant lay right across the vast stage, killed by his fall down the beanstalk. Somebody mounted the body and opened the pocket of the giant's jerkin. " Why, he's got the whole British Army in his pocket," was the cry as out of the pocket came hundreds of children in martial array, horse, foot and artillery—a British army in double miniature.

The autumn drama was " The Price of Peace " (Cecil Raleigh). Here the scenic novelties were a ward in St. Thomas's Hospital, the Terrace of the House of Commons with Members taking tea, the interior of the House of Commons, and of Westminster Abbey. Two scenes were especially topical, one in Battersea Park at the height of the cycling craze and one in a Skating Rink, another popular fancy. Collins was nothing if not topical.

The pantomime was " The Sleeping Beauty and the Beast," with Elaine Ravensberg, Madge Lessing, Leno and Campbell, and Fred Emney. There was a wonderful representation of the Enchanted Castle as the inmates awoke from their century of sleep.

In 1901 the drama was " The Great Millionaire," there being scenes in the Carlton Hotel and on the cliffs at Paignton. The pantomime was " Blue Beard," with Leno and Campbell, Elaine Ravensberg, Julia Franks, Fred Emney and Little Zola.

In the spring of 1902 an immense production of Lew Wallace's "Ben Hur," complete with Roman galleys and chariot races, was staged at Drury Lane. The autumn drama was "The Best of Friends."

In 1903 Sir Henry Irving appeared in a version of "Dante," written or prepared by his son, Laurence Irving, who had adapted it from the French of Sardou. It was a big, spectacular production, but not one of Irving's best efforts by any means. Later he appeared as Shylock to the Portia of Ellen Terry at a matinée in aid of the Actors' Association.

The autumn drama was "The Flood Tide." ·This time Collins took his audiences to the Hotel Metropole at Brighton, to the banks of a reservoir, and to the Black Mere, flooded by the bursting of a dam and sweeping all before it, a grand piece of stagecraft. There was also the paddock at Kempton Park, and the Paris Boat Train.

The ensuing pantomime of 1903, "Humpty Dumpty," was to be the last that great pair, Dan Leno and Herbert Campbell, played in. Louise Willis was principal boy, Marie George principal girl (she fell ill and Mabel Love replaced her), Ruth Lytton, George Bastow, Hugh Ward, and an important newcomer, Harry Randall.

Meanwhile the clouds were gathering round the bright light of Dan Leno. The great little man was working too hard. On top of his Drury Lane engagement, he worked the halls for the rest of the year. And as a result his mind was beginning to give way. In November, 1901, he had appeared before King Edward VII at Sandringham, and thereafter they called him "The King's Jester."

For a while he went into retreat. Thus it was good news indeed to the whole nation when it was announced later that his health had improved and that he would, as usual, be in the Drury Lane pantomime. But he was not quite the same, and in 1903 he was again under treatment. However, he again threw off his malady, for on Boxing Night he and Campbell duly appeared together in "Humpty Dumpty." And Dan got an uproarious welcome.

In the finale of that show, Leno and Campbell, hand in hand, had the little jingle to speak:

> And we hope to appear
> For many a year
> In the panto at old Drury Lane.

Before the next pantomime was in rehearsal, both these great men were dead. The supreme pantomime partnership was finished.

During 1904, after a season of Moody Manners opera, there were some alterations to the stage and the building of the theatre. It seemed that those changes were ominous, as if indeed they had broken the spell of luck for Arthur Collins. There was no autumn drama.

Collins was at his wits' end to find two men who could replace Leno and Campbell. It was well-nigh impossible, for there are no such things as replicas in the "profession." If it had been easy to find another couple like that, then the first pair would not have been worth anything. They were so wonderful because they were so unique. It was not a question of money. Dan Leno's pantomime salary at the end was £240 a week. Other comedians since have received twice as much and not been a fraction as funny.

Harry Randall was retained, for he had proved himself. He was a first-class comedian, if a little hard; but good as he was, he was not in the Leno class. Arthur Collins took a chance and engaged a great comedian from the legitimate theatre, James Welch. Queenie Leighton was Principal Boy, Marie George Principal Girl, and there were Fred Eastman, Hugh Ward, Tom Wootwell, Ruth Lytton, and Tom Hearn. But disaster hung over the whole thing. For once, under Collins, the Drury Lane pantomime failed, as it had once before under Harris. Collins's choice of Welch, who was a newcomer to pantomime, was influenced because of the public outcry at the number of music-hall performers enrolled for pantomime. Brilliant Jimmy Welch, one of the finest actors, simply did not fit into pantomime.

Sir Henry Irving gave another short season in 1905, playing "Waterloo," "Becket," "The Merchant of Venice" and a number of other pieces. And in the autumn, Hall Caine provided the drama with "The Prodigal Son," in which George Alexander, Henry Neville and Kate Rorke appeared. There were fine scenic effects and the play was a success all round.

In that year Sir Francis Burnand, Hickory Wood and Collins wrote the pantomime, "Cinderella." Queenie Leighton was again Principal Boy, May de Sousa Principal Girl, and the comedy was reinforced by Walter Passmore, Harry Randall, Tom Wootwell, Arthur Williams. Pollie Emery and Emily Spiller were the Ugly Sisters, and for the first time came Harry Fragson, the Anglo-French comedian, who played "Dandini." He was a success, especially in an Entente Cordiale duet, "The Two Cochers," he of Paris and Randall of London. It was at the time when L'Entente Cordiale was a topic of the day.

The stage jubilee of the one and only Ellen Terry was celebrated on the boards of Drury Lane on June 12th, 1906, and a wonderful gathering of stars and celebrities acclaimed her. Again Hall Caine provided the autumn drama, this time with "The Bondman." Mrs. Patrick Campbell was the leading lady, which led to plenty of fireworks at rehearsals.

The pantomime was "Sinbad." In it Collins played almost the same team: Queenie Leighton, Marie George, Walter Passmore, Fred Emney and Harry Fragson. Since the trouble over "The White Cat," Collins had purged the pantos to eliminate vulgarity.

According to stage superstition, white cats are unlucky, but there was a scene in this show which, in another form, lasted on the music-halls for many years. Harry Randall and Fred Emney played two old women, gossiping over cups of tea, which got stronger and stronger as "extraneous" matter was added from a bottle, and in the end the friendly chat developed into a slanging match. They built this up into a riotous farce, and played it on the music-halls as "A Sister to Assist 'Er." At the Lane, it became a fashion to drop in just to see this scene. Fred Emney was a magnificent comedian.

By now it seemed that luck had returned to the Lane. Although the season of 1907 started badly with an outside production, "The Last of His Race," a Red Indian drama which scored the lowest run for Old Drury (fourteen performances), Cecil Raleigh's and Henry Hamilton's autumn drama, "The Sins of Society," was a big hit. There was some fine stuff in this. One big scene showed a troopship sinking during a tremendous storm, with the troops lined up facing their end and singing the National Anthem. It was inspired by the tragedy of "The Birkenhead." In this play, that fine actor, Lyn Harding, as the villain, "Noel Ferrers," instructed Constance Collier, playing the adventuress, how to cheat a pawnbroker when "popping" a diamond tiara by substituting lumps of coal for the jewels. This was taken from a recent "cause célèbre," which had resulted in a young nobleman being sent to prison. It thrilled the house. King Edward came to see the Drury Lane drama as usual, and at curtain fall he went back-stage. He told Lyn Harding and Constance Collier that this scene was in the worst of taste. The players were considerably discomfited, but the authors (who were not present) and Arthur Collins, remained unperturbed. " The Sins of Society" continued a huge success despite the Royal censure, and it was playing to capacity when taken off to make room for the annual pantomime.

The pantomime (1907-8) was "The Babes in the Wood," with Agnes Fraser as Principal Boy, Madge Vincent, Walter Passmore and Marie George, Neil Kenyon, Harry Fragson, Lennox Pawle and the Pender Troupe of Giants.

CHAPTER 36

HISTORY IS MADE AGAIN

FIRE, which had devastated Drury Lane on two previous occasions, assailed it again in 1908, but this time it was confined to the back stage premises. Although the damage was thus localised, it was sufficient to keep the theatre closed until the autumn drama, which was " The Marriage of Mayfair."

" The Marriage of Mayfair " was sensational. Lyn Harding, again the Lane Villain, plotted to steal the Crown Jewels from the Tower of London. In a scene depicting the Tower, the Ceremony of the Keys was reproduced with absolute fidelity. Later in the play, Harding, to make his escape from pursuing justice, had to ride a horse over an Alpine pass and be overtaken and swept to death by an avalanche. This was a scene after Collins' own heart. He let himself go. So realistic was the avalanche that one night the poor horse was indeed killed and Harding had a narrow escape. Actually, he used to ride the horse up the slope, make an unseen getaway into the flies, whilst a specially engaged acrobat did the extremely thrilling death fall over the precipice in his place.

The pantomime that year was " Dick Whittington." Queenie Leighton was again Principal Boy, Marie Wilson Principal Girl, and in the cast were Truly Shattuck, Wilkie

Bard, Johnnie Danvers, Aubrey Fitzgerald, and Marie George.

In 1909, the Lane was again to make history. It had an Italian Opera Season in the spring, but the autumn drama was the record-breaking play "The Whip." The work of the famous combination, Cecil Raleigh and Henry Hamilton, "The Whip" was the beau ideal of all that a Drury Lane melodrama should be. It had ancestral halls with Hunt breakfasts, bachelor chambers where dirty work was hatched, jockeys whose sisters had been "betrayed" by the villain, a hero who lost his memory and did not remember to whom he was engaged, and a heroine who wanted to ride "The Whip" (which was a racehorse) in defiance of Jockey Club rules. Also there was a handsome, ruthless adventuress, a drunken curate who was her dupe, an Army Captain who stopped at nothing to gain his ends, a genial trainer, and his bluff and breezy "lady friend." The horse box containing the favourite "slipped" on the railway outside the tunnel just as an express was due, the horse being rescued in the nick of time by the good angels who arrived by motor car. Horse box and train were smashed to splinters amid terrific din, steam and conflagration. And finally there was a horse race on the stage with real horses and jockeys thundering along to the winning post.

This was Drury Lane fare as it should be; melodrama in excelsis. In the splendid cast were Cyril Keightley as the villainous Captain Sartoris; Nancy Price as the wicked, scheming "Mrs. D'Acquilar" Basil Gill as the drunken curate, Madge Fabian as the betrayed girl, Fanny Brough as the outspoken lady friend of the trainer; whilst the trainer himself, "Tom Lambert," was played by George Barratt, who gave one of the best performances ever seen at Drury Lane in drama.

Things had seldom gone smoothly at an Augustus Harris first night, either of pantomime or drama, and that was another legacy which Collins inherited. On the first night of "The Whip" the great race scene brought the house to its feet cheering, but lo and behold something went wrong. "The Whip" was down the field; it failed to pass the post first! For no apparent reason, the judge's box shot into the air, and the judge (a super) was left standing like a jack-in-the-box whose position had been reversed, a truly astonished and terrified man. The curtain fell quickly, and the short last scene was played at top speed. Then Arthur Collins came forward, complete master of the situation. "Ladies and gentleman," he said to a cheering house, "perhaps some of you may have noticed that to-night 'The Whip' did not win. Owing to a misunderstanding with the judge's box, however, I may tell you that it was no race. It will be run again to-morrow night, and judging by your applause, for many nights to come; and on those occasions I can promise you that 'The Whip' will be the winner." A masterpiece of quick thinking and cool demeanour typical of Collins. He was right about the result, for "The Whip" was the greatest winner the Lane had known. It ran until the panto, it was revived after it, running for 388 performances in all. It toured all over the country and made fortunes for many.

"Aladdin" arrived at Christmas, with Marie George, Ida Rene, Truly Shattuck (who was a large handsome American), George Graves, Wilkie Bard and George Ali. Graves made his first entrance in an aeroplane surrounded by live chickens, and when, for no reason whatever, all the huge crowd, including himself, found themselves at the North Pole, he described that remote spot as "The Margate of the North."

The following year, 1910, "The Whip" was revived. The theatre, however, was closed for three nights from May 6th owing to the death of King Edward VII. The pantomime was "Jack and the Beanstalk."

For some time past, the pantomimes of Arthur Collins had been showing a more imaginative note than those of Harris. The magnificence and spaciousness were still there, but a lighter and more fantastic touch was creeping in; and that was all to the good. This version of "Jack and the Beanstalk" started on Leith Hill, with Dolly Castles, the principal boy, as a "Boy Scout" who, sleeping by her camp fire, dreamt the story. Again there was the vast mechanical giant, who could only be seen in sections. His huge legs and feet trod down whole streets, his mighty hands appeared and abducted the Princess, an awesome sight indeed. There was also a forest in flames. The cast was brilliant—Dolly Castles, Julia James, George Graves, Harry Randall, (back again), George Barrett, Austin Melford, and Barry Lupino.

"The Sins of Society" was revived in the spring of 1911. There was a Command Performance of "Money" to celebrate the Coronation of King George V. And the pantomime was, in that winter of 1911, "Hop-o'-My-Thumb." This had Violet Loraine as principal boy, Daisy Dormer, Renee Mayer ("Hop"), George Graves, Will Evans, Barry Lupino, Austin Melford and Frederick Ross. A very lovely scene showed the Land of Lost Memories.

That year there was an autumn drama called "The Hope." In this it was again decided to include a horse race, to challenge that most successful effect in "The Whip." But the producers decided to go one better. In "The Whip," the race had been run across stage, now horses were to run head on at the audience! It was believed that the result would be paralysing. And, as rehearsed, it certainly was. So much did it excite the company that they could hardly wait to see its impact on the astonished audience. Came the first night. There had been a terrifying earthquake scene, with Sicilian palaces and streets crashing into dust, people "perishing by the thousand," and the villain meeting his just deserts amidst the carnage and ruin. This scene had been inspired by the Messina disaster.

Then the action sped back to England for the great race which was to make all end happily. A short scene was being played in front, whilst masked by a black velvet curtain, the horses were strapped on their moving track, the jockeys mounted, the tracks started up and the horses began to gain speed. All the company gathered in the wings to watch. The supers in the crowd stood expectantly waiting the stage manager's word to cheer. The cue came, the stage manager blacked out on the short front scene, and gave the signal. The horses galloped for their lives, their hooves thundering and drumming like a vast orchestra of percussion; the supers cheered themselves hoarse; principals in the wings, carried away with excitement, did the same. The race ran its short course, and the stage manager blacked out. Then all waited for the thunder of applause which was to be the reward of their labours. From the front of the house came just dead silence. Everyone was struck with blank amazement. It was the worst anti-climax ever known. What had gone wrong? Then the stage manager found out. In his excitement over the race, he had forgotten to give the signal for the removal of the black velvet curtain! The audience, sitting dumbfounded in their seats at the racket back-stage, had not seen a single thing! But it was all right the next night.

"Ben Hur" was revived in 1912, with its Eastern pageantry, its almost religious atmosphere, its chariot races, (real horses and real chariots, of course) and the scene below deck in the Roman Trireme, showing the slaves pulling at the oars. In this revival the part of a Centurion was played by Jack Glyn, one of Drury Lane's best known characters.

In 1912, there was staged a modern morality play called "Everywoman." And, when pantomime time came round, a drastic break with tradition was essayed. For the Principal Boy was played by a man, Wilfred Douthitt. The show was "Sleeping Beauty," with Florence Smithson as Beauty. There were also George Graves, Will Evans, Barry Lupino, Renee Mayer, Charles Rock (a fine straight actor) and the Poluski Brothers. George Graves played "The Count of Monte Blanco," and made his first appearance marvellously made up as a scarecrow. He had mice in his pockets, mushrooms sprouting all over him, a bird's nest on his head, and a golf ball in his ear!

In 1913, Drury Lane saw another great actor, Sir Johnstone Forbes-Robertson, bid farewell to the stage. His season lasted from March 22nd to June 6th, and included "Hamlet," "The Passing of the Third Floor Back," "Sacrament of Judas," "The Light that Failed," "Mice and Men," "Caesar and Cleopatra," "The Merchant of Venice" and "Othello." It was with "Hamlet" that he opened the season and with "Hamlet" that he closed it to scenes of leave-taking which have not been paralleled since. This was a different affair to Macready's relieved farewell. Forbes-Robertson, after his last curtain, and in response to insistent demands, came into the front of the house, down amongst the audience, shaking them by the hand, and taking a personal farewell of as many as he could. Many of the audience wept, as did the great actor.

There was a most exciting season of Russian opera and ballet in 1913 sponsored by Sir Joseph Beecham (nine operas and fourteen ballets). This awakened London to the real significance of Russian art. The autumn drama was "Sealed Orders." The crux of this was a great hoax which had been carried out during the year by some undergraduates who, masquerading as Indian Rajahs and their suites, had spoofed many high officials.

Apart from the hoax, "Sealed Orders" was extremely

topical. For round about that time the chief topic of gossip everywhere had been a mystery airship, which was said to cruise over England at night, and was generally believed to be German. Collins presented not only the airship in mid-air with a terrific fight in which the villain met his doom, but anti-aircraft guns (of which the public knew next to nothing) in action, finally bringing down the airship into the sea. There was a scene at Chelsea Flower Show, in which the plot thickened, for the " papers " had to be got out of England.

The pantomime was a revival (with new scenes) of " The Sleeping Beauty "—with " Reawakened " tacked on to the title. The cast was almost the same as the previous year, but Forrester Harvey came in as an addition and Stanley Lupino also played in Drury Lane pantomime for the first time. He always swore that the ghost of Dan Leno appeared to him.

The fateful year of 1914 saw " Sealed Orders " revived in the spring, and another of Sir Joseph Beecham's opera and ballet seasons.

Then, on August 4th came the declaration of war. So, playing for safety, Collins put on " Sleeping Beauty " again, this time " Rebeautified." George R. Sims was the collaborator in this very successful pantimime. There were, however, changes in the cast. Bertram Wallis was a very masculine and handsome principal boy, and Ferne Rogers was " Beauty."

In 1915, the war atmosphere was oppressive. Collins, doubtful about the outlook, revived " Sealed Orders." But he did a new pantomime, " Puss in Boots " by George R. Sims, Frank Dix and himself. Business was pretty bad, and Collins feared the loss of the huge sum which a pantomime entailed. So he approached the company and asked if they would agree to half salaries. They all agreed with one exception, who struck out for and received full salary right through the run. But the panto succeeded, and ran until Easter. Although there was no liability on the part of the management, at the end of the last week every member of the cast received a cheque for an amount which brought his or her salary up to par for the entire run. That was Arthur Collins's way.

The following year, 1916, saw the Lane break new ground in the shape of presenting its first moving picture. This was on a scale suitable for the theatre, for it was the

302

D. W. Griffith's masterpiece of silent cinematography "The Birth of a Nation."

That, too, was the year of the Shakespeare Tercentenary Celebrations and a great matinée performance of "Julius Caesar" and Shakespearean tableaux was given. "Julius Caesar" was played by the veteran Frank Benson, who had done so much for the stage. King George V, who was present, made up his mind during the show that he would confer a knighthood on Benson, and commanded that he should be brought to the box for the accolade. His Majesty, although in uniform, was not wearing a sword. Nor could a sword be found in Drury Lane. Those in the property room had, as a loyal gift, been handed over at the outbreak of war. All that remained were obviously unworthy stage "props," entirely unsuitable for such an occasion. So two men sped through the back streets and burst, panting and out of breath, into the shop of a famous outfitters on the corner of Bedford Street, Covent Garden. There they gasped out their request for the loan of a sword, and tried to explain what it was for. Their story seemed incredible to the assistants in the shop. A 'phone call to the theatre convinced those in charge of the shop, and enabled the two sword-seekers to speed back to the theatre, breathless again but triumphant, bearing the precious piece of steel in their keeping. They arrived just in time, and the great actor knelt in the Royal Retiring Room to rise—Sir Frank Benson.

The pantomime for that year was "Puss in Boots" and again there were alterations. The male principal boy was no more, instead a great actress played this part. It was Madge Titheradge, and a marvellous principal boy she made. Lennie Deane, afterwards to be a principal girl in her own right, played "Puss."

There followed another Griffith picture—"Intolerance," with a full orchestra under the baton of Philip Page, now a dramatic critic. There was no autumn drama, a revival of "The Birth of a Nation" taking its place. From September to November, Sir Thomas Beecham gave a splendid season of opera; and for the ensuing pantomime "Aladdin," the celebrated F. Anstey joined Dix and Collins in the book.

The following year, 1918, was curious. From March 2nd to April 6th, Sir Thomas Beecham gave opera, and again from June 3rd to July 27th. In August there was a musical play produced in conjunction with J. L. Sacks, called "Shanghai." On September 27th, to celebrate the 21st year of the management of Arthur Collins, there was a special performance of "The Pageant of Drury Lane" by Louis N. Parker, with music by Percy Fletcher.

Then on November 11t came the Armistice, and the pantomime following "Shanghai" (which ran up to December 7th) was "Babes in the Wood." The principal boy was Marie Blanche, Florence Smithson was principal girl, the Babes were Stanley Lupino and Will Evans.

Sir Thomas Beecham did opera again in 1919, and C. B. Cochran staged Rostand's "Cyrano de Bergerac." There was a season of "La Fille de Madame Angot" (in English) which ran from July to August. In the autumn there was drama again—"The Great Day," by George R. Sims and Louis N. Parker. And at Christmas "Cinderella" came on. This was destined to be the last Drury Lane pantomime for many years. In it were Marie Blanche, Florence Smithson, du Calion, Harry Claff, Will Evans, Stanley Lupino (a fine "Buttons"). Lily Long and C. Denier Warren were an hilarious pair of Ugly Sisters.

A great change now overtook Drury Lane. Sir Alfred Butt joined the board and became joint managing director with Arthur Collins, and his far reaching plans included nothing less than complete reconstruction of the theatre.

But in 1920, before this work was put in hand Anna Pavlova gave a season of ballet, and the capacity of the theatre was taxed to its utmost. In June "The Garden of Allah" was produced, the first big show under the new régime. The idea of this play being staged—it was of a very different texture from the usual Drury Lane drama, and was adapted by its author Robert Hichens and Mary Anderson—was that of Sir Alfred Butt.

Arthur Collins produced it in the grand manner. But tradition was to assert itself in one of the old-time first-night mishaps. The two leading roles were played by Godfrey Tearle and Madge Titheradge. "The Garden of Allah" ran from June 24th, 1920, to April 2nd, 1921. The big scene was a most realistic representation of a sandstorm in the desert. And on the first night, the realism was overdone, for the audience shared in it, against their will. Someone decided that pea-flour was the best stuff to represent sand, and accordingly pea flour was used. There had been a gauze between the auditorium and the stage at the dress rehearsal. But on the first night the gauze was not there, with the result that pea-flour invaded the front of the house—in great clouds. It covered the occupants of the front rows of the stalls, magnificent in all their first-night glad-rags, and reduced them to choking, sneezing rows of pale yellow ghosts. Yet none of them bore malice, none complained, so great was the occasion and the success of the play. And nobody joined in the final applause more loudly than those devoted victims of this sorry mishap.

The success of "The Garden of Allah" drove panto-mime temporarily from its traditional home. For at Christmas, 1920-21, the Drury Lane pantomime of "Cinder-ella" was played at Covent Garden. This swapping of theatres caused unfortunate confusion. The man responsible for the advertising had not made it clear that the panto-mime was at Covent Garden. The huge pictorial posters which, as usual, flooded London, bore in big type "Drury Lane Pantomime" and the words Covent Garden in very small type. The public having missed seeing the small type went straight to Drury Lane and booked what they intended to be their pantomime seats as usual. The box office, not suspecting the misunderstanding, just handed out tickets—for Drury Lane. Then, when the pantomime began, the tragedy was discovered. Harrassed fathers and mothers, surrounded by crowds of disappointed children, in tears, found themselves destined to see "The Garden of Allah" instead of pantomime delights. Fortunately, the man who ran Covent Garden was equal to the occasion. He made reservations of blocks of seats at the first whisper of the calamity, organised a system of guides to bring the aggrieved families from the Lane to the Garden, and fixed everybody up. So the children smiled again.

In 1921, great changes were witnessed in Drury Lane, both in building and in personnel. The work of recon-struction, foreshadowed earlier, took from April 2nd, 1921, until the theatre was reopened in the April of 1922. J. Emblin Walker and F. Edward Jones were the architects, and the work was carried out by that finest of theatre specialists, Charles J. Hyde. They gave London a new Drury Lane, and one to be proud of, as majestic and lovely as anything which had gone before it, and far more con-venient than any of its predecessors. The old boxes, from which the line of sight was almost non-existent, were either thrown into the circle or replaced by that rare thing, a private box from which every inch of the stage can be seen. New entrances were made to the stalls. The reconstruction cost over £100,000.

But before the old theatre was handed over to the renovators, one very important function took place which remains to be chronicled. This was the establishment of "Warriors' Day," which was inaugurated on January 18th, 1921.

Every theatrical celebrity was on the stage, and the meeting was addressed by many of them, as well as by Field Marshal Earl Haig and Admiral of the Fleet Lord Beatty. The Prince of Wales (Duke of Windsor) presided, and there was a little hitch over his arrival. A Reception Committee had been appointed to receive and look after His Royal Highness. They were all clustered at the Royal Entrance, expectant and eager. The time of arrival came, but no Royal Personage. This was most unusual. One of the smaller fry attached to the Committee, a theatre manager, had an idea. He thought there might have been a mistake, and that the Prince might have gone to the front entrance. He mentioned this to Sir Alfred Butt, who dispatched him at once to find out. His guess had been right. When he arrived after a brisk sprint through the long corridors from back stage (distances are considerable at Drury Lane) he saw the Prince in solitary state, being escorted up the Grand Staircase by a waiter!

CHAPTER 37

THE LANE'S NEW TRADITION

A FEW more stories remain to be told before we leave those old pantomime nights at Drury Lane.

First to be recalled to mind is the famous monkey of 1916, engaged to play in a skit on "Romance" in the show. This simian actor, purchased for Collins in Seven Dials by Frank Foulsham, then the publicity man for the theatre, seemed quiet at first, but he did not take to the greasepaint; and a day soon came when he was reported missing. A search was instituted, and he was found enjoying freedom in the vast "flies" of the theatre, and easily resisted all attempts at capture. A trap eventually did the trick, but the monkey was dismissed for breach of contract in absenting himself without leave, and Frank Foulsham took it back to the shop from whence it had come. "Oh, it's back again, is it?" said the shopkeeper. "I'm not surprised." "What do you mean?" asked Foulsham. "It's been back twice before," replied the shopkeeper. "It broke up the flats of its last two owners."

Nor must George Graves' dressing room be overlooked. Visitors going there found themselves in a kind of crazy chamber. Chairs collapsed when sat upon, cigarettes thrust upon them exploded, pencils refused to write and turned on those wielding them, coat hangers proffered for their coats shut up and threw the garments on the ground, and when the thoroughly startled visitor was offered a drink, he found the liquor pouring all over his waistcoat from cleverly concealed small holes in the chasing on the glass. Royal personages came, saw, even suffered, and laughed good naturedly.

One afternoon, just after the matinee of a pantomime, a clergyman in full clerical clothes and with a heavy black beard asked one of the footmen if he could see Mr. Collins. He was most pressing. The footman did not try to worry Arthur, but found "Dickie" Lindo, the second in command, who came down to the vestibule to see the parson.

That worthy explained that he always came to see the pantomime, and was coming that night. The clergyman had a request. After seeing the show that night, he wanted to go behind the scenes. More, he wanted to be taken into the dressing room of the chorus girls, and he wanted to take one of them out to supper. Lindo explained that it could not be done. "But I have my wife's permission," argued the cleric. "That may be," said Lindo, getting a bit irate, "but you have not the permission of Theatre Royal, Drury Lane." It was the clergyman's turn to get annoyed, and to let out a string of the most vivid abuse—real Billingsgate. The shocked and horrified Lindo called the footman and told him to turn the intruder out. The clergyman promptly closed with the liveried official and as he did so off fell his hat and off came his beard—and there stood revealed that master of comedy and make-up, Will Evans, who was actually in the pantomime.

There was a wonderful act drop specially painted for Drury Lane to commemorate the Command Performance given before the Kaiser Wilhelm and King George the

307

Fifth, when the German Emperor came here to unveil the memorial to Queen Victoria outside Buckingham Palace. It was a work of art which showed the two Monarchs, the Kaiser on a white horse, facing each other, with London in the background and the figure of Peace hovering over them. After use, the original painting was installed on the first landing of the Great Staircase, much admired by all beholders. But needless to say it vanished in 1914. The original is in the possession of Horace Collins, brother to Arthur, who conducted the publicity side of the Lane so well for some years, and who is now the most efficient secretary to the Society of West End Managers.

Arising out of that picture, those who saw it will never forget the very lovely scene Arthur Collins used in "The Babes in the Wood" in 1918. The war was only just over. The scene was called "The Pageant of Peace," and the great critic A. B. Walkley, was ecstatic over it—as was everyone else. Everything was white, stage, scenery, vast columns reaching to the skies, so were all the dresses. Figures in white bore the National Colours of the Allies. It was a gleaming field of snowy Peace. But into it burst one solitary figure, dressed in ebony, bearing a war eagle on her shield. She rushed at the massed crowds of wearers of white, hesitated, paused, and fell to her knees conquered, the shield crashing down and the great war sword breaking into splinters. It was typical of the defeat of the forces and power of Germany, the war maker. The effect was startling; and every night the building echoed to deafening cheers. Walkley's criticism says, "Surely the old playhouse can never, in its long history, have had so fine a chance of responding with some symbolic expression so apt, so perfect in beauty, to the deepest feelings of man and woman gathered within its walls. One false, one vulgar touch, would have ruined the whole, but there was none."

There was a delightful custom at Drury Lane in prewar days. On Christmas Eve, the traditional night for the pantomime's opening, a great Christmas Tree was always placed in the Rotunda, smothered in toys and decorations, with a Fairy Queen towering level with the next storey, on its topmost branch. And by it stood one of the footmen, in his Royal livery, scarlet coat with gold lace, snowy shirt, black satin breeches, pink silk stockings and black buckled pumps, and powdered hair. Children entering were de-

lighted. Open eyed and open mouthed, they gazed at the
finest Christmas Tree they had ever seen. Their eyes
feasted on the wealth of toys which loaded it. They could
hardly be persuaded to pass it by to go in and see the
pantomime. The footman usually caused a bit of con-
jecture, but the majority held he was Father Christmas.
The Tree was dismantled and taken away on Twelfth Night,
and the toys brought joy into the hearts of little ones in
hospital, whom Drury Lane never forgot.

The new "Old Drury" opened its doors on 22nd April,
1922, with "Decameron Nights," by McLaughlin and Boyle
Lawrence, a finely conceived, magnificently mounted and
produced version of a Boccaccio story. There was a thrill
when the nude figure of a woman was rescued from the sea
by an old monk and carried into the monastery—the woman
was lovely Margaret Bannerman. Owen Roughwood and
H. A. Saintsbury had a most exciting and perfectly arranged
rapier and dagger duel, and the whole thing was on a scale
of splendour worthy of the old theatre—and the new. But
there was no pantomime.

In 1923 came a nasty flop; a curious trick show from
Middle Europe called "Angelo." Although very cleverly
staged, it ran for only 29 performances. It was almost the
last production of Arthur Collins. Then came "Ned Kean
of Old Drury," with that fine actor H. A. Saintsbury as
Old Drury's own Kean. Although a first-class drama by
Arthur Shirley, it failed to attract. Everyone grieved
when the notice went up. Then, on what should have been
its last performance, came another scene of Old Drury
drama. A gentleman stood up in the stalls, made a speech
in praise of the play, and said he thought it so good that he
would personally make himself responsible for the expenses
if the run were continued. So the reprieved show ran on a
little longer, but even that magnificent gesture could not
save it. The generous playgoer was a Mr. Greenlees, proprietor of a famous whisky and a regular patron of Drury
Lane. The fact was that public taste was changing again—
it was the Macready period repeating itself. As tragedy
had died then, a post-war generation, tired of alarums and
excursions, and out for a good time, was sick of drama. "Ned
Kean" was withdrawn after 61 performances. It deserved
a much better fate.

Arthur Collins was to do one more drama in the good
old fashioned way. It was called "Good Luck," and was

written by Seymour Hicks and Ian Hay. Seymour Hicks took the script along to the Lane, whistling gaily up the stairs, and into Collins' office. "There you are, Arthur, there's the play," said he. "What's it all about?" asked Arthur Collins. "Oh," replied Seymour airily, "the heroine rides the horse to victory in the last scene." "Right!" said Arthur. "We'll do it." And do it they did. There was much more to it than that. There was a mutiny in a prison, a convict's escape over Dartmoor, a ship dashed to pieces on the cliffs by a raging sea, and a representation of the bathing pool at Maiden Erlegh, the late Solly Joel's (a big Lane shareholder) country home, with bathing belles complete. Collins brought all his old magic to bear and it ran from 27th September, 1923, until 10th May, 1924—260 performances.

This was Collins' last show. He was tired and wanted rest. The times were changing, a new London and a new theatre had grown up which was not his London or his theatre. So after 43 years' official connection with the theatre and 27 years of control, Arthur Collins said goodbye. He had loved The Lane and served it well. He was a charming man, this dark, keen-eyed companionable genius of the theatre, a man who hated to be alone, who loved the company of his fellow-men and colleagues. He talked almost unceasingly and he talked well.

It was his joy to tell long stories, carrying on far into the night, and often he was to be found still talking at three in the morning, either in a dressing room or in his suite at the Savoy. He would go to Romano's to lunch, if there were no rehearsals on, and all well at the Lane, and when dinner time came round, it was not out of the way for him still to be there, coversing with his luncheon guests. He respected and loved his old chief and master, Sir Augustus Harris. He was a most loyal friend, and found jobs for his cronies, often creating them specially; and he would keep deserving cases in work so that they could qualify to join the Drury Lane Fund and make their old age safe. Yet he could be, and was, very scathing to those whom he considered in fault; and once, during the Drury Lane pantomime at Covent Garden, gave such a lecture and "telling off" to Jimmy Glover that that big man, trying to make a dignified and reproachful exit from a dressing room, fell backwards down a flight of stairs and nearly stunned himself. But he was just and fair to a degree. He closed

310

an epoch, and he left with it. Unlike Gus Harris, he never fell foul of a critic. In the morning, after a new Lane production, he would read all the Press notices carefully and then write a personal letter to each critic thanking him (whether the notice had been good or bad) and if suggestions had been made therein would say he was giving them his deep attention. But he rarely made any of the alterations suggested. He did not have to. He was nearly always right, and when he was wrong, it was so small an affair that it did not matter.

Arthur Collins took into retirement with him a name which was respected and loved, and a brilliant record of success and achievement in that glorious theatre which stands second to none. He lowered his colours only to the passing of time; when conditions altered, he went too. And he carried with him also, as a message from all in Drury Lane as well as from tens of thousands of playgoers, the title of the last play he produced—" Good Luck." When Arthur Collins left, Sir Alfred Butt was joined, for a short period, by Basil Dean, who undertook stage production.

The first play produced by the new régime was " London Life " by Arnold Bennett and Edward Knoblock, which only ran 39 performances, from 3rd June, 1924, to 5th July, 1924. Then another film came to Drury Lane, " The Thief of Bagdad," featuring Douglas Fairbanks. This filled the theatre from 24th September to 23rd November of that year, being shown 112 times.

The Christmas of 1924-25 was marked by the return of Shakespeare to Drury Lane. The Bard had, for some time, made only fitful appearances at the National Theatre, the last time being in Forbes Robertson's farewell season. That Christmas, Basil Dean staged " A Midsummer Night's Dream." It was a distinguished production, with a fine cast and many imaginative ideas. It ran from 26th December, 1924, until 7th March, 1925, 96 performances in all. Basil Dean then left Drury Lane.

Sir Alfred Butt now inaugurated a new Drury Lane tradition—that of big musical plays. He started off with " Rose Marie," with Derek Oldham as the hero and Edith Day as the heroine. The comedy was in the very safe hands of little Billy Merson, who, as " Hard Boiled Herman," scored a big success. Edith Day proved an ideal Drury Lane heroine. At the dress rehearsal of the play, the ticket agencies refused to do a "deal" for seats. They did not believe it would succeed, and said so unequivocally. Sir Alfred had every faith, and so had the producer, Oscar Hammerstein II. He told "The Trade," as they are called in the theatre, that they were entirely wrong. He said he was just leaving to go back to America and that he would be returning in exactly a year's time; and when he came back, he declared, "Rose Marie" would still be running. He was right. It ran from 20th March, 1925, until 26th March, 1927—851 performances. And all through that long run of packed houses, the ticket agencies had no special privileges at all. Sir Alfred Butt's policy was either that you were in or out. In this case they were out. There is no need to dilate on the joys of "Rose Marie," its music has gone into the national repertoire. King George V. came to see it three times during its first run, and again on its revival. "The Indian Love Call" was one of his favourite tunes. During convalescence after his serious illness, when a band played daily to him at Bognor Regis, that tune was always included in the programme.

Like its predecessors, Old Drury could still spring its surprises and have drama played off-stage within its precincts. A capacity audience, applauding a performance of "Rose Marie" to the echo one night, never dreamt, until they saw the papers next morning, that whilst they were enjoying themselves, a musical comedy star, Regine Flory, had committed suicide in another part of the building.

"Rose Marie" was succeeded by "The Desert Song," again with Edith Day as leading lady. That grand actor of musical plays, Harry Welchman, played the hero, "The Red Shadow." Once more Sir Alfred Butt's judgment was sound. He had seen the change in public taste which so many of his predecessors at the Lane had missed. "The Desert Song" ran for 432 performances, from 7th April, 1927, to 14th April, 1928.

The next offering was "Show Boat," a big show with a big cast, including Sir Cedric Hardwicke, Marie Burke, Edith Day as "Magnolia," and Paul Robeson. That magnificent voice of Robeson's was a great sensation, and during the run of "Show Boat" (May 3rd, 1928—2nd March, 1929) he gave special afternoon recitals to packed houses. "Show Boat" ran for 350 performances.

Then came "New Moon," on 4th April, 1929, with Evelyn Laye as leading lady, and some fine scenes on board ship. It did not have a long run—only 140 performances;

and " Rose Marie " was revived on 12th September to run
for another hundred shows.

Sir Alfred Butt then went back to pantomime. He
called in Julian Wylie, the Pantomime King, who at Christmas, 1929-30, staged a lovely production of " The Sleeping
Beauty," with Lilian Davies as Principal Boy, Eve Gray
as Principal Girl, and that magnificent comedian, G. S.
Melvin, in charge of the fun. Wylie loved publicity, and saw
to it that all the world was told that pantomime was back at
the Lane. One day at rehearsal he complained of feeling unwell. " What's the matter with you? " asked Herman Finck.
" I think it's vertigo," replied Julian. " Vertigo? " countered
Herman, " you mean ad-vertigo."

Julian brought back all the old Drury Lane pantomime
glories. He thought pantomime, he dreamt pantomime, he
talked pantomime all the year round; and to be at Drury
Lane was the height of his delight. " The Sleeping Beauty "
ran from 24th December, 1929, to 1st March, 1930, and was
a winner.

In 1931 " The Three Musketeers " was the attraction.
Produced on 28th March, it ran until 25th October. It was a
big, sweeping, colourful musical version of the Dumas story.
Denis King played D'Artagnan, and Raymond Newell
stopped the show on the first night with his singing of " Ma
Belle."

In 1931, too, Sir Alfred, who had so far drawn all his
big musical shows, except the " Sleeping Beauty " pantomime, from America, produced a home-made article. This
was " The Song of the Drum." Some of the music was by
Vivian Ellis. The cast included Derek Oldham, Marie
Burke, Raymond Newell, Bobbie Howes, Peter Haddon,
besides a host of others. It was a romance of India. That
has never been a successful background for stage shows—
why, there is no explaining. It was a beautiful production,
with snow-capped Himalayas, Eastern Palaces and Court-
yards, and a Bazaar which challenged the famous one in
" Kismet "; it was in every way a worthy Drury Lane effort,
but it only ran for 131 performances, from 9th January to
2nd May, 1931.

Sir Alfred Butt then left Drury Lane. He had succeeded in filling that vast playhouse for years, and in adding
to its prestige and prosperity, for the financial results were
excellent. He knew and understood the Theatre, and
managed it superbly. He was the fourth Member of Par-

liament to control it, the others being Collier, Polhill and Sheridan. He most certainly eclipsed the first two, and financially he far exceeded Sheridan's management. Even if he had found a Mrs. Siddons, it is doubtful if she would have appealed to the moderns.

After Sir Alfred Butt's departure, George Grossmith succeeded to power. The theatre was let to Stanley Scott, an extraordinary, volatile and enterprising young man, who imported a light opera by Franz Lehar, the composer of "The Merry Widow," and a foreign tenor who was only vaguely known in this country by reason of his gramophone records. A prominent publicity man, who had had a long connection with Theatre Royal, was engaged to put this singer on the map. He went to work with a will. Stanley Scott's exuberance sometimes ran away with him, and when he went down to meet the tenor at Dover, he assured him that the interest in his visit was so great that half London would be on Victoria Station to welcome him. The publicity man was there with a crowd of Press photographers. The station was certainly unduly crowded, and the publicity man, who was, as most of them are, of a modest nature, did not think it was due to his efforts on behalf of the tenor. So he asked the stationmaster what was up. He was informed that Alfonso of Spain, who had just abdicated from the throne, was on the same train. He was also told that Press photographers were barred. But that publicity man managed to persuade the stationmaster to allow the cameramen on the platform to take pictures of his tenor. The stationmaster saw no reason to refuse this and they were let through the barrier. So the photographers first got pictures of the abdicated monarch and then raced back to take pictures of the tenor. And the tenor beamed at the crowds. The next morning he went to Drury Lane in a large white car. On entering the theatre he went straight to the box office and shook hands with the box office staff. He said they were the men who mattered. They took the money.

Then rehearsals started in the foyer, under the direction of Felix Edwardes, the resident Drury Lane producer, who had done "Show Boat," "The Three Musketeers," "The Song of the Drum," "Rose Marie," and other shows at the Lane. All through the rehearsal the tenor lay low. None of the staff had any inkling of his real quality. In the cast were Hella Kurty, George Vollaire, Bruce Winston, and Cronin Wilson.

314

It was a Chinese play and a beautiful production, called
" The Land of Smiles." The first night came, and then
the tenor showed what he was made of—the very finest
quality and something which London had not savoured for
years. His name was Richard Tauber, and his singing all
through, but especially in " You are My Heart's Delight,"
made the first night a truly memorable one, even for Drury
Lane. That song, heard for the first time on the 8th May,
1931, won world-wide popularity. At the end of the show
there were scenes more like a Cup Final than a first night.
People stood on their seats and cheered.

" The Land of Smiles " ran from May 8th to July 18th
1931.

George Grossmith did not stop long at Drury Lane.
One of his troubles was the inability of the young lady on
the telephone switchboard to get his name right. She had
never heard of him before, and could not have cared less.
Her usual form of address was to call him " Mr. Green-
grass." But before he retired he arranged for a production,
under the banner of Charles B. Cochran, the great manager,
of Noel Coward's " Cavalcade." This was presented, Noel
Coward producing it himself, on October 13th, 1931. The
first night was memorable. And it was memorable, too,
to the Drury Lane staff, because for the first time for years,
there was a first-night hitch.

Under the control of William Abingdon, who had come
to the theatre as stage director with Basil Dean, and stayed
on when Dean left, such a thing had been unheard of.
There is not a better stage director, organiser or dis-
ciplinarian in any theatre in the world than " Bill " Abingdon, son of a great actor, and trained at His Majesty's
Theatre in the great days of Tree. But Drury Lane stage
is divided up into a series of lifts, which when not in use
become part of the stage itself. These can be raised, lowered
or tilted as required, and play a great part in the famous
Drury Lane " effects." On the first night of " Cavalcade "
one of them took it upon itself to stick and refuse to rise.
Actually, there was a wait of a very few minutes, but it
seemed like hours to the stage staff. Feverishly they rushed
below stage and worked like demons with crowbars and
other tools, thinking that the machinery had gone wrong.
Then the real reason was discovered. The supers required
in the scene had got on the lift before it was raised. Their
weight was too much, and the lift, very sensibly, refused to

315

try the elevation of such a mass. The supers were hustled off, and the lift went up as usual, and on went the show.

"Cavalcade" truly lived up to the Lane's reputation of topicality, even if it did so unwittingly. It was a play of about two decades of our history, and its production coincided with a political crisis of the first magnitude, when the country went off the gold standard. The Government fell, there was unrest and a feeling of insecurity everywhere. It was a very anxious time. And on the evening of 28th October, King George V, Queen Mary, the Prince of Wales, the Duke and Duchess of York (now our King and Queen) and the Duke of Kent went to Drury Lane, to see "Cavalcade." This was the only time that a private visit to a play was allowed to be publicised in advance—the rule is that nothing must be said until Their Majesties are in the theatre, except, of course, for Command Performances. As a rule, on private visits, the Royal Party times its arrival to synchronise with the rise of the curtain, and before entering the box, waits in the Royal Room until it is just going up and the lights have gone down. The idea is not to distract the public attention from the play. On this occasion, however, the King allowed the news of his visit to be published in advance, and on reaching the theatre, the whole of the Royal Party went straight into the box with the "house lights" full on, so that everyone could see them. They received a tremendous ovation. The idea of the King was to restore confidence. Here was almost the entire Royal Family going to the theatre, to Drury Lane, to see a play about England: so things could not be so bad. The gesture had a tremendous effect.

"Cavalcade" was a real success, running from October 13th, 1931, until September 10th, 1932. It was also true Drury Lane. Again we saw a troopship depart, again we saw a realistic railway station scene. We had a most imaginative representation of War with men marching, marching into the cauldron of death; we had a most moving glimpse of the funeral of Queen Victoria, the passing described from a balcony by Mary Clare, the leading lady. One heard the clatter of the horses' hooves and the jingle of chains and accoutrements as the cortège went by out of sight. That this effect, which moved many to tears, was produced by two property men, one just manipulating two halves of a coconut and the other shaking a chain, did

316

not matter at all. Nobody saw that, but they visualised one of the most solemn moments in history. Also a silent scene in St. James's Park of the public all dressed in deep black for the passing of the great Queen, whose death had stunned the nation, recalled memories to so many of how they too had been dressed in deep mourning by their parents at that time. Noel Coward played on the memories of his audience like a maestro. The final lines of the play, spoken by Mary Clare, have become almost proverbial. And its picture of the serried mass of players on the lifts with a background of the national flag stirred the deepest emotions.

" Wild Violets " was the next production, on October 31st, 1932, and it ran until July 8th, 1933. Produced by Hassard Short, this charming musical play was the only production in which a revolving stage has been used at Drury Lane. The staff there can work quicker than machinery, and the biggest scenes—and they are big scenes—get changed in an average of 1½ minutes. Charlotte Greenwood, that clever American actress, made a big success in " Wild Violets "; so did the English actress, Adèle Dixon.

A musical play, " Ball at the Savoy," followed. The cast included that burly comedian, Oscar Denes. It ran from September 8th, 1933, to January 13th, 1934.

Since " Cavalcade," runs were tending to shorten, and the Lane seemed to be losing its luck once more. Nor did the next production, a most elaborate one, break the spell. It was " The Three Sisters," which in spite of some good music, excellent scenes and a clever company including Charlotte Greenwood, Victoria Hopper, Adèle Dixon, Stanley Holloway, Esmond Knight (who lost his sight in the late war but has recovered sufficiently to act again), and Albert Burdon, failed completely.

Drury Lane was in the dumps again. A new General Manager was now appointed by the Board, H. M. Tennent, a tall, scholarly, distinguished looking man who was also a composer. He had been with Moss Empires, and had arranged productions for a most important producing concern. Whilst actually holding office at Drury Lane, he was to found a firm of play producers called by his own name, H. M. Tennent Ltd., which is one of the most distinguished and successful of its kind to-day, its direction being under Hugh Beaumont, Tennent's partner. Mr.

317

Tennent was faced with an empty theatre, and no attractions in sight.

Recalling Drury Lane tradition, he decided, very wisely, on pantomime. He called in once more Julian Wylie, who presented "Cinderella." It was a production worthy of Drury Lane. One of the scenes was a vast lake, into which marched an army of girls, entering the water and walking—down, down, down, until they were entirely submerged and lost to sight beneath the surface of the lake. It was an exciting scene and provided some thrills at rehearsals too. Once a bathing cap was seen floating on the surface and there was a moment of panic until it was discovered that the girl was safe ashore but had lost her cap in transit.

Almost on the eve of production Julian Wylie, the pantomime king with the heart of a child, died suddenly from overwork. If Wylie's shade was present that Christmas Eve, he must have felt proud. Phyllis Neilson-Terry was the principal boy. June played "Cinders," Clarice Hardwicke was "Dandini," that grand comedian Billy Danvers was "Buttons" (perhaps the best "Buttons" ever). Revnell and West, that amazing couple, were triumphant and real Drury Lane stars, as the Ugly Sisters. The Brokers' Men were The Three Sailors, one of the best acts that ever came from America; and in the chorus, making her début, was a young girl who bore a name old in Drury Lane history, the name of Pope. And there was a Leno at the Lane again—Dan Leno, worthy son of a great father; he gave an excellent rendering of "The Baron." Herbert Bryan had seen the last rehearsals through and finally staged the pantomime.

Mr. Tennant asked Ivor Novello, a young man of the theatre in whom he firmly believed, if he could do a show for Drury Lane. Over lunch Ivor immediately said that he had an idea. When he said it, he had not the ghost of one. But the pleased Tennent asked to be told, and the alert, nimble brain of Novello leapt to the challenge. He began to improvise and right on the spur of the moment he began to tell the story which was, in due course, to become "Glamorous Night," and start a new era of success and spectacle for Theatre Royal, Old Drury.

CHAPTER 38

END OF AN EPOCH

IVOR NOVELLO devised, wrote and composed "Glamorous Night" himself, thereby setting up a new record for Drury Lane.

But before it was produced, there were many snags and much excitement. That wonderful singer and actress, Mary Ellis, was engaged as leading lady. But Mary was in Hollywood, playing in pictures, and, in the true Hollywood way, nobody could or would give any idea as to when she was likely to be free. But to Ivor, obstacles are only there to be overcome. He sent her over the script; he had records made of the music she was to sing, and sent those over as well.

Delays and postponements occurred, and at one time it looked as though all hope was gone. But the picture finished—even Hollywood pictures have to do that—and Mary Ellis came over. She arrived word and music perfect, thanks to Novello's foresight.

Leontine Sagan, a most gifted actress and producer and a delightful woman, was engaged to produce the play, thus becoming the very first woman producer at Drury Lane.

A splendid cast was assembled. Besides Mary Ellis, there was Lyn Harding, villain of so many Drury Lane dramas and, one of the best of our all-round actors, and George Barrett, who had made such a triumph in "The Whip," was given a big part. Alas, when it came to rehearsals, he could not memorise the lines. His war service and injuries received on a minesweeper had disturbed the actor's most precious possession, his memory. It preyed upon him so that he shot himself in a railway train. Clifford Heatherly, the stage's most expert swordsman and a regular Drury Lane performer, succeeded to the part. Barry Jones, the actor who is nearly always fated to play Kings, had the part of a King in this, and played it in his own delightful manner. Trefor Jones was the tenor. Elizabeth Welch was engaged for special songs, and there was a crowd of other actors and actresses. Ralph Reader arranged the dances, and in addition, there was the Drury Lane chorus, the best ever assembled. Ivor Novello played the leading man's part himself.

He knew his Drury Lane, and knew the formula. What he gave in " Glamorous Night " was a very clever mingling of Drury Lane drama and Drury Lane musical play, with plenty of spectacle. It was a type of show never seen before, and it was to prove the ideal Drury Lane mixture; for it held all that was best of the old and new formulas. He struck the topical note, too, as did Gus Harris and Arthur Collins. One of the scenes showed a huge pleasure liner on fire and sinking. Not long before, s.s *Morro Castle* had met that sad fate. Another showed the interior of an " advanced " Broadcasting House, and in the final scene was a sample of television, talked about but never seen at that date. He even had real horses on the stage to complete the Drury Lane sequence. Great "sets" showed a suburban street, with a delightful mimed opening; the Square of a " Ruritanian " town called Krasnia; deck of a liner; the whole ship in flames; a mountain top with a gipsy wedding; and finally a Royal wedding seen by television.

Just before production there were fresh alarums and excursions, for British Actors Equity, then fighting for the " closed shop " principle, tried to enforce this at Drury Lane, but the matter was settled amicably.

There had been a good deal of debate amongst the know-alls of the theatrical profession as to whether Ivor Novello could do a show for the great theatre. " God knows it wants one badly enough," they said, " but is he the right man? " And indeed the condition of the Lane was parlous. The first night was 2nd May, 1934. Memories reverted to another fateful night, when the theatre was in straits and a man had arrived to put it right. On a January night in 1814, Edmund Kean had trudged through the snow, friendless, hungry, forlorn and disregarded, but supremely confident, to save Drury Lane. He had turned into that same stage door with not a friendly voice to greet him.

On that night in May, 1934, one hundred and twenty years afterwards, the plight of Drury Lane was much the same. But the scene at the stage door was different. Principals and chorus passed in, telegraph boys brought wires of good wishes by the handful, floral offerings arrived in lorry loads. Then, in the lull which occurs when the company are in and the overture has not begun, a slim lithe figure with a hat pulled down over his eyes, darted through the famous portal. The onlookers saw just a glimpse of him, but enough to shout " Good Luck." Inside, unlike Edmund Kean, he received smiles from everyone. But like Kean, much depended on him. If he succeeded that night, five hundred people would be in happy employment.

As the orchestra under Charles Prentice broke into the overture, the great battle for the survival and triumph of Drury Lane had begun.

How it ended everyone knows. It was indeed a Glamorous Night: The great glittering show hypnotised its smart, hardened first-night audience. For Drury Lane in front was as brilliant as Drury Lane back stage. All the players were acclaimed. Standing in line with his great company, Ivor returned thanks, giving Sagan, Reader and everyone their just due, in a modest speech which came straight from and went straight to the heart. It was a night never to be forgotten. Drury Lane, thanks to Ivor Novello, was itself again.

" Glamorous Night " ran from 2nd May, 1935, to 30th November 1935, and had to be taken off in its flood tide of success, because Mr. Tennent had arranged for a pantomime.

There are some amusing stories about the play's production. There was at Drury Lane young William Sutton, an assistant stage manager. To him was allotted the duty of "tester" for the effects. One of his jobs was to be locked in the cabin on the doomed liner, at rehearsals, to see how much he could stand in the way of maroon explosions, hot steam, red fire and smoke. He had to test it out for the rest of the company. It was not a pleasant job. In subsequent and other Novello productions, he was used as a tester for an avalanche, which he had to race as it swept downwards; as a passenger in a train which was blown up; and once he was given the cheery task of lying on the stage whilst an "earthquake" was in progress— to see where supers and small part people could throw themselves in safety whilst walls crashed, roofs fell and telegraph poles hurled themselves in all directions. But he did it all cheerfully and never got hurt.

The sinking of the ship in " Glamorous Night " was of course accompanied by the heartrending screams and shrieks of the doomed passengers. It was amusing to go back stage and see the ladies of the chorus sitting in the wings and in the Green Room, reading books or busy knitting, whilst without any emotion at all expressed on their faces, the most heartrending cries and sounds issued from their mouths.

On 28th May, 1935, that Queen of the Stage, Dame Marie Tempest, celebrated her golden jubilee as actress, at Drury Lane Theatre. There was a programme of all the stars, and the King and Queen (George V and Queen Mary) received Dame Marie in the Royal Room and tendered their congratulations in person. She had no greater admirers than they. A large sum was raised which was devoted to the foundation of the Marie Tempest Ward at St. George's Hospital.

The pantomime which displaced " Glamorous Night " was " Jack and the Beanstalk," staged by Prince Littler. This was a beautiful production scenically, with a truly gigantic giant's castle and kitchen, a troop of giant children, and once more a giant so vast as to be seen only in sections at a time. The scene of the growth of the beanstalk plus a flying ballet was one which equalled any former pantomime effect. And up that Beanstalk climbed the figure of Binnie Hale, who was Principal Boy. She had followed in her father's footsteps. At rehearsal she said : " Well, if I flop, at least I've played the Lane." She did not flop. Daughter of a Drury Lane comedian and one of the best comics of his day, and daughter of a famous Principal Boy, too—for Binnie's mother, Belle Hale, had been a grand one—Binnie had the theatre in her blood. She cut a brave figure in glittering armour defying the Giant. The cast included Marjorie Brown, charming as Principal Girl; Shaun Glenville, one of the very best and most experienced pantomime performers, who made a superb " dame "; Clifford Heatherley as " King "; Gavin Gordon as the Giant's henchman; Douglas Wakefield and Billy Nelson, (two real comics); and the harmless necessary cow was portrayed by the Griffiths Brothers, made up of one genuine Griffiths as the front legs, and Ronnie Tate, son of Harry Tate, as the hind legs. Good comedy was also supplied by Charles Heslop.

The " book " of " Jack and the Beanstalk " was written by Marriott Edgar, the creator of the famous young " Albert Ramsbottom " who was eaten by the lion. It

322

was Prince Littler's first introduction to Drury Lane. Today he controls it. It was a most worthy début.

It had been arranged by H. M. Tennent that Ivor Novello should do another show to follow the pantomime. But there was a disagreement with the Board, who argued about it and the casting, and the whole thing looked like falling through. The staff of Drury Lane had other ideas. Abingdon, Sydney Webb, Ronald Gray, the Secretary, and of another official went to work to heal the breach and support Tennent.

But meanwhile another show went on. It was called "Rise and Shine." Although everything possible was done for it, it did not live up to its title in any way. It had lovely decor and scenery, some good songs and a fine cast. But it never rose and it never shone. It had been provided with two big effects, a three-handed parachute descent and an avalanche, the latter a tried Drury Lane favourite. Both got cut out at rehearsals. There was, however, a gyroscope aeroplane which refused to rise at the dress rehearsal but fortunately obliged on the first night. Just before the production, the comedian originally selected broke down in health, and a substitute—a first-class substitute—was found at short notice. At twelve o'clock one Saturday he was watching cricket at Lord's, at one o'clock he was on the stage at Drury Lane, busy rehearsing. He gave an excellent account of himself, and afterwards became a great radio star whose catchword "What would you do, Chums?" told everyone it was Syd Walker speaking. But in spite of all that Binnie Hale, Jack Whiting, Grace Lane, Mary Honer and other clever people could do, with Ralph Reader as producer, it only ran for 44 performances.

Then Ivor Novello came back. Things had been arranged satisfactorily. He came back with "Careless Rapture." Everyone wondered if he could do it again. They were soon to find that he could. Once again he devised, wrote and composed the show, once again he played the lead. Leontine Sagan produced, Joan Davies did the dances, Dorothy Dickson was leading lady, Ivan Sampson, Walter Crisham, Olive Gilbert, George Elton and Zena Dare were in a large and brilliant cast. Once again Ivor was topical, and once again he gave the big scenic effects which are so truly Drury Lane. Another smashing success, running from 11th September, 1936, to June 5th, 1937. King

George VI's Coronation was suitably celebrated during the run.

"Careless Rapture" was produced on a Friday, which is treasury night in the theatre, and it devolved upon Albert Billings to pay out, despite all the other worries of a first night pressing upon him. Paying treasury at the Lane is never an easy job. It has to be timed to the moment so as to catch the people in their rooms, and it also involves a considerable distance of travel. That night Billing had not any means of gauging the correct times, but still he determined that the job must be done. Crossing the stage behind the scenes, he got involved in the earthquake effect. Things whizzed by him, maroons exploded under his feet, by his ears, all round him. He stood stock still, dazed and almost stunned, clutching his precious tray of treasury envelopes full of money. It was a dusty, hot and somewhat shaken treasurer who finally paid out all round, missing nobody, although the job took double the usual time. It took more than earthquakes on first nights to stop that excellent and efficient treasurer.

Then Novello proceeded to unleash his third Lane production. Speculation ran high. Could he do the hat trick? The answer was, Yes. The title was "Crest of the Wave." It was another true Drury Lane production. Again he devised, wrote and composed it all. The lyrics of all the three shows were from the inspired pen of Christopher Hassall. Again Dorothy Dickson was leading lady. Marie Lohr brought her talents to bear on a good comedy part and played it as only she can, with that delightful mixture of charm and comedy combined. There was Ena Burrell, Finlay Currie, and another actress who had been in all three Novello plays was dear old Minnie Rayner, Ivor's mascot, for whom he always wrote a special part. Walter Crisham was there again, to dance and sing, besides Peter Graves, clever Maidie Andrews, and Clifford Heatherley.

The ruined chapel scene was one of the finest and most imaginative ever mounted on Drury Lane's stage.

There was also a scene on board a great liner, which changed in the twinkling of an eye into a battleship, complete with 15-inch guns; a South American fiesta; a glimpse of Hollywood studios and the dwellings of the "stars"; and a most delightful finish on a quiet, homely Christmas note in the old English manner with a Christmas tree. The big scenic sensation was the smashing of a Transcontinental express, travelling at top speed: this was a typical Drury Lane effect in all its glory. In " Crest of the Wave," Ivor played two parts, both villain and hero. Some of the dances were arranged by Sokolova. It ran from 1st September, 1937, to 21st February, 1938. The success of Ivor Novello had banished pantomime again.

After this, Ivor wanted a rest, and took it in a manner typical of this man of the theatre, for he went on tour with the entire production and company of " Crest of the Wave." Under the enterprising guidance of that great showman, Tom Arnold, Drury Lane went to the big provincial cities and repeated its success everywhere.

Drury Lane reverted to melodrama, and melodrama in the old meaning of the word—drama with music.

This play was presented by O'Bryen, Linnit and Dunfee, and was called " The Sun Never Sets." It was a version of the Sanders of the River stories of the late Edgar Wallace, and was made into a play by his daughter Pat. It had been designed as a vehicle for Paul Robeson, but the great artist could not appear, which was, from the point of view of Drury Lane and the play, a tragedy. A substitute was brought from America, in the person of Tod Duncan. He was a good singer, and a good actor, but not a Paul Robeson. It was given a fine cast. Leslie Banks; Mackenzie Ward, Adelaide Hall, Stuart Granger, and Henry Oscar, with Edna Best as leading lady. There were hordes of negroes, " Leopard Men," Witch Doctors, Arab traders, and all the elements required for a Drury Lane big show. There was some excellent music by Kenneth Leslie Smith, and enough scenery and effects for two shows. Basil Dean produced. But a mistake was made by going into rehearsal without a completed " book." This was always being altered and rewritten during rehearsals, much of it by Richard Llewellyn, the author of " How Green was My Valley."

From the scenic point of view " The Sun Never Sets " was a masterpiece. There was a native village in which one could almost feel the burning tropical heat and smell the rank odour of the jungle. The finale showed the Residency in an African outpost of Empire on Christmas Day. All stood to attention whilst, over the radio, the King spoke to his people. A recording of the actual King's speech delivered on the previous Christmas Day was used (by special permission) and for the first time in history, the voice of a reigning monarch was heard in a play—and very fittingly at Theatre Royal.

All through rehearsals there had been storm and stress. The coloured performers were perpetually going on strike, and on one occasion at least violence loomed near. Bill Sutton was put in charge of these dark actors, to lead them through their paces. He fell foul of and stood up to a gigantic black actor three times his own size, who in private life was an all-in-wrestler. And Bill Sutton won.

The first night, despite the multiplicity of effects, went off without a hitch, but there was a bad contretemps on the second. In the course of the play Edna Best had to be carried off by savages. A huge negro seized her and swung her round, hitting her head against the proscenium arch with a resounding crack. There was a gasp of horror as she was rushed off stage. The poor negro lay on the ground and wailed, he expected instant death at the least. The first thing Edna did on regaining consciousness was to send word to him not to worry. The second thing she did was to demand to carry on.

A season of Russian ballet followed, "Ballet Russe de Monte Carlo," in which there was enough glamour for everyone. The ballets were superb, as was the dancing of Lifar, Markova and Massine. This special season ran from 12th July to 13th August, and seats were at a premium.

Then Ivor came back—this time not in a show of his own, but to satisfy a long ambition to play Shakespeare. The play selected was "Henry V," and it was sponsored by Tom Arnold, to whom the greatest credit is due. It was a beautiful production, with an endless army marching into Harfleur, a very exciting representation of the Battle of Agincourt; indeed, the whole execution was on the highest possible level. That fine actor and experienced Shakespearean, Lewis Casson (now Sir Lewis), produced for Tom Arnold. Ivor Novello played the King, greatly surprising his admirers, who knew him only as an actor of straight comedy and lighter rôles, though in his own production of "The Happy Hypocrite" at His Majesty's he had given a taste of what he really can do. He made a handsome, brave and manly King, speaking his great speeches faultlessly, and coming through the acid test with flying colours.

Alas, on top of the production, which got an enthusiastic Press, came the crisis of Munich; and a shadow fell on the world in general and the theatre in particular which no power could withstand. Even Shakespeare had to give way.

Tom Arnold did the pantomime of 1938-9. It was "Babes in the Wood," and it was in every sense of the word a real Drury Lane panto. Little did anyone realise that it would be the last one there for several years. Although the shadow of war was perceptible, Tom Arnold gave tens of thousands a happy Christmas. There were beautiful scenes in rapid succession, a very lovely woodland glade with a flying ballet, a bustling merry Nottingham Fair, a breath-taking Dresden China spectacle in which the Ganjou Brothers and Juanita showed their adagio art, and a gigantic staircase for the Finalé. Fay Compton was Principal Boy and Moya Macqueen Pope, of an Old Drury family, Fairy queen.

Then Ivor Novello came back again. All through the tour of "Crest of the Wave" he had been working on his next Drury Lane show. Much of the lovely music had been composed amongst the snow and ice of a Christmas season in Edinburgh. Ivor had done the hat-trick; was it possible to succeed at the Lane four times running?

That musical play, produced on 23rd March, 1939, was "The Dancing Years." It has now passed into theatrical history as the longest run of the war, and the second longest run of any musical play, only beaten by "Chu Chin Chow," which did not have to stand up to the blitz.

Once again Ivor Novello had Mary Ellis as his leading lady. In "The Dancing Years" she gave a performance both as singer and actress, which will never be forgotten. Peter Graves, Minnie Rayner, Barry Sinclair, Olive Gilbert—all the old hands—were there; and he added one more, dainty little Roma Beaumont, who had played on tour with him in "Crest of the Wave," and to whom at last he gave a chance of stardom at headquarters. Roma Beaumont took that chance with both her hands and both her twinkling little feet. That night a new star was born.

"The Dancing Years" was presented by Tom Arnold, who has completed a trilogy of productions at Drury Lane in the real traditional style.

By the end of August everyone knew war was inevitable. Theatre after theatre closed. On Friday, September 1st, the curtain fell at Drury Lane to a house of £35 in a theatre which could hold and had been holding, night after night, £750. It was the saddest night those at the Lane will ever remember. Outside the standard lamps were being dismantled, the lights were going out all over London, all over the world. Men and women were saying last goodbyes, in many cases final ones. The children were leaving London for safety, being taken from the horror and carnage which was to follow. Although the Declaration had not yet come, it was already War. The barrage balloons were going up, and the curtain at Old Drury came down. It descended on that scene of the promise of future happiness which concluded "The Dancing Years." That final scene may be prophetic.

But this was not the end of "The Dancing Years." That masterpiece was to go on, all over the kingdom and back to London to the Adelphi Theatre, there to brave out the blitz and only to end its London run (interrupted by the compulsory closing of theatres on the outbreak of war declared on 3rd September, 1939) when the flying bombs made theatre going impossible. And even then, in its fifth year, it went on tour again. But Tom Arnold had produced it originally at Drury Lane, and it was Ivor Novello's fourth success running in that famous theatre. It has had the longest run of any show produced at Drury Lane yet.

Thus ended, for the duration of the war, the history of Drury Lane as a theatre. Its last stage had been one of real glory, thanks to the genius of Ivor Novello. He had proved to be the man the grand old playhouse wanted.

The long tale of this playhouse, this centuries-stretched saga of the Drama, is nearly over, but not quite. There remains to be told the part that Theatre Royal played for its country during the greatest War of all time.

CHAPTER 39

ENSA TAKES OVER

DRURY LANE, which had lived through so many wars, was not to remain inactive for long.

On Friday, 8th September, 1939, there was a rather stormy inaugural meeting of ENSA (Entertainment National Service Association) at the offices of the Society of West End Managers in Charing Cross Road. There were ructions. In the midst of this wrangling, Basil Dean got up and went to the War Office, accompanied by the Public Relations Officer (who also acted in that capacity for Drury Lane). In a short time that official returned to the meeting, which was still in a state of high debate, and announced that ENSA had taken over Theatre Royal, Drury Lane, as headquarters. This put an abrupt full stop to all argument. There was nothing more to be said.

On Monday, September 11th, 1939, ENSA moved into Drury Lane. Although the old place was no longer to entertain the public, it was not going out of show business. Its function was merely switched for the benefit of the troops. There is no doubt that, but for this act of requisitioning, ENSA could never have got started so quickly. For at the Lane there was everything that was necessary—office accommodation, space, places for rehearsals, great workshops at the back of the stage, store rooms, wardrobe, electrician's shop, property room, and a stage big enough for all purposes. And the idea that all shows came from Drury Lane added glamour to the whole ENSA idea.

Sir Seymour Hicks, then Controller of ENSA, took over the Board Room (Sheridan's Room); Basil Dean, then Director of Entertainments N.A.A.F.I., now Director of National Service Entertainment, had the General Manager's office; Dan Leno's old room became a headquarters for equipment and R.A.F. Liaison under Lieutenant-Colonel Stanley Bell.

The old Guard Room, which had occasioned the dispute leading to the withdrawal of the military guard, remained in the occupation of William Abingdon, who became chief of equipment and chief of staff. Mrs. Siddons' dressing room was the headquarters of the publicity department. Garrick's room started as a general registry, but later became the centre of Theatre Control, under E. P. Clift. The time was to come when offices would spring up like mushrooms over every inch of available floor space, even invading the stage itself; while the Green Room, where so much had happened, including murder, was to become a cashier's office, and the space below the stage known as "The Elephant Hole" (because the elephants used in "The Great Ruby" had been stabled there) was to be converted into an air raid shelter. But rehearsals still went on in the old Ballet Room, where generation on generation of Drury Lane coryphees had practised their steps. Even the boxes became offices, nor even the sanctity of the Royal Retiring Room nor the Duke of Bedford's private room was to be spared from intrusion.

With the doings of ENSA, its virtues and its faults, this story is not concerned. But what happened at Drury Lane during its occupation is nevertheless very much our affair. Through its stage door poured crowds of artists of all ranks to offer their services. Many hundreds of the less important actors and actresses who could never in their wildest dreams have imagined they would be connected with Drury Lane, became familiar with it and made it almost their home. For the story of ENSA is largely the story of the little people of the " profession," little people who have done such a fine job of work. Out of that old stage door poured shows of all kinds, to struggle through the blackout to almost unknown destinations to all parts of the globe. It was a thrill to watch a party leave for hush-hush overseas destinations in the small hours of the morning (under the cover of deep " security "), when even the artists did not know the name of the ship on which they were to sail or their port of embarkation.

The stalls bar was converted into a broadcasting studio, from which numerous broadcasts were transmitted. For two solid years without a break a programme for overseas listeners called " London Carries On " announced proudly that it came from Drury Lane Theatre, whereas the origin of most programmes was anonymous. Not even the blitz stopped " London Carries On," which lived up to its title.

On November 28th, 1939, just before the departure for France of the first three troupes of entertainers ever to give shows to an army waiting the onset on the field of battle, their Majesties King George VI and Queen Elizabeth paid a visit to Drury Lane, to see things for themselves. It was another in that long list of Royal visits, but a most unusual one. The King and Queen came for three-quarters of an hour, but stopped for over two hours. They saw Jack Hylton with a big band in the Rotunda, playing in the shadow of the statues of Shakespeare, Garrick, Kean and Balfe. They saw companies arriving back from tours and other companies setting out. They saw Jack Buchanan supervising a show. They saw Henry Oscar rehearsing a play in the Green Room. They showed the greatest interest in a large map in which Sir Seymour Hicks had stuck red and blue flags to show where Ensa shows had been given.

330

When the Queen asked why some were red and some blue, the King told her the red ones had been put in because the blue ones had run out.

His Majesty offered to bet half-a-crown that Tommy Knox, the property man, and his boys, would not get a Minipiano into one of the small vans which the mobile parties used for travelling around. It was as well nobody took the bet, for he would have lost his money. The piano went in all right. Their Majesties spoke to the sewing women, and Kate, a Drury Lane veteran of the wardrobe, swelled with pride. They learnt conjuring tricks from Skeets Martin in the basement, while watching a troupe organised by Will Hay. The King said it would come in useful at Christmas.

They spoke with Dame Lilian Braithwaite about the shows she organised for hospitals, and with Sir Kenneth Barnes, and Alec L. Rea on general ENSA affairs. They inspected a device for generating electricity for the portable theatres, which was being worked by Bill Otter. In the ballet room they watched Ralph Reader and His Gang Show, the all-male company which was going up the front line. They inspected the company which Sir Seymour Hicks was taking over, which included himself, Dorothy Ward, Tom Webster, the famous cartoonist, Billy Russell, Claire Luce, and other performers, to all of whom they spoke. On the stage they met an old friend in the person of Leslie Henson (who had christened ENSA and who has done so much for it).

Henson had got together a show which, in memory of his famous troupe of the 1914-1918 war, he called "The Gaieties." It was a very starry affair too, with himself, Binnie Hale, Violet Loraine, Gavin Gordon, John E. Coyle and four Gaiety chorus girls in the company. The costumes had been designed by Norman Hartnell. The King and Queen sat in the stalls and watched a "run through." They joined in the chorus of one of the songs, "Goodbye, Sally" (written by another famous comedian, Arthur Riscoe), and then they went on the stage and chatted with the entire company, chorus girls included. A King and Queen, stage stars and chorus girls all in friendly conversation was something which even the stage at Drury Lane had not seen before. Before they left the King and Queen heard a short history of the theatre told them at their own request by the present historian. They were especially interested in the Ghost, who unfortunately did not oblige on that occasion.

There was another day in the Spring of 1940 when the great auditorium was packed from ceiling to floor by men from the Anti-Aircraft Service, men who had been standing-to since the previous September, and who, up to then, had had a pretty sterile time. It was to get hot enough for them later.

On this occasion the Duke and Duchess of Kent occupied the Royal Box. Sir Seymour Hicks, Stanley Holloway, Charles Coborn, Sidney Howard, and Will Fyffe were in the bill. And so was Gracie Fields. And one other, for Maurice Chevalier had flown over specially from Paris to sing characteristic songs in his own inimitable manner. It was a show worthy of Drury Lane, and it was the last full-sized one to be staged there during the war. It was for troops only. The King sent a telegram which General Pile, O.C.A.A., read to the men, and which they cheered to the echo.

Drury Lane Theatre was a big target in the blitz. It was frequently hit by incendiary bombs, but these were promptly dealt with, for it had its own A.R.P. organisation, of which the members were both expert and enthusiastic. Then came the terrible night of 15th October, 1940. The blitz was at its height, and the Covent Garden quarter was the target. At 11-55 p.m. a big bomb struck Drury Lane. It was a delayed action type, but something happened to it during its progress through the theatre, for it exploded at the back of the pit. It crashed through the roof, through the gallery, through the Ghost Walk in the Upper Circle, through the Grand Circle, and then burst at the rear of the pit. Its heavy nosecap penetrated the pit floor and fell into the stalls bar below, in-which members of the staff, waiting their turn for duty, were sleeping. Although covered with dust from debris and plaster, none of them was hurt. It was a miracle they escaped. The blast tore the bottom out of the grand circle, and all the decorations from the walls of the pit, it travelled forward across the auditorium, doing no damage, and finally struck the iron curtain, which held —it sagged, but it held. The old twenty-five feet-thick walls of the sturdy theatre took the shock and withstood it. There was not one casualty, nor was one working hour lost.

But more was to come. Through that same hole, a few minutes later, came an oil bomb which set alight the pit seats, the stalls, and the carpets. But the A.R.P. boys got the fire out. A guardian spirit must have protected Old Drury that night.

There was another very narrow escape too, later on in the blitz. Incendiaries were showering down. Several fell on the Lane. Everyone was busy extinguishing them. Afterwards, when the Chief Warden had an inspection, he found that one had fallen through the glass roof of the Paint Frame, hit the oak floor, exploded and started to burn. It had, however, melted a barrel of size, which in overflowing had put out the flames.

One daylight raid might have been lethal to the Lane. The sirens wailed, each A.R.P. squad was at its post. On the roof, the Chief Warden watched the German planes coming nearer and nearer. They were heading South-East, and must pass directly over the theatre. Fires were breaking out below in their wake and the incendiaries could be seen falling like great smuts everywhere. Just as the warden was about to give the word for action, as if by magic, the hail of bombs ceased. One fell in the roadway outside the theatre but did no damage. Theatre Royal was not to perish at Hitler's hands.

In the summer of the flying bombs Drury Lane had some narrow escapes, its windows and doors were shattered by blast, but it suffered no material damage. Its outside shows many scars from splinters, but the great pile stands quite intact.

The world-famous chorus is broken up—of its men, the majority went into the Forces, of the girls, most got married and have children who will, maybe, follow on one day at Drury Lane. Ronald Gray, the secretary, became a major in the Royal Army Pay Corps. He had served and suffered in the previous war.

But some still remain, those whom age or other reasons rendered unsuitable for active service. Cavell still watches over the stage door, while the burly ex-Guardsman Gert helps him. Harry Leggatt is still the faithful chief fireman, Mrs. Jordan the housekeeper; excellent Bill Otter is the chief electrician, and he, together with Ben Anderson and George Wright, did much good service in the Drury Lane A.R.P. Miss Easthope still presides over the switchboard. Tommy Knox is the property man who performs the impossible, as is always expected at Drury Lane. Mrs. Wisden, another Drury Lane stalwart, commands the wardrobe with other Lane veterans to help her. Joe Hart, the theatre's chief dayman, still looks after many of his old staff on the stage. And Sydney Forrest Webb is still the house manager, knowing every nook and cranny of the old place.

But many old faces have gone and will never return; the old times have gone with them. The control of the theatre itself has changed. The new Board of Directors is as follows: Charles Gulliver (chairman), Prince Littler (managing director), Emile Littler, A. Stewart Cruikshank, Stewart Cruikshank, T. Fleming Birch, and S. R. Newsome. They are men of standing and wide experience in the theatrical profession. Theirs is a great charge.

Theatre Royal, Drury Lane, is a curious place and a difficult proposition. It needs expert knowledge and careful handling. A show which might succeed in any other theatre in London, at Drury Lane may die the death. And a play which might fail elsewhere, becomes a crashing success.

Under its lofty roof it contains all things a theatre needs. Behind the vast stage is a great runway, which divides the stage from the workrooms, all of which are very spacious. Everything is to hand; it is a self-contained world of the theatre. In the days of peace, when a show was running, five hundred people found employment there. A self-contained community, they lived their lives there; they worked Drury Lane, they thought Drury Lane, they talked Drury Lane. So great is the absorption of that theatre, that they became almost oblivious to the outside world.

On its inside walls are blazoned the names of its great sons and daughters. In its vestibule the long list of its managers is inscribed in gold on a mahogany plaque. There is one too to commemorate the management of Arthur Collins. And for the future more are wanted—other names await inscription for good and faithful service.

In that vestibule, too, is another board which is the Theatrical Profession's Cenotaph for the war of 1914-18. On it shine the names of the actors who made the great sacrifice. But one name is there in error, the name of a man who was posted as missing, believed killed. So live and kicking was he that it was only when he was rehearsing

for " The Sun Never Sets " that the mistake was discovered. And the actor himself did not know his name was
there. The heroes of this war will be enshrined at Drury
Lane, too.

The purpose of this book has been to set down the
story of this great playhouse, a story which has never
before been gathered together as a whole. It is not meant
for experts, for erudite scholars of theatrical history. They
may—or rather, will—note many omissions, events not
chronicled, sufficient praise not bestowed, sufficient blame
not meted out. They will find many names missing from
the saga, and many which deserve more space. So this
book is not for them. The full history will be written when
the war-time restrictions of time and paper are things of
the past. It will take years to compile, but it will be done.

Here, however, is offered a sincere attempt to tell the
lovers of the drama, the playgoers and the general public,
some outline of that story which has been woven by the
centuries on the loom of Drury Lane . . . to record the
remembrance of the great names which have trodden its
stage or occupied its seat of power. It is an attempt to
show the tens of thousands who know its name, who pass it
by as they go about their business, who have been to see
its shows, that Drury Lane is something more than just an
old theatre where pantomimes used to be played, and which
evokes hazy memories of Nell Gwynne, David Garrick, Leno
and big musical plays. It is an attempt to show them that
Drury Lane is something far more than that, to prove that
in it they have a precious possession, a storehouse of
memories which it keeps alive, still active and sentient, and
that it continues adding daily to its wonderful record of
time and achievement. Drury Lane is to the Drama what
the Tower of London, Windsor Castle, St. James's Palace,
Westminster Abbey and St. Paul's Cathedral are to the
general history of England; it is a pulsating memorial of
the past, the present, and the future. It is more than a playhouse, it is a national treasure, and should be loved and
revered as such.

And here ends this outline of history of a Theatre which
is unique, not only in London, but in the whole world. No
other capital city can show its rival. It outshines in age, in
romance, in stability of location the Comedie Francaise
itself. It is the heart and life's blood of the history of our

Drama, it is part of the history of our proud city, it is part of the history of our race itself.

Drury Lane stands alone, serene and unchallenged; dreaming over the centuries that it has seen pass, and facing those to come with calm and confidence and high resolve. And whilst London lasts, may there always be that part of it which is known as Theatre Royal, Drury Lane.

———

Index of Names

Abingdon, William, 186, 315, 323, 329.
Abington, James, 178.
Abington, Mrs. Frances, 59, 177-180, 183, 184, 191, 195, 196.
Adam, Brothers, 177, 187.
Adam, William, 228.
Addison, Joseph, 124-127.
Aickin, 196.
Albertuzzi, 273.
Alexander, Sir George, 90, 295.
Ali, George, 299.
Alias, Charles, 286.
Allen, (Musician), 275.
Anderson, Ben, 333.
Anderson, James, 275-277, 280.
Anderson, Mary, 304.
Anderson, Professor, 283.
Andrews, 273.
Andrews, Maidie, 324.
Angelsey, Earl of, 25, 272.
Anne, Queen of England, 25, 70, 88, 106-108, 136, 137, 214.
Anstey, F., 303.
Argyll, Marquis of, 25.
Arne, Dr., 168, 181, 185, 254.
Arne, Susannah Maria (see Cibber, S. M.)
Arnold, Samuel James, 226-228, 229, 232, 233, 235-237, 241, 242, 268, 269.
Arnold, Tom, 12, 325-328.
Astley, 271.
Arundel, Thomas, Earl of, 17.
Auber, 268, 273.
Ayscough, G. E., 192.

Baddeley, Robert, 25, 191, 196-198.
Baddeley, Mrs., 191, 192.
Bagges, Zaccary, 82, 99, 118.
Balfe, Michael, 264, 269, 270, 272, 279, 330.
Banks, John, 64.
Banks, Leslie, 325.
Bannerman, Margaret, 309.
Bannister, Jack, 182, 184, 229, 239, 241
Bannister, Mrs., 182.
Bard, Wilkie, 297-299.
Barnes, Sir Kenneth, 331.
Barrett, George, 298, 299, 319.
Barry, Mrs. Elizabeth, 12, 59, 60, 67, 70, 71, 79, 81, 83, 110, 113, 115, 118, 131, 135.
Barry, Spranger, 12, 163, 169-172, 174, 182, 245.
Barry, Mrs. Spranger, 182, 207.

Barrymore, 223.
Barton, Frances, (see Mrs. Abington)
Bastow, George, 294.
Bate, Dr., 186.
Bateman, Thomas, 26, 29.
Baxter, Richard, 22, 24, 26, 28.
Bayley, Thomas Haynes, 273.
Beard, 183.
Beatty, Admiral Lord, 306.
Beatty-Kingston, W., 287.
Beaumont, Hugh, 317.
Beaumont, Roma, 327.
Bedford, Duke of, 214, 227, 290, 291, 330.
Bedford, Earl of, 23.
Beecham, Sir Joseph, 301, 302.
Beecham, Sir Thomas, 303, 304.
Beeston, William, 18, 20, 25, 27, 41.
Beethoven, 287.
Behn, Aphra, 65, 76, 84, 99.
Bell, Richard, 42, 56.
Bell, Lt.-Col. Stanley, 329.
Bellamy, Miss, 171, 172, 182.
Benedict, 279.
Bennett, Arnold, 311.
Bennett, George, 275.
Benson, Frank, 303.
Berry, 151, 161, 170.
Best, Edna, 325, 326.
Betterton, Matthew, 68, 70, 71.
Betterton, Thomas, 12, 22, 26, 43, 48, 53, 54, 59, 60, 65-72, 75, 76, 78-85, 87, 93, 95, 96, 99, 106, 114-118, 126, 131, 133, 135, 153, 160, 176, 191, 213.
Betterton, Mrs. (see Sanderson).
Bettini, 281.
Betty, ("Infant Roscius"), 220.
Beverley, 282, 291.
Bickerstaffe, Isaac, 184.
Bicknell, Mrs., 99.
Billings, Alfred, 324.
Bilton, Belle, 289.
Birch, T. Fleming, 334.
Bird, Theophilus, 24, 26, 27.
Blagden, Nicholas, 24, 26, 28.
Blakes, 161, 170.
Blanchard, E. L., 286-288.
Blanche, Ada, 286, 289, 291.
Blanche, Marie, 304.
Bohemia, Queen of, 25.
Bolingbroke, Lord, 126-128.
Bolton, George, 281.
Booth, Barton, 120, 125-131, 135, 137, 138, 140-142, 144, 150.
Booth, Charles, 12, 32, 39, 41, 59.
Booth, Junius Brutus, 249, 250, 255.
Boswell, James, 180, 217.

x   337

Grimaldi, John, 223.
Grimaldi, Mrs., 183.
Grossmith, George, 314, 315.
Gulliver, Charles, 334.
Gwynne, Nell, 12, 27, 30-33, 44-53, 54, 64, 102, 335.
Gye, 280, 281.

Hackett, Walter, 218.
Haddon, Peter, 313.
Hadfield, James, 219.
Haig, Fieldmarshal Lord, 306.
Hains, Joe, 41-43, 61.
Hale, Binnie, 322, 331, 333.
Hale, Belle, 322.
Halifax, Lord, 85.
Hall, 99.
Hall, Adelaide, 325.
Hallam, Thomas, 149, 150, 169.
Hamilton, 281.
Hamilton, Henry, 289, 292, 296, 298.
Hamilton, Mrs., 185.
Hammerstein, Oscar, 312.
Hammond, W. H., 273, 274.
Hancock, Thomas, 26, 28.
Handel, 146, 156, 225, 276.
Harding, Lyn, 296, 297, 319.
Hardwicke, Sir Cedric, 312.
Hardwicke, Clarice, 318.
Harley, Robert, (Earl of Oxford), 126.
Harley, Lady Jane, 229.
Harper, 159.
Harris, (actor), 42.
Harris, Sir Augustus, 12, 13, 228, 284-292, 298, 300, 310, 311, 320.
Hart, Charles, 12, 21, 23-28, 32, 39, 41-44, 46, 49, 51, 53, 56, 59-61, 63-67.
Hart, Joe, 334.
Hartnell, Norman, 331.
Harvard, 151, 161, 170, 185.
Harvey, Forrester, 302.
Harvey, Lady, 30.
Haverley, 287.
Hassall, Christopher, 324.
Hassard, Short, 317.
Hawtrey, Charles, 288.
Hay, Ian, 310.
Haynes, James, 274.
Hazlitt, William, 209, 241, 248, 253.
Hearn, Tom, 295.
Heatherly, Clifford, 319, 322, 324.
Henderson, John, 12, 198, 199, 202.
Henson, Leslie, 331.
Herbert, Sir Henry, 20, 21, 23, 60.
Hewat, Sir Thomas, 137.
Hewett, William, 23, 24.
Hewitt, Agnes, 289.
Hichens, Robert, 304.

Hicks, Seymour, 310, 329-332.
Highmore, John, 144, 146-148.
Hill, Capt., 74.
Hill, Aaron, 122, 171.
Holland, Actor, 184.
Holland, architect, 214, 215.
Holland, Lord, 226, 228.
Hollingshead, John, 114.
Holloway, Stanley, 317, 332.
Honer, Mary, 323.
Hookham, 273.
Hopkins, 185, 195, 211.
Hopkins, Miss P., 196.
Hopper, Victoria, 317.
Horton, Mrs. 132, 147, 162.
Horton, Miss P., 275.
Howard, Edward, 47.
Howard, James, 48.
Howard, Sir Robert, 23, 24, 31.
Howard, Robert (dramatist), 47.
Howard, Sidney, 332.
Howes, Bobbie, 313.
Huband, 99.
Huddart, 237.
Huddart, Miss, 281.
Hudson, James, 275.
Hughes, Mrs. Margaret, 22, 26, 31, 60.
Hughes, Miss, 221.
Hughs, 42.
Huntley, Grace. 289.
Hull, Thomas, 185.
Hyde, Charles J., 305.
Hylton, Jack, 330.

Incledon, 254.
Ireland, William, 217.
Ironmonger, Richard, 228.
Irving, Henry, 12, 142, 288, 294, 295.
Irving, Laurence, 294.

Jacks, Clara, 289.
James I, 15, 25.
James II, 42, 49, 53, 61, 62, 70, 75, 76, 92, 113.
James, Julia, 299.
James, Mrs., 42.
Jefferson, 182, 183.
Jeffreys, Judge, 76.
Jerrold, Douglas, 241.
Jersey, Lord, 244.
Joel, Solly, 310.
Johnson, Benjamin, 83, 99, 109, 151.
Johnson, Doctor Samuel, 12, 156, 157, 164, 165, 166, 170 171, 180, 206.
Johnstone, Edwin, 272.

341

346

List of Plays

347

The Laſt Time of the Company's performing this Seaſon.

At the Theatre Royal in Drury-Lane,

This preſent MONDAY, June 10, 1776,

The W O N D E R.

Don Felix by Mr. GARRICK,

Col. Briton by Mr. SMITH,

Don Lopez by Mr BADDELEY,

Don Pedro by Mr. PARSONS,

Liſſardo by Mr. KING,

Frederick by Mr. PACKER,

Gibby by Mr. MOODY,

Iſabella by Miſs HOPKINS,

Flora by Mrs. WRIGHTEN.